Palgrave Studies in the History of Economic Thought

Palgrave Studies in the History of Economic Thought publishes contributions by leading scholars, illuminating key events, theories and individuals that have had a lasting impact on the development of modern-day economics. The topics covered include the development of economies, institutions and theories.

The series aims to highlight the academic importance of the history of economic thought, linking it with wider discussions within economics and society more generally. It contains a broad range of titles that illustrate the breath of discussions — from influential economists and schools of thought, through to historical and modern social trends and challenges — within the discipline.

All books in the series undergo a single-blind peer review at both the proposal and manuscript submission stages.

For further information on the series and to submit a proposal for consideration, please contact Wyndham Hacket Pain (Economics Editor) wyndham.hacketpain@palgrave.com.

The series is dedicated to the memory of former editor and distinguished economist Geoff Harcourt.

Maria Cristina Marcuzzo

Economic Theories, Protagonists and Facts

Collected Essays in the History of Economic Thought

palgrave
macmillan

Maria Cristina Marcuzzo
Department of Statistical Sciences
Sapienza University of Rome
Rome, Italy

ISSN 2662-6578 ISSN 2662-6586 (electronic)
Palgrave Studies in the History of Economic Thought
ISBN 978-3-031-63948-7 ISBN 978-3-031-63949-4 (eBook)
https://doi.org/10.1007/978-3-031-63949-4

Cover illustration: Alan Copson Pictures / Alamy Stock Photo

This Palgrave Macmillan imprint is published by the registered company Springer Nature Switzerland AG.
The registered company address is: Gewerbestrasse 11, 6330 Cham, Switzerland

Acknowledgements

I would like to thank Wyndham Hacket Pain, Senior editor at Palgrave Macmillan for encouragement and support in preparing this volume. I am very grateful to Iolanda Sanfilippo for her help in all stages of the process and for her excellent editorial assistance, without which I would have not been able to publish this collection. Needless to say my greatest debts goes to my co-authors, in particular Annalisa Rosselli, a friend and a precious collaborator for over 45 years.

CONTENTS

List of Figures

List of Tables

CHAPTER 1

Introduction

This volume—containing articles and book chapters published between 1989 and 2017—is the sequel to two previous collections (Marcuzzo 2012, 2019) with which it shares approach and inspiration. In this introduction I would like to make more explicit what have been my guiding spirit and motivations in pursuing research in the history of economic thought in general and in the Cambridge and classical political economy traditions in particular.

The first is dissatisfaction with how economics has evolved during my academic life, which is now close to 50 years long, in abandoning the historical dimension in favour of modelling and mathematization. I am certainly guilty of sheer ignorance in both skills, but I believe this is not the reason for my distaste. Things have gone too far in that direction and the suspicion arises that this is not for entirely scientific reasons. Much has been written on what might have caused this turn in the discipline and I need only to refer here to Mirowski (1991).

The second element is that I have been earlier on persuaded that the criticism levelled against neoclassical economics by Keynes and Sraffa is both sound and thorough. Thus, I have followed their lines of thought, both in revealing their ideas and pursuing their approach in assessing later developments. Despite the differences between them, they embrace a vision of economics and provide tools of analysis which are close and which I find still unsurpassed.

M. C. Marcuzzo, *Economic Theories, Protagonists and Facts*, Palgrave Studies in the History of Economic Thought, https://doi.org/10.1007/978-3-031-63949-4_1

The third element is following what I consider "good" history of economic thought method. It is a combination of archival findings, textual exegesis, analytical accuracy, contextual framing, and biographical insights. These are all necessary ingredients that may not be found in each and every individual exercise, but I consider the tools of the trade, which I have constantly kept at hand in my work.

In what follows I give a short summary of each chapter and at the end I will give some concluding remarks on what I see as the significance of this collection as a whole.

The first section *History of economic thought: which are the issues?* includes 4 articles published between 2008 and 2016.

The purpose of the first paper—*Is history of economic thought a "serious" subject?*—is to clarify the nature of research in the history of economic thought. In reviewing which are the "techniques" that are involved in the discipline, four broader categories are identified: a) textual exegesis; b) rational reconstructions; c) contextual analysis and, with a sort of catch-all definition, d) historical narrative. After examining these different styles of doing history of economic thought, the paper addresses the question of its appraisal, namely what good history of economic thought is and how we should appraise it. I argue that there is a distinction to be made between doing economics and history of economic thought. The former requires the greatest possible respect for contexts and texts, both published and unpublished; the latter entails constructing a theoretical framework that is in some respects freer, not bound by derivation from the authors. Finally, the paper draws upon *Econlit* records to review what had been done in the subject in the preceding two decades.

The second paper—*A slender trunk and many branches. The history of economic thought in perspective, past and future*—looks at the styles and trends that have shaped the subject in the most recent years, but also peers into the past to trace its roots and ancestry. Within the history-of-ideas approach which does not fall into the Whig fallacy (linear progress from error to truth) there are two branches. The first is the search in the past for what has been lost and can no longer be found in modern theory; it is part of a program to build an alternative economic theory and is in fact synonymous with doing non-mainstream economics. The second does not necessarily entail heterodox implications and is mainly concerned with interpreting work in context. I argue that the revival of Keynes and Keynesian economics is an interesting case of the quest for an alternative branch in the history of ideas approach, which however does not make full use of scholarly investigation into Keynes's writings and unpublished material, failing therefore to grasp Keynes's message fully. My point is that the historians of economic thought have proved better equipped to appraise Keynes's wide range of proposals and not to make do with simple-minded so-called Keynesian policy. I claim that the "exit" strategy from Economics and Departments of Economics, as envisaged by some eminent scholars, for the survival of the history of economic thought, may be shortsighted since our "voice" may still have an audience and hearing in the aftermath of the present disillusionment with mainstream economic theory.

In the third paper—*A methodological agenda for new economic thinking*—I examine the suggestions made to set up the agenda for the development of alternative paradigms, concentrating mainly on the views emerging from the *Institute for New Economic Thinking* that brought together economists of various orientations, skills and persuasion, all disillusioned (to varying degrees) with the present state of economics and committed to promoting change in the way economics is practiced in research and teaching. I then examine the main lessons to be drawn from the work of Keynes and Sraffa, which seem to me an essential part of the criticism of mainstream economics, and I raise some issues against the existing career models and system of evaluation of research in economics.

The fourth paper, co-authored with Giulia Zacchia,—*Is history of economics what historians of economic thought do? A quantitative investigation*—presents a quantitative investigation into the history of economic thought. We propose an empirical study with the aim of describing the dynamics of changes in HET in recent years, detecting three trends: 1) a sort of 'stepping down from the shoulders of giants', namely a move towards studies of 'minor' figures and/or economists from a more recent past; 2) the blossoming of archival research into unpublished work and correspondence; 3) less theory-laden investigations, connecting intellectual circles, linking characters and events. Using data from *Econlit* we show the evolution of the overall publication of history of economic thought articles (1955–2013) and of history of economic thought fully or partially specialized journals (1993–2013); for the latter, by devising proxies which are amenable to quantitative assessment, we demonstrate that there is some evidence to support these claims.

The second section—*Ricardo, money and monetary systems*—includes 4 articles written over a longer stretch of time between 1987 and 2014. The first two focus on Ricardo's monetary theory, while the last two on the nature of the monetary system which Ricardo witnessed and analysed.

The first paper of this section, co-authored with Annalisa Rosselli,—*Ricardo's theory of money matters*—deals with three common criticisms of Ricardo's monetary theory: commodity money, the neutrality of money, and its long-term nature. The first is that the identification of money with gold prevents Ricardo from grasping the meaning of money-money and, consequently, from understanding its properties. The second portrays Ricardo as the champion of the quantitative theory of money who rejects the real effects of nominal variables. The third criticism is that Ricardo gives exclusive attention to the permanent effects, ignoring the short-term effects. Our interpretation challenges these points and offers an alternative interpretation of Ricardo's monetary theory.

The second paper—*On the notion of temporary and permanent causes. The legacy of Ricardo*—considers the distinction made by Ricardo between "permanent" and "temporary" causes, which he sometimes refers to also as "stable" and "accidental" causes, to derive implications useful to distinguish his approach from subsequent developments of the notions of short-period and long-period equilibrium. I then trace the change of focus in the concept of "permanent" forces brought about by Alfred Marshall—from whose insights Richard Kahn and John Maynard Keynes drew inspiration for their short-period analysis—which paved the way to fundamental changes in the method and theory. I argue that Ricardo's distinction maintains a heuristic value, *vis-à-vis* the distinction between short and long period, which is part of the common language in standard economics.

The last two papers in this section are a study of the monetary system contemporary to Ricardo. In the first, co-authored with Annalisa Rosselli,—*Profitability in the international gold market in the early history of the Gold Standard*—by looking at the available evidence on the London gold market in the late eighteenth century and early nineteenth century, we present a new formulation of the gold points and describe the market behaviour behind gold movements. While there is evidence that the merchants' behaviour sustained the purchasing power parity of gold in terms of currency, there is none to support the view that the gold flows realized the purchasing power parity of gold in terms of traded commodities. Therefore, the equilibrium condition imposed by both the monetary approach and the specie-flow mechanism seem unnecessarily restrictive.

The last paper of this section, also co-authored with Annalisa Rosselli,—*Metallic standards and real exchange rates*—has two purposes. The first is to provide a general framework of analysis of exchange-rate variations and profitability conditions in bullion trade under monometallic and bimetallic regimes. The second is to offer an example of its application, by constructing the series of the relevant indicator for the London-Paris markets during 50 years of the early history of the Gold Standard. We show that the variation in the market rate of exchange from the relevant parity is a good indicator of the conditions prevailing in the bills of exchange market and, therefore, of the state of the balance of payments, provided two conditions are met: first, the parity from which the deviations of the market rate of exchange are calculated must be the parity assumed as the term of reference by economic agents engaged in actual transactions; and second, allowance must be made for the component due to the conditions of the demand for bullion. We provide, as an example, computation of an indicator which is the measure of the deviation of the market rate of exchange from the real par, which satisfies both requirements. While its sign tells us whether the market is favourable or unfavourable to the domestic currency, its value—compared with the costs of shipping bullion—tells us whether an outflow or an inflow of bullion is likely to occur.

The third section of this collection—*Cambridge economics: past and present*—has also four papers, published between 2007 and 2019.

In the first—*Is there a Cambridge approach to economics?*—I argue that "the Cambridge approach to economics" is not a cohesive and a fully-fledged system of thought, but rather a legacy with many threads. Several aspects of method, "style" and content of the economics associated with the Cambridge tradition, whose imprinting is to be traced to Marshall, make it well recognizable, when compared with the so called "mainstream" economics and other schools of thought. The "style" aspect of the Cambridge economists as a group lies in their particular type of communication—written and oral—that led to very close forms of interaction, not devoid of diversity and dissent; in the physical and temporal closeness, helped in part by relatively unconventional lifestyles upon which profound personal ties were threaded and woven. I investigate the features of this approach under the headings of divergences, differences, and communalities. I conclude that the Cambridge tradition has handed down to us a legacy resting on two pillars. The first is rejection of the "classical" conclusion that market forces are always at work to bring the economic system to full employment of resources, implicated by the belief that there is no discontinuity between individual and aggregate behaviour, so that what is good for a single player in the market is good for the whole. The second is the Sraffian theme that the market, taken as synonymous with supply and demand, is a misleading arena for representation of the rules of production and distribution. Both pillars are needed to travel the road towards an alternative economic theory and economic policy.

The second paper in this section—*Luigi Pasinetti and the Cambridge economists*—is a tribute to Luigi Pasinetti as a historian of economic thought in general, but in particular with regard to his work on the Cambridge economists, and his interpretations mainly of Sraffa and Keynes, but also of Richard Kahn, Joan Robinson and Nicholas Kaldor. With them he shared everyday Cambridge life, and he is universally associated with them in terms of a common "school"—the Cambridge school. The purpose of the paper is not to provide a systematic account, but to offer some illustrations of Pasinetti's style of doing history of economic thought and how it developed over time. It is argued that the theoretical framework to which Pasinetti has dedicated so much of his intellectual efforts is built on his understanding of what Cambridge economics was about and how its scope and aims should be pursued and integrated. As such it is a personal construction which stands, alongside the individual contributions by the Cambridge economists with whom Pasinetti associates himself, as a milestone in the landscape of non-mainstream economics.

The third paper—*The "Cambridge" critique of the quantity theory of money. A note on how quantitative easing vindicates it*—revisited the arguments against the quantity theory in the "Cambridge" tradition of John Maynard Keynes, Richard Kahn, and Nicholas Kaldor, and defends their soundness and topicality. Through quantitative easing markets have been flooded with liquidity, at the time of expansionary monetary policy rather than inflation we witnessed a general deflation because of the liquidity trap environment in which the banking system operated.

The final piece in this section, co-authored with Eleonora Sanfilippo,—*Dear John, Dear Ursula (Cambridge and LSE, 1935). Eighty-eight letters unearthed*—tells the discovery of the eighty-eight letters which were unearthed while sifting through the Hicks papers at the Library of University of Hyogo, Japan, in December 2003. They were written between September and December 1935, when John Hicks had left the London School of Economics (LSE) for Cambridge, having been appointed University lecturer and Fellow of Gonville and Caius College, while Ursula (then Webb) was at the LSE, where she had been a student from 1929 and was currently a member of the staff. The letters cover the three months preceding their wedding, which took place in London, on December 17,

1935. It is a daily exchange, with just the odd interruption marking the days when they would visit each other (mostly at weekends) either in Cambridge or in London. It is a portrait of a marriage in the making, a picture of an academic milieu and a glimpse into British society of the 1930s.

The last section—*Cambridge protagonists: Keynes, Joan Robinson and Sraffa*—contains four papers published between 2011 and 2018.

Krishna Bharadwaj, who is the subject of the first paper of this section—*On alternative notions of change and choice. Krishna Bharadwaj's legacy*—following upon the work and insights of Sraffa, made substantial contributions to our understanding of what is implied in the neoclassical notion of change and its related notion of choice; in this respect, she appears closer to the spirit of Sraffa's critique of neoclassical theory than many others. She also supplemented important elements in building an alternative approach, based on classical political economy, which is free from the need to employ marginal magnitudes and does not require hypothetical or potential changes to determine the resting positions of economic variables. Moreover, she rescued the notion of choice from the parable of 'preferences' and gave to it more meaningful contents, allowing for consideration of habits, customs, and power relationships.

The second paper, co-authored with Annalisa Rosselli—*Sraffa and his arguments against 'marginism'*—takes as a starting point the subtitle of Sraffa's most celebrated work, *Production of commodities by means of commodities. Prelude to a critique of economic theory*. Given that no later work was ever published by Sraffa, we are left to wonder what would have come after the prelude. The paper suggests that the core of the critique might have been the marginal method itself. By carefully distinguishing between published and unpublished work, we show that Sraffa's opposition to the marginal method follows several threads, some of which were developed over a period of nearly thirty-five years, such as the belief that economic theory should use only measurable and observable magnitudes, the critique of the "fundamental" symmetry between production and consumption, and the disagreement with the Marshallian concept of equilibrium. Although none of the arguments reached a stage that Sraffa considered satisfactory enough to be worth publishing, our reconstruction sheds light on his research program and on otherwise rather obscure passages in his works.

The third paper—*Joan Robinson's challenges on how to construct a Post-Keynesian economic theory*—examines some of the challenges raised by Joan Robinson in constructing a post-Keynesian economic theory, with the intent to provide some assessment of their relevance today. Rather than dwell on her criticisms of neoclassical economics and of the Neoclassical synthesis, on which much has already been written (even though, unfortunately, not taken on board by mainstream economics), the focus here is on her arguments on the way to construct a post-Keynesian economic theory, possibly now forgotten or at any rate neglected. It is argued that there is still much to be learnt by reviving them today.

In the last paper—*Fighting austerity. Why after 80 years the General Theory is still relevant today*—I maintain that the guiding spirit of the Keynesian Revolution is that full employment is a goal which can be pursued not by following the free market rules, but by reshaping them by means of public intervention. This message was widely accepted for thirty years from the end of the Second World War by all the advanced countries which actively engaged in full employment and welfare policies, and subsequently abandoned with the neo-liberal Restoration which saw the dogmas of individualism and de-regulation prevailing. In reclaiming the topical importance of the *General Theory*, we should take into consideration the changed circumstances of today's world when compared to those of twenty—let alone eighty—years ago, although there are notable similarities between the Great Depression of the 1930s—Keynes's world—and our contemporary crisis. However, his prescription for a better society is still relevant: it lies in setting rules and limitations in the market arena, not letting individual self-interest prevail, and putting some governing bodies in charge of filling the gap when deficient aggregate demand occurs, so that the acquisition of material goods and the fruition of the enjoyments of life be not a privilege of the few but the conquest of civilization.

There are some general considerations I present here as concluding remarks. The history of economic thought is not an easy subject, it requires first a true passion for past ideas and commitment to restore them, like ancient man-made objects to their original shape. The main concern should not be to show their relevance for today, in any specific and detailed manner, but to provide a frame of mind in which today's problems and concepts could be seen through different eyes.

Economic theories do not follow a path leading from error to truth, they are embedded in the context in which they originated and are propagated, in which multifarious aspects are involved, such as ideology, political and social environment, state of the techniques, just to name a few. Digging into the past is a sure means to become aware of this, in order to keep them in mind when we confront the present.

The papers in this collection show that I have travelled both these two routes. I discussed the work of Ricardo, Keynes, Sraffa, Bharadwaj and Robinson, in their own context, in some cases pointing to what in my view are misunderstandings or misinterpretations, in others claiming their relevance as an antidote to mainstream economics. I have also made a plea for a recognition of the importance of the history of economics thought, reviewing the variety of approaches in which it is practiced, and at the same time openly declaring my own preferences and inclinations. My wish and hope are that even readers who may have different views will be interested and engaged.

Roma, March 2024

References

Marcuzzo, M.C. 2012. *Fighting Market Failure. Collected essays in the Cambridge tradition of economics*. Abingdon: Routledge.

Marcuzzo, M.C. 2019. *Essays in Keynesian Persuasion*. Newcastle upon Tyne: Cambridge Scholars Publishing.

Mirowski, P. 1991. The When, the How and the Why of Mathematical Expression in the History of Economic Analysis. *Journal of Economic Perspectives*, 5 (1): 145–157.

PART I

History of Economic Thought: Which Are the Issues?

CHAPTER 2

Is History of Economic Thought a "Serious" Subject?

In her 1932 booklet dedicated to Piero Sraffa, Joan Robinson addressed the question of whether economics is a serious subject. She did so in the form of an apologia of the economist "to the mathematician, the scientist and the plain man". A serious subject in the academic sense, she claimed, "is neither more nor less than its own technique" (Robinson 1932: 3). The point she wanted to drive home was that in economics any attempt at more ambitious endeavours (for instance making realistic "assumptions", and giving up abstract and simplified models) is doomed to failure, since the right techniques to tackle the complexity of the real world are often unavailable.

For my address as the first woman president of the European Society for the History of Economic Thought (ESHET) I decided to look to Joan Robinson, for two reasons: firstly as a homage to a great woman

This is a revised version of my presidential address to the XXII Conference of the European Society for the History of Economic Thought (ESHET), held in Prague, May 15–17, 2008. I wish to thank, without implicating them, Duncan Foley, Wade Hands, Nerio Naldi, Alessandro Roncaglia, Annalisa Rosselli, and Fernando Vianello, for their comments to an earlier version.

Originally publ. in: *The Erasmus Journal for Philosophy and Economics*, 1 (Autumn), 2008, pp. 107–23.
Reprint by Springer Nature Switzerland 2024 with kind permission

M. C. Marcuzzo, *Economic Theories, Protagonists and Facts*, Palgrave Studies in the History of Economic Thought,
https://doi.org/10.1007/978-3-031-63949-4_2

economist, and secondly to clarify the nature of research in the history of economic thought (HET). By reviewing which "techniques" are involved in our discipline, my aim is to find out whether for the historian of economic thought, too, there is any need for an apologia to the economist, the historian and the general audience at large.

For this purpose, I identify four broader categories in which HET can be classified: a) textual exegesis; b) "rational reconstructions"; c) "contextual analysis"; and, with a sort of catch-all definition, d) "historical narrative".

Although I refrain from endorsing a ranking of these techniques, my preferences—or, better, my favourite way of doing HET—deriving from my own personal experience and practice, will become apparent. Finally, I will draw upon *Econlit* records to review what has been done in our subject in the last two decades in order to frame some considerations on how our past may impinge on the future.

Textual Exegesis It could be argued that textual exegesis (TE) is the technique *par excellence* for doing HET.[1] In return for the toil and trouble of the scholarship—namely the laborious and punctilious skill required in this type of exercise—it accords its practitioners the right to establish the "true" meaning of given texts. This technique defines the scope and method of the professional activity of a historian of economic thought, within the accepted hermeneutic codes. Stigler (1965) has given us his recipe for good textual exegesis in HET, which encapsulates the demarcation criterion for deciding its scientific character, and which consists of reviewing texts in the light of the interpreter's contemporary economic knowledge. What is required is the ability to reconstruct the general position of "the theoretical core of an author's work [...] in a manner compatible with contemporary economic theory" (Emmett 2003: 525). Since for Stigler "the meaning of the text is determined not by the individual interpreter or even the original author, but by the scientific community of economists" (Emmett 2003: 525), it follows that doing HET is in all relevant respects no different from doing economics, and that any economist will, at least in principle, be endowed with the necessary skills.

Outstanding examples of the Stigler type of TE approach to HET are Hollander's large scale enterprise in interpreting classical political economy and Patinkin's investigation into Keynes's major works.[2] Far from being uncontroversial, in both cases the interpretations were challenged precisely on the grounds of their readings of the texts being framed by inappropriate theoretical contexts.[3]

Hollander's reconstruction of Ricardo's corn ratio theory of profit and Patinkin's identification of the principle of effective demand in Keynes's early 1930s writings are good examples of trying to make sense of the relevant passages or sentences by employing the logic of the particular neoclassical theory which was standard at the time the interpreter was writing.

Rational Reconstructions Rational reconstructions (RR) were the favoured and, indeed, the most popular technique for doing HET in the 1980s and 1990s. The ideas and insights of Smith, Ricardo, Marshall, Keynes, and Schumpeter were reconstructed in the light of either contemporary problems or modern economic analysis.[4] In just a few praiseworthy cases, investigations were undertaken with philological zest, contextualization, and excursus into unpublished materials, but in most cases the "reconstructions" were made to stand on the shoulders of the contemporary understanding of the issues addressed by past authors.

RR differs from TE in significant respects, the most important of which consists in the reformulation of the arguments of past authors into a modern theoretical framework, rather than "the construction of a theoretical position from the past author's work that can be contrasted with current knowledge" (Emmett 2003: 525).

But what exactly is the technique identifying the RR mode of doing HET? Formalisation, model building, or other translations into more rigorous economic language are called for. Unlike TE, which is a search into the *meaning* of a text, RR is a *translation* of the ideas of past authors into concepts recognisable to modern eyes by dressing them up with modern tools. Since the two exercises are somewhat different, so are the techniques involved.

A related point is whether RR is used to support existing economic knowledge or to challenge current theory. In the former case, the past is sifted for the predecessors of modern theory and present ideas—I call this a "quest for ascendancy"; while in the latter case the past is searched for what has been lost and can no longer be found in modern theory—I call this a "quest for an alternative".[5]

RR is thus not just a variety of "Whig" history, whereby present-day theory is appointed the judge *of the past*, but can also be practised as a search *into the past* for alternatives. Pasinetti's (1974) early work on Ricardo and Keynes can be seen as an outstanding example of the RR approach; alongside Hicks' or Samuelson's incursions into HET, with their reconstruction of Hume-Ricardo-monetary trade theory or Hicks's work on the contributions to monetary theory by classical political economists and Keynes.[6]

However, the pursuit of precursors of contemporary concepts and theories sometimes gives way to what I dub "HET seasoning". This is the technique of identifying ascendancy, or seasoning current economic analysis with references to authors of the past: Keynesian, Schumpeterian, Wicksellian are adjectives intended to add "flavour" to models, such as fixed-price or short-period AS-AD, or endogenous growth, or to interest rate determination in dynamic disequilibrium.

This "HET seasoning" can be performed with more or less concern for the source from which it is derived. For example, when the terms Marshallian or Keynesian are used in analysis of current economic facts or problems, they are interpreted *as if* the theory explaining them were the same as that formulated by Marshall or Keynes. Thus short period unemployment (i.e., Keynesian equilibrium) or external economies (i.e., dynamic competition) identify special cases of what is assumed to be a more general framework of analysis. Thus, within the RR perspective, historians of economic thought are seen to give their "serious" contribution to the advancement of knowledge whenever they *adapt* original concepts to fit contemporary analysis.

The RR mode ceased to be seen as a legitimate and respectable mode of doing HET with the rise of an alternative competing technique—historical reconstruction—which endowed HET with a more distinct character and autonomy as a discipline, but was also a factor in alienating the community of historians of economic thought from that of the economists. Historical reconstructions meant mastering a new technique involving, besides the published work, perusal of manuscripts and letters, and in general a familiarity with archival research methods, thus situating HET more firmly in the past rather than the present.

In fact, by making the past its present, HET's scope and concerns shift from textual exegesis and translation into modern economic language, to a more complex, puzzle-solving type of investigation; it requires acquaintance with facts, circumstantial and presumptive evidence, which have legitimacy per se, and not as a subsidiary to economic analysis. There are, however, two varieties of historical reconstruction, which share a straightforward endorsement of the historical method and a common suspicion of rational reconstructions, but differ in some significant respects. The first, I call "contextual analysis" and the other, for want of a better name, "historical narrative".

Contextual Analysis By context I mean the set of questions and answers which framed theories and concepts, the intellectual interlocutors to whom they were addressed and 'the state of the art' at the time of their conception. The framework consists of facts regarding time, place and circumstances, about which knowledge and information have first to be dug out and then used to make sense of what is being interpreted or, as far as possible, illuminated.

The first conundrum is a matter of source evaluation; in historical investigations we are always confronted with this problem, but as far as HET is concerned there are two aspects to consider: firstly, how related materials, for instance correspondence, stand vis-à-vis purely scientific work (whether published or unpublished); and secondly, in each individual case, the importance of exploring archives rather than relying on published material alone.

Correspondence is the material upon which biographers build their narrative, providing clues to facts, circumstances and above all motives. Moreover, correspondence helps us place ideas in time and context, and thus leads us to ask questions which would probably not have been asked in those terms.

The second conundrum is theoretical legitimacy: the role of archives in filling the gaps in our knowledge of the personal and intellectual lives of the economists concerned is also unquestionably valid, but what is their value in increasing our grasp of their *theories*? My answer, drawing on my own work—mostly done jointly with Annalisa Rosselli—is that "papers and correspondence" afford insight into the *motivations* behind the choices of a particular set of questions, assumptions or tools. These are not always explicitly stated in the published version, where the solutions discarded and definitions abandoned are left out. Archives therefore allow us to travel the road towards a theory rather than, as it were, visit the final destination.

Sraffa's contextual analysis of Ricardo's theory of value and distribution, conducted using unpublished drafts, parliamentary speeches, and correspondence, besides published works, remains the unsurpassed model of scholarship and mastery of this technique (Sraffa 1951–1973). It is the model which has inspired much of my work on the Cambridge approach to economics, attempting to capture the lives and works of Keynes, Kahn, Joan Robinson, and Sraffa in *their* contexts, drawing on the evidence of the intertwined relationships they formed and the conditions of their times; my aim has been more to grasp their individual and shared concerns, rather than to fit their contributions into a unified core of doctrine.

Historical Narrative More recently, rational reconstructions and philological inquiries have been directed towards "minor" or lesser-known figures, in order to answer to the need to survey the broader picture. It is a sort of "stepping down from the shoulders of giants", searching for less theory-laden investigations, connecting intellectual circles, linking characters and events, mapping "tribes and territories". HET thus appears to be progressively diverted from economic ideas and concepts *strictu sensu*, bringing in new perspectives and evidence from hitherto unexplored sources, crossing the boundaries of a single discipline to leap into the broader realm of intellectual history.

Browsing the programmes of the most recent ESHET and HES conferences, or the works awarded recognition as best articles or books by HET societies, this trend can easily be detected. Sessions (or research) on the major classical or neoclassical authors (with the possible exception of Keynes) have shrunk in number and more and more intellectual energy is being devoted to penetrating the less explored territories.

This is a trend which holds particular appeal for young scholars, and it may indeed be a source of misapprehension for those who think that relations with the economic profession should be reinforced, and not loosened. However, some very interesting insights and reconstructions are coming in from these investigations, enlarging and broadening the scope of HET. One should welcome these new openings and encourage the upcoming generation to lead the way.

HET Appraisal After this very brief overview of the techniques and styles of doing HET, I will now turn to the question of its appraisal. What is good HET? How can or should we appraise it?

This issue was raised by Roy Weintraub in his editorial piece in the HES list (Weintraub 1996). HET, he argued, requires a style of scholarship that is standard among historians (use of primary sources, circumstantial evidence, background knowledge, and so forth), but not among economists.

His conclusion was that a "good" economist is not necessarily a "good" historian of economic thought and vice versa.

This line of argument has become increasingly popular since the 1990s,[7] being applied to criticise both mainstream and non-mainstream economists as prone to writing mainly "internalist" or even "whig" histories, drawing on their economics rather than mastering the historians' skills.

I personally believe that good HET shows the capacity to be versed in *both* economic theory and historical methods. It is the combination of these two skills and not simply being knowledgeable in one or the other that makes the difference in the quality of our scientific output. However, I would claim that there is a relevant distinction to be made between doing economics and doing HET.

The task of the "historian" entails close adherence to the reconstruction of theories, personal contributions and the relevant circumstances, requiring the greatest possible respect for contexts and texts, both published and unpublished. The task of the "economist", working on texts and documents but, when expedient, also taking a certain distance from them, entails constructing a theoretical framework that is in some respects freer, and not bound by derivation from the authors. In this respect the theoretician is licensed to compose differences, connecting levels associated with different designs and conceptualisations in diverse authors or in the work of one and the same author.

An example of this distinction between historical and theoretical work which, significantly, has divided and continues to divide the economists working in the Cambridge tradition, has to do with compatibility between the approach of Keynes and the Keynesians, on the one hand, and that of Sraffa and the neo-Ricardians on the other. I feel that in our work as historians we must not be afraid of letting the differences emerge: rather, we must go on bringing to light all those elements of knowledge that offer an understanding of our authors in their historical backgrounds. In our theoretical work we are, in a sense, "freer" to interpret, integrate, and combine concepts and propositions that were quite distinct when formulated. This does not mean taking a cavalier approach to the historian's task but, rather, being clearer about the fact that a different aim is being pursued.

Whose HET? For an understanding of how HET has actually been practised as opposed to how it should be practised according to some declared norms, it may help to review what has been done in our field in the last 20 years or so. This I did by browsing *Econlit* on the basis of descriptors

B000-B590, which were introduced in 1991; although the classification and the chronology are far from being accurate and acceptable, this affords us a comprehensive overview of the extant HET literature.

Of course it has to be borne in mind that among the top ranked journals in our field only *History of Political Economy* has full *Econlit* coverage, while for *European Journal for the History of Economic Thought*, *Journal of the History of Economic Thought*, *History of Economic Ideas*, *History of Economic Review* the records start from the early 1990s.[8] However, these gaps are partly offset by the presence, up to the late 80s, of some HET articles in generalist journals such as *Journal of Political Economy*, *Economic Journal*, and even *American Economic Review* (Table 2.1).

Since more than one descriptor can be assigned to each individual record in *Econlit*, we can sum up all the B descriptor records only by making sure we have eliminated multiple attributions. This I have not attempted to do. However, within each descriptor we can compare the numbers and identify the time profile of each of them.

In the great majority of cases, *Econlit* records only articles from journals and edited volumes, and books which have been reviewed in JEL, in the latter case with a strong bias for those written in English. Notwithstanding all these limitations, we can get a reasonably reliable picture of HET output over the last 20 years. Tables 2.2 and 2.3 offer a bird's-eye view.

As to the *topics*, the highest score is for individual authors, B310–HT: Individuals (10941); followed by B410–Economic Methodology (3868); B220–HET: Macroeconomics (2292); B120–HET: Classical (including Adam Smith) (1760); B250–HET since 1925: Historical, Institutional, Evolutionary, Austrian (1714); and B520–Current Heterodox Approaches: Institutional, Evolutionary (1389).

As to *individuals*, about 40% (4540) of the records (10941) are for the top 5 of 50 most studied authors: Smith: 1366; Keynes: 1207; Hayek: 599; Marx: 535; Veblen 452; Sraffa: 381. We may note in passing that the "10 great economists from Marx to Keynes", according to Schumpeter's list (namely, Marx, Walras, Menger, Marshall, Pareto, Bohm-Bawerk, Taussig, Fisher, Mitchell, and Keynes) are very poorly matched in the *Econlit* ranking of records (Figs. 2.1, 2.2, 2.3 and 2.4).

As to the *time profile*, there is a general tendency for a fall in the numerosity of records, as can be seen by taking the top 5 ranked descriptors, i.e., those with the highest number of records: B310—History of Thought: Individuals (10941); B410—Economic Methodology (3868); B220—HET: Macroeconomics (2292); B120—HET: Classical (1760); with the

Table 2.1 HET *Econlit* descriptors post-1991

B000	Schools of Economic Thought and Methodology: General	**B250**	History of Economic Thought since 1925:Historical; Institutional; Evolutionary
B100	History of Economic Thought through 1925: General	**B290**	History of Economic Thought since 1925: Other
B110	History of Economic Thought: Preclassical (Ancient, Medieval, Mercantilist, Physiocratic)	**B300**	History of Thought: Individuals: General
B120	History of Economic Thought: Classical (includes Adam Smith)	**B310**	History of Thought: Individuals
B130	History of Economic Thought: Neoclassical through 1925 (includes Austrian, Marshallian, Walrasian)	**B400**	Economic Methodology: General
B140	History of Economic Thought through 1925: Socialist; Marxist	**B410**	Economic Methodology
B150	History of Economic Though through 1925: Historical; Institutional	**B490**	Economic Methodology: Other
B190	History of Economic Thought through 1925: Other	**B500**	Current Heterodox Approaches: General
B200	History of Economic Thought since 1925: General	**B510**	Current Heterodox Approaches: Socialist; Marxian; Sraffian
B210	History of Economic Thought: Microeconomics	**B520**	Current Heterodox Approaches: Institutional; Evolutionary
B220	History of Economic Thought: Macroeconomics	**B530**	Current Heterodox Approaches: Austrian
B230	History of Economic Thought: Econometrics; Quantitative Studies	**B590**	Current Heterodox Approaches: Other
B240	History of Economic Thought since 1925: Socialist; Marxist		

notable exception of Econometrics and Quantitative Studies, which has the lowest number of records. As to the ***dissertations***, although their number is small—totalling only 131 over the relevant period—they give us an interesting picture of the trend in the topics of research in the field (see Table 2.2). To be noticed is that the ranking slightly differs from that of the articles; while the top 2 ranked descriptors in both cases are B310 (History of Thought: Individuals) and B410 (Economic Methodology), the lowest numbers of dissertations are found in topics, such as B130 (History of Thought: Neoclassical through 1925), B210 (HET: Microeconomics) which are ranked among the first ten in the case of articles.

Table 2.2 Number of publications according to *Econlit* descriptors

CODE	*HET Econlit descriptors*	*No. PUBL.*	*No. DISS.*	*CODE*	*HET Econlit descriptors*	*No. PUBL.*	*No. DISS.*
B310	History of Thought: Individuals	10941	32	**B200**	History of Economic Thought since 1925: General	639	3
B410	Economic Methodology	3868	20	**B100**	History of Economic Thought through 1925: General	505	3
B220	History of Economic Thought: macroeconomics	2292	8	**B000**	History of Economic Thought and Methodology: General	450	
B120	History of Economic Thought: Classical	1760	9	**B190**	History of Economic Thought through 1925: Other	419	2
B250	History of Economic Thought since 1925: Socialist; Marxist	1714	11	**B530**	Current Heterodox Approach: Austrian	409	2
B130	History of Economic Thought Neoclassical through 1925	1539	1	**B230**	History of Economic Thought: Econometrics; Quantitative and Mathematical Studies	409	3
B520	Current Heterodox Approach: Institutional; Evolutionary	1389	8	**B290**	History of Economic Thought since 1925: Other	391	4
B210	History of Economic Thought: Microeconomics	908	2	**B300**	History of Thought: Individuals	254	1
B110	History of Economic Thought: Preclassical	856	3	**B500**	Current Heterodox Approach: General	149	2

(*continued*)

Table 2.2 (continued)

CODE	*HET Econlit descriptors*	*No. PUBL.*	*No. DISS.*	*CODE*	*HET Econlit descriptors*	*No. PUBL.*	*No. DISS.*
B240	History of Economic Thought since 1925: Socialist; Marxian	820	4	**B320**	Obituaries	134	0
B510	Current Heterodox Approach: Socialist; Marxian; Sraffian	794	8	**B540**	Feminist Economics	104	0
B150	History of Economic Thought through 1925: Historical; Institutional	743	1	**B590**	Current Heterodox Approaches: Other	45	0
B400	Economic Methodology: General	706	1	**B490**	Economic Methodology: Other	39	0
B140	History of Economic Thought through 1925: Socialist; Marxist	705	3	**B160**	History of Economic Thought: Quantitative and Mathematical	27	0

Table 2.3 Number of *Econlit* records on authors

Smith	1366	Samuelson	170	Edgeworth	87	Cantillon	42
Keynes	1207	Pareto	148	Kaldor	78	Kahn	42
Hayek	599	Malthus	147	Harrod	74	Turgot	42
Marx	535	Friedman	138	Thornton	73	Einaudi	34
Veblen	452	Hicks	131	Bentham	70	Galiani	33
Sraffa	381	Say	122	Quesnay	69	Modigliani	33
Schumpeter	376	Wicksell	121	Cournot	63	Neumann	29
Marshall	360	Kalecki	119	Arrow	62	Nash	27
Ricardo	281	Knight	107	Robertson	62	Mandeville	26
Walras	230	Jevons	106	Bohm-Bawerk	58	Wieser	23
Mill	206	Menger	104	Robbins	54	Petty	22
Fisher	196	Hume	98	Georgescu-Rogen	43		
J. Robinson	193	Pigou	93	Sismondi	43		

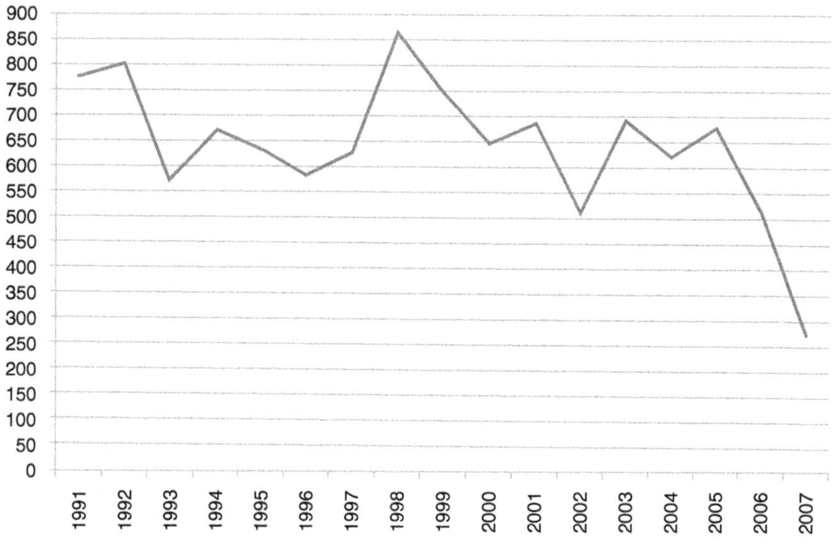

Fig. 2.1 B310: Individuals

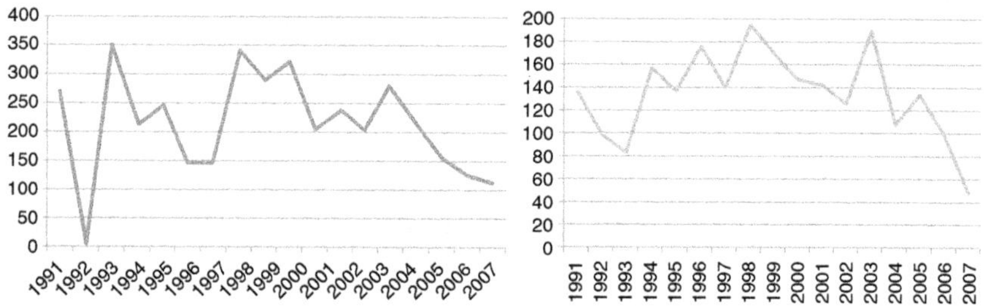

Fig. 2.2 B410: Economic methodology—B220: Macroeconomics

In order to be more significant, the exercise should be extended to the pre-1991 period, converting the old descriptors set to the new one; this would sometimes involve the arbitrary matching of topics and a large computation of records, which I have not attempted to do. Hopefully, however, what I have collected is sufficient to provide some evidence in presenting the outlook of our field in the last 20 years.

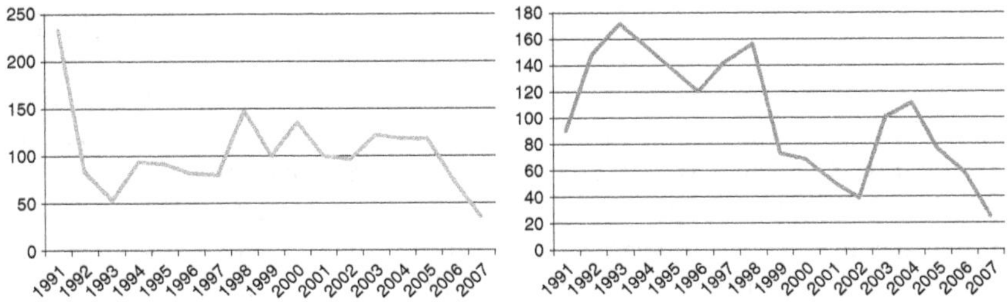

Fig. 2.3 B120: Classical (incl. Adam Smith)—B250: Socialist, Marxist since 1925

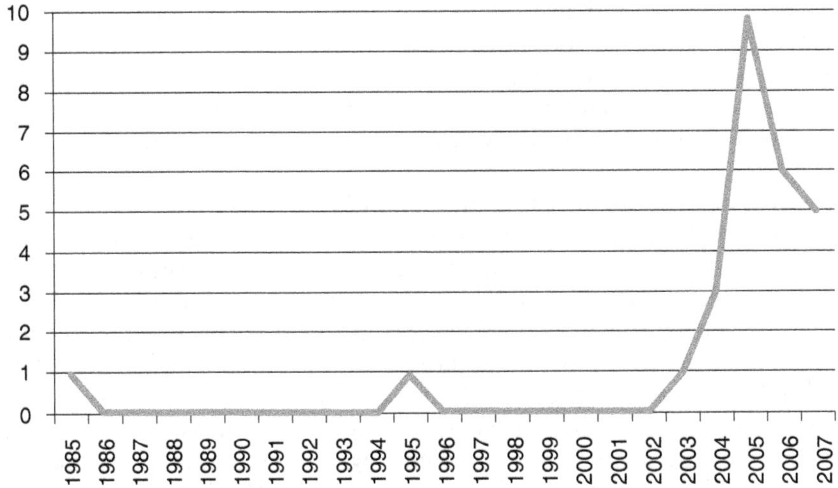

Fig. 2.4 B160: Quantitative and mathematical

Research Agenda Can the past activity in HET offer us some insights into its trend for the future? Are the gaps likely to be filled and how? I will venture to point to two areas in which I think we may expect some rise in interest and activity.

The first is feminist economics. HET could be an important tool in the work of exposing an impossible neutrality and pervasive gender-blindness.[9] A gender-sensitive reading of past works and theories could open our eyes to the gradual shifts in meaning of the terms, the slow movement of the boundaries of the discipline, the progressive exclusion from it of whole areas of economic activity (housework for example) and of concepts which, though meaningful, lack a quantitative dimension.

The second is the broadening of geographical areas in which we may see interest and country-related research activity blossom in HET. My recent travels to Mexico, India, Japan, and China have proved to me that HET is a vital key to connecting ideas, as well as preserving identity and individual intellectual histories, and this in turn shows that there are indeed ways and means to establish a multicultural rather than monocultural discipline.

HET may help to enhance the ability to speak the same economic language, a necessary requisite of any scientific communication, with awareness of the variety and diversification in approaches to economic ideas and problems.[10] National societies for the history of economic thought are already there for us to connect and they could play a prominent role in bridging economic cultures and national backgrounds. Personally, I am looking forward to increasingly globalised research activity in HET.

Conclusions I began my paper by asking whether there is any need for an apologia of the historian of economic thought, addressing this question to the economist, the historian, and the general audience at large.

To the economist, I would urge the importance of maintaining in the economics departments keepers of ideas and concepts born in the past, to preserve them from oblivion and the risks of being misused when uprooted from their context. Engaging in conversation and confrontation with contemporary economic discourse is an intellectual duty and while we should be wary of the consequences of alienating ourselves from it, we should make our case as boldly and fearlessly as possible. This is particularly true today, there no longer being a unified, mainstream core in economic analysis.

To the historian, I would plead the importance of ranking our priorities in fact finding and digging into unexplored sources; treasure hunts in economic archives do not have the same pay-off as in much intellectual history and should be done sparingly. Historical investigation should be a benchmark of scholarship for HET, not just another role-model, as mathematics or the natural sciences are for economists.

Finally, to the general audience at large I will make a plea for pluralism in economic analysis, in terms not so much of tools as of ideas. The critical awareness which HET cultivates of how economics is rooted in a given context of interests, ideology, and culture is the road to intellectual freedom and the recipe to advance our knowledge. HET is well placed to cater for the needs of the general public to have this clearly spelt out and understood.

Let me quote from Joan Robinson once again in conclusion: "Economics limps along with one foot in untested hypotheses and the other in untestable slogans. Here our task is to sort out as best we may this mixture of ideology and science" (Robinson 1964: 28).

This is the challenge, the duty, but also the pleasure of doing history of economic thought.

Notes

1. It may be objected that textual exegesis is a tool that can be applied to any type of HET research. For my purpose, however, it is used to indicate that specific approach centred on "making sense" of a text or a set of propositions.
2. For my purpose, it will suffice to refer here to Hollander (1979) and Patinkin (1982).
3. For Hollander, see Garegnani (1982) and Peach (1993); for Patinkin, see Kahn (1984).
4. See Blaug (1990).
5. See Marcuzzo and Rosselli (2002).
6. To give only two examples, see Samuelson (1971) and Hicks (1967).
7. See, for instance, the works by Schabas (1992), Hands (1994), and Henderson (1996).
8. HOPE (1969–present); EJHET (Autumn 1993–present); JHET (Spring 1990–present); HEI (1993–present); HER (Winter 1994–present).
9. For a recent attempt in this direction, see Marcuzzo and Rosselli (2008).
10. For a recent illustration of the same point, see Foley (2008).

References

Blaug, M. 1990. On the historiography of economics. *Journal of the History of Economic Thought*, 12 (1): 27–37.

Emmett, R.B. 2003. Exegesis, hermeneutics and interpretation. In *The Blackwell companion to the history of economic thought*, eds. J. Biddle, J. Davis, and W. Samuels. Oxford: Blackwell, 523–537.

Foley, D.K. 2008. The history of economic thought and the political economic education of Duncan Foley. Distinguished Guest Lecture, History of Economics Society Annual Conference, Toronto, June 27–30, 2008.
Garegnani, P. 1982. On Hollander's interpretation of Ricardo's early theory of profits. *Cambridge Journal of Economics*, 6 (1): 65–77.
Hands, D.W. 1994. The sociology of scientific knowledge and economics: some thoughts on the possibilities. In *New directions in economic methodology*, ed. Roger Backhouse. London: Routledge, 75–106.
Henderson, J.P. 1996. Whig history is dead: now what? *The History of Economics Society Website*. HES Archives. http://eh.net/pipermail/hes/1996-November/004822.html (accessed November 2008).
Hicks, J.R. 1967. *Critical essays in monetary theory*. Oxford: Clarendon Press.
Hollander, S. 1979. *The economics of David Ricardo*. Toronto: University of Toronto Press.
Kahn, R.F. 1984. *The making of Keynes's General Theory*. Cambridge: Cambridge University Press.
Marcuzzo, M.C., and A. Rosselli. 2002. Economics as history of economics: the Italian case in retrospect. *History of Political Economy*, 34 (Annual Supplement): 98–109.
Marcuzzo, M.C., and A. Rosselli. 2008. The history of economic thought through gender lenses. In F. Bettio and A. Verashchagina (eds.), *Frontiers in the Economics of Gender*. London: Routledge, 3–20.
Pasinetti, L. 1974. *Growth and income distribution. Essays in economic theory*. Cambridge: Cambridge University Press.
Patinkin, D. 1982. *Anticipations of the General Theory? And other essays on Keynes*. Oxford: Blackwell.
Peach, T. 1993. *Interpreting Ricardo*. Cambridge: Cambridge University Press.
Robinson, J. 1932. *Economics Is a Serious Subject: The apologia of an economist to the mathematician, the scientist and the plain man*. Cambridge: Heffer and Son.
Robinson, J. 1964. *Economic philosophy*. Harmondsworth: Penguin, Pelican Books.
Samuelson, P.A. 1971. An exact Hume–Ricardo–Marshall model of international trade. *Journal of International Economics*, 1 (1): 1–18.
Schabas, M. 1992. Breaking away: history of economics as history of science. *History of Political Economy*, 24 (1): 187–203.
Sraffa, P. (ed., with the collaboration of M. Dobb). 1951–1973. *D. Ricardo. Works and correspondence*, 11 vols. Cambridge: Cambridge University Press.
Stigler, G.J. 1965. Textual exegesis as a scientific problem. *Economica*, 32 (128): 447–450.
Weintraub, R. 1996. Legitimate contribution to H of E. *The History of Economics Society Website*. HES Archives. http://eh.net/pipermail/hes/1996-September/005765.html (accessed November 2008).

CHAPTER 3

A Slender Trunk and Many Branches. The History of Economic Thought in Perspective, Past and Future

3.1. To discuss the future of the history of economic thought (henceforth HET), I thought I would have to start by looking at its *past,* i.e. how it was conceived and practised by the Great Masters and moulded into a canonical form; then I would have to move on to assess the *present,* i.e. the current practices and the major players; and finally I would have to look for clues to divine its *future.* I soon discovered that, following this path, I would never get beyond the first stage, so much could be said about the earlier phases of the subject—so I decided to take an intermediate route, looking at the styles and trends that have shaped the subject in the past twenty years or so. In doing so, however, I peer into past history, to trace their roots and ancestry. As for the future of the history of economic thought, I can only make some tentative guesses as to which branches are likely to grow faster and burgeon with blossom and fruits.

3.2. According to Cannan 'the greatest part of an economist's duty will be upsetting false theories' (quoted in Maloney 1991: 70), and this provides the rationale for studying the history of economic thought. This sentence

Originally publ. in: H.M. Krämer, H. Kurz, H.-M. Trautwein (eds.), *Macroeconomics and the History of Economic Thought. Festschrift in honour of Harald Hagemann*, Abingdon: Routledge, 2012, pp.171–80.
Reprint by Springer Nature Switzerland 2024 with kind permission

M. C. Marcuzzo, *Economic Theories, Protagonists and Facts*, Palgrave Studies in the History of Economic Thought,
https://doi.org/10.1007/978-3-031-63949-4_3

can be, and in fact has been, interpreted to mean that (a) there is not a linear progression from error to truth, so that ideas in the past may be used to counteract the present economic ideas; and (b) there is a linear progression from error to truth, so that our present knowledge can be employed to expose the errors made in the past.

Most historians of economic thought have left behind them (b), which remains a feature of those economists who endorse Stigler's belief that the market of ideas is efficient (false ideas do not survive) and/or follow the Whig style in doing history (the past is read through the lenses of the present). They share the belief that in many respect economics is akin to natural science, and the common perception that past scientific theories have no relevance today.

An outstanding example of branch (a) within the 'history of ideas' approach is the tradition stemming from Marx to Sraffa. Sraffa attended Cannan's lectures at the LSE in 1920s, and during the same period he read Marx's *Theories of Surplus Value*; ever afterwards he engaged in the quest for what had been 'submerged and forgotten' with the advent of marginalist theories in the 1870s, namely the classical approach to value and distribution. In his 'Advanced theory of value' course—given in Cambridge between 1929 and 1931—he challenged the Marshallian view of a continuity of approach in the history of economics; he showed how the notion of cost of production was transformed from the classical school to the marginal school, leading to unification with utility. For such unification to be possible—Sraffa argued—the notion of cost of production had to undergo a series of changes which made it unrecognizable in terms of the meaning given to it by the classics. The discovery that there are two notions of costs, which gave rise to two theories of distribution, paved the way to the development of an alternative approach to neoclassical economics, based on a return to classical Political Economy.

The Neo-Ricardian and Marxist approaches to HET share what I dub the 'quest for the alternative', i.e. the past is searched for what has been lost and can no longer be found in modern theory, in contrast to the 'quest for ascendancy', where the past is sifted for the predecessors of modern theory and present ideas, which is typical of the traditional Whig approach to HET (see Marcuzzo and Rosselli 2002).

In the Neo-Ricardian and Marxist branch, however, the role of HET is instrumental: it is part of a programme to build an alternative economic theory and in fact is synonymous with doing non-mainstream economics. In the words of Heinz Kurz (2006: 475),

> historians of economic thought are almost bound to be to a smaller or larger degree heterodox; [their task could be to] act as critics, interpreters and intermediaries who bring back to life the historical conditions in which the ideas under consideration emerged, whether vested interests played any role in this, which transfigurations these ideas underwent over time, and what they mean today and why they are still held by some people.

This heterodox implication, however, is not necessarily imbued in the history of ideas approach; for instance, in the Cambridge tradition of historiography (Skinner 1969), 'interpreting work in the context of available meanings at the time' (Emmett 2009: 19) may or may not foster consideration of how those ideas may be transplanted to the present day. The work of Donald Winch is representative of the "intellectual history" approach to HET: 'my work proceeds *from* individual authors and their text *to* the intellectual and cultural context that promise most by way of understanding what those authors were attempting to do' (Winch 1996: 20). More recent examples are Hont (2005) and Cook (2009).

The history of ideas and the intellectual history approaches to HET stress the importance of locating texts in their historical context, i.e. it is primarily a 'sustained scholarly attempt to understand the meaning that the text of past authors had for themselves and for their contemporaries' (Waterman 1998: 303). Now, the question that arises is how the meaning of the text is best captured and how the context is best reconstructed. Here again, different branches fork off from the trunk.

3.3. Textual exegesis is as old as the discipline itself, and hermeneutic issues have long been debated. While Stigler (1965) defined it as the ability to reconstruct the general position of the theoretical core of an author's work in a manner compatible with contemporary economic theory, it has been recognized that this approach is limited in scope, and even distorting. Brown (1993) has offered an important contribution in this area, by drawing on literary criticism, while Gerrard (1991) has shown the subtle and complex conception of the nature and significance of interpretation.

By the end of the 1960, it was becoming increasingly accepted that 'texts, documents, and histories, and, consequently, the ideas contained therein, did not have stable meanings. They [...] took meaning from their contexts, and their contexts changed discontinuously as information environments (climates of opinion, epistemes) followed one another in chaotic fashion' (Neill 2002: 6).

Review of existing records and texts in order to provide evidence for interpretations and to explain developments of ideas, however, is not a simple matter, since the evidence is rarely unambiguous and interpretations are often constrained by the evidence available. It thus became expedient to turn to archives, which supplement and provide clues to the published works, filling the gaps in our knowledge. In fact, archival research into unpublished work and correspondence has blossomed among historians of economics and also economists in recent years, and has already yielded a rich crop of literature. How should we assess this activity and measure the value-added it holds for the profession?

In a recent paper (Marcuzzo and Rosselli 2008) we argued that archival research has allowed interpreters to have clearer insights into the development of ideas through time, their context in relation to interlocutors and opponents, and the nature of the problems addressed. The archival work which has been pursued in the last twenty-five years on the papers of Marshall, Keynes, Sraffa, Harrod, Hayek, J. Robinson and Kahn, to mention but a few, has produced scholarly articles and books which could not have been written on the basis of published material alone. The consequent success has attracted new practitioners and provided incentives to increase activity in research on the papers of the less famous, less familiar figures.

In that paper we gave warning that:

> it should not be encouraged to search archives in the spirit of a 'treasure hunt', or in other words in the hope that unpublished papers or unknown letters might unveil the true meaning of a concept or 'prove' one interpretation rather than another. These are very rare occurrences and it is, rather, the patient, persistent, sometimes unrewarding search for clues and facts which fits our discoveries into the pre-existing knowledge, as in a jigsaw. (Marcuzzo and Rosselli 2008: 216)

We are indeed witness to a growing industry of archive mining, which is undertaken to secure material which may be promising for an article for publication, and while all research findings are per se valuable, the instrumental end for which it is undertaken sometimes results in achievements that can ultimately prove meagre in terms of real significance.

3.4. The current revival of Keynes and Keynesian economics is an interesting case of the 'quest for alternative' branch in the history of ideas approach. A substantial literature has blossomed, in which the 'upsetting of the false theories' of rational expectation, efficient market hypothesis and calculable risk have been undertaken by rejuvenating the approaches taken by Keynes and Minsky. The case is interesting because the 'return to Keynes' plea is seldom matched by original research into his work, much being sheer rhetoric or relying on second-hand knowledge. I will illustrate here just a few cases and some issues.

The standard 'return to Keynes' argument is the need for fiscal stimulus to boost the economy from the depths of recession, and effectiveness of fiscal policies is back at the core of the dividing line between those who favour or oppose a 'return to Keynes', as it was in the 1970s between Keynesians and Monetarists. However, Keynes's original arguments have seldom been reappraised. The 'return to Keynes' in many cases turns out to be lip service, with very little original work done on those aspects of his work that are relevant to the present recession and crisis of economics. The strand of literature which has remained faithful to Keynes and is accused of 'preaching to the converted' relies, with few exceptions, on scholarly work done in the 1980s and 1990s.

The economics of Keynes is not just about government spending and injection of liquidity in times of crisis, but also about international cooperation on matters of finance, primary commodities and international payments to provide the appropriate framework to a market economy. It is the conviction that markets and economic behaviour are to be guided by a logic of coordination and rules, rather than left to the pursuit of individual interests and the freedom resulting from the lack of public intervention and regulation by the institutions. It incorporates a view of rational behaviour under uncertainty, where reasonableness as opposed to rationality is praised; while irrationality ('animal spirits' and 'herd behaviour') may at times dominate investment decisions or financial markets, ample room is left to rationality bounded by knowledge, judgement and experience.

Much of our understanding of Keynes's insights and prescriptions is the result of scholarly investigation into his writings and unpublished material undertaken by historians of economic thought; they have proved to be better equipped than economists to appraise Keynes's wide range of proposals and not to make do with simple-minded, so-called Keynesian policy.

3.5. There is another branch in the HET tree which has sprouted in recent years and can be characterized as the study of 'the interrelationships between economic ideas and their historical context, the influence of economic ideas on policy, and the public reputation, organization and professionalization of economics as an academic discipline and or science' (Coats 1993: ix). Outstanding examples are Clarke (1990), a reconstruction of the Keynesian revolution in a wider context where sociological, ideological and political elements are given a prominent role to play; and Mirowski (2002), showing how American orthodoxy was the product of further waves of physicists cascading over into economics in the Great Depression and the Second World War.

Rational reconstructions and philological inquiries have also focused on 'minor' or lesser-known figures, in order to answer to the need to fill out the broader picture. It is a sort of 'stepping down from the shoulders of giants', searching for less theory-laden investigations, connecting intellectual circles, linking characters and events, mapping 'tribes and territories'.

HET thus appears to be progressively diverted from economic ideas and concepts *stricto sensu*. In the papers presented at the most recent ESHET and HES conferences, or in the works accorded recognition as best articles or books by HET societies, this trend can easily be detected. Sessions (or research) on the major classical or neoclassical authors (with the possible exception of Keynes) have dwindled in number, and ever more intellectual energy is being devoted to penetrating the less explored territories. *Practices* rather than *ideas* have become the focus of analysis; papers on visualization, means and form of communication of economic ideas have become popular (see ESHET Conference 2010 call for papers; Levy and Peart 2010).

In my 2008 ESHET Presidential address I showed that this trend emerges from perusal of the B *Econlit* descriptor, i.e. History of Economic Thought articles published in JEL since 1991 (Marcuzzo 2008). In the past five or six years, in particular, there has been a fall in the numbers of records in all the top ranked descriptors, i.e. those with the highest number of records: B310—History of Thought: Individuals; B410—Economic Methodology; B220—HET: Macroeconomics; B120—HET: Classical; B250—Socialist, Marxist.

Robert Neill has recorded this sea change in the development of HET as an academic discipline, arguing that a new approach

> placed that discipline on a different footing, freeing it from intellectual dependence on the development of its subject, Economics. It acquired standing outside of Economics. It acquired a new task. The old tasks remained to be a handmaiden to, and a goad for theory. The new task was

> to assess the non-rational elements in the formation of theory and, on the basis of the assessment, to pass a hubris reducing judgement on theory as positive science. The result was a degree of separation between the History of Economics and Economics. (Neill 2002: 11)

Perusal of the contents of articles in HOPE (*History of Political Economy*), EJHET (*European Journal of the History of Economic Thought*) and JHET (*Journal of the History of Economic Thought*) in recent years yields interesting results. While there is still a fair number of articles 'clarifying what had been said, who had said it first, how it had been supplanted by something better, if it had, and who supported whom in favour of this or that view of the economic world and its policies' (ibid.: 8), it is apparent that the field is increasingly permeated by new perspectives and topics. Palma (2008), who tabulated the 1,236 articles published from 1993 to 2006, complains that only 5.9 per cent are dedicated to the period 1945 to today, and even less to contemporary mainstream theory (Table 3.1).

Table 3.1 Articles in HOPE, JHET and EJHET, 1993–2006

	History of Political Economy		*Journal of the History of Economic Thought*		*European Journal of the History of Economic Thought*		*Total*	
	Articles	*Rel. no. of articles (%)*	*Articles*	*Rel. no. of articles (%)*	*Articles*	*Rel. no. of articles (%)*	*Articles*	*Rel. no. of articles (%)*
Pre-classical	70	10.9	16	5.2	37	12.8	123	10.0
Adam Smith	38	5.9	17	5.6	22	7.6	77	6.2
1770–1870	77	12.0	37	12.1	47	16.3	161	13.0
1870–1900	37	5.8	36	11.8	31	10.8	104	8.4
1900–1945	114	17.8	57	18.6	43	14.9	214	17.2
1945–today	37	5.8	19	6.2	17	5.9	73	5.9
Cross-Section	61	9.5	42	13.7	39	13.5	142	11.5
Commentaries/ Replies	64	10.0	28	9.2	11	3.8	103	8.3
Other Methodology	144	22.4	54	17.6	41	14.2	239	19.3
Total	642	100.0	306	100.0	288	100.0	1,236	100.0

Moreover, although the contents of the 945 articles published from 2000 and 2009 in HOPE (382), JHET (283) and EJHET (280) *as described* by the JEL codes do not show any significant trend, with the possible exception of B100, B120, B190, B200 and B220[1] (see Fig. 3.1), this is certainly to be put down to the inadequacy of the descriptors, which do not capture changes in style and approach.

3.6. Since 1992 Margaret Schabas has argued that historians of economics should break away from the economics discipline and join forces with historians of science. Roy Weintraub has taken a very similar position, denouncing that economics may not be the place for HET: 'As the twenty-first century unfolds, it is less likely that economics will be a happy home for the history of economics [...] graduate students in economics are taught using the same textbooks in the United States, China, Italy, and Canada' (Weintraub 2002: 12–13), and HET is not part of it. He sees better possibilities in dialogue with those 'scholarly communities' with which history of economics shares 'permeable boundaries' such as economics, history, literature, philosophy, sociology, and science studies. This scepticism reflects the gradual disappearance of historians of economic thought in Canadian and US universities, as is evidenced in the nationality

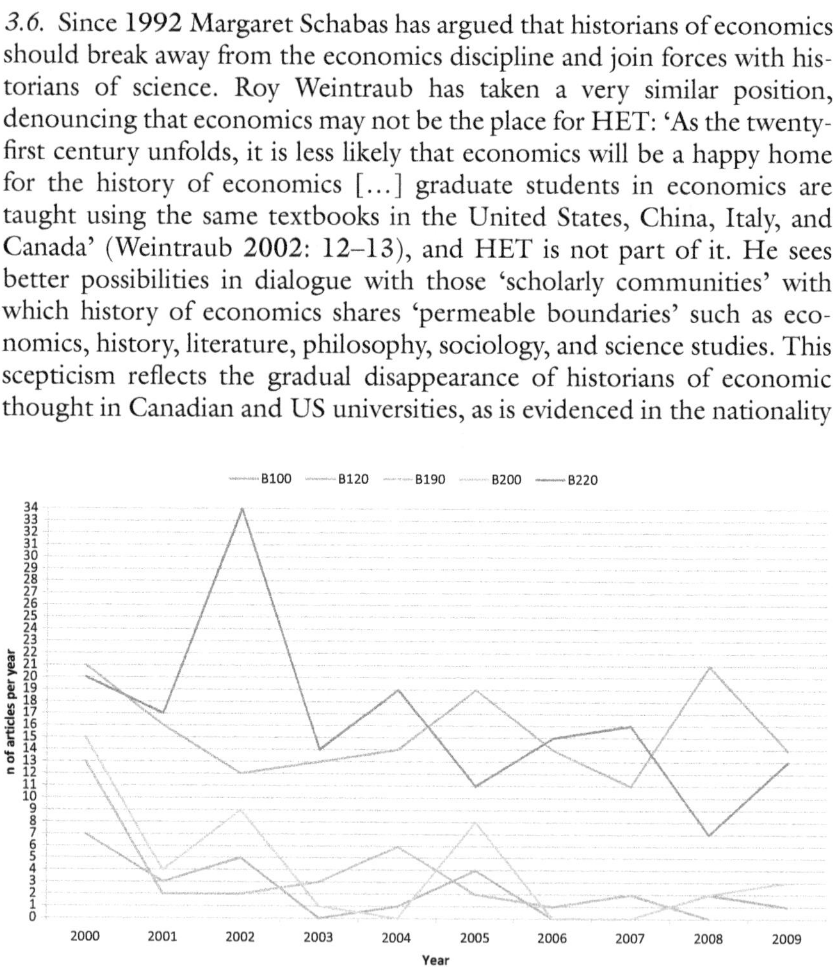

Fig. 3.1 JEL codes of articles in HOPE, JHET and EJHET, 2000–2009

of the authors of articles in HOPE, one of the leading journals in the field; Craufurd Goodwin, in his farewell address as editor, commented that:

> [there is] a steady increase in the proportion of authors in HOPE resident in countries where the elimination of HET from graduate education is, at least, less advanced. The proportion of American authors in HOPE has declined quite steadily over the four decades. In volume 1 it was over 75%. In volume 20 this had fallen almost to one half. By the latest full volume (41) Americans had fallen to about 15% of HOPE authors. (Goodwin 2010: 10)

On the other hand there is no doubt that historians of economic thought have formed a cohesive international community, which may not share the same views on what is the best academic strategy for the subject but has control of the bulk of the scientific output of the profession. Baccini (2009) studied the editorial proximity between journals through observation of the degree of overlap between their boards of editors, and discovered that the journals in the field have strong ties, forming a cohesive subgroup.

In his ESHET Presidential address Kurz took the opposite stance, arguing that 'there are strong reasons to try to regain lost territory within the profession' (Kurz 2006: 464). I also believe that the 'exit' strategy from Economics and Departments of Economics, for the survival of the history of economic thought, may be short-sighted since our 'voice' may still have an audience and hearing in the aftermath of the present disillusionment with mainstream economic theory.

There is another danger. If we agree with Philip Mirowski's diagnosis of the causes of present crisis, i.e. that:

> the first of which must be conceded to have been the exile of history and philosophy from any place within the contemporary economic orthodoxy [...] the areas where one found the greatest concentrations of sceptics concerning the shape and substance of the post-war American economic orthodoxy. (Mirowski 2010: 30)

and with George Soros' indictment that the study of financial markets:

> should not be treated as a physics laboratory but as a form of history. The course of events is time-bound and one-directional. Predictions and explanations are not reversible. Some timelessly valid generalizations can serve to explain events but not to predict them. (Soros 2010: 3)

then the danger of expelling history of thought from economics is even more serious—the danger of reproducing cohorts of economists who will not be able to ensure that the 'melt down' will not happen again.

Note

1. B100—History of Thought through 1925: General; B120—History of Thought: Classical (includes Adam Smith); B190—History of Thought through 1925: Other; B200—History of Thought since 1925: General; B220—History of Thought: Macroeconomics.

References

Baccini, A. (2009) 'Italian economic journals. A network-based ranking and an exploratory analysis of their influence on setting international professional standards', *Rivista Italiana degli Economisti*, 14(3): 491–512.

Brown, V. (1993) 'Decanonizing Discourses: Textual Analysis and the History of Economic Thought', in R. Backhouse, T. Dudley Evans and W. Evans (eds), *Economics as a Language*, London: Routledge, 64–65.

Clarke, P. (1990) *The Keynesian Revolution in the Making, 1924–1936*, Oxford: Clarendon Press.

Coats, R. (1993) *The Sociology and Professionalization of Economics. British and American Economic Essays*, London: Routledge.

Cook, S. (2009) *The Intellectual Foundations of Alfred Marshall's Economic Science. A Rounded Globe of Knowledge*, Cambridge: Cambridge University Press.

Emmett, R. (2009) 'History of Economics and History of Science. A Comparative Look at Recent Work in Both Fields', mimeo.

Gerrard, B. (1991) 'Keynes's General Theory: Interpreting the Interpretations', *Economic Journal*, 101: 276–287.

Goodwin, C. (2010) 'On Editing HOPE', mimeo.

Hont, I. (2005) *Jealousy of Trade. International Competition and the Nation-State in Historical Perspective*, Cambridge, MA: Harvard University Press.

Kurz, H. (2006) 'Whither the History of Economic Thought? Going Nowhere Rather Slowly?', *European Journal for the History of Economic Thought*, 13: 463–486.

Levy, D. and Peart, S. (2010), 'Economists, Crises and Cartoons'. Available online at http://papers.ssrn.com/sol3/papers.cfm?abstract_id=1547886

Maloney, J. (1991) *The Professionalization of Economics. Alfred Marshall and the dominance of Ortodoxy*, New Brunswick: Transactions Publisher.

Marcuzzo, M.C. (2008) 'Is History of Economic Thought a Serious Subject', *The Erasmus Journal for Philosophy and Economics*, 1: 107–123.

Marcuzzo, M.C. and Rosselli, A. (2002) 'Economics as History of Economics: The Italian Case in Retrospect', in E.R. Weintraub (ed.), *The Future of the History of Economics*, Annual Supplement, *History of Political Economy*, 34: 98–109.

Marcuzzo, M.C. and Rosselli, A. (2008) 'The Cambridge Keynesians: Kahn, J. Robinson and Kaldor', in R. Leeson (ed.), *Archival Insights Into the Evolution of Economics*, Vol. 1, London: Palgrave Macmillan, 196–220.

Mirowski, P. (2002) *Machine Dreams: Economics Becomes a Cyborg Science*, New York, NY: Cambridge University Press.

Mirowski, P. (2010) 'The Great Mortification: Economists' Responses to the Crisis of 2007—(and counting)', *The Hedgehog Review*, Summer.

Neill, R. (2002) 'J.J. Spengler's New History of Economics: From Hope to Acceptance'. Available online at www.upei.ca/~meill/web_papers/newhisec.html

Palma, N. (2008) 'History of Economics or a Selected History of Economics?' *Journal of the History of Economic Thought*, 30: 93–104.

Schabas, M. (1992) 'Breaking Away: History of Economics as History of Science', *History of Political Economy*, 24: 187–247.

Skinner, Q. (1969) 'Meaning and Understanding in the History of Ideas', *History and Theory*, 8: 3–53.

Soros, G. (2010) 'Presentation at the INET Conference @ King's College', 8–11 April. Available online at http://ineteconomics.org/initiatives/conferences/kings-college/proceedings

Stigler, G. (1965) 'Textual exegesis as a scientific problem', *Economica*, 32: 447–450.

Waterman, A. (1998) 'Reappraisal of *Malthus the Economist, 1933–97*', *History of Political Economy*, 30: 293–334.

Weintraub, R. (2002) 'Will Economics Ever Have a Past Again?', *History of Political Economy*, 34 (Annual Supplement): 1–14.

Winch, D. (1996) *Riches and Poverty: An Intellectual History of Political Economy in Britain, 1750–1834*, Cambridge: Cambridge University Press.

CHAPTER 4

A Methodological Agenda for New Economic Thinking

4.1 Introduction

The current economic crisis has drawn increased attention to the explanatory failures of modern economics. As market failure came to dominate discussion, idea failure was seen to play no secondary part. De Grauwe (2010) saw in this 'an intellectual framework that blinded economists and policy-makers', resulting from the systematic use of erroneous assumptions and hypotheses in current macroeconomics.

Which are the 'erroneous assumptions and hypotheses under scrutiny? There is some consensus that the assumption of full rationality, efficient markets and the macromodel of Dynamic Stochastic General Equilibrium (DSGE) models constitute the main culprit, and, in particular, the belief that the market adjustment will always tend to equilibrium. This belief is based on four principles:

> i) consumers always maximize their individual utility under a budget constraint; ii) producers always maximize their profits under a resource

Originally publ. in: In B. Dasgupta (ed.), *Non-Mainstream Dimensions of Global Political Economy. Essays in honour of Sunanda Sen*, Abingdon: Routledge, 2013, pp. 115–28.
Reprint by Springer Nature Switzerland 2024 with kind permission

M. C. Marcuzzo, *Economic Theories, Protagonists and Facts*, Palgrave Studies in the History of Economic Thought,
https://doi.org/10.1007/978-3-031-63949-4_4

> constraint; iii) markets may come up against some bumps here and there but in the end, after a few quarters, they always clear and iv) the representative agent was guided by rational expectations. Hence, a shock could move the economy away from 'steady state growth' but after a dynamic adjustment process that could take up to a few quarters it will always bounce back to the steady state. Hence, even assuming some lags due to sticky wages and prices, consumer habits and adjustment investment costs, as long as they assumed 'rational' behaviours of consumers and producers, rational expectations and an inherent market ability to clear, shocks will always generate an intertemporal trend towards equilibrium in DSGE models. [...] DSGE models did not include the financial sector because the predominant macroeconomic thought in the USA when they were created held that the financial market always cleared and no financial disequilibrium was possible – the so called '(?)efficient market hypothesis'. (Garcia 2011: 4)

In the face of the failure of DGSE models to predict, interpret and provide policy indication for the crisis, the profession reacted with a variety of responses which, for the purpose of my talk, I classify in three broad groups: (a) the Radicals, who question almost all the presuppositions upon which standard macro and micro economic models are built; (b) the Reformers, who claim some changes are called for within the existing macro and micro models; (c) the Conservatives, who believe that the crisis has not proved that what has been done in economics in the last decade is flawed, but, on the contrary, it indicates the path to follow.

These categories are, in fact, not hard and fast when it come to allocating individuals to any of these groups, with the exception perhaps of the Radicals and the Conservatives, but they serve the purpose of isolating the nature of the solutions proposed. Just to give a few examples of the positions described above, here are some quotations to illustrate the three positions. The radical stance can be summarized in the following proposition: 'Not distinguishing *uncertainty*, which is not calculable, from *risk*, which is, banks, embracing the assumptions of neoclassical or efficient markets finance with mathematical algorithms, believed that they were able to calculate risk with a "high probability of being right"' (Bresser-Pereira 2009: 12). According to this view, the consequence of embracing the assumption that all risks can be calculated, following the 'efficient market economics' has been to increase rather than reduce the frequency of financial crisis.

Blanchard (2008) can be taken as representative of the second group. In an often-quoted paper, he stated that 'the state of macro is good'. He openly admits that in the basic New Keynesian model there is no unemployment, but he believes that the problem can be 'fixed' by introducing a more sophisticated explanation of the *real* and *nominal* wage rigidity assumption as prevailing in the labour markets. Blanchard is also adamant that the model 'falls short of the mark' in assuming an 'arbitrage approach' to the determination of the term structure of interest rates and asset prices, leaving no room to the role that financial institutions play in the economy. He is optimistic about the future of the subject, declaring boldly that 'one can be confident that progress will happen rapidly'.

Chris Sims, the newly awarded Nobel prize-winner, has claimed (Sims 2010) that:

> It's not true that DSGE ignored the possibility of global instability. Though they have mostly been used in the form of local linearization around a stable steady state, their global stability properties have been studied by the people who develop and use them [...] [NK DSGE modelers] they are introducing simple forms of heterogeneity, agency problems, and financial intermediation, and coming up with models that promise to be nearly as manageable as existing DSGE's for fitting to data, yet usable to study the origins of the recent crisis and policy options for emerging from it.

Section 4.2 looks at the suggestions made to set up the agenda for the development of alternative paradigms, concentrating mainly on the views emerging from the Institute for New Economic Thinking (INET), which held its inaugural Conference at King's College in Cambridge in April 2010 on the theme 'The Economic Crisis and the Crisis in Economics', and the second in Bretton Woods on the theme 'Crisis and Renewal: International Political Economy at the Crossroads'.[1] These events brought together economists of various orientations, skills and persuasion, all disillusioned (to varying degrees) with the present state of economics and committed to promoting change in the way economics is practised in research and teaching. The participants were asked to analyse the present situation and to air opinions as to what should and could be done. It is impossible to do justice to all the ideas and suggestions made; my modest purpose here is to look into few of the proposals with a view to assessing their contributions towards addressing 'the failure of ideas' issue and setting up the agenda for new economic thinking.

In Sects. 4.3 and 4.4, I examine the main lessons to be drawn from the work of Keynes and Sraffa, which I consider to be an essential part of the criticism of mainstream economics; in Sect. 4.5, I raise some issues against the existing career models and system of evaluation of research in economics; finally, in Sect. 4.6 a few closing thoughts are offered as conclusions.

4.2 Research Guidelines

Those research guidelines which have focussed on rejection of the assumptions of extreme individual and markets 'rationality' and reliance on Dynamic Stochastic General Equilibrium (DSGE) have stressed various different aspects of the reasons behind this 'failure of ideas'. I find it useful to re-group them under four headings. a) Rationality; b) Interactions; c) Equilibrium; d) Formalism. I will briefly examine them in turn.

a. Rationality

One of the alternative approaches to replace 'rational expectations' in formulating the micro-foundations of models of aggregate outcomes comes from Frydman and Goldberg (2010) and their so-called Imperfect Knowledge Economics (IKE). They insist on recognition of the limits to the knowledge commanded by economists, market participants and policy officials alike and, (following Knight and Keynes), on acceptance that the complete set of outcomes of economic decisions and policies and their associated probabilities, can neither be inferred from past data nor known in advance. However, since individual decision-making displays some regularity, they claim (unlike Keynes) that it is possible to represent it with a mathematical model which allows for the probabilistic formalism. These regularities—the ways in which market participants make and alter their decisions—are better formalized with *qualitative* conditions than with deterministic models. In formulating these qualitative conditions, IKE 'incorporates observations concerning the social context within which individuals make decisions, including the historical record and conventions among market participants' (Frydman and Goldberg 2010). In this respect they attempt to go beyond psychology, which is the area that behavioural economists focus on in particular.

On the contrary, Buiter (2009) firmly believes that the future 'belongs to behavioural approaches relying on empirical studies on how market participants learn, form views about the future and change these views in response to changes in their environment, peer group effects, etc.' A similar views comes from Akerlof in presenting his notion of 'animal spirits' (purportedly drawn from Keynes) as alternative to the economic 'rationality' in the optimal choice assumed by the orthodoxy. Confidence, fairness, corruption, money illusion and stories are the 'real motivations for real people' (Akerlof and Shiller 2009) and the true drivers of human actions. According to this view, it is not limited knowledge or lack of information, which bound rationality and restrict the set of optimal choices; rather, it is the scope of human behaviour which extends beyond economic calculation.

b. Interactions

Can problems be solved by replacing rationality with more realistic behavioural assumptions? Some people have cast doubt on the idea, suggesting that the solution lies elsewhere. What seems to be missing in current macro analysis, according to these economists, is the study of *interactions* and *connections* between actors. Interestingly enough, the main accusation come from someone like J. Stiglitz, who has been one of the most active players in the history of macroeconomics of the last 20 years. Now, he claims that most of the problems posed by the crisis cannot be addressed within the representative agent model, which is the basis of current macromodels: 'It is not that it makes the wrong assumptions about behaviour but that the behaviours under examination are precluded by assumptions' (Stiglitz 2010). In fact, when there is a single agent, the informational asymmetries, externalities and predatory behaviours that have characterized recent events in financial markets by construction cannot be accommodated within the model. So what is the solution? Positive proposals have come from economists, such as Doyne Farmer of Santa Fè, who is committed to rebuilding macroeconomics from the 'bottom up' by collecting data on actual people to calibrate a rich model with millions of interacting agents. Farmer envisages the economy as a complex system, which requires the aid of powerful computers in order to model full complexity and make empirically testable predictions. This is achieved through simulation of the decision-making processes of households, firms, banks and government (Farmer 2010). The same claim is made by Brian Arthur, who draws the distinction between standard economics and complexity economics on the basis of the question asked: while the former is concerned with what is agents' behaviour in equilibrium with the pattern it creates, the latter asks how agents will react next and the pattern further unfold (Arthur 2011).

c. Equilibrium

A similar point is made by the economists who firmly believe that the dynamics of a complex system cannot be captured by the standard notion of equilibrium. We have two eminent economists, such as Axel Leijonhufvud and Duncan Foley, who insist on this point.

Leijonhufvud claims that the interesting distinction in macroeconomics is not between short-run and long-run effects, but between market processes that keep departures from equilibrium prices and outputs within more or less stringent bounds and those which do not, giving rise to deviation-amplifying movements. He objects to standard macro theory which attributes short-run problems to 'sticky wages' or other 'frictions', which, by their very nature, give way in the medium-to-long run, claiming that this is quite the reverse of what actually happens. He writes:

> The really serious short-run problems stem from instabilities and tend to be aggravated rather than helped by very flexible prices. Over the longer run, on the other hand, inflexibilities of one sort or another are at the root of imbalances that eventually will destabilize the system. (Leijonhufvud 2010)

So the dynamics of a complex system cannot be addressed with the notion that markets converge to stable equilibria. Similarly, Foley (2010) claims that the opportunities to introduce constructive new ideas into economics, are 'all connected in one way or another to the vision of the economy as a complex, adaptive system far from equilibrium'. However—he argues—'if one uses sophisticated mathematical methods to analyze a complex adaptive system far from equilibrium under the prior assumption that it is an equilibrium system, the sophistication of the mathematics is not going to correct the fundamental conceptual error'. Moreover, Foley argues, the mathematics employed by economists is of the wrong type:

> Where entropy maximization plays a central role in physicists' understanding of dynamic complex phenomena, economists are pointed toward stochastic optimization theories. Economics comes to a vision of the economy as an exact optimizing process rather than as a chaotic, self-organizing process that approximates orderliness. (Foley 2010)

d. Formalism

Questioning the excess of mathematics in the training and practice of economists has always been high in the agenda of the heterodoxy. The point has been made by several Post-Keynesian, Neo-Ricardian and Istitutionalist economists alike, before and after the recent 'failure of ideas'. In particular, Tony Lawson draws attention to the mismatch between the nature of social material and the conditions required for mathematical methods to have utility, which accounts for the failures of the formalist project in modern economics. The direction of new economic thinking must not be

> to a form of mathematical modelling identified as Keynesian, but to a form of analysis that takes its leave from Keynes' critique of such modelling, certainly from a critique of any *insistence* that modelling of a mathematical deductive type is the only way to proceed. (Lawson 2010)

Most of the suggestions made at the INET, however, fail to challenge the core of mainstream theory on this issue; indeed, the exceptions are very few (Dow 2010; Lawson 2010; Davidson 2011; Seccareccia 2011). I personally believe that the search for an alternative to orthodoxy should take stock of the radical rejection of the standard mode of thinking as accomplished in the methodological critique proposed by Keynes and Sraffa.

4.3 The "Return to Keynes"

In many aspects, it is Keynes (mostly revisited by Minsky) who has been invoked in the aftermath of the current economic crisis. However, this "Return to Keynes" euphoria (Bateman et al. 2010) has been short-lived. Indeed, the concept of uncertainty as opposed to risk, the argument that aggregate outcome is not just the sum of individual behaviour and the crucial role of aggregate demand as the determinant of employment and output, have come back to life in the popular and academic press, but there are signs of a reversal going on. This cycle is aptly described by Seccareccia:

> For a short period during 2009 and 2010, there was a 'Keynes moment' when all governments internationally implemented fiscal stimulus packages largely on the basis of Keynesian demand-side ideas regarding the merits of running budget deficits in times of recession. These ideas defended by policy makers tended to be in strong conflict with the views of most academic

> economists who had been trained for decades to believe that budget deficits are destabilizing because they would ultimately lead to higher interest rates accompanying higher rates of inflation. Since early 2010, this new policy framework seems slowly to have been abandoned. On the one side, there has been significant pressure coming from conservative politicians who are alarmed at the large size of the public sector deficits because of fears of non sustainability of the public finances. At the same time, there has been pressure from mainstream neoclassical economists who fear that long-term deficits would be destabilizing for the economy, because ultimately, it is argued, governments face an inter-temporal budget constraint, whereby current fiscal expansion must be followed ineluctably by future fiscal contraction. Although this view has been severely criticized by heterodox economists, policy makers seem to have reverted back to the pre-2008 policy position on the need for an 'exit strategy' and a return to balanced budgets. (Seccareccia 2011)

Discussion of the trade-off between the need to reduce government debt and the need to sustain aggregate demand in Europe and the USA, has proved that Keynes's lessons are difficult to learn and accept. The dividing issue between Keynesian and anti-Keynesian positions appears to be the relationship that is established between the size of the deficit and the level of income and unemployment. Since there is no theory to justify the 'right' size of deficit or the amount of government spending, the issue at stake is the scale of priorities: in times of recession and high unemployment the priority is to sustain the level of aggregate demand and to increase the level of income and employment. Only recently, with the tragedy of southern European countries risking default, has there been a shift towards concern for measures of growth and not just reduction of public debt. Paul Krugman and Joseph Stiglitz have increasingly become the most strenuous propagators of this view.

Indeed, the revival of Keynes has proved to be limited in breadth and scope, and many interesting features have remained wrapped in oblivion. There are issues that have not come to the forefront, such as Keynes's opposition to the economists' attempts to imitate the standard of scientific inquiry set by physics. It may, therefore, be worthwhile to rekindle his argument.

In his *General Theory*, after explaining that the level of employment oscillates around 'an intermediate position' below full employment and above the minimum subsistence employment (Keynes 1971–89, CWK VII: 254), Keynes adds:

> But we must not conclude that the mean position [of employment] thus determined by 'natural' tendencies, namely, by those tendencies which are likely to persist, failing measures expressly designated to correct them, is, therefore, established by laws of necessity. The unimpeded rule of the above conditions is a fact of observation concerning the world as it is or has been, and *not a necessary principle* which cannot be changed. (Keynes 1971–89, CWK VII: 254, my italics)

The point made here is that in economics 'we cannot hope to make completely accurate generalisations' (ibid.) because the economic system is not ruled by 'natural forces' that economists can discover and order in a neat pattern of causes and effects. The task of economics, according to Keynes, is rather to 'select those variables which can be deliberately controlled and managed by central authority in the kind of system in which we actually live' (ibid.).

Keynes strenuously opposed the economists' attempts to imitate the standard of scientific inquiry set by physics, asserting as the object of economic theory that of developing a logical way of thinking about factors which are 'transitory and fluctuating' (Keynes 1971–89, CWK XIV: 297). Economic theory is not required to discover absolute general laws, which the economic system obeys, but rather to explain decisions taken under different conditions of knowledge by different agents and the social context in which they operate.

In the *General Theory*, Keynes accepted many assumptions of the neoclassical theory—supply and demand analysis, profit maximisation, rising marginal costs, a given degree of competition—but he radically opposed the methodological implications that economic theory (even his own, for that matter) could claim universal validity and generality, regardless of the particular circumstances in which it might be applied.

This 'relativist'" stance, in Keynes's epistemology, can be illustrated by reference to the independent variables of *The General Theory*. In fact, while the liquidity preference, the propensity to consume, the marginal efficiency of investment, the wage unit and the quantity of money are presented as the 'ultimate independent variables', there is no suggestion that this distinction could ever be *general*; on the contrary, the division is said to be 'quite' arbitrary from any *absolute* standpoint (Keynes 1971–89, CWK VII: 247).

Keynes is thus challenging economics to abandon the 'modernist claim' to be a scientific study of society and become an investigation 'into problems which seek to bring about defined or desired end states (or solutions) and clarify values' (Parsons 1997: xiv). In fact, once the fallacy of the analogy of economic laws with physical laws is exposed, the possibility of promoting values and attitudes to change society as a whole becomes apparent. Keynes's struggle to promote reasonable collective behaviour is grounded on confidence in progress: 'it is many generations since men as individuals began to substitute moral and rational motive as their spring of action in place of blind instinct. They must now do the same thing collectively' (Keynes 1971–89, CWK XXVII: 453).

In conclusion, the most significant implication of Keynes's rejection of the mechanical view of economics as a discipline aiming to discover 'scientific' laws and be *wertfrei*, is the claim that 'moral thinking' and 'moral values' (Keynes 1971–89, CWK XXVII: 387) are embedded in any social philosophy, and the economist's quest is to find out how ends are better implemented and which institutions are more apt to the purpose of the social goal.

4.4 Lessons from Sraffa

I will now turn to Sraffa's criticism of the use made of the marginal method, which is used throughout neoclassical theory to determine the optimal choice of the economic agent. It is via this method that demand and supply functions of goods and factors are constructed, whereby prices and distribution are determined.[2] Serious objections to the generalized used of supply and demand analysis and the marginal method have not become part of the toolbox used to tackle the failure of ideas of standard economics. Unlike the situation with Keynes, there has been no 'Return to Sraffa' (either in academia or the media) for the simple reason that with the exception of a short period of time, when the capital controversy raged in the 1960s and 1970s, economists largely failed to acknowledge his importance. There is also another reason that accounts for this oblivion on the part of the profession: Sraffa wrote a great deal, but published very little. Now that his papers have become available,[3] we are in a better position to appreciate the scope and the breadth of his contributions.

In order to elucidate his criticism of neo-classical economics, Sraffa made a distinction between three types of magnitudes in economics: (1) those that are directly measurable in production and consumption processes (acres of land, tons of grain, etc.); (2) the purely subjective magnitudes (such as sacrifice or utility), which are not observable and cannot be measured; and (3) magnitudes—such as marginal productivity—which can be brought about by experiment only. Unlike counterfactuals, marginal magnitudes are propositions regarding happenings that can be subjected to experimentation.

I do not agree with Sen's interpretation (Sen 2003) that Sraffa rejected them as counterfactuals of the type 'what would have happened to European history if Napoleon had won at Waterloo'. This proposition cannot be made object of an *actual* experiment; on the contrary the experiment of measuring production upon adding the $n + 1th$ factor *can* be carried out, but it cannot be claimed that, thanks to the experiment, variation in production observed measures the marginal productivity. In fact, all marginal magnitudes share the nature of being a sequence of mutually exclusive alternatives (i.e. we cannot observe n and $n + 1$ units of factors at the same time) and therefore we have no certainty that the *ceteris paribus* clause holds.

By means of the experiment, measurement is made of the product obtained with $n + 1$ units as compared with that obtained in different circumstances in the preceding instance with n units. We measure only the difference between two average products, obtained in circumstances other than those obtaining before. There are no grounds to conclude that the marginal variation is the contribution of the marginal unit. Here is a relevant passage from Sraffa's unpublished writings, dated [October 1929]:

> [demand and supply curves, marginal productivities, which form the basis of Marshall's theory, (or, rather, Pareto's)] do not exist at any one moment, nor during any period of the recurrent steady process of production and consumption. They are alternatives, only one of which can exist in any one position of equilibrium, all the others being thereby excluded [...]. Therefore they cannot be found by merely observing the process or state of things, and measuring the quantities seen. They can only be found by experiments [...]. But the experiments have an entirely different significance: they actually produce facts which would otherwise not happen at all; if the experimenter did not step in first to produce them, and then to ascertain them, they would remain in the state of 'unknown possibilities', which amount to the deepest inexistence (*SP* D3/12/13/3). (quoted in Marcuzzo and Rosselli 2011)

The question may arise whether Sraffa's objections to the demand and supply function are tantamount to rejection of the hypothetical-deductive reasoning, the 'what-if?' thought experiment, which is the accepted scientific method of analysis in social and natural sciences. Cleary this is not the case. The objections are raised against the claim of generality and universality of the relationship between prices and quantities, or of the functional forms of demand and supply equations required for the existence and stability of equilibrium in neo-classical theory. These objections do not apply to reasoning based on observed magnitudes and measurable entities involved in the exchange and production processes, where the resting positions of the variables involved can be ascertained without invoking alternative either observable or measurable configurations.

Sraffa's lessons seem to be even more remote from the questions posed by the crisis, in the realms of both policy and theory. And yet we have recently seen renewed efforts which offer a positive contribution to understanding the roots of the crisis, combining Sraffa's and Keynes's teaching. For instance, it has been claimed that in the US the crisis originated from a distribution of income problem, i.e. a private debt, which increased to offset the fall in wages and salaries. So the remedy is to substitute public for private debt, increasing expenditure on health, education and housing, so as to restore an adequate and sustainable level of aggregate demand (Barba and Pivetti 2009).

In conclusion, I think that Sraffa's methodological criticisms of neo-classical theory of price and distribution still hold water, and that dropping the pervasive 'individual maximization' paradigm, together with the reasoning at the margin method, would greatly advance our understanding of economics; this is Sraffa's main lesson to be drawn against mainstream economic theory.

4.5 New Economic Practices

If a new way of thinking is to be generated in economics, it must be born from minds trained not only to mathematical or statistical skills, but refined through an understanding achieved by drawing upon the social sciences as well.

However, for this to come about, there must be appropriate incentives, which stimulate the production of innovative tools and rigorous reappraisal of the existing teaching and career models. Change in the systems for evaluating the quality of research in economics is needed, and it must take a new directional approach.

Reasonable as the 'publish or perish system' for progress in an academic career evidently is, it has nevertheless turned into a perverse sort of beauty contest, where the point is to hit on what the majority of economists (in the journals that count) think should be written. From exercises in evaluation carried out with various methods, it emerges that the journals' rankings are constructed on the basis of criteria that are, in part, debatable (for example, quality measured by the quantity of citations), and in some cases arbitrary. Comparison with evaluation processes for research in physics or biology (where the quality of scientific research is, in any case, subject to discussion) may result in something closer to parody than virtuous imitation. The idea of a universally valid criterion to measure the 'quality' of an article is, of course, a mere pipe dream, and examples of cases of *path dependence*, or a 'return' of popularity for a certain article or contribution are not hard to find. Insistence on the objectivity of evaluation, beyond the limits of a reasonable peer review consensus, inevitably brings us up against a whole series of difficulties. The literature on comparison of rankings in economics journals shows, with the possible exception of the top and bottom levels, just how great the margins of variability are.[4]

In the mid-1980s, the American Economic Association (AEA) launched discussion on the topic of educating and training new generations of economists, setting up a Commission on Graduate Education in Economics (COGEE) to study the matter. The Commission's Report was published in the *American Economic Review* in 1991 (Krueger 1991), but the findings it presented were so controversial that it was never accepted as an official document of the AEA. In fact, it brought into focus

> a number of problems in the profession such as a lack of focus on the inculcation of applied research skills, untoward emphasis on mathematics and axiomatic reasoning instead of analyzing institutions and historical change, inadequate attention to the training with respect to communication and writing skills, an absence of creativity, and excessive emphasis on conformity and homogeneity in professional discourse. (Bernstein 2008)

The Commission was given no further mandate. It would be an interesting, counterfactual, exercise to conjecture what the profession would have been like today if the analyses and recommendations of the AEA Commission had been acted upon. If research funding had been channelled into other areas and approaches, the state of the profession and, indeed, of the economy, might have been rather more comforting. Discontent with current practices in training and research in economics has been voiced in many quarters. In his written evidence to the US House Science and Technology Committee, David Colander explained why things are the way they are, with the following account:

> During that time[the last 30 years] the NSF and other research funding institutions strongly supported DSGE research, and were far less likely to fund alternative macroeconomic research. The process became self-fulfilling, and ultimately, all macro researchers knew that to get funding you needed to accept the DSGE modelling approach, and draw policy conclusions from that DSGE model in your research. Ultimately, successful researchers follow the money and provide what funders want, even if those funders want the impossible. If you told funders it is impossible, you did not stay in the research game. (Colander 2010)

In a similar vein, Judge Richard Posner, one of the most influential figures in the law and economics movement in the US, declared in a recent interview in the *New York Times* that:

> market correctives work very slowly in dealing with academic markets. Professors have tenure. They have a lot of graduate students in the pipeline who need to get their Ph.Ds. They have techniques that they know and are comfortable with. It takes a great deal to drive them out of their accustomed way of doing business.[5]

Among the unfavourable conditions that may thwart the development of a new economic thinking, a commentator of the inaugural INET conference mentions the:

> pressures to conform with the prevailing orthodoxy in economics [...] which in recent years have been given a new structure and force by formal systems for the assessment of research funding that place the primary emphasis on publication in a limited number of prestigious journals. (Conford 2010)

I believe that this a serious concern, which should rise to the top of any agenda for new economic thinking.

4.6 Some Conclusions

Mirowski (2013) argues—to my mind convincingly—that the 'remedies' generally proposed to overhaul the mainstream approach (behavioural economics, rejection of the efficient market hypothesis and extirpation of the Dynamic Stochastic General Equilibrium (DSGE) macroeconomic model) will not fix the problems with orthodox theory; these ultimately rest with the method and substance of neo-classical economics. I entirely agree that it would be more promising to consider the approaches that question more radically the presuppositions upon which standard economics is built. As the reader will have guessed, I side with the Radicals (and with those at INET) who question practically the whole set of presuppositions upon which standard macro- and micro-economics are built. While I appreciate efforts to reappraise existing methods and practice by proposing more sophistication in the tools of analysis, I am doubtful that much progress can be made along this path. My conclusion rests on three points. First, agreement about the pitfalls of orthodox teaching and research does not entail agreement on how to avoid erroneous representation and which alternative routes are open to us; there are conflicting views as to what is to be done, with the consequence that the search for an alternative is all the slower and harder. Second, recognition that there is indeed an identifiable neo-classical core of mainstream thinking to which methodological and substantive objections can be made, following in the footsteps of Keynes and Sraffa, is a necessary step in building the agenda for new economic thinking. While some recognition of the importance of Keynes is under way in orthodox camp, Sraffa's powerful critique is completely, and to my mind wrongly, neglected by the profession. My third point is the way economists are trained and that what is required to ascend the academic ladder matters as much as producing innovative and alternative ideas; to transform economics, we need to find incentives to break through the 'guild system' of the economic profession and make room for a change in practices.

Economists are required not to discover absolute general laws, which the economic system obeys, but rather to explain decisions taken under different conditions of knowledge by different agents in the varied social contexts in which they operate. The economists' box of tools contains some items that should be discarded, for no new economic thinking can come from pouring new wine into old bottles.

Notes

1. The second conference (2011) was held in Bretton Woods on the theme 'Crisis and Renewal: International Political Economy at the Crossroads'; the third conference (2012) was held in Berlin on the theme of 'Paradigm Lost: Rethinking Economics and Politics'. See www.ineteconomics.org.
2. This section of the paper draws on Marcuzzo and Rosselli (2011).

3. The Sraffa papers (*SP*) are kept in Trinity College, Cambridge. They number 115 archival entities consisting of notebooks, folders of notes, typescripts and proofs.
4. For an overview of the different rankings, see www3.eeg.uminho.pt/.../nipe/cempre+nipe-rank/
5. www.newyorker.com/online/blogs/johncassidy/2010/01.

References

Akerlof, G. and Shiller, R. (2009), *Animal Spirits. How Human Psychology Drives the Economy, and Why it Matters for Global Capitalism*, Princeton: Princeton University Press.

Arthur, B. (2011), 'Complexity Economics', INET, available online at: http://ineteconomics.org/initiatives/conferences/bretton-woods/agenda.

Barba, A. and Pivetti, M. (2009), 'Cambiamenti nella distribuzione del reddito. Disordine finanziario e crisi', presented to the conference 'The global crisis', January, 26–27, Siena.

Bateman, B., Hirai, T. and Marcuzzo, M.C. (eds) (2010), *The Return to Keynes*, Harvard University Press.

Bernstein, M. (2008), 'A Brief History of the American Economic Association', *American Journal of Economics and Sociology*, 67: 1007–1023.

Blanchard, O. (2008), 'The State of Macro', *Working Paper* 08-17, Cambridge: MIT.

Bresser-Pereira, L.C. (2009), 'The Global Financial Crisis and After: A New Capitalism?', *Texto Para Discussão* 240, San Paulo: Escola De Economia De São Paulo Da Fundação Getulio Vargas.

Buiter, W. (2009), 'The Unfortunate Uselessness of Most "State of the Art" Academic Monetary Economics", *Financial Times*, March 3.

Colander, D. (2010), Written Evidence Submitted to the Congress of the United States, House Science and Technology Committee, July 20th.

Conford, A. (2010), 'The Cambridge Diagnosis on the State of Economic Science', *Observatoire del la Finance*, www.obsfin.ch.

Davidson, P. (2011), 'The Keynes Plan, The Marshall Plan and the Imcu Plan; Designing the Future International Payments System Using the Past Principles of Keynes's Liquidity Theory and Soros's Reflexivity', INET, available online at: http://ineteconomics.org/initiatives/conferences/bretton-woods/agenda.

De Grauwe, P. (2010), 'The Return of Keynes', *International Finance*, 13: 157–163.

Dow, S. (2010), 'What Kind of Theory to Guide Reform and Restructuring of the Financial and Non-Financial Sectors? A focus on theoretical approach', INET, available online at: http://ineteconomics.org/initiatives/conferences/kings-college/proceedings.

Farmer, D. (2010), 'Toward Better Quantitative Models of Systemic Risk', INET, available online at: http://ineteconomics.org/initiatives/conferences/kings-college/proceedings.

Foley, D. (2010), 'Mathematical Formalism and Political-Economic Content', INET, available online at: http://ineteconomics.org/initiatives/conferences/kings-college/proceedings

Frydman, R. and Goldberg, M. (2010), 'Life After "Rational Expectations"? Imperfect Knowledge, Behavioral Insights and the Social Context', INET, available online at: http://ineteconomics.org/initiatives/conferences/kings-college/proceedings

Garcia, N. (2011), 'DSGE Macroeconomic Models: A Critique', *Economie Appliquée*, 1, January-March:

Keynes, J.M. (1971–1989), *The Collected Writings of J.M. Keynes* (CWK), ed. by D. Moggridge. London: Macmillan.

CWK VII, *The General Theory of Employment, Interest and Money.*

CWK XIV, *The General Theory and After: Defence and Development.*

CWK XXVII, *Activities 1940–1946. Shaping the post-war world employment and commodities.*

Krueger, A. (1991), 'Report of the Commission on Graduate Education in Economics', *Journal of Economic Literature*, 29: 1035–1053.

Lawson, T. (2010), 'Really Reorienting Modern Economics', INET, available online at: http://ineteconomics.org/initiatives/conferences/kings-college/proceedings.

Leijonhufvud, A. (2010), 'Instabilities', INET, available online at: http://ineteconomics.org/initiatives/conferences/kings-college/proceedings.

Marcuzzo, M.C. and Rosselli, A. (2011), 'Sraffa and his arguments against marginalism', *Cambridge Journal of Economics*, 35: 219–231.

Mirowski, P. (2013), *Never Let a Dire Crisis Go to Waste*, London: Verso.

Parsons, W. (1997), *Keynes and the Quest for a Moral Science. A Study of Economics and Alchemy*, Aldershot: Elgar.

Seccareccia, M (2011), 'Keynes's Legacy: Fiscal Activism through Public Investment as the Principal Macroeconomic Tool to Achieve Sustained Economic Growth', INET, available online at: http://ineteconomics.org/initiatives/conferences/bretton-woods/agenda.

Sen, A. (2003), 'Sraffa, Wittgenstein and Gramsci', *Journal of Economic Literature*, 41: 1240–55.

Sims, C. (2010), 'How Empirical Evidence Does or Does Not Influence Economic Thinking', INET, available online at: http://ineteconomics.org/initiatives/conferences/kings-college/proceedings

Stiglitz, J. (2010), 'An Agenda for Reforming Economic Theory', INET, available online at: http://ineteconomics.org/initiatives/conferences/kings-college/proceedings.

CHAPTER 5

Is History of Economics What Historians of Economic Thought Do? A Quantitative Investigation

5.1 Premise

There is no doubt that we have witnessed a change in the way history of economic thought, or history of economics, as some would prefer, has been pursued in the last 20 years or so. It is a perception that needs to be substantiated by research, but how should it best be done?

Almost 20 years ago,[1] Backhouse et al. (1997), while providing excellent research on 'what economists do', made a plea for more quantitative analysis of economists' output; recently the same approach and analysis—although on a much smaller scale and with more limited scope—is proposed by Duarte and Giraud (2016), who have the merit of being among

We are grateful to Liz Braunstein Associate Director, *EconLit* and Information Systems, for help in collecting the data and clarifying issues related to the JEL classification system. We received helpful comments on and criticism of earlier versions of the paper from Alberto Baccini, Roger Backhouse, Carlo D'Ippoliti, Pedro Duarte, Annalisa Rosselli and Andrea Salanti for which we are thankful. All responsibility for errors and omissions is ours alone.

Originally publ. in: (With Giulia Zacchia), *History of Economic Ideas*, 24 (3), 2016, pp. 29–46.
Reprint by Springer Nature Switzerland 2024 with kind permission

M. C. Marcuzzo, *Economic Theories, Protagonists and Facts*, Palgrave Studies in the History of Economic Thought, https://doi.org/10.1007/978-3-031-63949-4_5

the few who have carried out a quantitative exercise focussing on the sub-discipline History of Economic Thought or History of Economics,[2] rather than economics in general. Cherrier (2015a) concluded her brief but richly detailed overview of the issue of quantitative studies in history of economics by rightly pointing out that:

> Historians of economics' engagement with – or rebuttal of – quantitative techniques is underwritten by collective epistemological and practical debates. What kind of questions we want to answer with these techniques, which techniques are more appropriate to deal with history claims, what is a healthy balance between statistical and qualitative evidence are important questions.

This paper does not pretend to answer these important questions, but, building on previous work done by one of the authors (Marcuzzo 2008, 2012), attempts to contribute further elements to the ongoing discussion on some of the problems facing quantitative investigation into the history of economic thought (henceforth HET).

First, there is the question of the relevant sources. A tentative preliminary list would include: a) articles published in the specialized journals in the field; b) papers presented at the main conferences in the field; c) articles published in non-specialized journals and papers presented in other conferences; d) books; e) PhD dissertations, online blogs, pamphlets and other such evidence of work in progress. Not all these sources are easily available, and for the time being at least, a) is the most accessible and manageable.

Second, there is the issue of how to evaluate this evidence: the quantitative approach based on the descriptors which can be found in various databases, such as *Econlit, Repec, Scopus, ISI Web of Science* comes up against non-trivial problems including subject-identification, double counting and missing information, to mention just a few.

Let us take the case of the JEL code system. It is a classification system introduced by the American Economic Association in March 1911 (Cherrier 2015b); the current codes (from 1991) come in three levels. The first level is a single letter. There are 20 classes at this level. The second level consists of a single letter followed by a single digit. There are 128 classes at this level. At the third level, the code consists of a single letter followed by two digits. There are 757 classes at this level. In the case of HET, the first level is denoted by B, the second level has 5 classes, and the third level has 59 classes. Very few articles have only one descriptor, most of them coming with multiple descriptors from other classes or other one-digit codes. According to Rath and Wohlrabe (2015), the average sum of JEL categories per paper in Economics increased from around 1.6 in 1991 to 3.0 in 2013. Looking at three HET specialized journals (*History of Political Economy, Journal of the History of Economic Thought and European Journal of the History of Economic Thought*) we found that the average number of JEL codes per article had increased from 2.45 in 2000 to 3.84 in 2014.

The preliminary question for the use of JEL codes when assessing trends and patterns in the evolution of HET is to understand who assigns them and how. According to a former JEL editor, D. Ekwurzel:

> Subcategories for each subject classification were chosen by the editors and our Classification consultant with advice from economists who specialized in each subject area […]. Classifications are assigned to articles by graduate students in economics […]. All classifications are checked by senior classifiers for consistency. (quoted in Rubin and Chang 2003: 405)

This is confirmed in a private exchange with Liz Braunstein Associate Director, *Econlit* and Information Systems, who wrote in private correspondence with us that, when JEL codes are not assigned by authors, 'We have our own staff of professional classifiers, who review each article and assign appropriate 3-character JEL codes' (e-mail to MCM, July 6, 2015).

So it is somewhat misleading to say that the various B JEL codes can be used as: 'an indication of what has been considered as "history" by the economics profession […]' (Duarte and Giraud 2016: 435).

It is fair to say that Duarte and Giraud are aware that there are identification problems. In fact, they add:

> We are aware that JEL codes can sometimes be reported quite inappropriately: a few papers that historians of economics would obviously identify as contributions to their fields may have no B descriptor […] while a few items seem to mistakenly have a B-code. (Duarte and Giraud 2016: 11 fn)

Moreover, in her text analysis of seven top economics journals, Kosnik (2015) reports that 4800 keywords/phrases are considered to assign articles to field categories in the JEL Classification System and they overlap across the categories. This can explain why arbitrary classifications sometimes occur.

The point is that JEL codes should not be interpreted as entirely signalling the views of the authors of the articles, but rather as the result of a classification procedure finalized to provide a map of the economic discipline on the American Economics Association (AEA) website and to optimize the assignment of papers/articles submitted to referees.

Nevertheless, the descriptors available in *Econlit* are helpful in providing a picture of the evolving nature and trends of the discipline. It is clear that to capture changes in approaches and methods by quantitative analysis alone is a daunting task. Proxies can be devised, but one has to be cautious in interpreting the results.

5.2 HET JOURNALS AND ARTICLES

This paper offers a contribution in the direction of quantitative analysis of the state of the art of history of economic thought as a sub-discipline, by looking at:

a) journals that published at least one HET article from 1955 to 2013;[3]
b) HET articles published in journals from 1955 to 2013;
c) articles published in specialized HET journals, in the last twenty years (1993–2013).

We use *Econlit* because it is the largest database available; in 2011 it added indexed records for journal articles from 1886, amplifying the number of pre-1969 records. Despite the limitations previously identified, in order to trace trends in HET research over the last few decades, we decided to use the *Econlit Subject Classification System,* searching not by B JEL code (History of Economic Thought, Methodology, and Heterodox Approaches) but also by Subject Description Term (SU) 'History of Economic Thought'. The B JEL code was introduced in 1991 and so, to limit errors due to the conversion of equivalence between the present system and the pre-1991 JEL codes that used the older JEL numerical classification system, we prefer to use the Subject Description Term. We tested this by searching journal articles written before 1991,[4] controlling both for the numerical pre 1991-B JEL code equivalent (031)[5] and then using the SU 'History of Economic Thought'. We found that using the Subject Description Term instead of the JEL code we have 58% more information (in terms of number of journal articles), and in one single case we have 1,715 titles instead of 4,676.[6]

Moreover, we decided not to use the B JEL code in order to concentrate our analysis mainly on HET production, eliminating from our sample articles on the Methodology of Economics (B4) and in Heterodox Economics (B5).

According to *Econlit,* a total number of 930 journals published at least one HET article in the last 58 years, from 1955 to 2013. There has been a marked increase in the number of journals publishing HET articles between 2000 and 2013: 747 journals (out of 1,519, the total number of journals recorded in *Econlit)* published at least one HET article in these years, 341 of these journals having been recorded for the first time in *Econlit* in the same years. One possible interpretation of this surprisingly high number of journals publishing HET articles can be based on the journal editorial choices that have appeared to favour, in recent years, a more interdisciplinary approach tending to involve a wider range of disciplinary areas at the same time, including the History of Economic Thought, rather than thematic specialization. A point to bear in mind is that we considered here journals that have had at least one HET article in the last 58 years.

Looking, now, at the relative number of journals, within our sample, and in particular journals that have 1 or more HET article per year (Fig. 5.1), the picture is completely different: there has been a steady decrease of the percentage number of journals with specific interest in

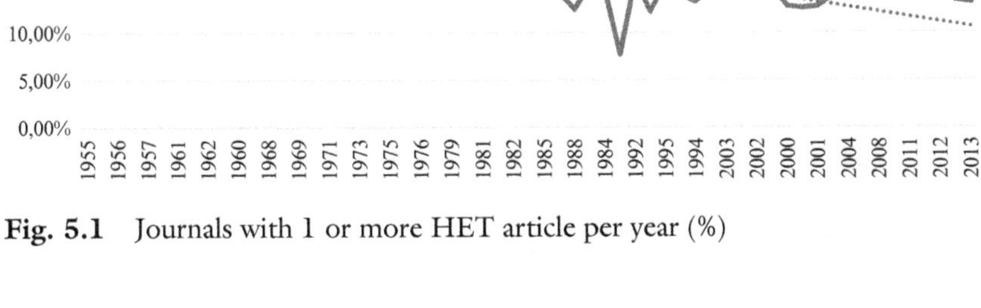

Fig. 5.1 Journals with 1 or more HET article per year (%)

History of Economic Thought, the main tendency being to publish HET outputs occasionally (less than one article per year).

When we consider articles, rather than journals, we find the largest increase in absolute numbers to have occurred in the earlier periods. Disregarding the pre-1969 years, there was an almost 90% increase in articles between 1985 and 1999, well above the 44% of the period between 2000 and 2013. Moreover, in recent years the share of HET articles has been decreasing, accounting just for the 1.6% of the total number of academic journal articles in 2013 (see Fig. 5.2). In relative numbers, the tendency is clear: we observe a steady decrease in both journals dealing with and articles about HET.

Turning to the journals with the highest number of HET articles per period, we found the highest concentration to be in the 1970s and 1980s. In fact, 48% of all HET production in the years 1970–1979 and 51.2% for the years 1980–1989 were published by just ten journals.[7] The concentration share decreased to 38.7% in the 1990s, 35.5% in the first decade of 2000 and to 29.2% in more recent years (2010–2013).

In order to restrict the effect of an increasing number of journals on the number of HET articles per period and to discover the actual trend, we consider 4 sub-periods (1955–1969, 1970–1984, 1985–1999 and 2000–2013) and examine separately the HET production of 38 journals[8] which published at least one HET article in all the four sub-periods considered—a total of 2,921 articles. We found that the largest number of

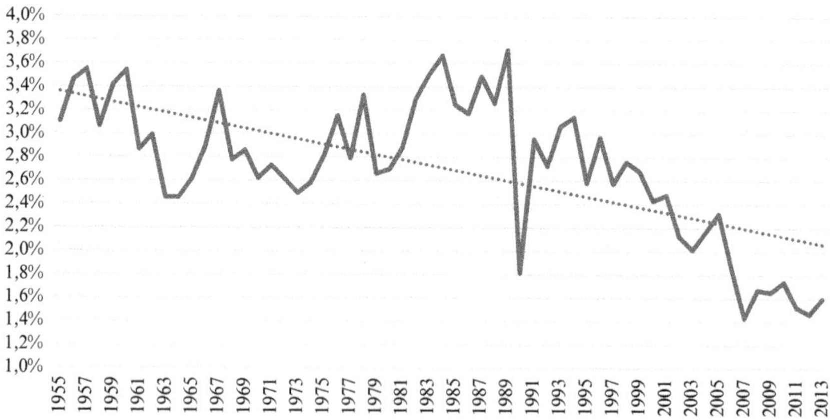

Fig. 5.2 HET articles in *Econlit* 1955–2013

articles was published in the period between 1970 and 1999 (64.5% of the total) with a gradual reduction in the number of HET articles from the year 2001; also the yearly average number of articles per journal was higher in the 1970–1999 period (1.6 per year) than in the later period 2000–2013 (1 article per year). Looking at the total number of articles published by the 38 journals, we see that the share of HET articles decreased from 4.9% in the period 1955–1959 to just 2.2% in 2000–2013; as Fig. 5.3 shows, the trend is similar to that described for all the journals considered (Fig. 5.2), even if the decrease in the share of HET articles is more evident for these 38 journals as from the end of the 1990s.

Our sample being heavily skewed due to the predominance of US journals, (52.4% of the articles analyzed were published in US journals), we checked the trend by country of publication (publishers' country as reported in the ISSN codes), not integrating UK in the Europe class as the English journals are heavily over-represented (Fig. 5.4). In all the cases, the share of HET articles was found to have decreased sharply in the recent period, although the trend is more marked for Europe.[9]

Finally, we present an analysis of the trend in publishing HET articles in the specialized journals. We look at HET articles in 10 journals with a high number of HET articles, distinguishing five highly specialized HET journals, or better, those journals that have, in the last twenty years, published more than 85% of articles with HET as subject, and those that have more than 20% of articles with HET as subject. The list of highly

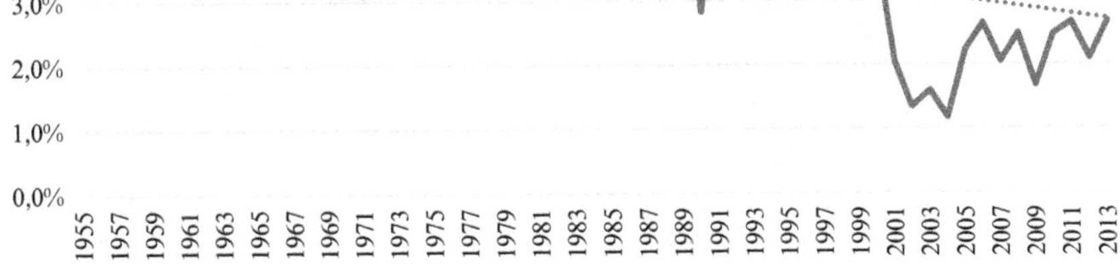

Fig. 5.3 Share of HET articles in 38 journals in *Econlit* 1955–2013

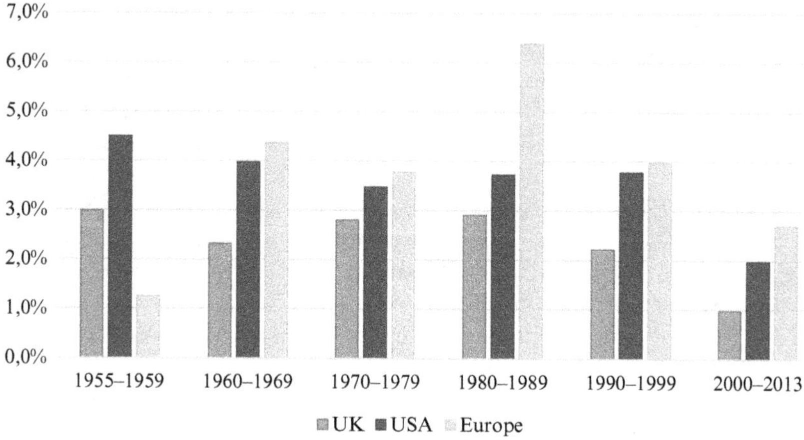

Fig. 5.4 Share of HET articles by country of publication

specialized HET Journals includes *History of Political Economy* (HOPE, started in 1969),[10] *Journal of the History of Economic Thought* (JHET),[11] *History of Economics Review* (HER),[12] *History of Economic Ideas* (HEI)[13] and *European Journal for the History of Economic Thought* (EJHET, started in 1993). Only two are official journals of HET associations (JHET of History of Economic Society, Usa and HER of History of Economics Society, Australia). The other three were founded by individuals and are owned by their respective publishing houses, although two of them have formal collaboration with HET associations (EJHET with European Society of the History of Economic Thought and HEI with Associazione per la Storia dell'Economia Politica, STOREP). We considered five other journals not specialized in HET but with a large share of HET articles (see Table 5.2): *Journal of Economic Issues* (JEI), *American Journal of Economics and Sociology* (AJES), *Cambridge Journal of Economics* (CJE), *Cahiers d'économie politique* (CEP), *Review of Political Economy* (ROPE).

To have the same time span for all the journals, we had to limit our analysis to the period 1993–2013. For the whole period, HET articles account just for 2% of all the articles recorded in *Econlit* and unsurprisingly, the 5 highly HET specialized journals published on average the largest number of HET articles, 24.4% (see Table 5.1). In absolute terms the highest score was obtained for the last few years: 3,173 records in 2000–2013 for the 10 journals and 2,185 articles in the 5 highly HET

Table 5.1 HET articles in the 5 highly specialized HET journals (1993–2013)

	HOPE	*EJHET*	*JHET*	*HEI*	*HER*	*Total*
Articles in 5 highly specialized HET Journals	948	550	542	502	396	2938
% of all HET articles in *Econlit*	7.88%	4.57%	4.50%	4.17%	3.29%	24.41%

Table 5.2 HET articles in the 5 journals with a large share of HET articles (1993–2013)

	JEI	*AJES*	*CJE*	*ROPE*	*CEP*	*Total*
HET articles in 5 journals with large share of HET articles	362	309	255	222	217	1365
% HET articles out of the total no. of articles in the 5 journals	23.4%	29,23%	23.16%	62,01%	34,28%	29.06%
% of all HET articles in *Econlit*	3.01%	2.56%	2.12%	1.84%	1.80%	11.34%

specialized journals. But in relative terms, as we saw in Fig. 5.2, the share of HET articles in *Econlit* has decreased over time, as has also the share of HET articles in the 10 journals and in the 5 highly HET specialized journals; this means that in recent years an increasing number of HET articles are reported in non-specialized journals, perhaps owing to the interdisciplinary approach favoured in several other journals.

Finally, we observe the average number of HET articles per journal in *Econlit* decreased from 3.5 between 1993–1997 to 2.92 between 2003–2007. Interestingly, the trend reverts between 2008 and 2013, when the average number per journal climbs to 5.5, roughly 1 article per annum, although the distribution is concentrated in a small number of journals (*Public Choice*, *Economies et Sociétés*, *History of Economic Thought*, *Economic Journal Watch*) (Fig. 5.5).

Looking at the 10 'HET-friendly' journals, the largest share (7.88%) was published in *History of Political Economy*, the smallest in the *Cahiers d'économie Politique*—just 1.80% (Tables 5.1 and 5.2). In the next section we examine the trends in these 10 journals.

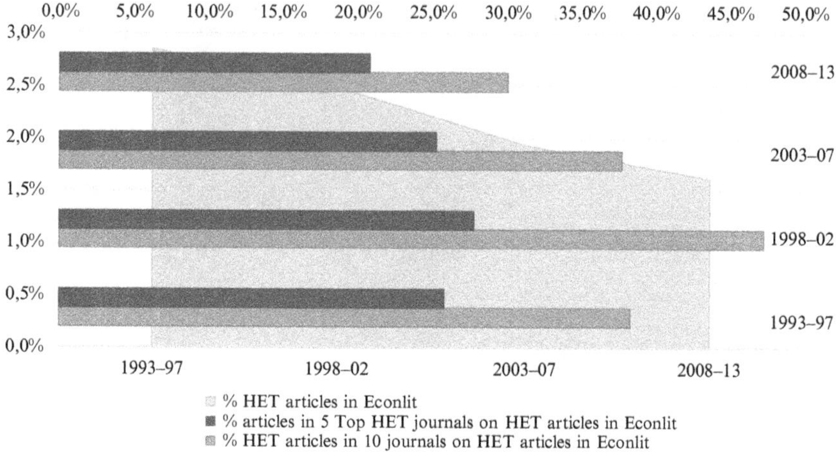

Fig. 5.5 HET articles 1993–2013

5.3 Searching for Trends and Patterns

In Marcuzzo (2008, 2012) three trends in the evolution of HET over recent years were detected: 1) a sort of 'stepping down from the shoulders of giants', namely a move towards studies of 'minor' figures and/or economists from a more recent past; 2) the blossoming of archival research into unpublished work and correspondence; 3) less theory-laden investigations, connecting intellectual circles, linking characters and events. In the following pages, we will try to substantiate these claims by devising proxies amenable to quantitative assessment for the period 1993–2013.

Mutating the Google Scholar motto, we proxy the 'shoulders of the giants effect', looking out for articles focussing on the economists who can be considered 'giants' in the history of economic thought (Smith-Ricardo-Marx-Mill-Marshall-Schumpeter-Wicksell-Walras-Keynes-Hayek).[14]

In the last two decades, the articles about the 10 'giants' in HET have accounted for 23.26% of all the scientific production in the HET specialized journals and for the 21.55% of the total number of HET articles recorded in *Econlit*. In general, the highest share of articles have been about Keynes and Smith; the distribution of the articles is almost the same among the highly HET specialized and less specialized journals, with the only exceptions of Marx, since interest in him goes beyond the HET scope and approach, and Schumpeter and Hayek (see Table 5.3).

Table 5.3 'Giants economists' in HET articles (1993–2013)

	5 highly specialized HET journals			*10 'HET-friendly' journals*			*Econlit*	
	Total	*Mean*	*% articles in highly specialized HET journals*	*Total*	*Mean*	*% articles in 10 'HET-friendly' journals*	*Total*	*% HET articles in Econlit*
Keynes	191	9.1	6.50%	281	13.38	6.53%	637	5.41%
Smith	165	7.86	5.62%	212	10.09	4.93%	480	4.08%
Hayek	61	2.9	2.08%	104	4.95	2.42%	384	3.26%
Marshall	59	3.24	2.01%	75	4	1.74%	168	1.43%
Ricardo	57	2.71	1.94%	87	4.14	2.02%	129	1.10%
Marx	53	2.52	1.80%	72	3.43	1.67%	286	2.43%
Schumpeter	42	2	1.43%	59	2.8	1.37%	183	1.55%
Mill	36	1.71	1.23%	43	2.04	1.00%	109	0.93%
Walras	28	1.33	0.95%	39	1.86	0.91%	105	0.89%
Wicksell	20	1.05	0.68%	29	1.48	0.67%	57	0.48%
TOTAL 'GIANTS'	712		24.23%	1001		23.26%	2538	21.55%

On the other hand, Ricardo and Marshall have less appeal in the non-HET specialized journals.

We tried to capture the 'stepping down from the shoulders of the giants' effect by calculating the percentage of articles that show the names of the 10 'giants' in the 10 HET 'friendly' journals relatively to the total number of articles about the same 'giants' in *Econlit.* In the last twenty years on average 39.4% of all articles have been published in the 10 HET 'friendly' journals. But looking at the trend (see Fig. 5.6) from 2001, we observe a reduction of interest in these topics, in particular in the last few years; for example, in 2013 there were only 28.8% of the articles including the 'giants' as topic.

The trend in pursuing archival research into unpublished work and correspondence was traced by searching for the words 'archives' or 'unpublished' in the abstracts of articles in *Econlit. We* restricted our search to the abstracts, since this is where authors usually mention what they see as the important aspects of the content and methodology of their papers. Once more, we consider the trend in the 'HET-friendly' journals relatively to the total number of articles with the same characteristics in *Econlit.* The

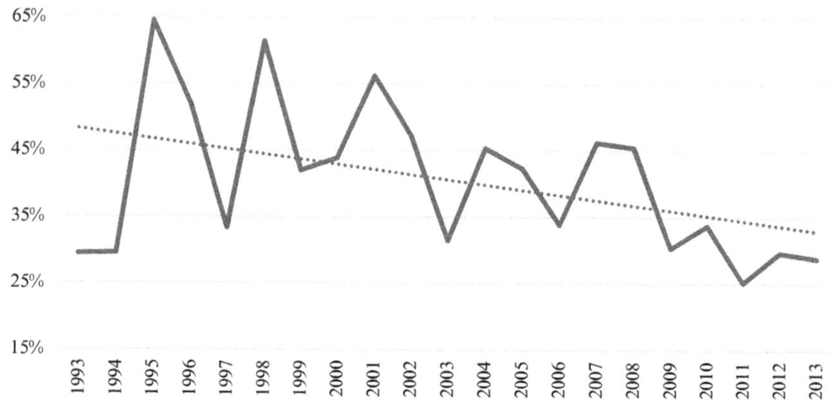

Fig. 5.6 The 'stepping down from the shoulders of the giants' effect in 10 HET 'friendly' journals 1993–2013

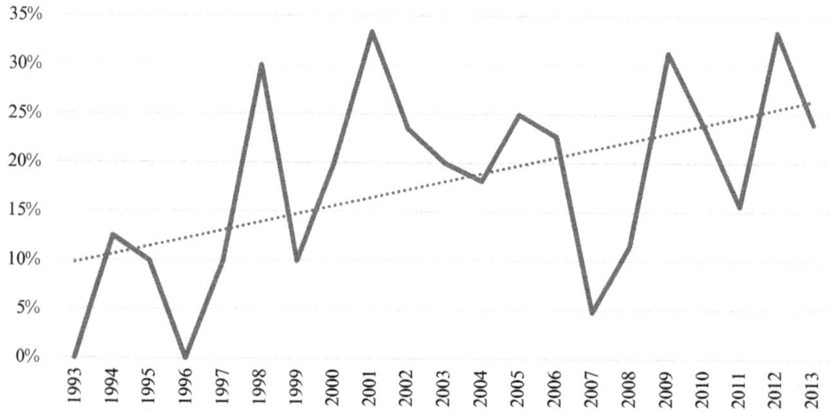

Fig. 5.7 Archival research trend in 10 het 'friendly' journals 1993–2013

articles on archival research represent on average of just 1.5% of all the articles so we were only able to consider a small number of articles (333 articles; 66 in the 5 journals with a large HET share). The trend can be seen in Fig. 5.7, although admittedly the numbers are small: the 'HET-friendly' journals tend to contribute to the archival research increasingly from 1996. Looking at the non-specialized journals, we also find an increase in the share of archival research in the HET records in the last few years, so we can conclude that this is common trend for HET publications in general.

Finally, we tried to find out whether a tendency to move out from the study of individual authors toward research into groups and networks is substantiated by any quantitative evidence. To track down articles that do not deal with any individual author—what we called 'not individual'—we selected the subject descriptor which allow us to exclude 'individuals'.

The share of articles not dealing with any individual author is higher for the highly HET specialized journals—on average 40 per cent of articles published in 1993–2013—while for the other 5 journals the percentage is lower (see Table 5.4). In Figure 5.8 we detect a clear trend in this direction in the last two decades: in the 'HET-friendly' journals there is a clear move out from the study of individual authors, in particular from 1997 to 2013.

Table 5.4 Articles with 'not individuals' in SU in 10 HET friendly journals

	HOPE	**EJHET**	**JHET**	**HEI**	**HER**	**Total**
SU: 'not individuals'	423	170	223	208	139	1163
%	44.62%	30.91%	41.14%	41.43%	35.10%	39.58%
	AJES	**CEP**	**CJE**	**JEI**	**ROPE**	**Total**
SU: 'not individuals'	50	37	78	124	46	335
%	16.18%	16.67%	30.59%	34.25%	21.20%	24.54%

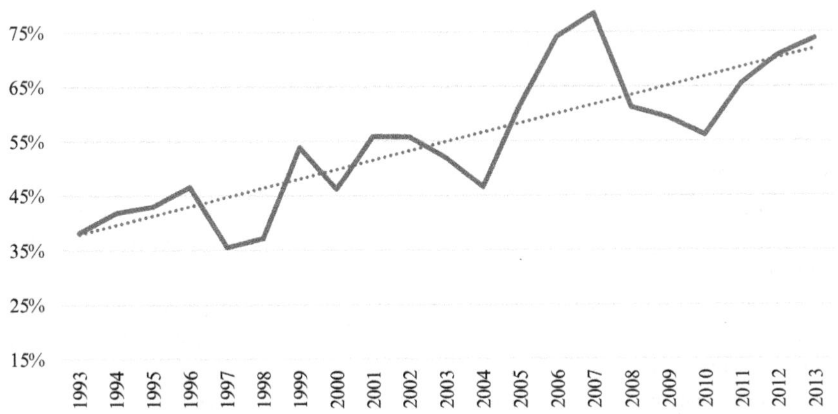

Fig. 5.8 'Moving out from the study of individual authors' trend in 10 HET 'friendly' journals 1993–2013

5.4 Conclusions

There are two good reasons in particular for the call for more quantitative analysis of HET output: a) to get away from a normative approach (what historians of economics should do) to positive description (what they do); b) to exploit the wealth offered by the existing database and web-related research engines, which make it possible to browse over a vast range of published material and works in progress. The latter, in particular, should enable us to detect trends, tendencies and also fashions and fads in our sub-discipline.

This demand for more quantitative analysis is part of a larger consensus on the usefulness of various metrics to evaluate research, which needs to have a basis in descriptive statistics to be performed on a large scale. Metrics, however, can be dangerous if not used with caution. As in the case of citation counts to measure the quality of a journal or, even worse, to assess the scientific output of an individual researcher, frequency distribution or trends of names or words over time give us an imperfect, or even distorted, picture and therefore afford limited understanding of the matter.

Review articles on selected topics do a much better job in telling us about the state of the art of the subject and indeed the disappearance of old topics and the appearance of new ones.[15] However, study of the over 3000 articles published in five highly HET-specialized journals in the last 20 years (to which one should add another 1500 published in the journals with a large share of HET articles) would be hard to handle.

Without some help from descriptive statistics, we may also come up against distortions and limitations due to the subjective nature of the evaluation, the impossibility of being fully knowledgeable of the topics, and so forth. Although quantitative analysis gives a very sketchy and imperfect picture, it provides a map, or a starting point for further investigations. As we see it, the field is open to the use of several other metrics, which could supplement what we have done in this article, such as the most cited papers, the authors with highest h-index, distribution of affiliation, gender composition and so forth.

We have pursued a somewhat modest aim with this paper, setting out to find some quantitative evidence of the three tendencies which we, as practitioners of the discipline, detected as characterizing the work of historians of economic thought in the last 20 years. This has entailed seeking quantitative confirmation in the articles published in the journals specialized in the field over the 1993–2013 period.

Our database shows in absolute terms a marked increase in the number of HET articles and journals which publish HET articles, but in relative terms a constant decrease of interest in HET.

We sought evidence of the tendencies in the style and content of doing HET with the help of proxies chosen among the available 'fields' in *Econlit* in articles published between 1993 and 2013 in the 10 Journals with articles with the highest HET content.

The 'stepping down from the shoulder of the giants' effect was captured by first singling out the '10 great economists'; the choice fell on Smith, Ricardo, Marx, Mill, Marshall, Schumpeter, Wicksell, Walras, Keynes and Hayek.

The tendency to get away from pure textual analysis of published texts into more historical investigations, making use of archival research or studies of unpublished material such as correspondence and related works, was traced by searching articles in 10 'HET-friendly' journals with the words unpublished' or 'archives' in the abstract.

Finally, to find out whether there has been an increase in the number of investigations attempting to discover networks, to trace the links between intellectual circles, rather than focussing on individual authors, we used the proxy variable in the subject descriptor term 'individuals' in *Econlit,* by employing the Boolean operator 'not'.

We cannot claim that the evidence we have presented in this paper entirely bears out the claims we have made about the main trends and tendencies in the work of historians of economic thought in the last 20 years or so. However, our quantitative investigation has certainly confirmed that the field has undergone significant changes in several ways.

First, we have the concentration of HET articles in a very small set of journals. This change was prompted by the almost contemporary establishment in the early 1990s of 3 HET-specialized journals, and the transformation of a fourth from a bulletin into a proper journal. Twenty years later we find 5 journals (comprising these 4 besides one founded in 1969) publishing a quarter of all HET articles recorded in *Econlit.*

Second, the move away from the focus on 'classical' authors is clearly detectable, although we need to do further investigation on which authors are most studied before we can see who or what became the fashionable topics of investigation.

Third, it is less evident that the subject has definitely moved into investigations using the tools of historical research, namely archives and unpublished material. Although we detected some evidence, the figures tell us—at least on the basis of the proxy we devised—that the authors studying and publishing articles on archives or unpublished material remain a minority.

Finally, on the basis of the indicator we have chosen, there is a clear abandonment of studies of individual authors in favour of interests in group, networks and such like.

These three trends are somewhat interrelated: an increased interest in archives and unpublished material implies studies on authors other than the 'giants', mainly because the literature on 'classical' authors is so vast that little unpublished material remains to be analysed. Moreover, the study of unpublished material, such as correspondence, would in itself imply an increased interest in groups and networks of authors rather than studies on individual authors. This paper represents a first attempt to identify and quantify these trends; we hope that it may be a starting point for further analysis, such as identification of new approaches and new 'schools' in History of Economic Thought.

We would like to conclude with some words of warning: quantitative investigations like the one performed here serve a useful purpose if they help to locate the areas to be investigated, and this can be done only by looking at the content of the papers. However, figures as high as 18,898 for the 1955–2015 period make assessment of the tendency in our sub-discipline on the basis of the perusal of the content of each article almost impossible. Quantitative investigation helps to clear the ground and make the figures appear more tractable, and therefore the task less daunting.

Notes

1. An even earlier plea for quantitative analysis, based on an input-output matrix of quotations and references, can be found in Earl (1987).
2. While we are aware that there may be a point in choosing either history of economic thought (HET) or history of economics (HE) to designate the sub-discipline, we adopt HET without any further qualification. See Backhouse and Fontaine (2014) for a discussion of the point.
3. We considered publications up to 2013 because not all the articles published in 2014 were fully recorded in *Econlit*. To avoid underestimating the output of certain journals, we decided not to include the years 2014 and 2015 in our analysis.
4. We concentrate our analysis on the period 1969–1990 because there were few observations pre-1969.

5. We have not considered the pre-1991 JEL code 036 since it is equivalent to the B4 code (Economic Methodology). For conversion tables see: *Journal of Economic Literature*, 1991, 29, 1, xviii–xxviii.
6. The main loss of information is in terms of HET studies on Individuals (50% of the articles that are not found using the JEL code but only searching for the SU), mainly (30%) concentrated in 4 journals: *History of Political Economy*, *Journal of Economic Issues*, *American Journal of Economics and Sociology* and *Journal of Post-Keynesian Economics*.
7. The six journals out of ten with the highest number of HET articles are the same in the two sub-periods 1970–1979 and 1980–1989: *American Journal of Economics and Sociology*, *History of Political Economy*, *Journal of Economic Issues*, *Review of Social Economy*, *Rivista Internazionale di Scienze Economiche e Commerciali*, *Science and Society*.
8. *American Economic Review*; *American Economist*; *American Journal of Agricultural Economics*; *Australian Economic History Review*; *Australian Economic Papers*; *Banca Nazionale del Lavoro Quarterly Review* (*PSL Quarterly Review*); *Bulletin of Economic Research/ ex Yorkshire Bulletin of Economic and Social Research*; *Business History Review*; *Canadian Journal of Economics*; *Economia Internazionale*; *Economic Development and Cultural Change*; *Economic Journal*; *Economic Record*; *Ekonomiska Samfundets Tidskrift*; *FinanzArchiv*; *Hitotsubashi Journal of Economics*; *Indian Economic Journal*; *Indian Economic Review*; *Jahrbucher fur Nationalokonomie und Statistik*; *Journal of Economic History*; *Journal of Economic Literature*; *Journal of Finance*; *Journal of Law and Economics*; *Journal of Money, Credit, and Banking*; *Journal of Political Economy*; *Journal of Regional Science*; *Kyklos*; *Land Economics*; *Metroeconomica*; *Osaka Economic Papers*; *Oxford Economic Papers*; *Quarterly Journal of Economics*; *Review of Social Economy*; *Scandinavian Economic History Review*; *Science and Society*; *Scottish Journal of Political Economy*; *South African Journal of Economics*; *Southern Economic Journal*.
9. In Europe, the recent introduction of national research assessments, that use purely bibliometric indexes as research quality proxies, has pushed HET and Heterodox Economics 'out of the official classification of what constitutes "economics" at all' (D'Ippoliti and Roncaglia 2015: 24).
10. See Goodwin (2010) for an insider account of the history of HOPE.
11. From HES website: 'In 1979 the Society began publication of a slim *Bulletin*, which became the *Journal of the History of Economic Thought* in Spring 1990, published by Carfax between 1997 and 2001, with Routledge from 2002 to 2007 and starting in 2008 with Cambridge University Press. From 1983 to 1998, selected conference papers were published in *Perspectives in the History of Economic Thought*, a hardcover series published first by Edward Elgar and then by Routledge. From 1999 on, selected

conference papers are published in one issue of the *Journal of the History of Economic Thought*'.

12. Started as a HETSA bulletin in 1980, HER became a journal in 1991.
13. From the Journal web: 'History of Economic Ideas is a new international series of *Quaderni di storia dell'economia politica,* a journal founded in 1983'. It took the present editorial form in 1992.
14. In order to find the relevant names, we selected the Named Persons (NP) field in *Econlit,* because it contains the names of economists who are the subjects of articles or reviews of their work that falls into the 'history of economic thought' subject category. There are 5 fields in *Econlit* where a personal name can be found, depending on the person's role in the work described: Author(s) (AU) Field; Source (SO) Field for editors of collective volumes; Reviewed Book (BK); Festschrift Honoree (FS) Field; Named Person(s) (NP) Field.
15. See Paganelli (2015) for a recent review article on Smith and the Scottish Enlightenment, with a quantitative assessment of the amount of the literature on the topic. Backhouse and Fontaine (2014) give a short but interesting review of the development of HET since the 1940s.

References

Backhouse R., Middleton R. and Tribe K. 1997, 'Economics is what Economists Do, but what Do the Numbers Tell Us?', mimeo.

Backhouse R. and Fontaine P. 2014, 'Introduction' in R. Backhouse and P. Fontaine, A *Historiography of the Modern Social Sciences,* Cambridge, Cambridge University Press.

Cherrier B. 2015a, 'Is There a Quantitative Turn in the History of Economics (and how not to screw it up)?', https://beatricecherrier.wordpress.com/2o15/o6/23/is-there-a-quantitative-turn-in-the-history-of-economics-and-how-not-to-screw-it-up/; accessed 4 December 2016.

Cherrier B. 2015b, 'Classifying Economics: a History of the JEL Codes', SSRN-id 2537382, http://papers.ssrn.com/s013/papers.cfm?abstract_id=2537382

Duarte P.G. and Giraud Y. 2016, 'The Place of the History of Economic Thought in Mainstream Economics, 1991–2011, Viewed through a Bibliographic Survey', *Journal of the History of Economic Thought,* 38 (4), 431–462.

Earl P. 1987, 'Unexploited Scope for Quantitative Work in the History of Economic Thought', HETSA Bulletin.

D'Ippoliti C. and Roncaglia A. 2015, 'Heterodox Economics and the History of Economic Thought', in T. H. Jo and Z. Todorova (eds) 2015, *Advancing the Frontiers of Heterodox Economics: Essays in Honor of Frederic S. Lee*, Abingdon, Routledge, 21–38.

Goodwin C. 2010, 'On editing HOPE, mimeo.

Kosnik L. R. 2015, 'What Have Economists Been Doing for the Last 50 Years? A Text Analysis of Published Academic Research from 1960–2010', *Open-Assessment E-Journal*, 9, 1–38.

Marcuzzo M.C. 2008, 'Is History of Economic Thought a Serious Subject', *The Erasmus Journal for Philosophy and Economics*, 1, 107–23.

Marcuzzo M.C. 2012, 'A Slender Trunk and many Branches. The History of Economic Thought in Perspective, Past and Future', in H. M. Krämer, H. Kurz and H. M. Trautwein (eds) 2012, *Macroeconomics and the History of Economic Thought Festschrift in Honour of Harald Hagemann*, Abingdon, Routledge, 171–80.

Paganelli M.P. 2015, 'Recent Engagements with Adam Smith and the Scottish Enlightenment', *History of Political Economy*, 47, 363–94.

Rath K. and Wohlrabe K. 2015, 'Trends in Economics Publications Represented by JEL Categories between 2007 and 2013', MPRA *Paper*, n. 66722.

Rubin R.M. and Chang C.F. 2003, 'A Bibliometric Analysis of Health Economics Articles in the Economics Literature: 1991–2000', *Health Economics*, 12, 403–414.

PART II

Ricardo, Money and Monetary Systems

CHAPTER 6

Ricardo's Theory of Money Matters

6.1 Misunderstandings

According to Hicks (1967), classical monetary theory has two main strands, one represented by Ricardo and the Currency School, who believed in relying at all costs (including deflation and unemployment) on automatic regulation of the quantity of money, the other stream by Thornton and Tooke, who favoured a permissive monetary policy and were prepared to accept a little monetary instability as the price of sustaining the level of economic activity and insulating the domestic economy from fluctuations in the balance of payments.

Clearly this interpretation reflects the general acceptance of the Keynesian approach to monetary theory in those years, when Ricardo "was that able but wrong-headed man" who "shunted the car" of monetary theory on to a wrong line. On the contrary, Thornton is the economist who understood that "money matters": a monetary economy is governed by uncertainty; in monetary affairs discretion is preferable to rules, since the economy is hardly ever in full equilibrium and the equilibrating forces of market mechanisms are slow or ineffective.[1]

Originally publ. in: (With Annalisa Rosselli), *Revue Economique*, 45 (5), 1994, pp. 1251–67.
Reprint by Springer Nature Switzerland 2024 with kind permission

M. C. Marcuzzo, *Economic Theories, Protagonists and Facts*, Palgrave Studies in the History of Economic Thought, https://doi.org/10.1007/978-3-031-63949-4_6

With the wide acceptance of monetarism and the monetary approach to the balance of payments in the early Seventies, Ricardo's monetary theory had a new lease of life. Ricardo appeared as the champion of the Quantity Theory approach (Mason 1977: 477), which had been unwisely discarded on the advent of the Keynesian Revolution (Humphrey and Keleher 1982: 102). In launching their counter-attack against Keynesian economics and the latter's criticism of the quantity theory approach, monetarists insisted on continuity with the classical and Ricardian monetary theory (Keleher 1991: 145), which needed to be amended only in so far as to allow for short-run effects of monetary disturbances (Humphrey 1974: 13). In fact, the neoclassical re-statement of the quantity theory admits the short-run non-neutrality of money, which—according to this view—Ricardo considered unimportant because of his concern with long-run equilibrium analysis.

In the meanwhile, the so-called "surplus approach" also launched reappraisal of Ricardian economics, but with regard to the theory of value and distribution alone. The implicit message in this literature was that, as far as Ricardo's monetary theory was concerned, there was not much worth recovering from what had been submerged and forgotten since the advent of neoclassical analysis.

The main concern of the surplus approach in interpreting Ricardo's theory was to demonstrate that Classics and Neoclassics had two distinct theories of output determination and value and distribution. Consequently, Ricardo's monetary theory was interpreted mainly with a view to confirming these differences. Thus, it was claimed that in Ricardo causation runs from prices to the quantity of money, while the reverse applies in neoclassical analysis where an entirely different argument is offered to assert the neutrality of money in the long run.

The quantity of money in classical theory was seen as being determined by the value of gold in terms of commodities and by the prices of commodities to be circulated, both being determined by their cost of production, while in neoclassical theory the value of gold and the prices of commodities are determined by the quantity of money (Green 1982: 63, 1992: 84).

Moreover, classical theory holds Say's Identity (saving is always identical with investment) while neoclassical theory offers Say's Equality (saving is always brought to equality with investment through variations in the rate of interest). It follows that only in neoclassical analysis is the level of output determined by the theory of supply and demand at the level of full employment, while in classical (Ricardian) analysis the level of output is given by the level of accumulation and cannot be assumed to be brought by market forces to the level corresponding to the full employment of labour (Garegnani 1983a: 23–28).

However, acceptance of Say's Identity and the consequent assumption of a fixed level of output left Ricardo with no choice when there was a change in the quantity of money. With prices given by costs of production, only if the velocity of circulation is allowed to be variable can effects of changes in the quantity of money on output be ruled out. But this possibility—so the surplus approach argument runs—was perceived by classical economists either as inconsistent with the acceptance of Say's Identity, which implies that every purchase is a sale so that the possibility of hoarding does not arise, or as an *ad hoc*. Thus Ricardo's monetary theory, when compared with his value and distribution theory, appears either uninteresting or possibly wrong.

The authors of this paper presented a different interpretation of Ricardo's monetary theory from all those set out above (Marcuzzo and Rosselli 1991). We maintained that Ricardo's theory of money merits revaluation, although for reasons that are different from those purported by monetarists, and that it matters as much as his theory of value and distribution. The purpose of this paper is to further substantiate these claims.

6.2 Interpretations

The main charges brought against Ricardo's monetary theory are: 1. the commodity-money fallacy; 2. the neutrality of money; 3. the long-period view, i.e. exclusive attention to permanent and general phenomena to the detriment of analysis of short period disturbances. We shall take these in turn.

6.2.1. The Commodity Money Fallacy One of the reasons why Ricardo's monetary theory is considered insufficient and outmoded lies in the alleged Ricardian identification of money with gold. Ricardo is held responsible for a number of fallacies, and in the first place for basing his monetary theory upon the shaky foundations of a defective value theory, i.e. the labour theory of value. Secondly, he is criticized for basing the determination of money prices both on the quantity of money and on the labour-theory of value, without being aware of their inconsistency (Laidler 1975: 217; Glasner 1985: 57; De Vivo 1987: 186). Finally, he is accused of not having really understood the change introduced by the suspension of convertibility, which forced the acceptability and the general usage of paper money as means of payments.[2] This latter view ascribes Ricardo's fault to a commitment to commodity-money, arguing that he was impervious to the idea that a generally accepted means of payments could be something which has no value or can be produced at almost zero costs.

We see this interpretation as a serious misunderstanding, since the role of gold in Ricardo's theory is not as money, but as the standard of money, i.e. the means to measure the value of money. We argued elsewhere (Marcuzzo and Rosselli 1991, ch. 3) that Ricardo's analysis pivots on the distinction between the value of gold and the value of money: while the former obeys the general law of value, namely it is determined by its cost of production, the value of money depends upon its quantity and is measured by the purchasing power of money over gold, which is the standard of money. It is immaterial whether the circulating medium is made up of full bodied gold coins or of debased coins or paper-money (whether convertible or inconvertible): the value of money is always determined by the quantity of gold bullion that one unit of currency can buy on the domestic and foreign markets, according to the prices of gold and the exchange rate.

In fact, the gold content of coins does not necessarily play any role in determination of the value of money. Debased or clipped coins can circulate at the same value as full-weight coins as long as their quantity has not been increased beyond what Ricardo calls its "natural level". (We shall come back to what this meant for Ricardo later on.) Therefore, although the gold content of a unit of currency decreases, the value of money may not decrease as the price of gold on principle may not increase.[3] And the value of money depends only upon the quantity of gold bullion which money can buy on the market and not on the number of coins (and of units of currency) necessary to make up a given weight of gold.

It follows that the value of money affects the determination of commodity prices through the money/gold ratio, not the gold/commodities ratio, as can be seen in the following equation:[4]

$$P_{money/commodities} = P_{money/gold} \cdot P_{gold/commodities} \tag{6.1}$$

In contrast, attributing the pivotal role to the commodity money not as the *measure* of value, but as the origin of the value of money, has a different implication altogether, money prices being only relative prices expressed in terms of gold and gold not the standard of money but simply a *numéraire*.[5] By doing so it becomes impossible to distinguish between a depreciation of the currency—which reflects the ratio of gold to money and depends on the quantity of money—and changes in the value of gold, which reflects the ratio of gold to all commodities. In Ricardo's own words: "If we adopted a currency without a standard [...] [the] depreciation could not admit of proof, as it may always be affirmed that commodities had risen in value, and that money had not fallen" (Ricardo 1951, vol. IV: 62).

Approaching the point in terms of an open economy (always the framework of Ricardo's theory) does not change the conclusion that the value of gold, namely the relative value of gold in terms of commodities, has no role to play in Ricardo's monetary analysis. It is not the equalization of the purchasing power of gold in terms of commodities that accounts for gold movements. Rather, the mechanism is to be found in the differences between the purchasing power of money over gold, that is to say in the differences between the money prices of gold at home and abroad. Gold, no less than any other commodity, is exchanged for money, not for other goods. It is not a change in the prices of commodities, but rather the discrepancy between the price of gold at home and abroad, due to a variation in the exchange rate, which signals arbitrage opportunities for gold importers and exporters.

Ricardo had many reasons to assume that the international price of gold—translated into domestic moneys through the exchange rate—was equalized across countries because the gold market was a highly organized market, where arbitrage could be enforced (Ricardo 1951, vol. III: 181, 1952, vol. VI: 54–55). Of course arbitrage exists for any commodity, as long as there is an organized market for that commodity. The law of one price tells us precisely this: if there is an organized market for a tradeable commodity, then the money price of that commodity is equalized across countries. Once the law of one price is assumed to hold for any tradeable, then the purchasing power of any commodity (gold included) in terms of any other commodity is equalized. The point is, however, that the condition for arbitraging in one commodity—the market signal which activates trading—is not given by the difference in the purchasing power of that commodity over any other, but rather by the difference in its money prices—translated through the exchange rate—across countries. As in Eq.

(6.1), the money price is the money to commodity ratio, not the commodity to gold ratio.

Ricardo had no reason to assume that the law of one price held *for all* international traded commodities, nor did his theory require that the purchasing power of gold over all international traded commodities be equalized across countries.[6] (We shall come back to this point in Sect. 6.3.) What matters here is that, according to Ricardo, in no circumstance was the signal for international gold movements given by its purchasing power in terms of commodities.

Many scholars of Ricardo see the gold/commodities ratio as playing a crucial role in the determination of the aggregate quantity of money. There is certainly enough evidence in Ricardo to show he was firmly persuaded that, whatever the composition of the circulating medium, the quantity of money that should circulate within a given country, ought to be equal to the quantity that would circulate if the entire circulation were made up of gold, but what exactly this quantity is remains unknown.

The point of having a standard is precisely this: the price signal bypasses the need for a quantity target.[7] The quantity of money is the "right" quantity whenever the market price of the standard shows no deviation from the official price, that is to say whenever the purchasing power of the currency over gold is kept constant. Ricardo defined the "right" quantity as the "natural" level, but he did not specify what this level was nor did he try to calculate it from the gold/commodities ratio.

In conclusion, it reveals a profound misunderstanding of Ricardo's thought to attribute him with a simple-minded monetary theory running thus: money is only gold, its value depending on its labour content, the price level being the ratio between gold and commodities, internationally equalized through international gold movements, and the quantity of money being adjusted so as to conform to the labour theory of value. We believe the correct interpretation of Ricardo's theory to be that gold is the *standard* of money, the reciprocal of the market price of gold at home and abroad, namely the quantity of gold purchased by one unit of currency, being the measure of the value of money. If this value is kept constant by variations in the quantity of money—through convertibility of bank notes into gold or control by the monetary authority—the quantity of money is maintained at its "natural level". The latter, however, is never calculated relating the cost of production of gold to the cost of production of commodities because such a figure—given the number of variables involved—is impossible to obtain.

6.2.2. The Neutrality of Money It is common opinion that Ricardo's theory is representative of the position according to which money is neutral, that is to say, variations in the nominal quantity of money have an effect only on nominal variables and never on real variables (O'Brien 1975: 164). Some qualify this position, admitting that Ricardo offers some evidence that monetary disturbances can have real effects in the short period (Humphrey 1990: 19).

However, since Ricardo was mainly concerned with long run effects or full equilibrium positions—so the argument runs—this qualification does not make much difference to the theory, which is seen as the Quantity Theory in its most rigid form (De Vivo 1987: 186).

The proposition that money is "neutral" is often supported by the adoption of a quantity theory of some form, but the exact nature of the relationship between neutrality of money and quantity theory has never been clearly explored in the literature. Unfortunately, while there can be little doubt about what the "neutrality" of money actually means, there are many views as to what the quantity theory is about. In fact, the quantity theory implies the neutrality of money, but it implies something else too, such as that there is proportionality between money supply and prices, that prices are entirely determined by the quantity of money, that money supply is exogenous, that the demand for money is stable and demand and supply of money are brought into equilibrium through variations in the price level (Humphrey 1974; Laidler 1991). Thus, while the proposition about the neutrality of money could on principle be maintained without any commitment to the quantity theory, the converse is not true.

As far as the neutrality of money is concerned, Ricardo undoubtedly held that an increase in the quantity of money would have no permanent effect on production, employment and interest rate. Production and employment are determined by the level of capital accumulation and the interest rate by the rate of profit of the economy. This is a natural consequence of his adherence to Say's Identity and his theory of distribution. However, it is not difficult to find evidence of cases envisaged by Ricardo where monetary disturbances have real effects: distribution effects due to the existence of contracts in money terms and fixed incomes (Ricardo 1951, vol. III: 136); alteration in the distribution of property and in the composition of the demand (Ricardo 1951, vol. V: 107–108); variation in relative prices, because of taxes fixed in money terms (Ricardo 1951, vol. I: 209) and, in the case of monetary contraction, effects on employment

(Ricardo 1951, vol. III: 94). So much is amply recognized in the literature. (Sayers 1953: 55; Hicks 1967: 161; Hollander 1979: 483–500; Ahiakpor 1985: 18–22). Thus, while we endorse the opinion that Ricardo was perfectly aware that an increase in the quantity of money may have "temporary" effects on the level and the composition of output, we are also inclined towards an interpretation of the distinction between "temporary" and "permanent" forces in Ricardo which is at variance with what is generally found in the literature. We wish to argue here that the emphasis on long run as opposed to short run effects is not due to a lack of understanding of the actual working of a monetary economy, but to the particular role Ricardo assigned to permanent causes, as we shall explain in more detail in the next section.

As for the quantity theory, interpreted as the proposition that necessary and sufficient condition for a change in money prices is a proportional increase in the money supply, certainly Ricardo never thought that *any* variation in prices *necessarily* implied a variation in the quantity of money. In other words, while the quantity of money always affects prices, variation in the quantity of money is not a necessary condition for a variation in prices. Price increases may just as well be caused by a decrease in the value of the standard, a rise in wages or tax increases (Ricardo 1951, vol. II: 412; vol. III: 328; vol. IV: 321; vol. VI: 233). In fact, Ricardo advocated a policy of reduction in the quantity of money only in case of depreciation measured in terms of the standard, and never in the case of an increase in prices, as we would expect if he held the strict Quantity Theory.

However, Ricardo's position seems less defensible if we look to the sufficient condition for a change in money prices: there is, in fact, overwhelming evidence that in Ricardo any increase in the quantity of money causes a proportional increase in prices. In the literature this is sometimes given as proof of his adherence to the Quantity Theory.

There are two ways to defend Ricardo from this charge, the first deriving from the textual evidence that the proportionality between an increase in the quantity of money and in prices is never said to be strict (Ricardo 1951, vol. V: 35). The second, and more important defence, is offered by Ricardo's explanation of the proportional increase in prices followed by an increase in the quantity of money. This effect is never accounted for with a direct link between the quantity of money and the level of prices but, rather, with the relationship between the quantity of money and the price of gold.

The only proportionality factor to be found in Ricardo is that between the quantity of money and the price of gold, since any increase in the quantity of money above the natural level brings about an exactly equal decrease in its purchasing power in terms of gold. In fact, the increase in the price of gold relative to the Mint Par is constantly used by Ricardo to evaluate the reduction in the quantity of money necessary to bring the price of gold to Par. (See, for instance, Ricardo 1951, vol. III: 123.)

As a consequence, but only as a consequence of this proportionality, if the relative values of commodities in terms of the standard are assumed to remain constant (see Eq. (6.1)), then the monetary prices of commodities vary in proportion with the quantity of money. But if the relative values of commodities in terms of the standard vary, for instance because there is a change in the conditions of production, then the proportionality between variations in prices and variations in the quantity of money disappear.

As evidence of this we can recall Ricardo's answer in 1823 to charges of being responsible for the 25–30 per cent fall in money prices, as a consequence of the reduction in money supply following the return to convertibility winch he had recommended. He contested that the reduction of the money supply he had advocated was only of the order of 3–4 per cent, since at the time this was the deviation of the market price of gold from its Mint price. He further claimed that the fall in money prices was not the consequence of a 25–30 per cent reduction in the money supply, but the result of the unwise policy of the Bank of England which had made heavy purchases of gold before the return to convertibility, thereby increasing the value of gold relatively to commodities and causing an unnecessary deflation (Ricardo 1951, vol. V: 354–5: 254–5).

6.2.3. Permanent Causes and Long-period Approach Perhaps the most common charge brought against Ricardo concerns his method, namely his search for permanent causes of economic phenomena. The charge has it that Ricardo's exclusive concern with full equilibrium or long-run positions shunted him on the wrong line, and that this is where his monetary theory fails to convince (Hutchinson 1978: 45–9; Laidler 1987: 291). The argument is that a good monetary theorist should be able to understand that monetary affairs are rooted in transitory forces such as uncertainty, confidence and expectations, which are better pictured as short period equilibria. Antipathy towards Ricardo's approach can be taken to the point of claiming, as some contemporary post-Keynesians do, that the approach based on long-period positions (common to Ricardo and neoricardians) stand in the way of full understanding of the working of a monetary economy.

The first point to clarify is whether the search for permanent causes is to be approached as a search for forces which tend to establish positions prevailing in the long-run, after a sequence of short-period positions during which all the variables involved in the adjustment process are not fully adjusted.

When reference is made to natural or normal values in Ricardo's theory, a distinction is made between "permanent" and "temporary" causes of economic events. This distinction pertains to the nature of the forces involved and not to the time sequence in which they are assumed to operate, and it therefore cannot be interpreted—although it often is in the literature—as a distinction between long and short-period equilibria.

A permanent cause should be interpreted as a sufficient condition for something to happen: its effects are certain regardless of the time interval necessary for their implementation.[8] Permanent causes are sufficient but not necessary conditions, since the same effects could be brought about by other causes that Ricardo labels as "temporary": neither necessary nor sufficient. They are not sufficient because either their effects are not certain and may well be offset by the working of more permanent forces or they are not necessary because a given effect cannot be unambiguously imputed to them.

The value assumed by certain variables, such as prices, rate of profit, wages and the quantity of money, when permanent forces prevail, is called by Ricardo their "natural" value. There is no lack of evidence that this is indeed fundamental to Ricardo's approach. For instance, a change in the conditions of production of a given commodity is a "permanent" cause of a change in its price, which means that the price will certainly change, although not every variation in commodity prices can be imputed to variations in the conditions of production. On the contrary, a change in demand is a "temporary" cause of a change in prices, not because its effect does not last long enough, but because it is not certain. Similarly, when discussing natural wages, Ricardo granted that money wages can be pushed downwards when the supply of labour grows faster than demand, but that if there is at the same time a change in the conditions of production of wage goods, making them more difficult to produce, their money prices rise and the overall effect is an increase, not a decrease, in money wages. The former can be taken as an example of a temporary cause while the latter—an increase in the price of wage goods—is a permanent cause of wage increases (Rosselli 1985).

It is our contention that the definition of the natural quantity of money in Ricardo is given by analogy with the definition of natural wages and natural prices. Thus the effects of a change in the natural quantity of money should be discussed in terms of the distinction between temporary and permanent causes.

The non-neutrality of money in the short-run as conceived by Ricardo cannot be interpreted as a temporary effect, namely as something which is not going to last. Rather, it should be interpreted as an uncertain effect, because, in the absence of a theory to deny the validity of Say's identity, the level of output is given. Alternatively, the non-neutrality of money should be interpreted as an effect which is offset by others deriving from a permanent cause. It is for this reason that temporary causes cannot be part of the theory: not because their effects are not recognized as part of reality, but because their effects are uncertain and volatile and can be offset by more certain and permanent ones. Again, taking as an example the case of the neutrality of money, Ricardo's position is that the level of output *may*, and not *must*, increase following an increase in the quantity of money.[9] The question is, then, not one of measuring "for how long" or "to what extent" an observed consequence follows from a given cause, before deciding whether it is a short or a long-run effect. The question for Ricardo is one of deciding which causes can be made object of a theory, namely of whether from a given cause he can derive consequences which are certain and therefore predictable.

Thus, it seems to us that a case can be made for claiming that Ricardo's distinction between temporary and permanent *causes* cannot be assimilated to the more familiar distinction between short-run and long-run analysis. While the former pertains to the question of which causes are eligible to become part of a theory, the latter pertains to the question of which *effects* come sooner or last less than others. On the contrary, if permanent causes are identified with long run forces, Ricardo's theory appears—as indeed it often appeared—meaningless.[10]

However, what still needs to be explained is, we believe, the criterion for choice among the different causes. Certainly, we are indebted to the "surplus approach" for a clear distinction of the notions of equilibrium in classical and neoclassical analysis, the former being defined as the equalization of the general rate of profit, while the latter is characterized by the equality of supply and demand in the relevant markets. As exponents of the surplus approach have pointed out, this distinction does not exhaust the differences between the two approaches, since "natural value" in classical analysis does not have the same meaning as "value taken by a given variable in the long-run" nor has "market value" the meaning "of the value the *same* variable takes in the short-run". In fact, the distinction between natural and market values, unlike the distinction between long and short run, is not "one of degree, relating to the period over which the equilibrating process was supposed to occur." (Garegnani 1983: 313).

In the surplus approach, however, the choice of a permanent cause is made dependent on its duration, as if the latter were synonymous with its permanency.[11] On the other hand, our interpretation of Ricardo takes permanency as a property independent of the length of time during which causes exercise their influence—although it is certainly true that causes which last longer are more permanent than others—because the definition of a permanent cause is not given by the length of its duration but by its place in the structure of the theory.

6.3 Comparisons

Once we have cleared up the misunderstandings about Ricardo's monetary theory, comparison with Thornton's theory also appears in a different light, and perhaps those self-assured claims that the latter had a "better" and "more" interesting monetary theory than the former should be revised (Peake 1978; Beaugrand 1981; Hetzel 1987). The point at stake is not of course that there are not differences between Thornton and Ricardo, which would be nonsensical, but that their differences were a matter of judgment and policy prescriptions, rather than of theory.

Ricardo and Thornton were on the same side in the Bullion Controversy in so far as they both advocated the return to convertibility. They shared the same view on the working of the Gold Standard, namely as self-regulating monetary regime as far as the quantity of money was concerned, although, neither of them tried to calculate the "right" quantity of money but, rather, relied on a price signal. For both authors the test for an "excessive" quantity of money was given by the discrepancy between the market and the Mint price of bullion, and—to some extent—by the difference between the market rate and the Par, defined as the ratio between the foreign and domestic official prices of gold or silver.[12]

However, Thornton was persuaded that, self-regulating as it might be, a monetary economy was not immune from confidence crises, and therefore there was the need for an active policy on behalf of a Central Bank. Conversely, Ricardo believed that discretion had to be checked by rules in order to avoid the otherwise inevitable abuse. As we know, in principle Ricardo won and the Bank Charter Act of 1844 was inspired by his ideas, but in practice the Bank of England turned increasingly to Thornton's prescriptions in the course of the XIX century.

It is noteworthy that the different role assigned by the two authors to the Bank of England derived from the same type of criticism of the behaviour of that body, taken to task for its aversion to risk and excessive prudence. The accusation by Thornton that the Bank of England in 1797 acted under panic and suspended convertibility instead of showing nerve and restoring confidence by providing the system with liquidity, is parallel to Ricardo's that the Bank of England acted irresponsibly in 1819 before the return to convertibility, causing general deflation, because it bought gold to increase its reserves, instead of selling it to prevent a rise in its price. But they held different views as to the best remedy to prevent misconduct on the part of the Bank of England. While Ricardo thought that the best remedy was to relieve the Bank of England of the responsibility of issuing notes (Diatkine 1994), Thornton believed in transforming it into an establishment which had, by statute, a commitment towards the public in general (see Hetzel 1987; Ciocca and Sannucci 1990).

To substantiate our claim that the differences between Thornton and Ricardo were not so much a matter of theory as, rather, of policy prescriptions, let us compare their views on depreciation.

Unlike other contemporaries, both Ricardo and Thornton traced the cause of an increase in the price of gold bullion to depreciation of the exchange: it is because of its effect on the rate of the exchange and not because of an increased demand for all commodities (gold included) that an increase in the quantity of money determines an increase in the price of gold. When there was a great depreciation of the exchange—whatever the cause—it became profitable to export gold. Bullion merchants reacted to the signal of depreciated exchange by buying gold and exporting it; thus the demand for gold increased, and its price also tended to rise.

This was the mechanism which ensured that, in the Gold Standard, the quantity of money was kept at its "natural" level. An excess of money (what Ricardo and Thornton called an "overissue") directly affected the rate of exchange and only indirectly, and "probably by slow degrees" (Thornton 1978: 225), commodity prices. If there was convertibility, the profitability of the gold trade caused an outflow of gold, a reduction in the quantity of money and appreciation of the exchange rate. If convertibility was suspended—as happened in Ricardo's and Thornton's times—it caused an increase in the demand for gold and in the domestic price of gold up to the point where the exportation of gold was no longer profitable.

The same chain of causes and effects follows the depreciation of the exchange in the case of payment of a subsidy or of an import of com in abnormal circumstances. As we know, however, Ricardo and Thornton differed in their explanation of why—when England was in need of foreign currency-gold and not any other commodity became the preferred means of obtaining it, to pay for a subsidy or for an import of com, which at the time was called an unfavorable balance of trade.[13]

The question was to explain why a circumstance such as the following occurred:

$$\frac{P_{gold}\left(1+\tau_{gold}\right)}{P^{*}_{gold}} \leq \frac{P_i\left(1+\tau_i\right)}{P^{*}_i} \qquad i=1,\ldots\ldots n \qquad (6.2)$$

where:

n= number of traded commodities other than gold

τ_{gold}= transaction and transport cost for gold as percentage of the price

τ_i= transaction and transport costs for commodity i as percentage of the price

P_{gold}= domestic price of gold bullion

P_i= domestic price of commodity i

P^{*}_{gold} = foreign price of gold bullion

P^{*}_i = foreign price of commodity i

This inequality indicates that, in Ricardo's words, "gold was the cheapest exportable commodity" (Ricardo 1951, vol. III: 105), i.e. the cheapest way to acquire a unit of foreign currency.

What the literature sees as a difference in analysis it is to us rather a difference in their assessment of the circumstances. While Ricardo never conceded a point unless it was proved to be logically inconsistent with his theory, Thornton was more concerned with the qualifications required to apply the theory to circumstantial phenomena. The point is, of course, not the difference between the theoretician and the practical man, or between the pure and applied economist. It is rather between faith in economic theory as a quest for generalizations, which may sometimes obscure assessment of the importance of circumstances, and a need to provide an answer to a circumstancial problem, which may sometimes obscure the logic of the theory.

To account for (6.2), Thornton argued that the prices, P_i^*, English commodities could fetch on the foreign markets might have fallen or that the transport and transaction costs, τ_i, might have increased because of unrest and political turmoil, while Ricardo's explanation was that an "unfavourable" balance of payments was due to a general increase in domestic prices of English commodities, P_i, because of a depreciation of the currency.

Thornton saw an overissue as a "permanent" cause of the depreciation of the exchange rate and of gold outflows because, while not every exchange depreciation could be imputed to overissue, whenever there was an excessive quantity of money there was certainly going to be an exchange depreciation. (Thornton 1978: 221). Thus, the circumstances of the war or of a bad harvest provided the qualifications in application of the theory.

In contrast, Ricardo was convinced that the sole cause of exchange depreciation was monetary. It was his view of England as "world workshop" which distorted his assessment of the circumstances and confirmed, perhaps unwisely, his faith in the generality of his theory. Or, more likely, Ricardo held strongly that an excess of the quantity of money was a necessary and not only sufficient condition for gold outflows, because Thornton's explanation was inconsistent with Say's Identity. This law does not admit a simultaneous fall of all P_i^* due to a generalized "glut of commodities", and no temporary or accidental circumstances could change that.

6.4 Conclusions

Let us now summarize our arguments in favour of revaluing Ricardo's monetary theory and thus spell out more clearly precisely what we mean by saying that Ricardo's theory of money "matters".

The first reason is that it matters in order to understand what Ricardo's theory is about. Ricardo always applies his analysis to observed variables, which are monetary variables: money prices, money wages, the aggregate value of output in money terms. His aim is to explain what goes on behind changes in those variables and his purpose, therefore, is to decipher market signals. As an example, we can take Ricardo's study of the effects of change in the conditions of com production on the general rate of profit.

It would be very misleading to assume that the "com model", i.e. a model in which every thing is expressed in real terms, was the framework of Ricardo's theory of distribution, since his analysis makes sense only if all magnitudes are expressed in money terms (Vianello 1983; Rosselli 1985).

Underlying the *Principles* there are the assumptions that money is not depreciated and the value of the standard is constant, so that variations in money prices are caused only by changes in the conditions of production or in income distribution. These assumptions are acceptable because, *in another part* of the theory, the conditions under which they may occur are explained. Money is not depreciated whenever the market price of gold is in line with the Mint price of gold and the market rate of exchange in line with Par. The value of the standard is constant because Ricardo attributes to gold the property of being an "invariable" measure of value. Whatever the merit of the choice made by Ricardo, which is questionable and indeed was questioned by Sraffa (1951: xl–xlix), Ricardo's search for an invariable measure of value has undoubtedly always been a search for both a measure of the absolute value of commodities and a good standard of money. Thus, underlying his value and monetary theory there is the same quest for a standard to distinguish different causes of variations in prices. (Marcuzzo and Rosselli 1994).

The second reason why Ricardo's theory of money matters is because it enhances our understanding of the actual working of the Gold Standard. Unlike contemporary models, Ricardo's analysis does not grant this monetary regime the merit of maintaining price stability (Barro 1979; Bordo and Ellson 1985; Fremling 1986). The virtue of keeping the price of the standard of money fixed was not, to Ricardo's way of thinking, to ensure price stability, but to allow the distinction between changes in the value of money and changes in money prices. If the price of the commodity chosen as the standard of money is kept fixed, changes in money prices of commodities can occur only because of changes in the relative value of commodities in terms of the standard. Thus, once the price of the standard is kept fixed, only if the relative value of the standard is constant is price stability ensured.

Ricardo believed that only variations in money prices which had a *monetary* origin could be avoided, while variations in money prices due to a change in the relative value of the standard in terms of commodities could not be prevented, as having their origin in a change in the conditions of production or in taxation or both. But these changes could not be avoided under any monetary regime.

Ricardo also offers a clue to understanding the role of prices during and at the end of the adjustment mechanism in the Gold Standard. In our reconstruction of Ricardo's theory, an increase in the discount activity of the Bank of England immediately affected the exchange rate, because merchants who had access to credit were chiefly engaged in international trade (Duffy 1982; Davis 1979). This is also supported by the Evidence given to the Bullion Committee by the Continental Merchant: in fact Ricardo commented approvingly on this Evidence, noting that it applied to a fully convertible regime.[14] The increased demand for foreign currency was initially satisfied by the exporters of commodities other than gold, up to the point when depreciation led to gold becoming "the cheapest exportable commodity". The export of gold and consequent contraction of the money supply as gold is taken out of circulation will cease as soon as there is at least one commodity which can replace gold as the "cheapest" exportable commodity. Whenever this happens the difference between the domestic price and the foreign price of gold once again makes it unprofitable to export gold. But Ricardo says nothing about prices of other commodities whether domestic or foreign.[15]

Thus, if we interpret Eq. (6.2) as describing the condition under which gold outflows occurred according to Ricardo's theory, we can see that it states only the necessary condition for gold outflows: the latter will come to an end only when the inequality no longer holds. Unlike the adjustment mechanisms envisaged by the specie flow and the monetary approach in contemporary models of the Gold Standard,[16] Ricardo's explanation of gold flows does not require the further condition of the equalization of the purchasing power of gold over internationally traded commodities. This is a sufficient condition for the absence of gold outflows although, when added, it does not help clarify the causes of gold movements. In conclusion, Ricardo's theory does not impose this constraint on description of the way in which the Gold Standard really worked, and thereby appears to account for the empirical evidence better than contemporary models (Marcuzzo and Rosselli 1987).

Praise is due to Ricardo's theory of money not for providing an answer to contemporary monetary problems, but for posing questions neglected in modern monetary theory. Whether monetary problems have changed in our times, or whether Ricardo's questions, by their very nature, can no longer be asked within the modern framework of analysis, is an issue doomed to remain unsettled as, probably, is endorsement of the claim which heads this paper.

Notes

1. According to Schumpeter (1954: 704n.) "[...] in matters of monetary as of general theory, Ricardian teaching is a detour and [...] it slowed up the advance of analysis, which could have been much quicker and smoother had Thornton's lead been followed—had Ricardo force not prevailed over Thornton's insight". See also Hayek (1978: 36): "Although Thornton's merits have long been overshadowed by the greater fame of Ricardo, it has now come to be recognized that in the field of money the main achievement of the classical period is due to Thornton".
2. See for instance Peake (1978: 204): "[R's] failure to distinguish between the abstract unit of account and the concrete forms of money made it impossible for Ricardo to come to grips with paper money as Thornton had".
3. Ricardo (1951, vol. I: 353): "On the same principle, too, namely, by a limitation of its quantity, a debased coin would circulate at the value it should bear, if it were of the legal weight and fineness, and not at the value of the quantity of metal which it actually contained. In the history of the British coinage, we find, accordingly, that the currency was never depreciated in the same proportion that it was debased; the reason of which was, that it never was increased in quantity, in proportion to its diminished intrinsic value".
4. See Ricardo (1951, vol. I: 149): "While gold is exclusively the standard in this country, money will be depreciated, when a pound sterling is not of equal value with 5 dwts. and 3 grs. standard gold, and that, whether gold rises or falls in general value".
5. On the distinction between a standard of money and a *numéraire*, and why gold was considered by Ricardo a good standard of money, see Marcuzzo and Rosselli (1994).
6. See Ricardo (1951, vol. I.: 147). For an alternative interpretation of Ricardo's view, see Humphrey and Keleher (1982: 154 and 322).
7. Ricardo (1951, vol. IV: 64): "The issuers of paper money should regulate their issues solely by the price of bullion, and never by the quantity of their paper in circulation. The quantity can never be too great or too little, while it preserves the same value as the standard". See also Ricardo (1951, vol. I: 357–358).
8. Also Roncaglia (1994) claims that a long-run position is not defined as an equilibrium established through time.
9. See Ricardo (1951, vol. III: 122–23): "[...] a depreciation of currency may, as far as it is considered as a stimulus to production, be beneficial or otherwise".
10. For a recent example of this position, see Peach (1993: 42): "Yet it was typical of Ricardo's natural style of reasoning that when he thought some-

thing should happen, he presumed it would happen, virtually without delay".

11. See, for instance, Garegnani (1983: 309), where permanent causes are said to be "non accidental conditions that are likely to emerge through a repetition of the situation".
12. See Thornton (1978: 192): "It is the maintenance of our external exchanges, or, in other words, it is the agreement of the mint price with the bullion price of gold which seems to be the true proof that the circulating paper is not depreciated". See Ricardo (1951, vol. III: 175).
13. For a detailed comparison of the theory of unilateral transfers by Ricardo and Thornton, see Marcuzzo and Rosselli (1991: 142–148).
14. "An increase of the circulating medium enables persons to make greater advances to foreigners, and more bills are thus brought into the foreign market; this must have the effect of lowering the exchange. Should, on the contrary, a scarcity of money exist here, it would become desirable to realize and accelerate the payment of debts due to this Country; advances now readily made to them would from necessity be curtailed, and the foreigner, who required a bill on this country, would be obliged to pay a higher price for that which was scarce then it were abundant" ([Ricardo 1951, vol. III: 353).
15. For the alternative view, see Frenkel (1976: 36–37).
16. The equalization of gold prices of commodities is compatible with both theories of the adjustment mechanism of the Gold Standard, namely the specie-flow theory and the monetary approach, because, like any sufficient condition, it does not unequivocally point towards a unique cause.

References

Ahiakpor, J.C. (1985). Ricardo on money: the operational significance of the non-neutrality of money in the short run, *History of Political Economy*, 17 (1), 17–30.

Barro, R. (1979). Money and the Price Level under the Gold Standard. *Economic Journal*, 89 (March), 13–33.

Bordo, M.D. and Ellson, R.W. (1985). A model of classical Gold Standard with deplection. *Journal of Monetary Economics*, 16, 109–120.

Beaugrand, P. (1981). *Henry Thornton: Un Précurseur de J.M Keynes.* Paris: Presses Universitaires de France.

Ciocca, P. and Sannucci, V. (1990). Henry Thornton, primo teorico della banca centrale. In H. Thornton, *Indagine sulla natura e sugli effetti del credito cartolare in Gran Bretagna*, It. tr., Torino: Cassa di risparmio di Torino, i–xxiv.

Davis, R. (1979). *The Industrial Revolution and British Overseas Trade.* Leicester: Leicester University Press.

De Vivo, G. (1987). Ricardo, David. In J. Eatwell, M. Milgate, and P. Newman (eds.), *The New Palgrave: A Dictionary of Economics*, London: Macmillan.
Diatkine, S. (1994). A propos de la position de David Ricardo concernant la liberté d'émission de la monnaie. In G. Deleplace (ed.), *Monnaie et étalon chez David Ricardo*, special issue (23) of *Cahiers d'Économie politique*, Paris: l'Harmattan, 79–99.
Duffy, I.P.H. (1982). The discount policy of the Bank of England during the suspension of cash payments 1797–1821. *Economic History Review*, 35 (1), 67–81.
Fremling, G.M. (1986). A Specie-Flow Model of the Gold Standard. *Journal of International Money and Finance*, 5, 37–55.
Frenkel, J. (1976). Adjustment Mechanisms and the Monetary Approach to the Balance of Payments: A Doctrinal Perspective. In E.M. Claassen, and P. Salin (ed.), *Recent Issues in International Monetary Economics.* Amsterdam: North Holland.
Garegnani, P.A. (1983). The Classical Theory of Wages and the Role of Demand Schedules in the Determination of Relative Prices. *American Economic Review*, 73 (2), 309–313.
Garegnani, P.A. (1983a), Notes on Consumption, Investment and Effective Demand. In J. Eatwell, and M. Milgate (eds.), *Keynes's Economics and the Theory of Value and Distribution.* London: Duckworth.
Glasner, D. (1985). A Reinterpretation of Classical Monetary Theory. *Southern Economic Journal*, 52 (July), 46–67.
Green, R. (1982). Money, Output and Inflation in Classical Economics. *Contributions to Political Economy,* 1, 59–85.
Green, R. (1992). *Classical Theories of Money, Output and Inflation.* New York: St Martin Press.
Hayek, F.A (1978). Introduction to Thornton, H. *An Enquiry into the Nature and Effects of the Paper Credit of Great Britain.* Fairfield: Kelley.
Hetzel, R.L. (1987). Henry Thornton: Seminal Monetary Theorist and Father of the Modern Central Bank. *Economic Review*, 73 (4), 3–16.
Hicks, J.R. (1967). Monetary theory and history: an attempt at perspective. *Critical Essays in Monetary Theory.* Oxford: Clarendon Press.
Hollander, S. (1979). *The Economics of David Ricardo.* Toronto: University of Toronto Press.
Humphrey, T.M. (1974). The quantity theory of money: its historical evolution and role in policy debates. *Economic Review*, 60 (May-June), 2–19.
Humphrey, T.M. (1990). Ricardo versus Thornton on the Appropriate Monetary Response to Supply Shocks. *Federal Reserve Bank of Richmond*, 76 (6), 18–24.
Humphrey, T.H., and Keleher, R.E. (1982). *The Monetary Approach to the Balance of Payments, Exchange Rates, and World Inflation.* New York: Praeger.
Hutchinson, T.W. (1978). *On revolution and progress in economic knowledge.* Cambridge: Cambridge University Press.

Keleher, R.E. (1991). The Use of Market Prices in Implementing Monetary Policy: The Bullionist Contribution. *Southern Economic Journal*, 58 (July), 144–154.
Laidler, D. (1975). *Essays on money and inflation*. Manchester: Manchester University Press.
Laidler, D. (1987). Bullion Controversy. In J. Eatwell, M. Milgate, and P. Newman (eds.), *The New Palgrave: A Dictionary of Economics*. London: Macmillan.
Laidler, D. (1991). The Quantity Theory is Always and Everywhere Controversial: Why?. *The Economic Record*, 67 (December), 289–306.
Marcuzzo, M.C. and Rosselli, A. (1987). Profitability in the International Gold Market in the Early History of the Gold Standard. *Economica*, 54 (August), 367–380.
Marcuzzo, M.C. and Rosselli, A. (1991). *Ricardo and the Gold Standard. The Foundations of International Monetary Order.* London: Macmillan.
Marcuzzo, M.C. and Rosselli, A. (1994). The standard commodity and the standard of money. In G. Deleplace (ed.) *Monnaie et étalon chez David Ricardo*, special issue (23) of *Cahiers d'Économie politique*, Paris: l'Harmattan, 19–31.
Mason, W.E. (1977). Winners and Losers: some paradoxes in monetary history resolved and some lessons unlearned. *History of Political Economy*, 9 (4), 476–489.
O'Brien, D.P. (1975). *The Classical Economists*. Oxford: Oxford University Press.
Peach, T. (1993), *Interpreting Ricardo*. Cambridge: Cambridge University Press.
Peake, C.F. (1978). Henry Thornton and the development of Ricardo's economic thought. *History of Political Economy*, 10 (2), 193–212.
Ricardo, D. (1951–1955). *Works and Correspondence*, ed. by P. Sraffa with the collaboration of M. Dobb, vols. I.–XI Cambridge: Cambridge University Press.
Roncaglia, A. (1994). On the compatibility between Keynes's and Sraffa's viewpoints on output levels. In G.C. Harcourt, A. Roncaglia, R. Rowley (eds.), *Income and Employment in Theory and Practise*. London: Macmillan.
Rosselli, A. (1985). The Theory of Natural Wage. In G. Caravale (ed.), *The legacy of Ricardo*. Oxford: Blackwell.
Sayers, R.S. (1953). Ricardo's Views on Monetary Questions. In A.W. Coats (ed.), *The Classical Economists and Economic Policy*. London: Methuen.
Schumpeter, J.A. (1954). *History of Economic Analysis*. New York: Oxford University Press.
Sraffa, P. (1951). Introduction. In D. Ricardo, *Principles of Political Economy and Taxation*. Cambridge: Cambridge University Press.
Thornton, H. (1978). *An Enquiry into the Nature and Effects of the Paper Credit of Great Britain*. Fairfield: Kelley.
Vianello, F. (1983). *On Ricardo's principle that the profits of the farmer regulate the profits of all other trades*. Modena: Studi e ricerche dell'Istituto economico, Università degli studi di Modena.

CHAPTER 7

On the Notion of Permanent and Temporary Causes. The Legacy of Ricardo

7.1 "Natural" Values and the "Natural" Quantity of Money

David Ricardo stated quite clearly what he thought to be characteristic of his own method in a letter to Robert Malthus:

> It appears to me that one great cause of our difference in opinion, on the subjects which we have so often discussed, is that you have always in your mind the immediate and temporary effects of particular changes—whereas I put these immediate and temporary effects quite aside, and fix my whole attention on the permanent state of things which will result from them. Perhaps you estimate these temporary effects too highly, whilst I am too much disposed to undervalue them. To manage the subject quite right they should be carefully distinguished and mentioned, and the due effects ascribed to each. (Ricardo to Malthus, 24 Jan 1817, in *The Works and*

I wish to thank three anonymous referees. While I have not always followed their advice, I am grateful for their comments and criticisms which helped me to revise and, I hope, to improve the paper.

Originally publ. in: *Journal for the History of Economic Thought*, 36 (4), 2014, pp. 421–34.
Reprint by Springer Nature Switzerland 2024 with kind permission

M. C. Marcuzzo, *Economic Theories, Protagonists and Facts*, Palgrave Studies in the History of Economic Thought, https://doi.org/10.1007/978-3-031-63949-4_7

Correspondence of David Ricardo [hereinafter *Works*, followed by the number of the volume] VII: 120)

In fixing his attention "on the permanent state of things," Ricardo was, in fact, trying to separate permanent from temporary effects by the nature of the causes occasioning them; however, his search for permanent causes has been interpreted as an exclusive concern with full equilibrium or long-run position (i.e., Hutchinson 1978: 45–46; Laidler 1987: 291). I take issue with the view that these permanent forces should be identified as those establishing long-period equilibrium; i.e., prevailing at the end of the adjustment process, after a temporal sequence of short-period positions. In this paper[1] I present an alternative view based on a different interpretation of "permanent" and "temporary" causes whose meaning is found not in the time scale, but in the hierarchy of the forces within the theory.

We can define a "permanent cause" as a sufficient condition for something to happen, regardless of the time interval necessary for its implementation. Permanent causes are sufficient but not necessary conditions, since the same effects could be brought about by other causes that are said to be "temporary"; these latter causes are neither necessary nor sufficient. They are not sufficient because their effects may well be offset by the working of other forces, and they are not necessary because a given effect cannot be unambiguously imputed to them.

When permanent forces prevail, the value assumed by certain variables, such as prices, rate of profit, wages, and the quantity of money, is called by Ricardo their "natural" value. For instance, a change in the conditions of production of a given commodity is a "permanent" cause of a change in its price, which means that the price will certainly change, although not every variation in commodity prices can be imputed to variations in the conditions of production. By contrast, a change in demand is a "temporary" cause of a change in prices, not because its effect does not last long enough, but because it is not brought about by a "permanent" cause. Ricardo wrote: "Having fully acknowledged the temporary effects [...] produced on the prices of commodities [...] by accidental causes [...] we will leave them out of our consideration, whilst we are treating of the laws which regulate natural wages and natural profits, effects totally independent of these accidental causes" (*Works* I: 91–29).[2]

When discussing natural wages, Ricardo granted that money wages can be pushed downwards when the supply of labor grows faster than demand, but, he said, if there is at the same time a change in the conditions of production of wage goods, making them more difficult to produce, their money prices rise and the overall effect is an increase, not a decrease, in money wages. The former can be taken as an example of a temporary cause, whereas the latter—an increase in the price of wage goods—is a permanent cause of wage increases (see Rosselli 1985). "Suppose com to rise in price because more labour is necessary to produce it. […] If, *as is absolutely certain*, wages would rise with the rise of corn […] profits would necessarily fall" (Ricardo, *Works* I: 110–111; italics added).[3]

Ricardo's definition of the natural quantity of money is given by analogy[4] with the definition of natural wages and natural prices. In order to see the analogy, first we need to clarify Ricardo's definition of the value of money as the purchasing power of a unit of currency over the standard: "Depreciation as applied to money must be understood to mean relative lowness as compared with the standard, and nothing else" (*Works* IX: 276); and "Commodities generally […] can never become a standard to regulate the quantity and value of money" (*Works* IV: 61).

The standard is that particular commodity that—in virtue of its own particular characteristics—is chosen to measure the value of money. If, then, gold is chosen as the standard, variations in the money price of gold are the measure of changes in the value of money. An increase in the price of gold (i.e., a change in the purchasing power of the currency over the standard) means a decrease in the value of money (i.e., a depreciation of the currency; conversely, for a decrease in the price of gold). From this premise, Ricardo drew a distinction between a change in money prices and a change in the value of money: by the former, he meant a change in the ratio of the currency (money) to commodities; by the latter, a change in the ratio of the currency to the standard.

If the standard is gold, the price of gold measures the internal value of the currency, while the rate of exchange (the ratio between the official prices of gold at home and abroad, assuming that the other countries have also adopted a gold standard) measures the external value of the currency. Whenever the market price of gold shows no deviation from the official price, and the market rate of exchange (the price of foreign bills of exchange) is close to the par of the exchange, the purchasing power of the currency over gold—therefore, its value—is equalized at home and abroad.

This configuration of the system is attained when the quantity of money is at its "natural" level. This is not a quantity that can be given a numerical value—targeted by the monetary authority—but, rather, is a benchmark signaled by the foreign and domestic value of money, on the evidence of which it can be seen when that level is not attained. When both the market price of gold at home and the market rate of exchange deviate from their official values, provided the internal and external convertibility of the currency are maintained, forces are at work that will restore that level.

Once the price of the standard is fixed in terms of the currency, its quantity will adjust so as to keep the value of money (in terms of the standard) constant. If the price of the standard is not fixed (i.e., the external and/or internal convertibility of the currency into gold are suspended), the quantity of money is no longer self-adjusting and the concept of a "natural" level becomes meaningless. In those cases where the quantity of money did not adjust to its "natural" level, the "uniformity in the value of money" could not be maintained (Ricardo, *Works* IV: 69); rather, its "value must be constantly vacillating" (Ricardo, *Works* III: 139).

For Ricardo, this was a most undesirable state of affairs:

> In the present state of the law [Bank of England's notes were no longer convertible into gold at an official price] they [bank directors] have the power, without any control whatsoever, of increasing or reducing the circulation in any degree they may think proper: a power which should neither be entrusted to the State itself, nor to any body in it; as there can be no security for the uniformity in the value of the currency, when its augmentation or diminution depends solely on the will of the issuers". (Ricardo, *Works* I: 359)

A currency without a standard, according to Ricardo, "would be exposed to all the fluctuations to which the ignorance or the interests of the issuers might subject it" (Ricardo, *Works* IV: 59).

With unbounded variations in the price of gold, the rate of exchange and the prices of all commodities were affected. A monetary disturbance was then introduced into the system of prices, altering the market signals that direct capital from one sector to another, disrupting the rules of production and distribution of the social product. However, Ricardo did not see a "real" disturbance as equally distorting. Changes in the *value* of gold—as opposed to changes in its *price*—signaled that gold ceased to be a good standard; a change in the relative value of commodities signaled a change in their conditions of production or the necessary adjustment in the process of capital competition.

Thus, the quantity of money is at its "natural" level whenever the market price of the standard shows no deviation from the official price; that is to say, whenever the purchasing power over the standard is kept constant (*Works* III: 105, 193). If gold is the standard, the quantity of money is kept at its natural level by a market mechanism. An increase in the quantity of money immediately lowers the exchanges, making the purchasing power of the standard in terms of the domestic currency higher abroad than at home, thereby making the export of gold profitable. The ensuing reduction in the quantity of gold brings the quantity of money back to its natural level.

Thus, changes in the quantity of money involving changes in its purchasing power in terms of gold at home and abroad are "temporary," because market mechanisms will bring the quantity of money to its natural level, thereby restoring the equality of the purchasing power of money at home and abroad. Changes in the quantity of money deriving from a change in the condition of production of gold, on the other hand, are permanent, because they cause a change in its natural level.

Let us take an example to illustrate the point. It is common opinion that Ricardo's theory represents the position according to which money is neutral; that is, variations in the nominal quantity of money have an effect on nominal variables, but only in the short period on real variables. Thus, Ricardo is seen as the champion of the quantity theory of money and of long-period analysis (O'Brien 1975: 164; Humphrey 1990: 19; Laidler 1991, *passim*).

Even if the quantity theory is interpreted as the proposition that a necessary and sufficient condition for a change in money price is a proportional increase in the money supply, it is certainly true that Ricardo never thought that any variations in prices necessarily implied a variation in the quantity of money. In other words, whereas the quantity of money always affects prices, variation in the quantity of money is not a necessary condition for a variation in prices. Price increases may just as well be caused by a decrease in the value of the standard, a rise in wages, or tax increases (see *Works* II: 412; III: 328; IV: 321; VI: 233). In fact, Ricardo advocated a policy of reduction in the quantity of money only in the case of depreciation measured in terms of gold, and never in the case of an increase in prices, as we would expect if he held the strict quantity theory. He wrote: "The issuers of paper money should regulate their issue solely by the price of bullion, and never by the quantity of their paper in circulation. The quantity can never be too great or too little, while it preserves the same value as the standard" (*Works* IV: 64).

But, is the change in the quantity of money a sufficient condition for a proportional change in money prices? The answer is no. The only proportionality factor to be found in Ricardo lies between the quantity of money and the price of gold, since any increase in the quantity of money above the natural level brings about an exactly equal decrease in its purchasing power in terms of gold. As a consequence, but only as a consequence of this proportionality, if the relative values of commodities in terms of gold are assumed to remain constant, then the monetary prices of commodities vary in proportion with the quantity of money. But, if the relative values of commodities vary—for instance, because there is a change in the conditions of production—then the proportionality between variations in prices and variations in the quantity of money disappears.

Thus, the non-neutrality of money in the short period conceived by Ricardo cannot be interpreted as a *short-run* effect, as something which is not destined to last. Rather, it should be interpreted as an *uncertain* effect because, in the absence of a theory to deny the validity of Say's identity, the level of output is given. Alternatively, the non-neutrality of money in the short period should be interpreted as a temporary effect, which is offset by others deriving from a permanent cause. This is why temporary causes cannot be part of the theory: not because their effects are not recognized as part of reality, but because their effects are uncertain and volatile, and can be offset by more certain and permanent ones (Marcuzzo and Rosselli 1994).

In conclusion, the question in Ricardo's theory is, then, not one of measuring "for how long" or "to what extent" an observed consequence follows from a given cause, before deciding whether it is a temporary or permanent effect. The question is one of deciding which causes can be made the object of a theory; whether, from a given cause, consequences can be derived that are certain. For Ricardo, the distinction between temporary and permanent pertains to the question of which *causes* are eligible to become part of a theory, and not to the question of which *effects* endure or fail to endure. Ricardo takes permanency as a property independent of the length of time during which causes exercise their influence because the definition of a permanent cause is given not by the length of the duration of its effects but by its place in the structure of the theory.[5]

7.2 "Normal" Values

Marshall made a change in terminology, revealing in itself of a change in meaning, from "natural" to "normal" values.[6] He maintained that "it is to the persistence of the influences considered, and the time allowed for them to work out their effect" that we should refer "when contrasting Market and Normal price" (Marshall 1920: 289). Moreover, he asserted that "the term normal implies the predominance of certain tendencies which appear likely to be more or less steadfast and persistent in their action over those which are relatively exceptional and intermittent" (Marshall 1920: 28).

For instance, producers adapt the level of production to expected demand if, and only if, the expected supply price is sufficient to make it worthwhile to produce that quantity. The price, "the expectation of which is sufficient and only just sufficient" (Marshall 1920: 310), to produce that quantity is the "normal" supply price. Given his definition, not surprisingly, Marshall applies the term "normal supply price" *equally* to the short and to the long period, the only difference being that in the long period, "supply means what can be produced by plant, which itself can be remuneratively produced and applied within the given time" (Marshall 1920: 315).

As Michel De Vroey (2000: 248) put it:

> The triggering event to which the firms' managers must react is a shift in demand. Three possibilities have to be disentangled in this respect: the first possibility is that the shift is accidental. That is, its expected persistence is too short to make it worthwhile to change the amount of variable factors used. The second possibility is that the shift is expected to last long enough for this specific purpose, yet to be too short to make changes in capacities worthwhile. When this is the case, short-period analysis comes into play. Finally, the shift in demand may be expected to be long enough to make an overall change in factors worthwhile. The long-period analysis then becomes relevant.

Marshall's distinction aims to qualify causes according to the persistence of their effects in time, whereas Ricardo aims to single out causes that can provide a sufficient explanation of given effects. For Marshall, it is the *persistence in time* of a known cause that is the criterion for attributing the term "normal" to the value assumed by a given variable, but, for Ricardo, it is the *certainty of their effects* that leads to identification of those causes that are responsible for "natural" values. Since the purpose of economic analysis is, according to Marshall, to determine the "immediate and ultimate effects of various groups of causes" (Whitaker 1975: 97) through close study of the time element, the distinction between short and long period is derived not from the nature of the forces determining observed effects, but from the length of time necessary for the *same* forces to work their effects. As Marshall says:

> In each [situation] price is governed by the relations between demand and supply. As regards *market* prices, Supply is taken to mean the stock of the commodity in question which is on hand, or at all events "in sight". As regards *normal* prices, when the term Normal is taken to relate to *short* periods of a few months or a year, Supply means broadly what can be produced for the price in question, with the existing stock of plant, personal and impersonal, in the given time. As regards *normal* prices when the term *Normal* is to refer to *long* periods of several years, Supply means what can be produced by plant, which itself can be remuneratively produced and applied within the given time; while lastly, there are very gradual or *secular* movements of normal price, caused by the gradual growth of knowledge, of population and of capital, and the changing conditions of demand and supply from one generation to another. (Marshall 1920: 314–315)

Since the forces that govern the economic system are supply and demand, the crucial factor becomes "the period of time which is allowed to the forces of demand and supply to bring themselves into equilibrium with one another" (Marshall 1920: 274). See, for instance:

> The actual value at any time, the market value as it is often called, is often more influenced by passing events, and by causes whose action is fitful and short-lived, than by those which work persistently. But in long periods those fitful and irregular causes in large measure efface one another's influence so that in the long run persistent causes dominate value completely. (Marshall 1920: 291)

Marshall's distinction between short and long period is based on the *nature of the decisions* involved, which reflects what individuals take as given and what they expect in different periods of time.

> For short periods people take the stocks of appliances of production as practically fixed; and they are governed by their expectations of demand in

> considering how actively they shall set themselves to work those appliances. In long periods they set themselves to adjust the flow of these appliances to their expectations of demand for the goods which the appliances help to produce. (Marshall 1920: 310–311)

It is the nature of the *decisions* involved, characterized by the time horizon to which they apply, that sets the boundary between the long and the short period. Accordingly, economic theory can take as constant those factors over which decisions can be postponed and take them as variables only when describing situations in which they are a matter of decision by economic agents.

7.3 The Role of Beliefs and Expectations

From Marshall's definition of short period, Kahn drew a further implication.[7] He noticed that the possibility of considering machinery and the organization of production as constant from the point of view of the short period arises from the fact that, in both cases, the decision to alter them is the same and depends on whether demand conditions are or are not considered "normal."[8] Accordingly, depending upon whether changes in demand are *believed* by entrepreneurs to be transitory or permanent, as compared with the level considered as normal, the decisions to modify the plant or the organization will or will not be taken. Although the short period cannot be "shorter" than the length of the productive process or longer than the time necessary to modify productive capacity, the time necessary to modify productive capacity depends not only on technological factors, but also on the prevailing conditions—depression or boom—which mold expectations regarding the return to "normal" conditions of demand. Thus, for Kahn, the nature of the short period is seen not as a conceptual experiment, but as a question of fact: the life of fixed capital is considerably longer than the period of production (Kahn 1932, ch. 2: 2, 1989: xiii). He wrote:

> If there were a complete range of continuous variation in the lives of the different means of production the notion of short period could not be employed. But, in reality as far as the range of variation is concerned between raw materials on the one hand and productive plant, on the other hand, there is a desolate and sparsely populated area. As a general rule, the life of physical capital is illustrated either by the mayfly or by the elephant. (Kahn 1989: xiii)

One aspect of the rationale for an "economics of the short period" is, therefore, rooted in the nature of the production process, which gives meaning to a time interval where productive capacity is given and only its utilization varies. In fact, there are changes that occur rapidly (such as output and employment) and others that occur only slowly (such as alterations in fixed plant) (Kahn 1932, ch. 2: 6). The other aspect characterizing the short period is rooted in expectations of changes in demand relative to the level perceived as "normal."

The level of demand that individuals take as "normal" is the benchmark against which observed variations are evaluated and expectations about its future course are formed. The two aspects are combined to explain why, in the short period, productive capacity is not altered. This is so because a change in the conditions of demand is not perceived as permanent. In fact, the "ideal" short period is defined as a situation where "any change that occurs is not expected to be permanent" (Kahn 1932, ch. 2: 10). In a depression, however, short-period equilibrium implies expectations that demand will return to its normal level, since suspending production or reducing the productive capacity to zero would be tantamount to acknowledging that demand must remain permanently low. In a boom, by contrast, short-period equilibrium implies that expectations are such that an increase in production is preferred to building up capacity until the increase in demand is perceived as "permanent."

Since what matters are expectations regarding the normal values of certain variables—in particular, the level of demand—it follows that the short period need *not* be a "short" time interval or only a temporary state before the long period forces work out their effects. It is, rather, a position that is maintained as long as the set of decisions, depending upon the expected values of selected variables, does not change (Dardi 1996). When the demand for an industry's output alters, according to Kahn, there are changes where responsiveness is immediate and changes where responsiveness is slow, but there is no continuous range of variation between "responsiveness" and "irresponsiveness." Changes that occur rapidly (output and employment) "do not very much depend on what has occurred in the past or what is expected to occur in the future" (Kahn 1932, ch. 2: 12). They are reversible changes as opposed to changes "which by definition have not time to occur in the short period [and which] depend on what has occurred in the past and what is expected to occur in the future" (ibid.).

In conclusion, according to Kahn, we have causes that have different effects according to whether they are *perceived* by economic agents as permanent or persistent on the basis of what is believed to be the normal value of a given variable. It is the divergence between the expected and the "normal" values of selected variables that explains why the short period may not be just a temporary situation.

7.4 The Short-period Method

In a letter to Keynes, Dennis Robertson referred to "your and Kahn's s[hort] p[eriod] method" (Keynes 1979: 17) to characterize the peculiarity of their approach. It was indeed Keynes who further developed short-period analysis with the more general purpose of accounting for decisions taken under different conditions of knowledge. These different conditions are manifested in what individuals expect in any given situation, and such expectations typically differ from individual to individual. The case in point is illustrated by the theory of liquidity preference, whereby

> the individual, who *believes* that future rates of interest will be above the rates assumed by the market, has a reason for keeping actual liquid cash, whilst the individual who differs from the market in the other direction will have a motive for borrowing money for short periods in order to purchase debts of longer term. (Keynes 1973a: 170; italics added)

More generally, the role assigned to expectations in *The General Theory* is to account for the possibility of an equilibrium at less than full employment. This equilibrium is not described as a situation characterized by "wrong" expectations, since "the theory of effective demand is substantially the same if we assume that short-period expectations are always fulfilled" (Keynes 1973b: 181). Thus, the short period is not a situation where expectations are not fulfilled, but a situation in which expectations generate "a state of things" (Dardi 1994) that conforms to them.

In a departure from Ricardo, Keynes attempted to capture the effects of decisions taken in an "uncertain" environment and provide an explanation not of "permanent causes," but of "motives, expectations, psychological uncertainties," which are, by definition, accidental and unstable (Keynes 1973b: 300).

For Ricardo, the predictive power of the theory is enhanced by severely limiting its domain, by drawing a distinction:

> between field of analysis, where necessary quantitative relations could be found between rates of remuneration, and between these rates and relative prices, and other fields where no such necessary relations could be established, and where actual relations had to be studied in their multiplicity and diversity according to circumstances. (Garegnani 1983: 312)

In Keynes—since "the material to which it [economics] is applied is, in too many respects, not homogeneous through time" (Keynes 1973b: 296)—it is the search for permanent causes that is severely limited. As he wrote: "The object of a model is to segregate the semi-permanent or relatively constant factors from those which are transitory or fluctuating so as to develop a logical way of thinking about the latter, and of understanding the time sequences to which they give rise in particular cases" (Keynes 1973b: 296–297).

And, as Jan Kregel put it:

> [...] [Keynes's theory] is not limited to a period of time so short that the capital stock cannot change. Rather it attempts to avoid analysing everything at once by applying a method which identifies a single aspect of the broader whole for analysis. The choice of the problem will then determine which aspects of the system should be given, not in the sense they are thought as unchanging, but that 'the effect or consequences of changes in them' are not taken directly into account. The capital stock is not assumed unchanged *over actual time;* rather any changes in it are left to one side to be considered later. (Kregel 1983: 96)

I will not take up here the question of whether the arguments set out by Keynes in the *General Theory* can be extended to the long period, or indeed the reasons why short-period analysis came to predominate in economics, but will now turn to Kahn's and Keynes's definition of short period vis-à-vis Ricardo's and modern usage, respectively.

7.5 The Nature of the Distinction Between the Short and the Long Period

In standard macroeconomics, the long period is usually identified with an "optimal" position towards which the economic system "naturally" tends if the necessary flexibilities are guaranteed. On the contrary, the short period is a temporary position characterized by some rigidities that prevent the system from entering into the optimum state. In standard microeconomics, the short period is a situation in which the productive capacity is given, and it is the level of utilization of this given capacity that is allowed to vary. The long period, on the other hand, is a situation in which also the productive capacity can change to adjust to the level of demand. It has been noted that since the two definitions are not identical, modern usage of the terms is marked by confusion and ambiguity, and strikingly so in the textbooks (Hamouda 1984; Kyer and Maggs 2006; Sanfilippo 2011).

The standard macroeconomics short period is a temporary position of the level of income and employment of resources, which can become permanent if rigidities (prices, wages, interest rate) are not removed, unlike the Kahn-Keynes version, which is characterized by expectations preventing the system from moving on to a different equilibrium, which is not necessarily the long-period equilibrium. While, in standard macroeconomics, the short period-long period distinction aims to separate temporary from permanent configurations, in the Kahn-Keynes definition of the short period, there is no such implication. In Ricardo, the distinction between temporary and permanent effects pertains to the nature of the causes occasioning them, and there is no implication that a temporary effect can become permanent if sufficient time is allowed for the causes to exercise their full force unimpeded.

The questions arising here are two: a) is Ricardo's approach to the short period the same as in standard macroeconomics? and b) can long-run positions be made the object of economic theory, or is, rather, the Kahn-Keynes short-period equilibrium more appropriate to deal with an economic system characterized by uncertainty and fundamental instabilities?

This issue was at the root of the controversy between Joan Robinson and Pierangelo Garegnani in the late 1970s, and it is interesting to take a new look at their arguments at a distance of nearly thirty-five years.

Robinson objected to the method based on comparisons in classical political economy and followed by Piero Sraffa (because "there is no causation and no change" [Robinson 1980b: 132]) as showing no substantial difference from the neoclassical equilibrium method in their neglect of time. Timeless analysis implies disregard of uncertainty and expectations, which are the guiding forces of economic behavior, according to Joan Robinson, fully persuaded as she was that the "Keynesian revolution destroyed the basis of [the] concept of long-period equilibrium and put nothing in its place" (Robinson 1980a: 130).

Robinson's argument rests on the distinction between a long-period approach, in which correct foresight regarding output composition and the pattern of prices that maximize profits is the fundamental assumption, and a short-period model, where there is no correct foresight. In the latter case, she wrote: "there are individual expectations which need not be consistent with each other and which may turn out later to have been mistaken [...]. The consequent interaction of individual decisions is seen in the total composition and prices of the total flow of output and its distribution" (Robinson 1980c: 89–90).

Garegnani contested Joan Robinson's argument that expectations and uncertainty prevent the attainment of long-period equilibrium, in the first place retorting that the point of normal position method is the *tendency* towards it, and then going on to raise the issue of the incorrectness of expectations, which may be assumed to characterize Ricardo's theory of accidental causes making market prices deviate from natural prices. Revision of expectations is, in fact, the moving force in the process of tendency to the long-period position. This tendency, Garegnani wrote, was "supposed to be the result of objective experiences, independent of the normal levels of the variables being in the 'minds of the dealers' from the beginning" (Garegnani 1989: 351).

So the two points of view held respectively by Robinson and Garegnani seem to indicate an incompatibility between Ricardo's method of analysis and that of Kahn-Keynes, which is at the root of the division between Neo-Ricardians and Post-Keynesians. In the next section, I wish to suggest that there is one aspect that shortens the distance between the two approaches, but not between them and the neoclassical theory.

7.6 Dividing Lines

The question of whether Ricardo's method is compatible with acceptance of the Kahn-Keynes short-period equilibrium—which differs from the neoclassical (Marshallian) notion of a temporary situation, the latter differing in turn from Ricardo's notion of temporary cause—revolves around the role of demand and supply in these approaches.

Ricardo did not deny that these forces were at work in influencing prices; what he denied was that supply-and-demand functions could be employed to derive a precise, quantitative relation between prices and quantity. Garegnani explained quite clearly the difference between classical effectual demand and the neoclassical demand function:

> The notion of demand schedule requires that the price-quantity relationship be determinate for all prices in the relevant range, and not only for the 'natural' or 'normal' price, which, however, is the only one that we may expect to experience under the non-accidental conditions that are likely to emerge through a repetition of the situation. We are therefore dealing with a much stricter notion than the immediately plausible one according to which an accidental fall in the quantity supplied below its normal level is likely to be accompanied by a rise in the price, and vice versa: in this notion no attempt would be made to determine the magnitude of such a rise, considered as depending on accidental factors. (Garegnani 1983: 309)

Similarly, there is no supply schedule in Ricardo's theory; that is, a well-behaved quantitative relation between price and quantity, derived from average and marginal costs.

So the first dividing line is between Ricardo's permanent positions and the neoclassical full equilibrium. Since supply-and-demand functions have no role to play in the case of Ricardo, the two concepts cannot be taken as identical. The second dividing line is in the meaning attributed to the short period, which Ricardo and neoclassical theory interpret as a temporary situation, while, for Keynes, on the contrary, it is not. Keynes's short-period equilibrium is not, in fact, a temporary situation that will eventually become a long-period equilibrium via flexibility of prices, wages, and interest rate, as it is taken to be in neoclassical theory. If expectations are such that the level of demand is perceived to remain low, no price mechanism is at work to pull the system out of short-period unemployment equilibrium, since the level of income at which the system comes to rest is set only by the level of aggregate demand.

We have seen that Ricardo's temporary situations are defined relative to the nature of the causes occasioning them: in the case of prices, these are the changes in the quantities supplied and demanded; in the case of wages, they are the supply and demand of labor; while, in the case of the natural quantity of money, they consist of deviations in the market price from the official price of gold. These causes will produce temporary, not permanent, effects, like those produced by a change in the cost of production in the case of the price of commodities, the price of necessities in the case of wages, and the value of gold in the case of the natural quantity of money. So the dividing line is not only between the neoclassical theory and Ricardo, who sees different forces are at work in determining short- and long-run equilibria, but also between Ricardo and Keynes, the latter holding that short-run equilibrium can be a permanent situation.

There is, however, an aspect of Ricardo's method of analysis—the importance attributed to the hierarchy of causes in the groundwork of the theory—which is retained by Keynes, who also holds that there are some causes which are more "important" than others. For instance, in Keynes, the level of aggregate demand, whatever the reasons underlying it, is a permanent cause holding the level of income at a level below that of full employment; no flexibility in the rate of interest, prices, or wages will have the same effect as a high level of aggregate demand for the attainment of full equilibrium, as is the case in neoclassical theory.

Ricardo's legacy can thus be seen in the device allowing for the separation of causes by means of which it is possible to separate propositions that have the nature of sufficient conditions, regardless of the time interval necessary for their implementation. This is a case of the effect of the conditions of wage-goods production on profit, dominating all other circumstantial causes. See, for instance, Ricardo's letter to Malthus, 16 September 1814:

> I agree with you that when capital is scanty compared with the means of employing it, from whatever causes arising, profits will be high. *Whether temporary or permanently must of course depend upon whether the cause be temporary or permanent.* It is however very important to ascertain what are cause which make capital scanty compared with the means of employing it,—and how far when ascertained they may be considered temporary or permanent. It is in this enquiry that I am led to believe that the state of the cultivation of land is almost the only great permanent cause. There are other circumstances which are attended with temporary effects of more or less duration, and frequently operate partially on particular trades. The state of production from land compared with the means necessary to make it produce operates on all, and is alone lasting in its effects. (*Works* VI: 133; italics added)

A similar methodological stance can be found in Keynes's approach, where an increase in effective demand is a sufficient condition for an increase in employment, while a reduction in money wages is not. He wrote:

> The reduction in money-wages will have no *lasting* tendency to increase employment except by virtue of its repercussion either on the propensity to consume for the community as a whole, or on the schedule of marginal efficiencies of capital, or on the rate of interest. There is no method of analysing the effect of a reduction in money-wages, except by following up its possible effects on these three factors. (1973a: 262; italics added)

Indeed, Keynes objected to the very idea that the economic system be governed by natural laws, and the 120 years that separate Ricardo's *Principles* (1816) from Keynes's *General Theory* (1936) saw the abandonment of faith in positivism and awareness of the advances in physics that challenged the Newtonian representation of the laws of the universe, and also their applicability to the realm of economic affairs. With his insistence on "motives, expectations, psychological uncertainties," which are, by definition, accidental and unstable, Keynes could hardly have endorsed Ricardo's faith in the similar nature shared by economic and physical laws.

Notwithstanding these profound epistemological differences, Ricardo's quest for a theory in which the hierarchy of causes is detectable in the structure of the arguments was also pursued by Keynes, who shared with Ricardo the recognition of its relevance and usefulness.

Notes

1. I draw on Marcuzzo and Rosselli (1994), Marcuzzo (1996, 2002), which also deal with several points taken up here.
2. See also: "Diminish the cost of production of hats, and their price will ultimately fall to their new natural price, although the demand should be doubled, trebled, or quadrupled" (*Works* I: 382).
3. See also: "A tax [...] on raw produce, and on the necessaries of the labourer, [...] would raise wages. Wages would *inevitably and necessarily* rise; and in proportion as they rose, profits would fall" (*Works* I: 159; italics added).
4. The word "analogy" is used to indicate the similarity, rather than the identity, of the meaning "natural" when applied to a quantity, rather than to a price. It is the idea of a benchmark that market mechanisms tend to establish

whenever temporary or accidental causes make prices (or wages) or the quantity of money deviate from it.

5. See, for instance: "A commodity can only *permanently* rise in price, either because a greater quantity of capital and labour must be employed to produce it, or because money has fallen in value" (*Works* I: 417; italics added); and "It is the cost of production which must *ultimately* regulate the price of commodities, and not, as has been often said, the proportion between the supply and demand" (*Works* I: 382; italics added).
6. As Krishna Bharadwaj (1986: 37) remarked: "The shift to supply and demand theories yet retained the significance of 'long period' positions as distinct from the 'short period'; the tendency towards a uniform rate of profit and wage was retained. However, market prices became synonymous with 'short period' prices and natural prices with 'long period' prices; the main theoretical shift being that both were now represented as values attained in equilibrium through the balancing of symmetrical but opposite forces of supply and demand, only under different conditions."
7. Kahn, perhaps more than any other economist, was preoccupied with the precise definition of the short period; he chose it as the title of his fellowship dissertation, "The Economics of the Short Period," written between October 1928 and December 1929. It was first published in Italian in 1983 and in English only in 1989. In the following two or three years, Kahn presented his thoughts on short-period economics in a book bearing the same title as the dissertation, which, however, remained unfinished and is still unpublished. Of the eleven chapters planned, on the evidence of the contents list, chapters 1, 3, and 4 remained unwritten, and chapter 7 was left unfinished. The extant copy, which was found among Kahn's papers in King's College archives, can be dated to the last quarter of 1932.
8. Note that the meaning of "normal" is here slightly different from that given to it by Marshall, since to the subjective element—i.e., what is *perceived* as normal—is given more emphasis.

References

Bharadwaj, K. 1986. *Classical Political Economy and the Rise to Dominance of Supply and Demand Theories.* Calcutta: University Press India.

Dardi, M. 1994. Kahn's Theory of Liquidity Preference and Monetary Policy. *Cambridge Journal of Economics*, 18: 91–106.

Dardi, M. 1996. Imperfect Competition and Short-Period Economics. In M.C. Marcuzzo, L.L. Pasinetti, and A. Roncaglia (eds), *The Economics of Joan Robinson.* London: Routledge, pp. 29–35.

De Vroey, M. 2000. Marshall on Equilibrium and Time: A Reconstruction. *European Journal of the History of Economic Thought*, 1: 245–269.

Garegnani, P. 1983. The Classical Theory of Wages and the Role of Demand Schedules in the Determination of Relative Prices. *American Economic Review*, 73: 309–313.

Garegnani, P. 1989. Some Notes on Capital, Expectations and the Analysis of Changes. In G.R. Feiwel (ed.), *Joan Robinson and Modern Economic Theory*. London and Basingstoke: Macmillan, pp. 344–367.

Hamouda, O. 1984. On the Notion of Short-Run and Long-Run: Marshall, Ricardo and Equilibrium Theories. *British Review of Economic Issues*, 6: 55–82.

Humphrey, T.M. 1990. Ricardo versus Thornton on the Appropriate Monetary Response to Supply Shocks. *Federal Reserve Bank of Richmond*, 76: 18–24.

Hutchinson, T.W. 1978. *On Revolution and Progress in Economic Knowledge*. Cambridge: Cambridge University Press.

Kahn, R.F. 1932. "The Economics of the Short Period." Unpublished manuscript.

Kahn, R.F. 1989. *The Economics of the Short Period*. London: Macmillan.

Keynes, J.M. 1973a. *The General Theory of Employment. Interest and Money*. Vol. VII of *The Collected Writings of John Maynard Keynes*. Edited by D. Moggridge. London: Macmillan.

Keynes, J.M. 1973b. *The General Theory and After: Defence and Development*. Vol. XIV of *The Collected Writings of John Maynard Keynes*. Edited by D. Moggridge. London: Macmillan.

Keynes, J.M. 1979. *The General Theory and After: A Supplement*. Vol. XXIX of *The Collected Writings of John Maynard Keynes*. Edited by D. Moggridge. London: Macmillan.

Kregel, J.A. 1983. Conceptions of Equilibrium, Conceptions of Time and Conceptions of Economic Interaction. In G. Caravale (ed.), *La crisi delle teorie economiche*. Milano: Franco Angeli, pp. 55–101.

Kyer, B.L. and Maggs, G.E. 2006. A Note on Time Periods in Macroeconomics. *Atlantic Economic Journal*, 34: 235–236.

Laidler, D. 1987. Bullion Controversy. In J. Eatwell, M. Milgate, and P. Newman (eds), *The New Palgrave: A Dictionary of Economics*. Vol. 1. London: Macmillan, pp. 289–294.

Laidler, D. 1991. The Quantity Theory is Always and Everywhere Controversial: Why?. *The Economic Record*, 67 (December): 289–306.

Marcuzzo, M.C. 1996. Short Period Economics in Retrospect. In P. Arestis, G. Palma, and M. Sawyer (eds), *Capital Controversy, Post Keynesian Economics and the History of Economic Theory: Essays in Honour of Geoff Harcourt*. Vol. I. London: Routledge, pp. 398–409.

Marcuzzo, M.C. 2002. David Ricardo and the 'Natural' Level of the Quantity of Money. In B. Schefold (ed.), *Exogenität und Endogenität. Die Geldmenge in der Geschichte des ökonomischen Denkens und in der modernen Politik*. Marburg: Metropolis, pp. 171–185.

Marcuzzo, M.C. and Rosselli, A. 1994. Ricardo's Theory of Money Matters. *Revue Economique*, 45: 1251–1267.
Marshall, A. [1920] 1964. *Principles of Economics*. 8th ed. London: Macmillan.
O'Brien, D.P. 1975. *The Classical Economists*. Oxford: Oxford University Press.
Ricardo, D. 1951–1973. *The Works and Correspondence of David Ricardo*. Edited by P. Sraffa, with the collaboration of M.H. Dobb. Cambridge: Cambridge University Press.
Robinson, J.V. 1980a. Debate: 1970s. In *Further Contributions to Modern Economics*. Oxford: Blackwell, pp. 123–130.
Robinson, J.V. 1980b. Retrospect 1980. In *Further Contributions to Modern Economics*. Oxford: Blackwell, pp. 130–134.
Robinson, J.V. 1980c. Time in Economic Theory. In *Further Contributions to Modern Economics*. Oxford: Blackwell, pp. 86–95.
Rosselli, A. 1985. The Theory of Natural Wage. In G. Caravale (ed.), *The Legacy of Ricardo*. Oxford: Blackwell, pp. 239–254.
Sanfilippo, E. 2011. The Short Period and the Long Period in Macroeconomics: An Awkward Distinction. *Review of Political Economy*, 23: 371–388.
Whitaker, J.K. 1975. *The Early Economic Writings of Alfred Marshall 1869–1890*. London: Macmillan.

CHAPTER 8

Profitability in the International Gold Market in the Early History of the Gold Standard

8.1 Introduction

The distinctive feature of the Gold Standard was the equilibrating mechanism of gold movements which, by altering the world distribution of gold from deficit to surplus countries, restored international balance of payments equilibria. Although, on average, the occurrence of gold movements was in fact less frequent than expected, it was the implicit discipline of gold flows that gave to the Gold Standard its equilibrating mechanism.

The adjustment paths followed by the Gold Standard have been widely analysed in the literature, though the issue of what was the dominant

An earlier version of this paper was written while both authors were Visiting Fellows of Political Economy, University College, London, and was circulated as Discussion Paper 1985/15. We are indebted to David Blake, Meghnad Desai, Ghislain Deleplace, Morris Perlman, David Pierce and an anonymous referee for very helpful comments. We would also like to thank the participants to the Money Workshop at the University of California, Los Angeles, to the International Trade and Finance Seminar at Stanford and to the Non-neoclassical Economics Seminar at Harvard-MIT for very stimulating discussions when this paper was presented.

Originally publ. in: (With Annalisa Rosselli), *Economica*, 54, 1987, pp. 367–80. Reprint by Springer Nature Switzerland 2024 with kind permission

M. C. Marcuzzo, *Economic Theories, Protagonists and Facts*, Palgrave Studies in the History of Economic Thought,
https://doi.org/10.1007/978-3-031-63949-4_8

mechanism does not seem to have been settled (Schwartz 1984: 6). But the microeconomics of gold movements—i.e. who are the agents and what is the relevant market behaviour behind the occurrence of gold flows in the early history of the Gold Standard—has not been analysed. In the most recent interpretations of the Gold Standard the focus has been rather on the evolution of the 'management' of the Gold Standard by the Bank of England and on the violations of the rules of the game, in response to movements of gold, by central banks in the pre-1914 Gold Standard (Bordo 1984: 94–98).

In this paper we discuss the profitability of gold flows when the development of an organized international gold market centred in London was on its way, and when the basis for the rise of the Gold Standard as an international monetary system, which gave London a 'special position' within the system, was laid.

The purpose of the analysis is to lay down the necessary and sufficient conditions of profitability of gold imports and exports from the point of view of individual agents, both when the Bank of England was committed to exchange her notes at a fixed gold price (until 1797), and when she was not (1797–1821). Besides the expected result that the rise of the Gold Standard depended on the development of integrated markets, our analysis produces a less familiar result. By looking at gold flows from the point of view of individual agents, we show that the equilibrium condition imposed by *both* the monetary approach and the price-specie-flow mechanism (i.e. such that gold flows will come to an end only when the equalization across countries of the purchasing power of gold in terms of commodities is attained) is unnecessarily restrictive. We claim instead that the stopping rule for gold movements can be limited to the attainment of the purchasing power parity of gold over each currency, i.e. when each currency buys on the domestic market no more and no less gold than it buys on the foreign markets.

In Sect. 8.2 we review the available evidence on the London gold market in the early history of the Gold Standard. In Sect. 8.3 we develop an alternative formulation of the gold points. In Sect. 8.4 we allow for the possibility of institutional frameworks in which the price of gold is not fixed. Finally, in Sect. 8.5 we derive the main analytical conclusion of the paper, namely, the distinction between the necessary and sufficient conditions for gold movements to take place.

8.2 The London Gold Market

We do not have reliable data on the gold market in the early history of the Gold Standard in England, i.e. before the middle of the nineteenth century. One of the reasons why the evidence about international gold movements is so scanty may be the fact that it was a trade in which secrecy mostly ruled (Sutherland 1932: 369), and that the export of bullion was illegal in most countries. However, we do have a fairly good idea of how the market in precious metals worked from the middle of the eighteenth century up to the first quarter of the nineteenth century. The evidence comes from two types of sources: from the evidence given to the British Parliamentary Committees, notably the Bullion Committee (1810) and the Resumption of Cash Payments Committees (1819), and from the ledgers and papers of merchants engaged in the bullion trade.

Spain and Portugal shared the monopoly of the supply of silver and gold respectively, as they had complete control over the mines of these metals in their colonies. During the eighteenth century the centre of the international gold market shifted from Amsterdam to London, where the export of foreign gold or 'sworn off' gold (i.e. upon oath that it did not come from the melting of domestic coins) had been legalized since 1663 (Shaw 1896: 162). By the middle of the eighteenth century, London was already the chief gold importer from Portugal, given the strong trade relationship that England enjoyed with Portugal (see Shillington and Wallis Chapman 1908). Smuggling gold from Portugal was an ongoing business for British ships which called at Lisbon whenever the fleet from Brazil arrived (Godinho 1950: 193). Precious metals were also smuggled from South America, through the West Indies, by British merchants, who at the same time handled the shipping of silver to the East Indies. London quickly became the world transhipper of gold and silver and, after 1815, the largest gold market in the world. This occurred not only because of the low freight charges that British ships could offer, but especially because London was becoming the best organized market, both in gold and in foreign exchange (dominated by specialized intermediaries: Christelow 1947: 19–20), and the City was becoming the commercial and financial centre of the world (see Chapman 1977, 1979).

In the early days of the Gold Standard in England the pre-eminent bullion broker in the City was the House of Mocatta and Goldsmid, which was later to be followed by the House of Rothschild. Mocatta and Goldsmid would fix the price of gold, which was then published twice a week in the *Wetenhall Bulletin*. The prices and the quantities transacted (with the names of buyers and sellers) were registered in two separate books, according to whether the transaction was on behalf of the Bank of England or between individual merchants, at the Bullion Office of the Bank of England.[1] The Bank of England daily declared its buying price (Jastram 1977: 16), that is, the price at which the Bank would buy gold. But as Mocatta and Goldsmid were the only sellers to the Bank of England, and as sellers to Mocatta and Goldsmid were not informed of the names of the buyers (i.e. whether it was the Bank or a merchant), the market price of gold and the Bank price were the same.[2]

Most of the gold that was sold through Mocatta and Goldsmid was exported, but the number of buyers, that is, the number of houses that could afford to be in the gold export trade, was small: it was reckoned to be 20 by A. Goldsmid in his evidence to the Bullion Committee (British Parliamentary Papers 1810: 42). The number of sellers was much higher: it was made up partly of merchants who were consignees of the gold coming from Portugal, partly of merchants specializing in the import trade in precious metals coming from Africa and Jamaica, and partly of merchants who bought and sold underweighted coins and gold objects.

By looking at the papers of merchants trading with Portugal and Brazil, it has been possible to gather further information about the gold trade. For the years 1741–1774 we have the records of an English bullion merchant trading with Portugal. It is clear that the bullion trade differed from any other commodity trade in one major respect. Owing to the high level of competition, the margins of profit were low and therefore the commission fees were lower than in other foreign sectors. For instance, in the foreign trade with Portugal in the middle of the eighteenth century, the factorage was estimated at around 2 per cent, while in the bullion trade it was rated at 0.33 per cent (Sutherland 1932: 382). Insurance costs, particularly during wartimes, were high, and in general the risks involved in this commerce were numerous, as is well documented by the correspondence of a British merchant in Brazil (Heaton 1946: 18).

The profit in the bullion trade derived from the existence of different conditions in the bullion market and in the world foreign exchange market. Familiarity with market imperfections and the knowledge of the institutional framework surrounding each particular market were the crucial elements in what was considered the 'most difficult art of merchandising' (Postlethwayt 1757: 91).

Bills of exchange were the alternative to shipping gold, and therefore the price of foreign bills of exchange, i.e. the exchange rate, was the chief concern of a merchant in the bullion trade. This was clearly recognized by Ricardo in his *The High Price of Gold Bullion*:

> No person ever exports or imports bullion without first considering the rate of exchange. It is by the rate of exchange that it discovers the relative value of bullion in the two countries between which it is estimated. It is therefore consulted by the bullion merchant in the same manner as the price-current is by the other merchants, before they determine on the exportation or importation of other commodities. (Ricardo 1951: 73)

The market of foreign bills of exchange depended on the conditions prevailing in the commodity trade and in the capital flow sector of the economy. The supply of foreign bills of exchange was regulated by domestic exports (commodities and capital inflows), while the demand for foreign bills of exchange on the domestic market was regulated by domestic imports (commodities and capital outflows).

The foreign exchange market in London from the end of the seventeenth century was a highly organized market, which was to become increasingly dominated by specialized intermediaries (brokers and dealers).[3] Arbitraging among different foreign currencies and gold prices in the international markets of the world, exploiting discrepancies in the price of bills, the price of gold and the rate of discount, was the business of a specialized class of economic agents who found in London the chief market place for their transactions. They could supply foreign bills of exchange, when the demand was high, by undertaking the risk of exporting gold, or they could buy bills of exchange to import gold as soon as the rate of exchange made this trade profitable.

According to Blake, the merchants in the bullion trade

> [are] remarkable for their shrewdness and the small profits upon which they transact their business; and as soon the premium on a foreign Bill exceeds, by a very small amount, the expenses of the transit of bullion, the certainty of the profit compensates in some degree for its smallness, and the opportunity, when it occurs, is seldom neglected. (Blake 1810: 23)

After the Napoleonic wars, the bill on London had become the chief means of remittance in international transactions. Bills on London were quoted in every foreign exchange market, while relatively fewer currencies were quoted in the London Royal Exchange.[4] This in turn had an impact on the way in which international gold transactions were carried out.

8.3 International Gold Transactions Options

The conditions under which it is profitable to export or import gold can be looked at from different viewpoints. We start by looking at the profitability of importing gold in the domestic market, say, from the point of view of a merchant in London. There are two ways to carry out this particular transaction.

A. The merchant in London buys a foreign bill of exchange, sends it to his correspondent abroad and asks him to ship gold to London.
B. The London merchant's correspondent abroad sells a bill drawn upon the London merchant, then buys gold in the foreign market and ships it to London.

The profitability conditions for A and B require that (8.1) and (8.2) respectively hold, where the left-hand sides describe the cost and the right-hand sides describe the revenue from the transaction for each pound initially spent, when one looks at the matter from the point of view of the London merchant's account:

$$1+i_{t(A)} < \frac{E_m}{p_0^*\left(1+\tau_0\right)} p_0 \tag{8.1}$$

$$1+i_{t(B)} < E_m^* \frac{1}{p_0^*\left(1+\tau_0\right)} p_0 \tag{8.2}$$

where

τ_0 = cost of shipping gold (brokerage, insurance, commission and freight) as a percentage of the price

E_m = price of a 'sight bill' in the domestic foreign exchange market; i.e. units of foreign currency for 1 unit of domestic currency = market rate of exchange

E_m^* = price of a 'sight bill' in the foreign exchange market abroad

p_0^* = price of gold bullion in the foreign market (per ounce)

p_0= price of gold bullion in the domestic market (per ounce)

$t_{(A)}$= time interval between the purchase of the foreign bill and the sale of the gold imported

$t_{(B)}$= time interval between the payment of the bill and the sale of the gold imported

i_t= rate of interest for t days in the domestic money market.

In (8.1) we assume that the London merchant buys a sight bill on the foreign country from which gold is imported, at a cost of £1. The loss of interest during the interval, $t_{(A)}$, from the time when the bill is purchased and mailed until the gold is bought, shipped and sold, as measured by the domestic market rate (i_t) must therefore be added to the cost of purchasing the bill.[5] If E_m is the amount of foreign currency that can be bought with one unit of domestic currency, then $E_m / \{p_0^*(1+\tau_0)\}$ is the amount of gold that the correspondent will buy and ship to the London merchant.

In (8.2), the correspondent abroad sells a sight bill on London, say, for £1. Gold must be sold in London before the bill comes due. But if either the delivery or the sale of gold is delayed, there will be a loss of interest from the day the bill comes due to the day the revenue from the sale of gold becomes available. The loss of interest is given by $i_{t(B)}$.[6]

It is clear that $t_{(A)} > t_{(B)}$. Moreover, in (8.2) the only uncertainty concerns the domestic price of gold at the time of its delivery in the domestic market as E_m^* and p_0^* are observed variables, while uncertainty about p_0 and p_0^*,[7] which are both expected prices, is a feature of (8.1). It follows that, in principle, (8.2) is always preferred to (8.1).[8] This is particularly true when the time interval required to complete the transaction, in an age well before the transport revolution, is very long.

There is then the question of whether a particular foreign currency is quoted in the domestic market. We know, for instance, that bills on Hamburg and on US cities were hardly quoted in the Royal Exchange until the second quarter of the nineteenth century, either because all the transactions related to the US market were carried on in pounds (Einzig 1970: 173), or because the market for that pair of currencies was more developed abroad, as was the case with Hamburg.[9] So, if we look at the profitability conditions for a merchant in the United States, it follows that only option A is viable. Likewise, if the transaction involved a London merchant with his foreign correspondent in the United States, then only option B is viable.

Generally speaking, it follows that, on the assumption that $E_m = E_m^*$, B will always be preferred to A because in B the opportunity cost of the investment, measured by i_t, is minimized, given that $t_{(B)} < t_{(A)}$. Moreover the uncertainty about p_0^* is zero.

The assumption $E_m = E_m^*$ may appear too strong. In fact, there were significant fluctuations of E_m^* both below and above E_m, so that the difference between the rates of exchange at a certain point in time could offset the greater cost of A.[10] Given, however, that E_m and E_m^* could not be known simultaneously, random discrepancies between E_m and E_m^* did not play a crucial role in the choice between A and B.

We turn now to the question of the profitability of exporting gold from the domestic market, again from the point of view of a merchant in London. Once again, there are two ways to carry out this transaction:

C. The London merchant buys gold on the domestic market. This gold is shipped to his correspondent abroad who will sell it in the foreign market and remit a bill on London to him.
D. The London merchant sells a bill of exchange denominated in foreign currency, drawn by him on his foreign correspondent, and ships gold to the foreign market.

Transactions C and D are profitable if (8.3) and (8.4) hold, respectively, where the left-hand sides are the costs and the right-hand sides the revenues involved in transaction C and D, respectively, for each unit of foreign currency:

$$\frac{p_0\left(1+\tau_0\right)\left(1+i_{t(C)}\right)}{p_0^*} < \frac{1}{E_m^*} \tag{8.3}$$

$$\frac{p_0\left(1+\tau_0\right)\left(1+i_{t(D)}^*\right)}{p_0^*} < \frac{1}{E_m} \tag{8.4}$$

where

i_t^* = rate of interest for t days in the foreign money market

$t_{(C)}$ = time interval from the time gold is purchased and shipped abroad until the time when the bill remitted comes due

$t_{(D)}$ = time interval between the payment of the bill and the sale of gold in the foreign market

While the domestic price of gold, p_0, is an observed variable, p_0^* and E_m^* are expected prices. Sudden changes in p_0^* could turn a profitable gold export into a loss.[11]

In (8.3), the loss of interest for $t_{(C)}$ days (i.e. the time necessary to complete the transaction) must be taken into account as a cost sustained by the London merchant and added to the shipping costs. It is measured by $i_{t(C)}$, i.e. by the rate of interest prevailing in the domestic money market.

In (8.4), $1/E_m$ is the revenue from the sale of a bill for one unit of foreign currency. The cost to the London merchant of buying and shipping gold to pay for the bill when it becomes due is given by

$$\frac{p_0\left(1+\tau_0\right)\left(1+i^*_{t(D)}\right)}{p_0^*}$$

allowing for delays in the sale of gold in the foreign country. For simplicity's sake, we assume that τ is the same in each direction.[12]

It is clear that $t_{(C)} > t_{(D)}$. From (8.3) and (8.4) it follows that D is preferred to C if (8.5) holds:

$$E_m\left(1+i^*_{t(D)}\right) < E_m^*\left(1+i_{t(C)}\right) \tag{8.5}$$

In this case, it is impossible to decide whether C is more profitable than D even under the assumption $E_m = E_m^*$, given that $i_t^* \neq i_t$, But it is safe to say that uncertainty about E_m^* at the moment in time when gold is to be sold and a bill has to be remitted accounts for the preference given to D.[13]

8.4 The Gold Points

With respect to the early history of the Gold Standard, inequalities (8.1), (8.2), (8.3), and (8.4) qualify the proposition that gold movements will occur when the market rate of exchange hits the 'gold points'. Gold points are said to be reached when deviations of the rate of exchange from parity (from below or above) are higher than the costs of shipping gold. The par of exchange between two currencies was defined as the ratio between the bullion content of the respective coins, or (which amounts to the same thing) as the ratio between their mint prices.

But as there was no institutional enforcement of the par of exchange—i.e. no central authority in charge of maintaining a fixed rate of exchange between two currencies—there was scope for a wide oscillation of the market rate of exchange around parity. Determining whether the 'premium' or 'discount' of a bill of exchange, at which they were usually quoted, was large enough to make bullion a cheaper remittance than buying foreign currency required a tiresome calculation.[14] First, if two currencies were on different standards, as was often the case, the computation of the deviations of the market rate of exchange from par was complicated by the necessity of calculating the actual parity, i.e. of taking into account the change in the ratio of gold to silver with respect to their mint ratio in both markets. This was called the 'real exchange'. The real exchange of a Gold Standard currency with a Silver Standard currency obviously became more favourable to the former whenever gold appreciated in the foreign market. The real rate of exchange differed from parity as much as the market gold/silver ratio differed from the mint ratio. Second, the price of gold bullion itself was not fixed, even when it was adopted as standard of the currency.

The Gold Standard actually arose in England in 1717 when the gold/silver ratio in the market proved to be lower than the mint ratio, although it was formally introduced only one hundred years later. During these one hundred years another step was taken which favoured the Gold Standard, by instituting a new coinage and declaring that silver was legal tender up to £25 by tale, and beyond that by weight. In the 1816 Act, gold coin 'made according to the indenture of the Mint' was made 'the sole standard measure of value and legal tender for payment, without any limitation of amount' (56 Geo III c. 68), and silver coin was declared to be legal tender only up to 40 shillings.

In the meantime, from February 1797, the Bank of England had suspended cash payments and its notes were not to be payable at demand at a fixed gold price until May 1821, even if guineas continued to circulate at their face value until 1810. Hence, in the discussion of gold movements in the early history of the Gold Standard, two general cases have to be considered.

In the first case, the price of gold is bounded and can vary only within a very limited range. The price of gold was such that

$$p_M - \varepsilon \leq p_0 \leq p_M + \eta \tag{8.6}$$

where

p_M = official (mint) price of gold

ε = Bank of England Commission or seignorage expenses. The loss of interest while waiting for the gold to be coined can also be considered as seignorage

η = monetary compensation for the risk involved in melting domestic coins, which was against the law

This general form encompasses different institutional frameworks which marked the early history of the Gold Standard. These are reflected in the values taken on by ε and η. The value of ε was never high in England where coinage at the Mint was free. Only in 1816 was a seignorage imposed on silver coinage in order to depress the price of silver bullion (Officer 1983: 589).

As for η, after 1797 guineas could not be obtained from the Bank. Therefore the monetary compensation for the risk had to be higher than before to induce people to search for guineas in order to melt them down. Obviously, $\eta = 0$ when gold in bar can be obtained from the Bank at the mint price.

The second case is given by

$$p_M - \varepsilon \le p_0 \le \frac{1}{m} + \eta \qquad m < \frac{1}{p_M} \tag{8.7}$$

where

m = actual bullion content of 1 unit of domestic currency.

(8.7) is the general form to describe monetary regimes in which the price of gold varies over a wider range. In the case of inconvertible paper money, $m = 0$ and the price of gold is not bounded from above.

The distinction envisaged in (8.6) and (8.7) is more general than the distinction between convertible and inconvertible monetary regimes. In fact, monetary regimes described by (8.6) include the case in which there was inconvertible paper money (as long as there were guineas in circulation), and monetary regimes described by (8.7) include also the case of a pure metallic circulation (as long as it consisted of debased coins). This distinction is therefore more suitable to describing institutional frameworks such as those prevalent in England from the middle of the eighteenth century to the first quarter of the nineteenth century.

Excluding times in which there were 'runs' on gold arising from widespread panic, the oscillations of the price of gold around the mint parity were chiefly determined by changes in the exchange rate. When the rate of exchange becomes so 'unfavourable'—for reasons that will be discussed later—that gold can be exported at a profit, the price of gold rises. But once an increase in the price of gold has taken place, the exchange can fall even further.[15]

Under the assumption that the foreign country was on a silver standard and the domestic country was on a gold standard, the range of variations of the exchange rate below and above the 'real parity' can be written as

$$\Delta E_{XP} = -\left(\tau_0 + i^*_{t(D)}\right) + \left(\Delta q^*_0 - \Delta p_0\right) \tag{8.8}$$

$$\Delta E_{MP} = \left(\tau_0 + i_{t(A)}\right) + \left(\Delta q^*_0 - \Delta p_0\right)$$

where

ΔE_{XP} = maximum depreciation of the exchange rate relatively to the 'real parity'

ΔE_{MP} = maximum appreciation of the exchange rate relatively to the 'real parity'

Δq^*_0 = percentage variation of the foreign price of silver relative to its mint price

Δp_0 = percentage variation of the domestic price of gold relative to the mint price.

These are simply the 'export and import points' which bound the profitability conditions of gold movements. To explain what makes the exchange rate reach the gold points, a theory of the exchange rate is required.

8.5 Stopping Rules for Gold Movements

In order to explain *why* the exchange rate has become so low or so high as to make gold the most preferred traded commodity, a comparison has to be made between the profit in the bullion trade and the profit in any other commodity trade; in what follows we analyse only the case of gold exports, as the case of gold imports is perfectly symmetrical.

Let us define the following, under the assumption that there are *n* traded goods:

p_i= domestic price of commodity i
p_i^* = foreign price of commodity i
t_i= time interval between the payment of the bill drawn against the shipping of the commodity i (i = 0, 1, ..., 0, n) and the sale of the same commodity in the foreign market
τ_i= costs of shipping commodity i (i = 0, 1, ..., 0, n) as brokerage, freight, insurance and commission calculated as percentage of the price.

The profitability condition of gold exports has been expressed by Eq. (8.4), which can be rewritten in a more familiar form as

$$p_0^* - E_m p_0 \left(1+\tau_0\right)\left(1+i_{t(0)}^*\right) > 0 \tag{8.9}$$

where $t_{(0)} = t_{(D)}$.

We postulated that whenever (8.9) holds there are economic agents who are ready to export gold. But in order to explain why the excess demand for foreign bills of exchange in the domestic market (which is responsible for the fall in the exchange rate) is matched by bills drawn against the shipping of gold and not of any other commodity, a further condition is required. This is that there be no other commodity more profitable to export. It is expressed by Eq. (8.10):

$$\frac{p_0\left(1+\tau_0\right)\left(1+i_{t(0)}^*\right)}{p_0^*} < \frac{p_i\left(1+\tau_i\right)\left(1+i_{t(i)}^*\right)}{p_i^*} \tag{8.10}$$

where i = 1, 2, ..., n.

From inspection of (8.10), there can be only five possible causes that explain why, from a situation of zero gold movements, gold is exported:

I. Increase in the shipping costs τ_i ($i = 0, 1, \ldots, n$): an increase in shipping costs affects bulky commodities more than gold, which has a high value/volume ratio.
II. Increase in the foreign price of bullion p_0^*: this may occur when a new parity has been fixed or a new coinage has been introduced in the foreign country.
III. Decrease in foreign prices $p_i^* \rightarrow \left(i = 1, \ldots, n\right)$: gold prices are more 'sticky' than commodity prices.

IV. Increase in the prices of all commodities except gold in the domestic market $p_i \rightarrow (i = 1, \ldots, n)$.
V. Increase in $t_i \rightarrow (i = 1, \ldots, n)$: gold always has a market: it has superior marketability compared with most commodities, and therefore it has the lowest arbitrage cost.

While I and II can be said to be exceptional causes of the fall of the exchange rate in the domestic market and of gold outflows, III, IV and V depict the chain of causes that describe the adjustment mechanisms of the classical Gold Standard. It is clear in fact that III and IV on one side, and V on the other, are the alternative explanations of the adjustment mechanisms of the Gold Standard as they are envisaged by the price-specie-flow theory and by the monetary approach, respectively.

The specie flow theory would argue that gold outflows are generated as a consequence of a change, for whatever cause, in the relative prices of traded commodities. If gold flows are the effect of prices of traded commodities in terms of gold being higher at home than abroad, the equilibrating mechanism of gold flows consists in restoring equilibrium by increasing foreign prices, p_i^*, and lowering domestic prices p_i $(i = 1, \ldots, n)$. It follows that gold flows will stop if (8.10) no longer holds, i.e. when either p_i or p_i^* or both have changed.

On the contrary, a theory that assumes that prices of internationally traded commodities can never vary, relies on the explanation of gold outflows given by V, i.e. by the fact that gold has the lowest arbitrage cost. If there is an excess demand for foreign bills of exchange, it is gold that will be exported, thereby supplying the market in foreign bills of exchange, because it can be sold abroad more easily than any other commodity. It follows that gold outflows will come to an end only if the costs of arbitraging in any other commodity are no longer higher than the cost of arbitraging in gold, i.e. when (8.10) no longer holds.

From the evidence we have on the structure of payments in the British international trade during this period (imports were paid in cash or on a short-term basis, while British commodities were exported on long-term credit: Nishimura 1971: 34), from what we know about the role of London mercantile houses and merchant banks in the network of international settlements (Davis 1979: 61), and from the evidence of the credit policy of the Bank of England towards them (see Duffy 1982), we can infer that the exchange rate was highly sensitive to the state of liquidity and that gold flows into and out from England in the early history of the

Gold Standard might have occurred independently from changes in domestic prices relatively to foreign prices in terms of gold.

From what has been said, it can be concluded that (8.10) states the *necessary* condition for gold outflows, and therefore it states that gold outflows will come to an end only when changes in any of p_i^*, p_i, τ_i, t_i, p_0^* have died out. But the adjustment mechanisms envisaged by both the specie flow and the monetary approach introduce a further condition for the attainment of equilibrium, i.e. the equalization of the purchasing power of gold over internationally traded commodities. This is a *sufficient* condition for the absence of gold outflows, which, when added, does not help to clarify the causes of gold movements. In fact, the equalization of gold prices of commodities is compatible with two theories of the adjustment mechanism of the Gold Standard, because, like any sufficient condition, it does not unequivocally point towards a unique cause.[16] Our conclusion is that it is more useful to stick to the stopping rule given by (8.10) and to rely only on the equalization of the purchasing power of each currency in terms of gold at home and abroad,[17] which does not impose a constraint on the description of the way in which the Gold Standard really worked.

8.6 Conclusions

While much attention has been given in the literature to the working of the Gold Standard from the later part of the nineteenth century, relatively less attention has been given to its rise in England during the eighteenth century.

The Gold Standard is usually said to have started in England in 1717, when the new mint ratio between gold and silver favoured gold and therefore silver disappeared from circulation (Jastram 1977: 12–13), or in 1821, when the Bank of England resumed at the old gold parity cash payments that had been suspended during the Napoleonic wars (Bordo and Schwartz 1984). But it was the development of the City as the financial and commercial centre of the world, with its network of correspondents and its developed credit market, that provided the conditions for the rise of the Gold Standard as an integrated system.

In this paper we have modelled our analysis of the market behaviour behind gold movements on the London market, which from the beginning of the nineteenth century became the most important international market for commodities, financial assets and gold (see Chapman 1984:

6–26). Mercantile houses and merchant banks that engaged in the export and import of gold were ready to supply foreign bills of exchange, which the branch house or the correspondents were ready to honour, whenever gold turned out to be profitable merchandise to export (and vice versa for imports).

Looking at the matter from the point of view of the individual merchant, we see that gold was traded against foreign currency, and the overall result was the enforcement of the law of one price in the case of gold; i.e. the price of gold in terms of each currency could never differ in the domestic and foreign markets. While there is evidence that merchants' behaviour sustained the purchasing power parity of gold in terms of currency, there is none to support the view that gold flows realized the purchasing power parity of gold in terms of traded commodities. Therefore we maintain that the former alone was the market mechanism on which the gold standard was based during the first decades of its history.

Notes

1. Evidence of John Humble before the Bullion Committee (British Parliamentary Papers 1810: 146).
2. Evidence of Aaron Goldsmid before the Bullion Committee (British Parliamentary Papers 1810: 58) and evidence of Isaac Goldsmid before the Lords Committee on the Resumption of Cash Payments (British Parliamentary Papers 1819: 255).
3. See Evidence of Isaac Goldsmid before the Commons Committee on the Resumption of Cash Payments (British Parliamentary Papers 1819: 205).
4. In the 1790s there were 17 rates of exchange quoted in the London Exchange (see Cope 1983: 33–34).
5. The loss of interest was a crucial element in the transaction. See a letter to N. M. Rothschild from M. M. Warburg & Co., merchant bankers in Hamburg, in 1830: 'We could have cheaper freight costs with a schooner, but if one considers the possibility of bad weather and contrary winds, you could receive the gold 8 days later, which represents a considerable loss of interest on such a large sum; we have therefore decided not to take freight costs into consideration, and to ship it by steamer [...]' (quoted in Rosenbaum and Sherman 1979: 27).
6. This is clearly explained by the British Consul in Lisbon in 1741, who complained of the captains of the British ships who, 'if they have not already got the sum which satisfies their avarice, let the consequences be

ever so ruinous to those merchants who have already put their money on board, and want to have it delivered in London to answer the bills drawn by a packet-boat that has sailed, they will still remain here two months longer [...]' (quoted in Boxer 1969: 466).

7. There is no uncertainty about p_0^* if the correspondent is instructed by the London merchant to buy gold only when the price is p_0^*. In this case the entire transaction may require an even larger interval to be completed. But the loss of interest from the time the bill is cashed until gold is bought is now measured by the difference—which can be positive or negative—between the domestic and the foreign rates of interest.
8. The evidence that option B was actually chosen by merchants in the Anglo-Portuguese bullion trade is provided by Fisher (1971: 97).
9. Evidence of Mr '———', continental merchant, to the Bullion Committee (British Parliamentary Papers 1810: 74).
10. It can be shown that

$$\frac{1-h}{1+h+c} \leq \frac{E_m}{E_m^*} \leq \frac{1+h+\min\left(i_T, i_T^*\right)}{1-h-c}$$

where

h = brokerage fee on the purchase and sale of a bill as a percentage of its price;

c = commission of the correspondent, as a percentage of the bills purchased or sold;

T= time necessary to complete the arbitrage.

We assume that the brokerage fees and the commissions are the same in the domestic and the foreign markets. When $E_m > E_m^*$ a merchant in London can make a profit by buying a bill of exchange denominated in the foreign currency and sending it to his correspondent abroad.

The latter will buy a bill denominated in sterling and send it to the merchant in London. Likewise, a foreign merchant can make a profit by buying sterling at home and ordering his correspondent in London to change pounds into the currency of his own country. The arbitrage costs include, in addition to brokerage fees and commissions, the loss of interest for the time necessary to complete the transactions. When $E_m < E_m^*$, the arbitrage costs do not include any loss of interest. A merchant in either country can make a profit by drawing a bill on his correspondent in the other country, who, in turn, will draw on him to pay for the bill when it comes due.

11. See the account of N. M. Rothschild of the successes and failures, according to the fluctuations in the price of gold in Russia, of his gold exports to Petersburg (evidence before the Commons Committee on the Resumption of Cash Payments, British Parliamentary Papers 1819: 163).
12. But this was not the case if, for instance, the export of (foreign) gold was legal from one country—as in England and in France after 1755 (see Shaw 1896: 163)—but illegal from the other, in which case it was more risky to export it. This was the case for Portugal.
13. See Evidence of C. Lyne before the Bullion Committee (British Parliamentary Papers 1810: 61). See also Cole (1929: 396).
14. Gold points have often been miscalculated, because no attempt was made to calculate the true costs of shipping gold. Even a recent attempt by Clark (1984) has not been entirely satisfactory, as pointed out in Officer (1985).
15. See evidence of A. Goldsmid before the Bullion Committee (British Parliamentary Papers 1810: 55) and evidence of N. M. Rothschild before the Commons Committee on the Resumption of Cash Payments (British Parliamentary Papers 1819: 163).
16. See evidence of A. Goldsmid before the Bullion Committee (British Parliamentary Papers 1810: 55).
17. McCloskey and Zecher (1984: 126): 'That in one respect [namely, purchasing power parity] the models [the price-specie flow mechanism and the monetary approach, sub-specie purchasing power parity] happen to have the same outcome in the long run should not be allowed to obscure that the two exhibit radically different behaviour in most other things.'

References

Blake, W. (1810). Observations on the Principles which Regulate the Course of Exchange; and on the Present Depreciated State of the Currency, London: Lloyd.

Bordo, M.D. (1984). The Gold Standard: the traditional approach. In Bordo and Schwartz (1984).

Bordo, M.D. and Schwartz, A.J. (eds.) (1984). *A Retrospective on the Classical Gold Standard, 1821–1931*. Chicago: University of Chicago Press.

Boxer, C.R. (1969). Brazilian gold and British traders in the first half of the eighteenth century. *Hispanic American Historical Review*, 49, 454–472.

British Parliamentary Papers (1810). *Committee on the High Price of Gold Bullion. Minutes of Evidence*, Vol. III. London.

British Parliamentary Papers (1819). *Committees on the Expendiency of the Bank Resuming Cash Payments. Minutes of Evidence*, Vol. III. London.

Chapman, S.D. (1977). The international houses: the continental contribution to British commerce, 1800–1860. *Journal of European Economic History*, 6, 5–48.

Chapman, S.D. (1979). British marketing enterprise: the changing roles of merchants, manufacturers, and financiers, 1700–1860. *Business History Review*, 53, 205–233.
Chapman, S.D. (1984). *The Rise of Merchant Banking*. London: Allen & Unwin.
Christelow, A. (1947). Great Britain and the trades from Cadiz and Lisbon to Spanish America and Brazil, 1759–1783. *Hispanic American Historical Review*, 27, 2–29.
Clark, T.A. (1984). Violations of the gold points, 1890–1908. *Journal of Political Economy*, 92, 791–823.
Cole, A.H. (1929). Evolution of the foreign exchange market of the United States. *Journal of Economic and Business History*, 1, 384–421.
Cope, S.R. (1983). *Walter Boyd. A Merchant Banker in the Age of Napoleon*. London: Alan Sutton.
Davis, R. (1979). *The Industrial Revolution and British Overseas Trade*. Leicester: Leicester University Press.
Duffy, I.P.H. (1982). The discount policy of the Bank of England during the suspension of cash payments, 1797–1821. *Economic History Review*, 35, 67–81.
Einzig, P. (1970). *History of Foreign Exchanges*. London: Macmillan.
Fisher, H.E.S. (1971). *The Portugal Trade. A Study of Anglo-Portuguese Commerce*. London: Methuen.
Godinho, V.M. (1950). Le Portugal, les flottes du sucre et les flottes de l'or. *Annales*, 5, 184–197.
Heaton, H. (1946). A merchant adventurer in Brazil 1808–1818. *Journal of Economic History*, 6, 1–23.
Jastram, R.W. (1977). *The Golden Constant, The English and American Experience 1560–1976*. New York: John Wiley.
McCloskey, D.N. and Zecher, J.R. (1984). The success of purchasing power parity: historical evidence and its implications for macroeconomics. In Bordo and Schwartz (1984).
Nishimura, S. (1971). *The Decline of Inland Bills of Exchange in the London Money Market 1855–1913*. Cambridge: Cambridge University Press.
Officer, L.H. (1983). Dollar-sterling mint parity and exchange rates 1797–1821. *Journal of Economic History*, 43, 579–616.
Officer, L.H. (1985). Integration in the American foreign exchange market, 1791–1900. *Journal of Economic History*, 45, 557–585.
Postlethwayt, M. (1757). *The Universal Dictionary of Trade and Commerce*. London.
Ricardo, D. (1951). *Works and Correspondence*, Vol. III. Cambridge: Cambridge University Press.
Rosenbaum, E. and Sherman, A.J. (1979). *M.M. Warburg and Co. 1798–1938. Merchant Bankers of Hamburg*. London: Holmes & Meier.
Schwartz, A.J. (1984). Introduction. In Bordo and Schwartz (1984).

Shaw, W.A. (1896). *The History of Currency 1252–1896*. 2nd edn. London: Wilsons and Milne.

Shillington V.M. and Wallis Chapman, A.B. (1908). *The Commercial Relations of England and Portugal*, London: Routledge and Sons.

Sutherland, L. (1932). The Accounts of an Eighteenth Century Merchant. *Economic History Review*, 3, 367–387.

CHAPTER 9

Metallic Standards and Real Exchange Rates

Introduction In the late eighteenth and early nineteenth centuries, the international monetary system relied on the merchants' response to profitability conditions for the import and export of gold and silver to bring about the adjustment mechanism of the monetary system. Price arbitrage in the trade of precious metals gave rise to a unified bullion market and paved the way to the late-nineteenth- century monetary order.

From the merchants' point of view, profitability conditions for the export and import of the precious metals, involved knowledge of the price of gold and silver, at home and abroad, and of the rate of exchange

The first version of this chapter was presented at the Cliometric Session of the Eleventh International Economic History Congress, Milan 1994. We are indebted to D. McCloskey for helpful comments. The second version was presented at the workshop on "Monetary Standards and Exchange Rates," held in Perugia in 1995. We are grateful to M. Flandreau, L. Officer and G. Tattara for comments and to G. Deleplace for stimulating criticism. Financial assistance from the Italian National Research Council is gratefully acknowledged.

Originally publ. in: (With Annalisa Rosselli), in M.C. Marcuzzo, L. Officer and A. Rosselli (eds.), *Monetary Standards and Exchange Rates*, London: Routledge, 1997, pp. 81–105.
Reprint by Springer Nature Switzerland 2024 with kind permission

M. C. Marcuzzo, *Economic Theories, Protagonists and Facts*, Palgrave Studies in the History of Economic Thought,
https://doi.org/10.1007/978-3-031-63949-4_9

(Marcuzzo and Rosselli 1987, 1991). But what was the right rate of exchange?

The "observed" variable was the market rate of exchange, which was the price of the domestic currency in terms of foreign currency as established in the market for bills of exchange. For the occurrence of gold and silver flows what mattered was the difference between the market exchange rate and the cost of obtaining the same amount of foreign currency through exporting gold (or silver).

Variations in the price of bills of exchange reflected both the conditions prevailing in the market for bills of exchange—which in turn reflected the conditions of the balance of payments—and conditions prevailing in the market for gold and silver; the latter being influenced by the employment of the two metals in monetary and nonmonetary uses.

It follows that behind any variation of the market rate of exchange two different sets of forces were at work: excess demand of bills and changes in the price of gold and silver. In this chapter we present a general framework of analysis which will allow us to distinguish between the two causes of changes in the exchange rates and thus offer a contribution to the interpretation of the working of the gold standard in its early history.

Monetary Standards and Monetary Regimes In addressing the issue of the causes of changes in the exchange rates, the first point to clarify is what the standard of the currency is and which monetary regime it defines. When gold or silver are chosen as standard, there is an official value of the unit of currency in terms of a given quantity of bullion, or—amounting to the same thing—an official price of bullion. Whenever there is a mechanism by which the market price of bullion is brought in line with the official price, the metal chosen as the standard becomes a special commodity in two respects.[1] First, the prices at which the standard metal are bought and sold on the market are relatively stable; second, any outflow or inflow of the standard metal leads to a variation in the quantity of money.

When this mechanism is absent or becomes ineffective—because, for example, convertibility is suspended—the price of the standard metal is not bounded and there may be no change in the quantity of money for any outflow or inflow of the metal. In these circumstances, however, the standard metal may retain its function as standard of money (i.e., the purchasing power of the currency over the standard measures the variations in the value of money) although, in all other respects, it does not differ from any other commodity.[2]

When both countries have a monometallic regime, either the standard is single and the same in each country (i.e., both are on either a gold or a silver standard) or the standard is single but different in the two countries (i.e., one country is on gold and the other on silver). When the standard is single, the other metal may be entirely demonetized, i.e., there is no coinage in other metal than the standard. Otherwise, the regime may be only *de facto* monometallic, because there continues to be an official price of the other metal. For instance, coins of a given nominal value are minted from a given quantity of bullion, but these coins are valued according to their weight and are not legal tender, or are legal tender only for a limited sum.

We shall analyse the two cases of monometallic regimes with the same and with a different standard in turn.

Exchange Rates in Monometallic Regimes: The Case of a Single and Identical Standard Let us start with the case of two countries having the same standard, which we assume is gold. The gold parity is then defined as the ratio between the gold content of their respective units of currency. Only when there is a change in the official gold content of a currency does the parity change. Normally it remains constant for long periods of time and becomes the center around which the market exchange rate oscillates.

In pure conditions of "perfect convertibility," namely, when gold can be bought and sold at its official price, the parity represents the cost (net of transport costs) of making international payments by remitting gold. When there are coins in circulation, "perfect convertibility" requires—besides the condition that the Mint be open to the public—that two very special conditions hold.

First, there must be no coinage expenses, not even in the form of loss of interest during the time required to have the coins delivered. Thus the price of a given quantity of gold could never fall below the nominal value of the coins made out of that bullion, because no seller of gold would accept a price lower than that which could be obtained from the Mint.

Second, melting of coins is not prohibited, and is costless. Thus the market price of a given quantity of gold could never rise beyond the nominal value of the coins of equal weight, because any buyer of gold would always have the option of melting the coins to obtain bullion.

Moreover, when convertible paper-money also exists, conditions of "perfect convertibility" require that the buying and selling price of gold in paper money both coincide with the official price of gold.

Historically, perfect convertibility has never existed. There has always been a difference between the buying and selling price of gold at the central bank (say, the Bank of England) and there have always been coinage and melting expenses. Consequently, the market price of gold has diverged from the official price. Besides the "official" parity, it is therefore necessary to take into consideration the effective cost of exchanging domestic currency for foreign currency on the basis of the respective market gold prices. The latter was known as "real" or "commercial" parity (British Parliamentary Papers 1819).

The "official" gold parity, X_g, when the rate of exchange is defined in terms of foreign currency for one unit of domestic currency, can be expressed as

$$X_g = \frac{p_M^*}{p_M}$$

where

p_M^* = official (Mint) price of gold abroad

p_M = official (Mint) price of gold at home.

The "real" or "commercial" gold parity, R_g, can be expressed as where

p^* = market price of gold abroad

p = market price of gold at home.

Let us consider the percentage deviations of the market price of gold bullion from the official price at home ($\boldsymbol{p}$) and abroad ($\boldsymbol{p}^*$) and of the market rate of exchange, determined by supply and demand of bills of exchange, from the official gold parity ($\boldsymbol{e}$) and from the "real" gold parity ($\boldsymbol{t}$). We define the following (bold letters always stand for percentage deviations)

$$\boldsymbol{p}^* = \frac{p^* - p_M^*}{p_M^*} \tag{9.1}$$

$$\boldsymbol{p} = \frac{p - p_M}{p_M} \tag{9.2}$$

$$e = \frac{E_m - X_g}{X_g} \quad (9.3)$$

$$t_g = \frac{E_m - R_g}{R_g} \quad (9.4)$$

where E_m is the exchange rate on the domestic market and t_g represents those variations in the exchange rate that reflect the conditions prevailing in the market for foreign bills of exchange. The value of t_g is bounded by the so-called "gold points," i.e., by transaction and transport costs of remitting gold to the foreign country.

To what extent does commercial parity differ from official parity? From the definitions given above, it follows that e, the percentage deviation of the market rate of exchange from the official parity, X_g, is given by[3]

$$e = t_g + p^* - p \quad (9.5)$$

As long as market mechanisms are at work at home and abroad to enforce the equality of the market to the official price of gold, p and p^* are close to zero. When domestic convertibility is suspended or coins are debased, however, the market price of bullion can be significantly higher ($p > 0$), because it is not possible to obtain gold at the official price by melting coins of legal weight or by converting banknotes. In contrast, when seignorage is high, $p < 0$, because coined gold fetches a premium over bullion that can be as high as seignorage.

The divergence between the official and the market price of gold represents either a loss or a gain for the bullion merchant, which must be distinguished from the other transaction costs of a gold remittance for at least two reasons. First, unlike transport and transaction charges, which tend to remain constant through time, it is a variable and not a relatively fixed cost, depending on the conditions of demand for bullion. Second, the amount of loss or gain involved is a function of the difference between the market and the official price of the standard. In this respect, it is a rough measure of how far Gold Standard differs in practice from its pure and ideal form.

Exchange Rates in Monometallic Regimes: The Case of a Single but Different Standard

The Relevant Parity

Let us turn now to the case of two countries on a single but different standard, such as gold and silver. It is necessary to modify Eq. (9.5) in order to incorporate a modified concept of parity. Since in each country the unit of currency is officially equivalent to a given quantity of bullion, we can still define an "official" parity on the basis of the official price of the respective standard. As we shall see, it is not a fixed parity, since it varies with every variation in the market ratio between gold and silver, both at home and abroad. Moreover, given that there are two standards, we have two parities, one for gold and the other for silver. We shall label each of these parities as the "true par" (Officer 1985: 566), corresponding to what the classical authors called the "computed exchange" (Marcuzzo and Rosselli 1991: 104–13).

The purpose of defining an "official parity" in the case of two different standards is threefold. First, to indicate that in each country there is an official price of either metal; second to compare this monetary regime with others in which the price of one or both metals is fixed; third, to be able to distinguish between two different causes of variations in the market exchange rate. By comparing the market rate of exchange with an official parity, we do not confine ourselves only to the conditions prevailing in the market for bills, but allowance is made for a "monetary" cause of the movements of the exchange rate due to the difference between the market and the official price of either metal.

Let the parity be defined with respect to gold as E_g and the parity defined with respect to silver as E_s and, furthermore, let us assume that the domestic country is on the gold standard and the foreign country on the silver standard.

In order to define E_g, we know that the quantity of gold which is officially equivalent at home to one unit of currency is given by $\frac{1}{p_M}$. This quantity of gold can buy abroad the quantity of silver given by $\frac{1}{p_M}\frac{p^*}{q^*}$, where q^* equals market price of silver abroad. By multiplying the latter by the foreign official price of silver, q_M^*, we obtain E_g units of foreign currency, that are equivalent to 1 unit of domestic currency, so that

$$E_g = \frac{q_M^*}{p_M}\frac{p^*}{q^*} \tag{9.6}$$

Similarly, one unit of foreign currency is officially equivalent abroad to $\frac{1}{q_M^*}$ units of silver, which—when sold on the domestic market—obtains $\frac{1}{q_M^*}\frac{q}{p}$ units of gold. By multiplying the latter by the domestic official price of gold, we obtain $\frac{p_M}{q_M^*}\frac{q}{p}$ units of domestic currency. So that, given our definition of the rate of exchange as units of foreign currency per one unit of domestic currency, we get

$$E_s = \frac{q_M^*}{p_M}\frac{p}{q} \tag{9.7}$$

Adopting the same notation as in the previous section, we define

$$\boldsymbol{q} = \frac{q^* - q_M^*}{q_M^*} \tag{9.8}$$

Denoting $\boldsymbol{e}_g$ the deviation of the market rate of exchange from E_g, we obtain from (9.6) and (9.8)

$$E_m = E_g\left(1+\boldsymbol{e}_g\right) = \frac{p^* q_M^*}{q^* p_M}\left(1+\boldsymbol{e}_g\right) = \frac{p^*\left(1+\boldsymbol{e}_g\right)}{p_M\left(1+\boldsymbol{q}^*\right)} \tag{9.9}$$

By definition we have

$$E_m = R_g\left(1+\boldsymbol{t}_g\right) = \frac{p^*\left(1+\boldsymbol{t}_g\right)}{p_M\left(1+\boldsymbol{p}\right)} \tag{9.10}$$

Neglecting second order terms, by comparing (9.9) and (9.10), we obtain

$$\boldsymbol{e}_g = \boldsymbol{t}_g + \boldsymbol{q}^* - \boldsymbol{p} \tag{9.11}$$

In other words, although the parity is no longer fixed, in the difference between the market rate of exchange and parity we can still distinguish that component due to the condition of the market for bills of exchange, $\boldsymbol{t}$, from the components due to the conditions of circulation, $\boldsymbol{q}^*$ and $\boldsymbol{p}$.

Similarly, defining e_s as the deviation of the market rate of exchange from E_s and t_s as the deviation of the market rate of exchange from the "real" silver parity R_s we have

$$E_m = R_s\left(1+t_s\right) \tag{9.12}$$

and we obtain

$$e_s = t_s + q^* - p \tag{9.13}$$

There is only one case in which the two parities, E_g and E_s, coincide, namely when $\frac{p}{q}=\frac{p^*}{q^*}$; in this case obviously also $t_g = t_s$ and $e_g = e_s$. However, in general, the gold/silver ratios differ and to this case we now turn.

The Gold/Silver Ratios

When the gold/silver ratios are not equal in every country, we may have larger differences between them than those between the foreign and domestic individual prices of gold or silver. In fact, arbitrage opportunities offered by the difference in the gold/silver ratios are fewer, since they imply transaction costs double those implied in the arbitrage in one bullion market alone. For example, an arbitrage operation may involve the purchase of gold, the shipment and sale of gold abroad, the purchase of foreign silver, the shipment and sale of foreign silver in the domestic country. This can immediately be seen if we denote the transaction costs involved in a gold shipment (as percentage of the total value) by c_g and the transaction costs involved in a silver shipment by c_s, assuming that costs are the same in both directions. So that, when all arbitrage opportunities have been exploited, the variation interval of the ratio is given by[4]

$$\left(1-c_g\right)\left(1-c_s\right)\frac{p}{q} < \frac{p^*}{q^*} < \frac{p}{q}\left(1+c_g\right)\left(1+c_s\right)$$

or, if $c_g = c_s = c$

$$\left(1-2c\right)\frac{p}{q}<\frac{p^{*}}{q^{*}}<\frac{p}{q}\left(1+2c\right)$$

Thus, the difference between the gold/silver ratios, although constrained by the level of transaction costs, could still be relevant.

The divergence of $\frac{p}{q}$ from $\frac{p^{*}}{q^{*}}$ gives rise to different profitability conditions for the remittance of precious metals. Thus, unlike the case in which both countries are on the same standard, we must here find out which is the relevant t (i.e., whether $\boldsymbol{t_g}$ or $\boldsymbol{t_s}$) as indicator of the conditions prevailing in the market for bills of exchange.

It is always the metal undervalued at home, relatively to the other country, to be preferred in making an international payment, since it yields a greater amount of foreign currency in exchange for the bullion corresponding to one unit of domestic currency.[5] If the most economical means to obtain foreign currency for a domestic merchant is shipping gold, then the relevant parity—to ascertain the most profitable alternative to buying a bill of exchange—is the gold parity and the merchant who wants to purchase foreign currency must choose between buying a bill of exchange and shipping gold. Conversely, whenever gold is undervalued at home, the merchant who wants to sell foreign currency must choose between importing silver or selling a bill of exchange in the domestic market. In this case, the relevant parity to ascertain the most profitable alternative to selling a bill of exchange is the silver parity. Obviously, if $\frac{p}{q}>\frac{p^{*}}{q^{*}}$, the opposite applies.

However, unlike the case in which both countries are on the same standard, the maximum and minimum levels that the market rate of exchange can reach have to be defined accordingly. The maximum depreciation is a situation in which the export of bullion represents the alternative to the purchase of a bill on the foreign currency, while the maximum appreciation is a situation in which the import of bullion represents the alternative to the sale of a bill on the foreign country. In fact, as shown by Eqs. (9.11) and (9.13), the minimum and maximum values of the exchange rate depend on the maximum values of $\boldsymbol{t_g}$ and $\boldsymbol{t_s}$.

It is clear that this maximum value is determined only by transportation and transaction costs, since coinage and melting expenses are included in the calculations of the deviations of the market price of the standard from its official price.[6] The reason for excluding coinage and melting expenses from the calculation of the "gold points" is that they represent the maximum deviation of the market price of the standard from its official price, whereas in fact that deviation can be less than its maximum value, according to the conditions prevailing on the bullion market.

Given that $E_g \geq E_s$ if and only if $R_g \geq R_s$ there are two ways to find out whether t_g or t_s apply and to calculate their value. The first is to calculate the deviations of the market exchange rate from the official parities, E_g and E_s, then to add algebraically the deviations of the market price of the standard from its official price, according to (9.11) and (9.13). The second, which is exactly equivalent, is to calculate the deviations of the market exchange rate directly from the commercial pars, R_g and R_s.

However, the official and the commercial parities have a different role in our search for the forces which explain the behavior of the exchange rate on the basis of historical evidence. The parities most used in practice were the official parities, because they represented a widely accepted term of reference. The market rate of exchange was always compared with the official parities—computed by taking into account the deviations of the market prices of the standard from their official prices, when the purpose was to ascertain whether the currency was depreciating or appreciating.[7]

On the contrary, the parities which were relevant to decide whether gold or silver are more profitable than bills of exchange in transacting foreign currency on the basis of gold/silver ratios, transaction and transportation costs, were the commercial pars, R_g and R_s.

Finally, in order to find out the maximum and minimum value of the exchange rate we must distinguish two cases: first, when $\frac{p}{q} < \frac{p^*}{q^*}$, second when $\frac{p}{q} > \frac{p^*}{q^*}$.

If $\frac{p}{q} < \frac{p^*}{q^*}$—and therefore $E_g > E_s$ and $R_g > R_s$—that is to say, when gold is less valued at home than abroad, then the market rate of exchange finds its lower limit (maximum depreciation) in R_g, diminished by the costs of shipping gold (see Fig. 9.1). In fact, nobody would be prepared to obtain fewer units of foreign currency than those that could be obtained by remitting gold. When the rate of exchange reaches this minimum level, it is profitable for the resident in the domestic country to export gold instead of buying a bill of exchange.[8]

The upper limit (maximum appreciation) is given by R_s augmented by the costs of shipping silver, because as soon as the exchange rate rises to higher levels, it becomes profitable to import silver. So that

$$R_g\left(1-c_g\right) \leq E_m \leq R_s\left(1+c_s\right) \tag{9.14}$$

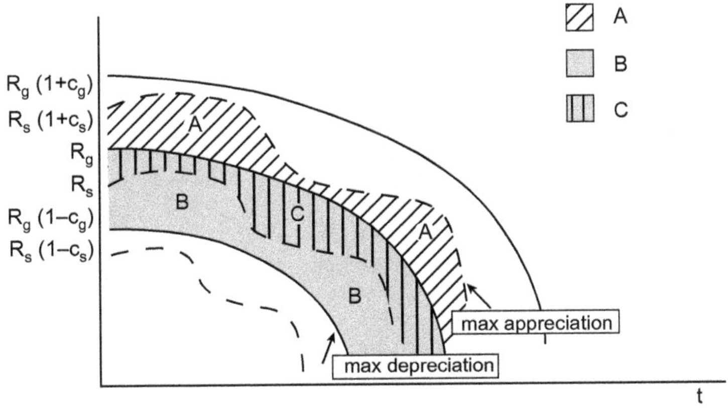

Fig. 9.1 Range of variations in the market rate of exchange when $\frac{p}{q} < \frac{p^*}{q^*}$

Conversely, if $\frac{p}{q} > \frac{p^*}{q^*}$, the profitability conditions are reversed: $E_g < E_s$ and $R_g < R_s$. The upper limit of the exchange rate (maximum appreciation) is set by the gold parity, while the lower limit (maximum depreciation) is set by the silver parity.

Thus we have

$$R_s\left(1-c_s\right) \le E_m \le R_g\left(1+c_g\right) \tag{9.15}$$

If transport costs for gold and silver are equal, then the fluctuation margins of the market rate of exchange are narrower than in the case of a single standard in both countries, given that $R_g \neq R_s$.[9]

In summary, when two countries have a single but different standard, variations in the market ratios between gold and silver in the two countries are relevant for three reasons. First, because they alter the gold or silver parity, which varies as the gold/silver ratio varies, as shown by (9.6) and (9.7). Second, they make either gold or silver parity the relevant parity to ascertain the profitability conditions for shipping one of the two metals. Third, they set the fluctuation margins of the exchange rate.

Exchange Rates in a Bimetallic Regime In a bimetallic regime both gold and silver are standards of money. Historically, this meant that both silver and gold coins circulated as money and/or banknotes were convertible into either metal.

In the bimetallic case we have two official parities. Besides X_g, the official gold parity, we have an official silver parity, X_s:

$$X_s = \frac{q_M^*}{q_M}$$

From the above definitions it follows that $X_g = X_s$, if and only if the official gold/silver ratio is identical in both countries.

Bimetallism works when the official gold/silver ratio is such that there are no gains to be made from the exportation of either of the two metals. Otherwise one metal alone would become the standard. As in the case of monometallism, there is a market mechanism which ensures the equality of the market and the official price of the standard. In bimetallism, however, the equality of the official and market prices of the metals obstructs the mechanism preventing the outflow of the undervalued metal. As we have seen, if $\frac{p}{q} < \frac{p^*}{q^*}$, there is a tendency for the undervalued gold to be exported and for silver to be imported provided that the difference between the ratios is higher than the arbitrage costs. If the prices of gold and silver could freely fluctuate, then the scarcity of gold and the abundance of silver at home would raise the price of gold, relative to silver, so that the difference in $\frac{p}{q}$ and $\frac{p^*}{q^*}$ would fall below the transaction costs.

On the contrary, if the two prices are kept fixed, because successfully kept at their official level, then the equalizing mechanism is prevented from working.[10] It is then apparent that a bimetallic regime is more difficult to manage than a monometallic regime.

Conceptually, however, the framework of analysis of the oscillations of the market rate of exchange around parity does not differ from what we illustrated in the previous section, and we need only to substitute X_g for E_g and X_s for E_s.

Here too the oscillation margins of the market exchange rate are set by the export and import points of the standard, the transportation charges relative to one metal defining the upper limits, and the transportation charges relative to the other metal the lower limit. To find out which is the relevant metal in setting the upper and lower limit, we must know the relationship between $\frac{p}{q}$ and $\frac{p^*}{q^*}$. The same applies to the choice of the metal to ship rather than selling or buying a bill and the price of which enters into the calculations of the merchants in trading on the market for bills of exchange.

However, unlike the previous case, the relevant parities, X_s and X_g, are fixed and reflect only the ratio between the official prices of the two standards in both countries.

Computation of $\boldsymbol{t_g}$ *and* $\boldsymbol{t_s}$ Deviations in the market rate of exchange from gold or silver parity can be employed as significant indicators of conditions in the market for bills of exchange if allowance is made for that part representing the deviations in the market price from the official price of the respective standard. We defined $\boldsymbol{t_g}$ and $\boldsymbol{t_s}$ as the deviation of the market rate of exchange from the "commercial" gold and silver par, respectively. In order to employ $\boldsymbol{t_g}$ and $\boldsymbol{t_s}$ as indicators of the conditions prevailing in the market for bills and therefore of the state of the balance of payment between the two countries, we have to solve the question of which is the relevant t.

The assumption that equilibrium in the market for foreign bills of exchange is characterized by $\boldsymbol{t_g} = 0$ (or $\boldsymbol{t_s} = 0$) needs some justification. As noted by Viner (1937: 379) for the Gold Standard, any exchange rate within the gold points—whenever $\boldsymbol{t_g}$ is less than the transaction costs of shipping gold—is an equilibrium rate. According to this view, the market can be said to be out of equilibrium only when gold flows occur, since the equality between supply and demand would require a level of the exchange rate which is beyond the gold points and therefore unattainable. Clearly, the rate of exchange at which $\boldsymbol{t_g} = 0$ (or $\boldsymbol{t_s} = 0$) is not the only equilibrium rate, within the gold points, that is the only rate at which demand is equal to supply, but is the relevant exchange rate which, in our model, provides the unifying term of reference. This is a homage to the tradition which views the normal ratio between two currencies as determined by their purchasing power over their respective standards.

However, by normal value it is not meant the average value of the market rate of exchange under the assumption of a uniform distribution within the interval of the gold points (as in Officer 1985; see also Officer 1997). In fact, the latter coincides with the condition $t = 0$ only when transaction costs are equal in both directions.

In the case of a monometallic regime in which both countries have the same standard (say gold), a value of t_g greater than zero means an excess supply of foreign currency in the home market; conversely a value for t_g less than zero means an excess demand for foreign currency and therefore an "unfavorable" rate of exchange for the domestic currency.

In the case of a bimetallic regime, in which each country has a different standard, as we have seen, the metal which is more profitable to export is not the one which is more profitable to import. Once more, we assume that there are two countries and that the domestic country is on the gold standard while the foreign country is on the silver standard. The profitability conditions for the domestic merchant in deciding which is the most economical way to remit a payment to the foreign country are not the same as those confronting the seller of a bill denominated in the foreign currency in the domestic exchange market.

We shall start by assuming that we have the situation depicted in Fig. 9.1, that is to say that $\frac{p}{q} < \frac{p^*}{q^*}$ (the shape of the two curves could be any).

For the buyer of a bill denominated in foreign currency, the term of reference is the gold par, because shipping gold is the alternative to buying a bill, while for the seller of foreign currency the term of reference is the silver par. In these circumstances, we have then three occurrences.

$$t_g > 0 \text{ and } t_s > 0 \tag{I}$$

The market rate of exchange lies within the area A of Fig. 9.1, corresponding to an appreciation. We know for sure that there is an excess supply of the foreign currency and therefore t_s is a measure of the appreciation of the domestic currency.

$$t_g < 0 \text{ and } t_s < 0 \tag{II}$$

The market rate of exchange lies within the area B of Fig. 9.1, corresponding to a depreciation. We know for sure that there is an excess demand for the foreign currency and therefore t_g is a measure of the depreciation of the domestic currency.

$$t_g < 0 \text{ and } t_s > 0 \tag{III}$$

The rate of exchange lies in the area C, that is to say it is bounded from above by R_g and by R_s from below. The very concept of a favorable rate of exchange becomes meaningless, since in this case—given that the rate of exchange is lower than the gold par but higher than the silver par—it implies that it is favorable to both buyers and sellers of foreign currency.

To give meaning to the concept of a favorable exchange, it would be necessary to take one parity arbitrarily as the term of reference, or an average between the two. We discarded the idea of taking an average between the two parities for two reasons. First, because it was not a term of reference for merchants and brokers; second, because it requires *ad hoc* assumptions. In fact, when there are two parities, a gold par and a silver par, the midpoint of the interval bounded by the "bullion points"—which is equal to the average value of the exchange rate under the assumption of its uniform distribution in the interval—coincides with the average between the two parities only when the transaction costs involved in shipping either metal are equal in both directions when measured not in percentage but in absolute value.

Thus, lacking any argument to choose one par rather than the other, we are left with the only option of labeling the corresponding values as indeterminate.[11]

An Example: London on Paris 1821–1870 We shall employ the conceptual framework set out above to study the behavior of the market exchange rate in London on Paris for the 50 years that saw the official beginning of the Gold Standard in England and the *de facto* end of bimetallism in France, when convertibility of banknotes was suspended.[12] The aim of our chapter is to show that behind the fluctuations of the exchange rate there may be two types of forces at work. By employing equations (9.5) and (9.13) we can interpret the market signal of the exchange rate, imputing its variations partly to the conditions of circulation ("monetary factors", $\boldsymbol{p}$ and $\boldsymbol{q}^*$) and partly to the conditions of the balance of payments ("real factors", $\boldsymbol{t}$).

In the period under consideration Great Britain was on the Gold Standard. The official price of gold was £3 17s 10 ½d., per oz. troy (equal to 31.1 grams) of standard gold (22 carats). Since 1816 silver had not been legal tender for any sum above 500 shillings. There were gold coins in circulation and banknotes were convertible in gold coins at the Bank. Gold could also be sold to the Bank at a price slightly lower, or coined at the Mint at no cost beyond the interest involved in the time span before coins were delivered.

In France, since 1803, the franc (FF) had been convertible both in gold and in silver. The official price of gold was 3444.44 FF per kg. Gold could then be sold to the Banque de France at the buying price of 3434.44, or be coined at the Hotel de la Monnaie, obtaining 3444.44 FF from which 10 F had to be deducted to cover coinage expenses. Similarly, the Banque de France's buying price for silver was 218.89 FF per kg and its selling price 222.23, the difference being imputed to coinage expenses of 3.33 FF per 1 kg of silver.

Although the prices at which gold and silver could be sold were fixed and generally known, this did not apply to the prices at which gold and silver could be bought. The Banque de France had the right to choose the metal in which to convert its banknotes. It followed that the price of the other metal could rise on the market, since the prospective buyer who did not succeed in obtaining it from the Bank, in principle, was willing to pay up to the sum corresponding to the nominal value of the coins plus the cost involved in melting them.

Figure 9.2 shows, for Paris, yearly averages of the deviations of the market price of silver from the official price and the yearly averages of the deviations of the market price of gold from its Mint price. The data are taken from Schneider et al. (1991, henceforth SSZ), who give the first quotation available for each month and a yearly average, derived from contemporary sources such as commercial bulletins and newspapers.

A certain degree of flexibility in gold prices facilitated the task undertaken by France of maintaining a bimetallic regime with no preference for either metal. In fact, flexibility in the price of gold allowed the gold/silver ratio in France to be brought in line with the international ratio. Moreover, the task of pursuing a bimetallic regime was facilitated by the choice, made by France in 1803, to set its official gold and silver prices so that the $\frac{p_M^*}{q_M^*}$ ratio, set at 15.5, was an average value of those prevailing in its neighbouring countries: 14.5 in the Netherlands, 15.21 in England, 16 in Spain and Portugal (Thuillier 1983: 117), the consequence being that a country, for instance Spain, that could gain from an undervalued silver, shipped silver to the Netherlands rather than to France, thus leaving the gold/silver ratio in the latter country unaffected.

As we pointed out earlier, there are two pars of exchange in London on Paris. The first is the gold parity, defined as the ratio between the official gold prices, being equal to

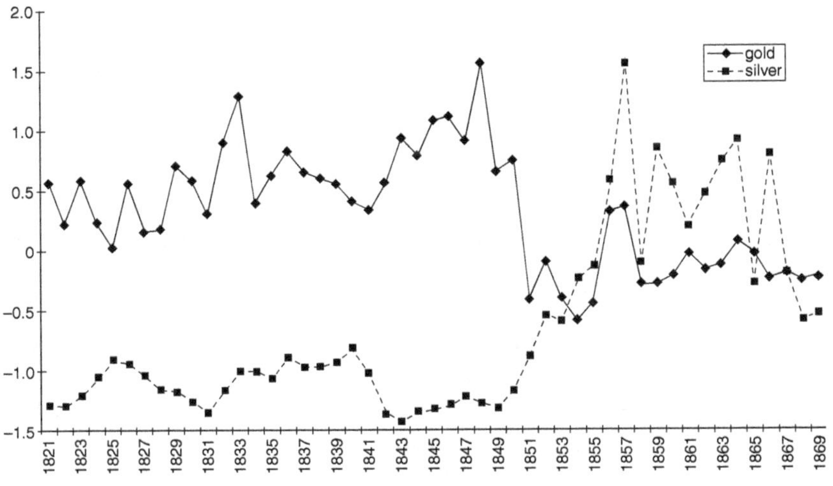

Fig. 9.2 Percentage deviation of the market price of gold and silver from the official price, Paris 1821–1870. (*Source*: Our elaboration from Schneider et al. (1991))

$$X_g = 25.22\,\text{FF} / £$$

if we follow the traditional way of quoting francs per pound.

The second is the silver parity, E_s (see equation 9.7) which can be calculated through the gold/silver price ratio in London, which in turn is derived from the prices of gold and silver in that market. The latter were regularly published in London twice a week in the Lloyd's and Wetenhall's Lists, on the basis of "Average Amount of Sales and Purchases of the Bank of England, or Merchants on Tuesday and Friday in each week."[13] They were based on actual transactions, the minimum amount being £1500 and their source was the House of Goldsmid, brokers for the Bank of England. (In fact most of the transactions were carried out at the Bank.) Although they did not appear as official publications, those quotations were taken by contemporaries as the most reliable data available.

The latter Lists are the source of the quotations given by SSZ (1991). Since the prices are given for standard silver and standard gold in London,[14] we have had to convert them into prices for fine silver and gold. Especially in the case of silver, however, many data are missing,[15] although we have been able to fill a fair number of gaps using the data presented by

Boyer-Xambeu et al. (1995, henceforth XDG), who employed the series derived from the Course of Exchange published in London by J. Castaing and other sources available from the microfilm of the Goldsmiths'-Kress Library of Economic Literature. In a couple of instances we completed the missing entries for silver by using the Soetbeer (1880) data, which are given as the highest and lowest quotation in the month, by taking the average between the two.[16]

The comparison between the gold/silver ratio in London and Paris allows us to find out whether $\frac{p}{q}$ is less or greater than $\frac{p^*}{q^*}$. As examination of Table 9.1 shows, the differences between the ratios are small and when negative they show that in London gold was favored in exports and silver in imports. The prices of gold and silver in London and Paris allow us to calculate the gold par, X_g, the silver par, E_s, and the commercial pars R_g and R_s, which are shown in Fig. 9.3.

The data for the market rate of exchange of London on Paris are taken from SSZ, referring to sight bills, taken from Wetenhall's List.[17] As from 1834, we no longer have quotations for sight bills, but only for short-term bills, i.e., for less than 15 days. In order to conform the short-term series of bills to that of the sight bills it would be necessary to discount the price of a short-term bill for the number of days passing between when a bill is presented for payment in Paris and when it is due. This is why a short-term bill is at discount in comparison with a sight bill. The relevant interest rate would be the one prevailing in London, but since the latter remained below 5 per cent throughout the period, and well below for most of the period, it is legitimate to consider the two series as equivalent.[18] As in the former case we completed the missing entries with data taken by XDG, who derived their series from the Course of Exchange published in London by J. Castaing and other sources available from the microfilm of the Goldsmiths'-Kress Library of Economic Literature.[19]

The main result of our investigation are presented in Table 9.2, where the relevant $\boldsymbol{t_g}$ and $\boldsymbol{t_s}$ are calculated, on the basis of the date available.[20] Its examination suggests that throughout the period, with few exceptions, the pound appreciated for reasons due to the state of the balance of payments.

It must be noted that the "indeterminate" cases cover situations which may be very different. The rate of exchange may be such that it is equally profitable to import gold and to export silver (for instance, as in June 1821, probably as a consequence of the return to gold by Great Britain). This case is "indeterminate" because the market rate of exchange lies

Table 9.1 Differences in gold/silver ratios in London and Paris (monthly data), 1821–1869

	Jan	*Feb*	*March*	*April*	*May*	*June*	*July*	*August*	*Sept*	*Oct*	*Nov*	*Dec*
1821	0.092	0.054	0.074	0.196	0.191	0.427	0.332	0.219	0.210	0.326	0.211	–0.042
1822	0.135	0.141	0.271	0.136	NA	0.194	0.171	0.012	0.091	0.085	0.152	–0.031
1823	0.122	NA	0.162	0.139	0.186	–0.025	0.077	0.154	0.102	0.112	0.049	0.006
1824	0.063	0.067	0.039	0.029	–0.055	–0.006	–0.054	–0.161	NA	–0.133	–0.077	–0.209
1825	–0.067	–0.127	–0.127	–0.202	–0.178	–0.112	–0.084	–0.127	–0.145	–0.185	–0.137	–0.516
1826	–0.184	–0.300	–0.233	0.102	0.164	0.088	0.149	0.202	0.198	0.155	NA	–0.069
1827	0.072	0.075	0.080	0.018	0.078	0.029	NA	NA	–0.078	–0.079	NA	NA
1828	–0.122	–0.120	–0.072	NA	0.011	NA	0.072	–0.005	–0.080	–0.018	–0.006	–0.077
1829	–0.018	0.001	0.055	0.140	0.017	NA	0.060	0.060	–0.040	0.014	–0.005	0.130
1830	0.128	0.126	0.133	0.073	0.121	–0.038	0.154	–0.028	–0.002	0.016	–0.002	0.159
1831	0.014	–0.025	–0.030	–0.005	0.073	0.041	0.021	–0.027	–0.027	–0.083	–0.023	NA
1832	NA	NA	NA	NA	NA	NA	NA	NA	NA	0.100	0.109	0.421
1833	0.182	0.127	0.119	0.143	–0.120	0.139	–0.136	–0.265	–0.310	–0.065	–0.118	0.200
1834	0.022	0.051	–0.009	0.025	0.029	0.019	0.037	–0.222	–0.214	0.052	0.070	0.080
1835	0.039	0.052	–0.024	0.007	–0.015	–0.017	0.006	–0.026	–0.189	–0.013	–0.009	0.006
1836	0.074	0.002	–0.061	–0.023	–0.082	–0.166	–0.146	–0.212	–0.139	–0.098	–0.155	–0.057
1837	–0.067	–0.148	–0.135	0.514	0.060	0.071	0.108	0.108	0.127	0.120	0.058	0.091
1838	0.090	0.075	0.078	0.078	0.118	0.105	0.094	–0.009	0.069	0.088	0.088	–0.014
1839	–0.055	–0.157	–0.150	–0.061	–0.071	–0.112	–0.086	–0.115	–0.154	–0.109	–0.149	–0.099
1840	–0.071	–0.057	–0.057	–0.065	–0.106	–0.127	–0.149	–0.167	–0.132	–0.198	–0.158	–0.061
1841	–0.037	–0.110	–0.084	0.007	–0.068	–0.140	–0.108	–0.085	–0.088	–0.089	–0.021	0.011
1842	0.007	–0.018	0.060	0.075	0.152	–0.054	–0.112	0.172	–0.025	0.043	0.142	0.054
1843	0.049	0.032	0.023	0.082	0.039	0.045	0.016	0.036	0.028	0.012	0.029	0.012
1844	0.043	0.037	–0.006	0.023	0.007	–0.025	0.029	–0.040	–0.041	–0.070	–0.032	–0.005
1845	0.038	0.020	0.002	0.064	0.045	0.069	0.068	0.076	–0.008	0.028	–0.102	0.059

(*continued*)

Table 9.1 (continued)

	Jan	*Feb*	*March*	*April*	*May*	*June*	*July*	*August*	*Sept*	*Oct*	*Nov*	*Dec*
1846	0.028	0.067	0.067	0.067	0.102	0.038	0.038	0.006	0.006	0.016	–0.074	–0.264
1847	–0.201	–0.189	–0.210	–0.252	0.187	–0.036	–0.013	–0.106	–0.044	0.008	0.061	0.064
1848	0.080	0.066	–0.347	–0.252	0.209	–0.111	–0.133	0.039	–0.094	–0.138	–0.187	0.091
1849	–0.026	–0.066	–0.017	0.007	–0.103	–0.066	–0.043	–0.053	0.083	–0.003	–0.032	–0.025
1850	–0.053	–0.080	–0.090	–0.098	–0.157	–0.089	–0.017	–0.060	–0.048	–0.074	–0.020	–0.271
1851	–0.347	–0.347	–0.287	–0.254	–0.254	–0.098	–0.067	–0.088	–0.014	0.079	–0.028	–0.067
1852	–0.059	0.009	0.040	0.033	0.110	0.109	–0.008	0.043	0.124	–0.078	–0.170	0.042
1853	–0.326	–0.289	–0.266	–0.254	–0.254	–0.107	–0.208	–0.238	–0.415	–0.270	–0.171	–0.232
1854	–0.192	–0.138	–0.222	–0.219	–0.189	–0.100	–0.111	–0.126	–0.115	–0.069	–0.104	–0.134
1855	–0.166	–0.166	–0.134	0.022	0.090	–0.104	–0.134	–0.175	–0.195	–0.146	–0.071	–0.151
1856	–0.132	–0.114	0.003	–0.027	–0.087	–0.090	–0.103	–0.163	0.007	0.019	–0.167	–0.167
1857	–0.219	–0.130	–0.085	–0.079	0.008	0.153	0.032	–0.086	0.032	–0.086	–0.086	–0.092
1858	–0.130	–0.180	–0.060	–0.142	–0.131	–0.190	–0.190	–0.051	–0.041	–0.101	–0.288	–0.208
1859	–0.105	–0.054	–0.075	–0.227	0.310	–0.114	–0.114	–0.231	–0.054	–0.114	–0.114	–0.114
1860	–0.139	–0.220	–0.153	–0.060	0.001	–0.108	–0.136	–0.146	–0.165	–0.133	–0.135	–0.002
1861	–0.104	–0.033	0.019	–0.007	0.088	0.046	0.113	0.089	0.028	0.052	0.037	–0.086
1862	0.013	–0.138	0.060	–0.169	–0.108	–0.070	–0.060	0.036	–0.113	–0.059	–0.157	0.054
1863	0.016	0.076	0.024	0.114	–0.045	–0.026	0.095	0.029	–0.016	0.012	–0.027	–0.036
1864	0.040	0.116	0.056	0.116	0.189	0.116	0.095	–0.079	–0.139	–0.035	–0.087	–0.200
1865	–0.200	–0.140	–0.146	–0.026	–0.022	–0.026	0.044	–0.030	0.032	–0.091	–0.151	–0.212
1866	–0.126	–0.051	0.050	–0.071	–0.010	–0.189	–0.007	0.301	0.239	0.551	0.178	0.125
1867	–0.005	–0.010	0.051	–0.010	0.051	0.077	0.051	0.052	0.113	0.043	–0.008	–0.019
1868	0.020	0.020	0.020	–0.041	0.020	–0.041	0.020	0.029	0.076	0.075	0.075	0.012
1869	0.028	0.098	–0.018	0.044	0.028	0.152	0.090	0.099	0.024	0.013	0.026	0.030

Source: Our elaboration from Boyer-Xambue et al.(1994), Schneider et al. (1991), Soetbeer (1880)

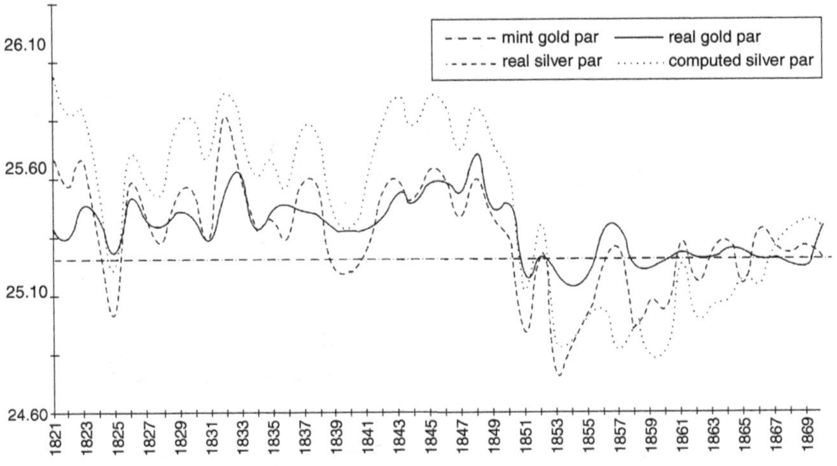

Fig. 9.3 London/Paris parties, 1821–1870 (FF per £). (*Source*: Our elaboration from Boyer-Xambue et al. (1994), Schneider et al. (1991), Soetbeer (1880))

between the silver and the gold par. However, in this case, it is higher not only than the gold par, but also than the gold import point and it is lower not only than the silver par, but also than the silver export point. This, in general, does not apply to all other "indeterminate" cases.

Finally, Table 9.2 could offer a way of testing how many times the gold and silver points were reached throughout the period, if we had a more detailed knowledge of the transaction costs involved in shipping gold and silver.[21]

Conclusions The purpose of this chapter is twofold. The first is to provide a general framework of analysis of exchange-rate variations and profitability conditions in bullion trade under monometallic and bimetallic regimes. The second is to offer an example of its application, by constructing the series of the relevant indicator for the London-Paris markets during 50 years of the early history of the Gold Standard.

We show that the variation in the market rate of exchange from the relevant parity is a good indicator of the conditions prevailing in the bills market and, therefore, of the state of the balance of payments, provided two conditions are met: first, the parity from which the deviations of the market rate of exchange are calculated must be the parity assumed as the

Table 9.2 Measure of excess demand in the London market for bills of exchange denominated in French francs, 1821–1870

	Jan	*Feb*	*March*	*April*	*May*	*June*	*July*	*August*	*Sept*	*Oct*	*Nov*	*Dec*
1821	1.73%	1.50%	1.84%	1.75%	1.72%	indet.	indet.	2.12%	indet.	indet.	indet.	0.53%
1822	1.32%	indet.	indet.	indet.	NA	indet.	1.20%	0.12%	0.76%	0.72%	indet.	0.25%
1823	1.62%	NA	2.02%	2.27%	1.66%	0.89%	1.07%	indet.	1.21%	1.48%	1.34%	0.67%
1824	0.84%	0.68%	0.64%	0.57%	0.38%	0.20%	0.63%	indet.	NA	indet.	indet.	indet.
1825	indet.	indet.	indet.	indet.	indet.	0.79%	indet.	indet.	1.13%	1.40%	1.21%	indet.
1826	indet.	indet.	2.38%	1.26%	1.06%	0.60%	indet.	indet.	indet.	indet.	NA	indet.
1827	0.84%	0.86%	0.68%	0.81%	0.63%	0.72%	NA	NA	0.70%	0.58%	NA	NA
1828	0.95%	indet.	indet.	NA	0.17%	NA	indet.	0.10%	indet.	0.14%	0.37%	indet.
1829	indet.	0.08%	indet.	indet.	0.79%	NA	0.67%	0.78%	1.03%	0.74%	0.86%	2.79%
1830	1.55%	1.33%	1.08%	1.14%	1.16%	0.87%	indet.	1.26%	0.67%	0.66%	0.09%	indet.
1831	–0.63%	–0.59%	–0.82%	–0.46%	–0.63%	–0.43%	–0.53%	–0.38%	indet.	indet.	0.20%	NA
1832	NA	NA	NA	NA	NA	NA	NA	NA	NA	0.83%	0.82%	indet.
1833	indet.	indet.	0.84%	1.06%	1.81%	1.05%	1.96%	2.16%	2.17%	0.71%	indet.	1.76%
1834	–0.32%	0.40%	–0.21%	indet.	0.21%	indet.	indet.	indet.	1.49%	0.57%	0.63%	indet.
1835	0.26%	indet.	0.41%	0.85%	0.10%	0.71%	0.55%	0.71%	1.71%	0.59%	0.37%	0.31%
1836	0.47%	0.35%	0.82%	0.29%	0.60%	indet.	1.11%	indet.	indet.	0.76%	indet.	0.54%
1837	0.82%	indet.	0.90%	indet.	0.57%	–0.54%	0.71%	indet.	indet.	indet.	0.43%	indet.
1838	1.17%	indet.	0.68%	indet.	0.76%	indet.	indet.	0.38%	indet.	indet.	indet.	–0.11%
1839	indet.	indet.	indet.	indet.	indet.	indet.	indet.	indet.	indet.	0.98%	indet.	indet.
1840	0.51%	indet.	indet.	indet.	indet.	indet.	indet.	indet.	indet.	1.33%	indet.	indet.
1841	indet.	0.72%	0.78%	0.32%	0.47%	indet.	1.06%	0.73%	2.03%	0.91%	0.47%	0.59%
1842	0.55%	0.56%	0.72%	0.73%	indet.	0.69%	0.95%	indet.	0.63%	0.73%	indet.	0.79%
1843	0.91%	0.43%	0.56%	0.67%	0.66%	0.60%	0.62%	0.48%	0.54%	0.63%	0.44%	0.54%
1844	0.58%	0.32%	0.50%	0.49%	0.24%	0.35%	–0.19%	0.58%	0.68%	0.78%	0.81%	0.78%

1845	0.56%	0.62%	0.87%	0.81%	0.70%	0.63%	0.69%	0.48%	0.69%	0.76%	1.45%	0.89%
1846	0.66%	0.92%	0.92%	1.31%	1.01%	0.50%	0.32%	0.50%	0.50%	0.46%	–1.98%	indet.
1847	indet.	indet.	indet.	indet.	1.53%	0.49%	0.86%	indet.	–0.28%	–0.23%	0.50%	indet.
1848	indet.	indet.	–2.57%	2.37%	–2.70%	indet.	indet.	–0.74%	indet.	indet.	indet.	–0.90%
1849	–0.38%	0.53%	–0.17%	–0.28%	indet.	indet.	indet.	indet.	indet.	–0.04%	0.23%	0.23%
1850	indet.	indet.	indet.	indet.	indet.	indet.	0.20%	indet.	indet.	indet.	–0.33%	2.49%
1851	indet.	indet.	indet.	indet.	indet.	indet.	–0.55%	indet.	indet.	0.55%	0.42%	indet.
1852	–0.60%	0.38%	0.48%	0.53%	indet.	–2.07%	indet.	0.41%	indet.	0.64%	indet.	–0.29%
1853	indet.	indet.	indet.	indcet.	indet.	indet.	indet.	indet.	indet.	1.80%	indet.	indet.
1854	indet.	indet.	indet.	–2.42%	indet.	indet.	indet.	indet.	indet.	0.52%	indet.	2.24%
1855	indet.	indet.	indet.	0.15%	indet.	0.93%	indet.	indet.	1.64%	1.67%	0.72%	indet.
1856	indet.	indet.	0.49%	0.49%	0.88%	0.80%	indet.	indet.	–0.14%	–0.72%	indet.	indet.
1857	indet.	indet.	indet.	indet.	–0.40%	–1.28%	–0.51%	indet.	–0.71%	indet.	indet.	1.00%
1858	1.08%	indet.	–0.48%	indet.	indet.	indet.	indet.	–0.38%	indet.	indet.	indet.	indet.
1859	indet.	indet.	indet.	indet.	–2.45%	indet.	indet.	indet.	indet.	indet.	indet.	indet.
1860	indet.	indet.	indet.	indet.	–0.21%	indet.	indet.	indet.	indet.	indet.	indet.	–0.15%
1861	indet.	indet.	0.54%	0.58%	–0.67%	0.55%	indet.	indet.	0.64%	0.63%	0.36%	0.61%
1862	0.26%	–2.36%	–0.72%	1.44%	0.86%	0.51%	0.75%	indet.	0.84%	indet.	indet.	–0.56%
1863	–0.28%	indet.	–0.23%	–0.76%	indet.	0.25%	indet.	0.36%	0.36%	0.15%	0.26%	0.45%
1864	indet.	indet.	indet.	–1.10%	indet.	–0.80%	–0.83%	0.77%	1.06%	0.61%	indet.	indet.
1865	indet.	indet.	indet.	indet.	–0.37%	–0.35%	indet.	indet.	indet.	0.72%	1.06%	indet.
1866	indet.	indet.	indet.	0.56%	–0.07%	indet.	0.09%	–2.08%	indet.	indet.	–1.25%	indet.
1867	–0.05%	–0.25%	–0.53%	indet.	–0.58%	–0.53%	indet.	–0.38%	indet.	–0.33%	–0.35%	–0.45%
1868	–0.28%	–0.23%	–0.33%	0.27%	–0.28%	0.27%	indet.	–0.23%	indet.	indet.	–0.53%	–0.13%
1869	indet.	–0.73%	0.12%	indet.	–0.23%	indet.	indet.	indet.	indet.	–0.13%	–0.22%	–0.29%
1870	indet.	indet.	–0.40%	indet.	NA	–0.08%	indet.	indet.	–0.67%	NA	NA	NA

Source: Our elaboration

term of reference by economic agents engaged in actual transactions; and second, allowance must be made for the component due to the conditions of the demand for bullion, which can fluctuate widely, as we saw on p. 84.

In this chapter we provide, as an example, computation of an indicator which is the measure of the deviation of the market rate of exchange from the real par, which satisfies *both* requirements. While its sign tells us whether the market is favorable or unfavorable to the domestic currency, its value—compared with the costs of shipping bullion—tells us whether an outflow or an inflow of bullion is likely to occur.

Notes

1. The most obvious mechanism is the convertibility of banknotes into coins or bullion. Generally, the same mechanism exists when the circulation is made up only of coins or of coins and paper, regardless of whether paper money is convertible or inconvertible (see Marcuzzo and Rosselli 1991: 123–128).
2. On the function of the standard as measure of the variations in the value of money see Marcuzzo and Rosselli (1994).
3. By rearranging (9.3) and (9.4) we have:

$$E_m = X_g(1+e) = \frac{p_M^*}{p_M}(1+e) \quad (9.3b)$$

and

$$E_m = R_g(1+t_g) = \frac{p^*}{p}(1+t_g) \quad (9.4b)$$

Substituting (9.1) and (9.2) in (9.4b), we obtain

$$E_m = \frac{p_M^*}{p_M}(1+e) = \frac{p^*}{p^*}(1+t_g) = \frac{p_M^*(1+p^*)(1+t_g)}{p_M(1+p)}$$

and by neglecting second order terms we obtain (9.5).

4. In fact, if $\frac{p}{q} < \frac{p^*}{q^*}$, namely if gold is undervalued at home, it is profitable to buy gold at home, ship and sell it abroad, buy silver abroad and ship it home, if and only if

$$\frac{qp^*}{p(1+c_g)q^*(1+c_s)} > 1$$

or

$$\frac{p^*}{p^*} > \frac{p}{q}\left(1+c_g\right)\left(1+c_s\right)$$

where $\frac{1}{p\left(1+c_g\right)}$ is the amount of gold that can be bought and shipped abroad with one unit of domestic currency. This amount of gold, when sold abroad at the price p^*, enables the merchant to buy $\frac{1}{p\left(1+c_g\right)}\ \frac{p^*}{q^*\left(1+c_s\right)}$ amount of silver, whose value at home is obtained by multiplying it by its price q. Therefore when the left-hand side of the above inequality is greater than one, this means that there is a positive gain in the arbitrage.

Similarly, if $\frac{p^*}{q^*} < \frac{p}{q}$ namely when silver is undervalued at home, it is profitable to buy silver at home and exchange it for gold abroad to be shipped back home, if and only if

$$\frac{q^* p}{q\left(1+c_s\right)p^*\left(1+c_s\right)} > 1$$

or, by rearranging terms:

$$\frac{p^*}{q^*} < \frac{p}{q}\left(1-c_g\right)\left(1-c_s\right)$$

5. Given that $\frac{p}{q} < \frac{p^*}{q^*}$ implies $\frac{q^*}{q} > \frac{p^*}{p}$ the amount of gold purchased by one unit of domestic currency $\frac{1}{p}$, fetches abroad a higher price than $\frac{1}{q}$ the amount of silver purchased by one unit of domestic currency.
6. Transportation and transaction costs include freight, insurance and commission.
7. See, for instance, Ricardo (1951: 31–33).
8. When transportation costs of shipping gold and silver widely differ, it is theoretically possible that R_s, diminished by transport costs, be higher than R_g, diminished by the transport cost, if transportation costs for silver are lower than for gold. However, this is a case that does not seem to be empirically relevant. For instance, in 1819 transport costs for gold and silver from London to Paris were approximately the same. See Evidence of

Richard Page, General Merchant, to the Resumption of Cash Payments Committee of the House of Lords (British Parliamentary Papers 1819: 150). However, later on there seem to have been slight differences (see Flandreau 1995: 104).

9. The same point is made in greater detail by Boyer-Xambeu et al. (1994, 1997).
10. Historically, we have examples of either metal in turn being left to fluctuate relative to its official value or of banknotes being converted into the metal chosen by the Bank and not by the public.
11. The case of $\frac{p}{q} < \frac{p^*}{q^*}$ is perfectly analogous: in case (I) t_g is the measure of the excess supply in the market for foreign bills of exchange and in case (II) t_s is the measure of the excess demand.
12. From the end of bimetallism to full adherence to the Gold Standard in France, gradual steps were taken: first the suspension of convertibility in 1870; then 5 Francs silver coin was no longer coined as from 1875 (Thuillier 1983: 330); finally silver was no longer coined as from 1876 (Shaw 1967: 196).
13. Evidence of Robert Mushett, First Clerk to the Master of the Mint, to the Committee on Resumption of Cash Payments of the House of Lords (British Parliamentary Papers 1819: 205).
14. In SSZ there is an apparent slip in the reference to the relevant gold and silver prices. They are quoted as "Feingold" and "Feinsilber" respectively, but in correspondence with the authors of the present paper it was confirmed that they are quotations of prices for *standard* gold and silver.
15. For the reason why the series of silver prices in London is incomplete see Flandreau (1995: 103).
16. Data for September 1839 and November 1867.
17. According to the Evidence given by Isaac Goldsmid to the Resumption of Cash Payments Committee, the Wetenhall's List reported the quotations made at the fixing of the exchanges on Post day and were not the "result of actual transactions, but a guide for the transactions to take place." The actual price of bills drawn on the Houses of the utmost credit could differ as much as 0.5 per cent from the quoted price (see British Parliamentary Papers 1819: 205).
18. The price of a short-term bill is higher than a sight bill, but for a 15 days bill, at a rate of interest lower than 5 per cent, the difference can never be more than 0.2 per cent.
19. The data are for Oct.-Nov.-Dec. 1833 and July 1840.
20. In fact, the calculation requires that five data be available: the market rate of exchange and the prices of gold and silver in London and Paris. We calculated the t_g and t_s utilizing also the data provided by XDG. Differences in the results were insignificant.

21. Between London and Paris, transportation and transaction charges were never, for most of the period under consideration, above 1 per cent. See Evidence of R. Page to the Resumption of Cash Payments Committee of the House of Lords (British Parliamentary Papers 1819: 149); Evidence of I. Goldsmid (ibid.: 258); Evidence of G. Gurney to the Committee of the Bank of England Charter (British Parliamentary Papers 1831–1832: 253–4). See also Flandreau (1995: 105, 1997).

References

Boyer-Xambeu, M.T., Deleplace, G. and Gillard, L. (1994), Régimes monétaires, points d'or et "serpent bimétallique" de 1770 à 1870, *Revue Economique* 45: 1139–74.

Boyer-Xambeu, M.T., Deleplace, G. and Gillard, L. (1995), Bimétallism, taux de change et prix de l'or et de l'argent 1717–1873, *Economies et Sociétés* 7–8.

Boyer-Xambeu, M.T., Deleplace, G. and Gillard, L. (1997), "Bimetallic snake" and monetary regimes: The stability of the exchange rate between London and Paris from 1796 to 1873, in M.C. Marcuzzo, L.H. Officer and A. Rosselli (eds.), *Monetary Standards and Exchange Rates*, London and New York: Routledge, 106–148.

British Parliamentary Papers (1819), *Reports from the Secret Committees of the Elouse of Commons and of the House of Lords on the Expediency of the Resumption of Cash Payments*, vol. III, London.

British Parliamentary Papers (1831–1832), *Report from the Committee of Secrecy on the Bank of England Charter* (1832), vol. VI, London.

Flandreau, M. (1995), *L'Or du monde: La France et la stabilité du système monétaire international 1848–1873*, Paris: l'Harmattan.

Flandreau, M. (1997), As good as gold? Bimetallism in equilibrium, 1850–70, in M.C. Marcuzzo, L.H. Officer and A. Rosselli (eds.), *Monetary Standards and Exchange Rates*, London and New York: Routledge, 150–176.

Marcuzzo, M.C. and Rosselli, A. (1987), Profitability in the International Gold Market in the Early History of the Gold Standard, *Economica* 54: 367–80.

Marcuzzo, M.C. and Rosselli, A. (1991), *Ricardo and the Gold Standard: The Foundations of the International Monetary Order*, London: Macmillan.

Marcuzzo, M.C. and Rosselli, A. (1994), The Standard Commodity and the Standard of Money, *Cahiers d'économie politique* 45: 19–31.

Officer, L.H. (1985), Integration in the American Foreign-Exchange Market, 1791–1900, *Journal of Economic History* 45: 557–85.

Officer, L.H. (1997), Integration in the American Foreign-Exchange Market, 1791–1931, in M.C. Marcuzzo, L.H. Officer and A. Rosselli (eds.), *Monetary Standards and Exchange Rates*, London and New York: Routledge, 211–228.

Ricardo, D. (1951), *Works and Correspondence*, in P. Sraffa (ed.), vol. VI, Cambridge: Cambridge University Press.

Schneider, J., Schwarzer, O. and Zellfelder F. (1991), *Währungen der Welt I. Europäische und nordamerikanische Devisenkurse 1777–1914*, vols I–III, Stuttgart: F. Steiner Verlag.
Shaw, W.A. (1967), *The History of Currency 1252 to 1896*, New York: Kelley.
Soetbeer, A. (1880), Edelmetall Produktion, "Ergänzbugsheft 5", Gotha: Petermann's Geographisches Mitteneilungen.
Thuillier, G. (1983), *La Monnaie en France au début du XIX siècle*, Geneva: Librairie Droz.
Viner, J. (1937), *Studies in the Theory of International Trade*, New York: Harper.

PART III

Cambridge Economics: Past and Present

CHAPTER 10

Is There a Cambridge Approach to Economics?

Introduction '*Cambridge* capital controversy', '*Cambridge* monetary theory of business cycle' and '*Cambridge* equation' are some of the geographical references used to characterize the economic theories and approaches that developed in Cambridge (UK) between the 1920s and the 1960s. The question that then arises is which are, if any, the shared aspects in these developments that point to the idea of a Cambridge approach to economics.

I have been arguing for some time that the group of economists renowned as representatives of the 'Cambridge school' (Keynes, Sraffa, Kahn and Joan Robinson) or the 'Cambridge Keynesians' with the inclusion of Kaldor, as they are also named (see Pasinetti 2007) should be best defined as a 'group' rather than a 'school'; the reason behind the distinction is to convey the idea of both cohesion and sharing, rather than adhesion to a common body of doctrine. The implication is that 'the Cambridge approach to economics' is an alternative to neoclassical economics, but is not as cohesive and a fully fledged system of thought; it is rather a legacy with many threads. Several aspects of method, 'style' and content of the

Originally publ. in: In A. Sinha and A. Thomas (eds.), *Economics and Its History*, Delhi: Routledge, 2019, pp. 122–35.
Reprint by Springer Nature Switzerland 2024 with kind permission

M. C. Marcuzzo, *Economic Theories, Protagonists and Facts*, Palgrave Studies in the History of Economic Thought,
https://doi.org/10.1007/978-3-031-63949-4_10

economics associated with the Cambridge tradition, and often traced back to Marshall, make it well recognizable, when compared with the so-called mainstream economics and other schools of thought. This is what will be presented in this chapter, drawing on my previous works (Marcuzzo and Rosselli 2005; Marcuzzo 2012).

The Cambridge Group The Cambridge group's profile should be seen against the framework provided by Marshall—the founder father of Cambridge economics—to whom institutionalization of the subject at the University was due. Be it in the form of criticism, refinements or extension, the approach taken by Marshall towards the multifarious aspects of economic life was taken by this group as a point of reference. The type of economics Marshall favoured involved the application of the tools of economic analysis to reality. Be it districts, trades or markets, his agents and markets were embedded in historically determined worlds. He devised the supply and demand apparatus not just as a mechanical tool designed to determine equilibrium price and quantity in each market, resulting from maximizing rules followed by consumers and producers. The apparatus was also a means to interpret situations in which expectations are fulfilled. Given their knowledge of the environment and the routines the various economic agents follow, on the basis of that knowledge, if they see no reason to expect a change, they behave in such a way that their expectations are confirmed. For Marshall it was not so much a matter of individual perfect foresight as the ability to adjust, through trial and error, to market twists and turns, assuming that individuals have varying decision-making skills.

While Marshall praised market mechanisms, albeit with many qualifications and footnotes to the contrary, the path was opened by the two intellectually leading figures of the group, Keynes and Sraffa, to expose the shortcomings of both the trust in markets and the faith in market theory inherited by Marshall.

Sraffa pursued the goal of exposing Marshall's inconsistencies arising from his method of representing the equilibrating forces of the market with a pricing mechanism of goods and factors of production based on marginal magnitudes. Keynes was more concerned with the inconsistency of expecting full employment of resources in the aggregate from individuals maximizing either utility or profit.

Kahn also accepted several Marshallian basic postulates, helped Keynes in proving that in general there is no level of effective demand sufficient to sustain full employment by forging the tools of the multiplier and the aggregate supply function and supported schemes to intervene in the market in the public interest.

On her part, while remaining a fierce Keynesian fighting against the 'bastard' (as she called it) progeny throughout her life, Joan Robinson was seduced by Sraffa's arguments favouring the classical (and Marx's) political economy as better equipped to explain capitalism, and took a more radical stance than the others in politics as well in academic debates.

Kaldor, owing to his economic growth models, theory of distribution and contributions to policy debates, became a leading figure of the post-war Cambridge economics and stood in the forefront of the fight against Monetarism in the 1970s.

This Cambridge group was embedded in what Mohit Sen called 'The Cambridge tradition of the equality of intellects, arrival at the truth through discourse and the careful nurturing of the minds of the young, encouraging without patronizing and guiding without compelling' (Sen 2003: 54). This 'Cambridge style' found expression both in the personal and professional lives of Cambridge dons and students, for whom public debate and discussion were founding elements in their life and in students' education.

What marked the Cambridge didactic system out was the personal relationship established with the students and the close attention given to their selection and. education. Some of the personal rapports of respect and friendship that characterized the interaction between the Cambridge economists began as relations between supervisor and student (as in the cases of Keynes with Robertson and Kahn and of Robertson and Shove with Austin Robinson). Even the relationship of Marshall with Keynes and Pigou had begun as a relation between teacher and pupil.

Keynes gave form and finish to his ideas by submitting them to the others; his own contribution to the work of the others remaining far more modest. For him dialogue yielded the desired results only if it ran along the lines that he traced out, and apart from the occasional comments and consultation, it was hard to draw him out on other grounds, like the theory of value or imperfect competition.

The relationship between J. Robinson and Kahn epitomizes the kind of intellectual collaboration that was typical of Cambridge. In the first place, it was a sharing of time and space, which also entailed a sharing of knowledge and the habit of exchanging ideas and mingling together. From the post-war period, until the end of the 1970s, both had fundamental roles in shaping the Cambridge that attracted students and scholars in great numbers from all over the world.

Sraffa was involved in all the intellectually important happenings at Cambridge, but found no company along his solitary path in quest of an alternative economic theory. Although it was Keynes who drew him to Cambridge and both Kahn and Robinson attended his lectures, the impact of his criticism of the Marshallian theory and his efforts to gain acceptance for an alternative approach were surprisingly ineffective until the early 1960s. His 1926 suggestion—the assumption of imperfect competition—developed in directions departing far from the approach that had inspired them. This may explain why he did not share his research pursuits with any economists in Cambridge, with the exception of Maurice Dobb.

Kaldor, like Sraffa, with whom he became a close friend, was not a born-and-bred Cambridge economist, having got his education in economics at the LSE. Unlike Kahn and Robinson, he converted to the Keynesian Revolution only after the publication of the *General Theory*, but once he was made a fellow at King's and a member of the economic faculty he mingled with the group, although the rivalry with Joan Robinson was in more than one occasion a cause of bitterness and academic quarrels.

To sum up, the 'style' aspect of the Cambridge economists as a group lies in the particular type of communication—written and oral—that led to very close forms of interaction, not devoid of diversity and dissent, in the physical and temporal closeness, helped in part by relatively unconventional lifestyles upon which profound personal ties were threaded and woven.

In what follows, I will investigate the features of the approach to be identified as 'Cambridge' under the headings of divergences, differences and commonalities, concluding with a short review of its heritage in subsequent developments.

Divergences 'Marshall's Principles were the Bible' (Robinson 1951: vii), Joan Robinson flashed out recalling the time when she went to Cambridge as an undergraduate in 1922. With the arrival of Sraffa a few years later, the landscape changed. He came to Cambridge in 1927, upon Keynes's invitation, on the strength of two articles, only one of which was in English (Sraffa 1926). Joan Robinson was later to say, 'He was calmly committing the sacrilege of pointing out inconsistencies in Marshall' (Robinson 1951: vii).

Sraffa brought to Cambridge two new research programs: (i) a reappraisal of the theory of value of classical political economy as antagonist to the Marshallian 'fundamental symmetry' of supply and demand, and based on a definition of cost as 'physical' cost, which does not include any subjective factors, such as 'sacrifice' and 'waiting'; (ii) investigation into the exchange ratios between commodities that enable the exchanges between productive sectors which warrant reproduction of the economic system.

The first line of research would have been known only to those who were attending his lectures on 'Advanced Theory of Value' (as Kahn and Joan Robinson did), while the early formulation of the second line of research was shown to Keynes and Pigou, who like Kahn and Joan Robinson for the first, did not make much of it and was not disclosed until 1960.

The interwar years were dominated by Keynes who, between his first book, *The Treatise on Probability* (1921), and his major work, *The General Theory of Employment, Interest and Money* (1936), produced other landmark contributions including the *Treatise on Money* (1930), *A Tract of Monetary Reform* (1923) and the two collections *Essays in Persuasion* (1931) and *Essays in Biography* (1933).

The making of the *General Theory* and its aftermath marked a watershed in Cambridge economics, which was transformed by it at least for those, like Kahn, Robinson and Kaldor who fully endorsed the tenets: the rejection of the 'classical' conclusion that market forces are at work to bring the economic system to the full employment of resources while the individual's pursuit of self-interest does not—contrary to Smith's parable of 'the butcher, the brewer and the baker'—produce a social good, but the unemployment and waste of resources. Aggregate economic behaviour does not have the same outcome as individual economic behaviour, so what is good for the individual may not be good for the whole.

Keynes's approach to human behaviour rested on the two pillars of expectations and conventions provided the key to understanding how opinions are formed and how they can be transformed through the joint effects of persuasion and artfully designed institutions. His conception of probability, while offering the key to rational or rather reasonable actions, does not lead to the idea that we can overcome uncertainty by devising formulae to transform it into calculable risk.

Keynes saw the main task of economic policy as 'managing' rather than 'transmuting' human nature. In the last chapter of the *General Theory*, he concluded that it is 'wise and prudent statesmanship to allow the game to be played, *subject to rules and limitations*' (Keynes [1936] 1971: 374, emphasis added). He brought new arguments and strength to the tradition of thought which Marshall and Pigou upheld, in favour of some State intervention against exclusive reliance on market mechanism, tracing out the implications of individual behaviour for the welfare of society, admitting failures and suggesting ways of improving the working of society.

After Keynes's death, Kahn, Robinson and Kaldor were engaged in extending the *General Theory* to the long period and were faced with unsettled issues of determination of growth, income distribution and technological change. The question of the measurement of the value of capital and therefore the determination of the rate of profit cropped up and remained unsolved until the publication of *Production of Commodities by Means of Commodities* (PCMC) in 1960 (Sraffa 1960).

Sraffa provided the theory of prices and distribution alternative to neoclassical theory in general, and of Marshall in particular: given the quantities produced and the technical conditions of production for each commodity, the prices are determined by a system of simultaneous equations, under the assumption that in a capitalist society the rate of profit must be equal in all sectors. The distribution of the surplus is not made dependent exclusively on the technical conditions of production and the relative scarcity of productive factors, since one of the distributive variables is determined outside the system of prices and could be influenced by other economic, or even political and social causes.

By drawing an inverse relationship between rate of profit and wage, Sraffa shows that the interests of labourers and capitalists are antithetical. The substitution of labour for capital, when the rate of profit rises relatively to the wage loses any meaning after it is showed that the same technique could be adopted as the most profitable at different rates of wages (the so-called reswitching).

PCMC came out as a surprise inside and outside Cambridge, with the possible exception of Joan Robinson who said that she had seen the 'light' in Sraffa's Introduction to Ricardo's *Principles*, which led her to write her 1953 article, which anticipated the capital controversy.

Keynes had been dead for a decade when PCMC was published, but had he lived long enough to see Sraffa's project disclosed to the world, he would never have endorsed it. No matter how highly he regarded Sraffa or how strongly he felt the need to have him in Cambridge, he was reluctant to abandon his Marshallian tools, and he was allergic to Marx. On the other hand, no matter how much Sraffa felt for Keynes (both personally and intellectually), he considered him a 'bourgeois intellectual' whose 'mentality' prevented him from appreciating Marx and understanding the working class issues (P. Sraffa to R. Palme Dutt, April 19, 1932 in Marcuzzo 2005). On his part, Sraffa remained 'secretly sceptical of the new [Keynes's] ideas', (Robinson 1978: xii) as Joan Robinson had observed then and afterwards, isolating himself from the Keynesian revolution and, in turn, depriving it of his own contributions.

Since the late 1960s, many attempts have been made to argue for or against the compatibility of the approaches adopted by Keynes and Sraffa. Neo-Ricardians (Sraffa's followers accused Keynes and his followers [post Keynesians] of not sufficiently shaking off several neoclassical traits [for instance, acceptance of the inverse relationship—based on the marginal productivity of factors—between investment and the rate of interest]) and the post Keynesians retorted that in Sraffa's system there is no room for money and uncertainty, which are the distinct features of a capitalist economy.

In fact, the critique that Keynes, Kahn, Kaldor and Joan Robinson raised against the neoclassical paradigm went together with their apparently unquestioning acceptance—at least at a disaggregate level—of marginal analysis. True, Kaldor and Robinson in later years rejected the notion of equilibrium, but without severing the connection with supply-and-demand theories. Kahn championed the 'marginal principle' for the determination of price and output for the single firm and he was instrumental in persuading Keynes to adopt the marginal approach in the *General Theory*. Keynes never rejected increasing marginal costs in the *General Theory* and this led him to adopt assumptions, such as the inverse relationship between employment and real wages, which brought conclusions that he later admitted were at variance with facts.

Sraffa's estrangement from Cambridge economics and his refusal to engage in the discussion of his own work with those who were among his closest friends can be accounted for by a political, social and cultural gulf. In Cambridge, Sraffa remained an isolated intellectual figure, feared and admired rather than actually understood. An example of the difficulty or even impossibility of 'penetrating' the insularity of a body of doctrine remained, notwithstanding the Keynesian Revolution, far away from Sraffa's background and frame of mind.

Differences Joan Robinson tried to incorporate Sraffa's prices into the Keynesian framework. Her encounter with Kalecki (who was in Cambridge during 1937–1939) and constant engagement with Sraffa made her more willing than Kahn to enlarge the Cambridge approach beyond the boundaries of Keynesian economics.

In her 1954 article, she drew attention to the 'profound methodological error' (Robinson [1954] 1964: 120) connected with the concept of quantity of capital outside the short period. She pointed out the neoclassical failure to distinguish between changes in the conditions of producing a given output, when the quantity of physical capital is altered, from changes in the value of that capital, due to variations in wages and profits. The implication is that 'different factor ratios cannot be used to analyse changes in the factor ratio taking place through time', because over time the value of the quantity of capital may change as a consequence of a change in distribution, and we will not be comparing the same quantities. She concluded that 'it is impossible to discuss changes (as opposed to differences) in neo-classical terms' (Robinson [1954] 1964: 129).

Robinson interpreted the 'points of view of difference and of change' as a distinction between legitimate and illegitimate comparisons between two equilibria, with different amounts of capital. Since changes in the value of capital may occur simply because of a change in the rate of profit, it is impossible to know whether the quantity of capital has changed in the transition from one position to another. Thus she drew the conclusion that equilibrium positions could only be compared as differences, and never described as changes from one position to another.

However, in the introduction to Ricardo's *Principles*, Sraffa takes the question of the measurement of the quantity of capital to pertain only to the question of measuring 'the magnitude of aggregate of commodities', i.e., to the *apparent* change in the quantity of output to be distributed whenever there is a change in its value due to a change either in wages or in profits.

Sraffa does not take it to pertain to the question of the impossibility of comparing two different aggregates of commodities at two different points in time because of the impossibility of singling out the effects of a change in distribution, as Joan Robinson seemed to take it. It is not the time element that makes the analysis of change impossible in neoclassical terms, but the circularity in the measurement of capital unless the rate of profit is determined simultaneously.

After the publication of *Production of Commodities,* Joan Robinson became aware of the misunderstanding of her reading of the introduction to Ricardo's *Principles,* but still defended her distinction between the 'two point of views of difference and of change' as resting on the distinction between logical and historical time, claiming that reasoning in logical time is common to both general equilibrium theory and Sraffa's system, while the language of Keynes is in historical time.

Joan Robinson's main line of attack on the neoclassical theory was levelled against the notion of equilibrium and the impossibility of dealing with historical time, rather than against the inconsistencies in the theory of supply and demand. She remained unconvinced by the theory of prices of production and objected to the method of *Production of Commodities,* because 'there is no causation and no change' and 'the argument is conducted strictly in terms of comparisons of logically possible positions' (Robinson 1980a: 132). She felt it to be more promising to rely on Keynes, who, 'at the opposite extreme to Sraffa, discusses only events' (Robinson 1980b: 139) and discusses them 'in terms of processes taking place in actual history' (Robinson 1979: xiv).

This issue gave rise to the controversy on the question as to where the dividing line of the alternative to neoclassical economics lay. There were those, like Garegnani (1979) who argued that the assumption of irreversibility in time was implicit only in the method of supply-and-demand analysis, in which the tendency towards equilibrium is described as movements along those curves. The same assumption is not made when comparing two long-term equilibrium positions determined by a 'classical' theory of prices and distribution. (Garegnani 1979).

Also K. Bharadwaj (1991), while agreeing that history, namely the process involving actual and irreversible changes as opposed to potential and reversible changes, has to be rescued from neoclassical theory and brought back into economic analysis, defended the method of comparison between long-term positions as a legitimate method of analysis of change. Robinson objected to the method of comparisons of classical political economy and to Sraffa's method as showing no substantial difference from the neoclassical equilibrium method in their neglect of disregard of uncertainty and disregard of expectations, which are the guiding forces of economic behaviour. K. Bharadwaj responded by making two objections to Robinson's criticism of the equilibrium (in the sense of the long-term position) method. First, the equilibrium concept does not entail that the corresponding prices and the uniform rate of profit actually rule at any particular moment in time. It is rather, the tendency towards it, driven by the forces that are believed to be persistent, that is argued for. Second, while not denying that uncertainty or expectations had a role to play, she followed Sraffa in defending an objective method of analysis, which does not to appeal to non-observable entities, such as individual utility functions, but instead to looks at customs, social norms and the like (see Marcuzzo 2014).

Commonalities I have so far pointed to the divergences and differences among these economists who did not always share the same interests, background or attitudes, but nevertheless convey a sense of belonging to a common world. Where can we find those commonalities, which will allow us to define a Cambridge approach to economics? My answer will have two parts: the first relates to certain features which we can detect in the authors whom I have selected as representative of Cambridge economics, and the second concerns the heritage in the research development which have evolved since their time.

Marshall's works represented the major theoretical reference point for this group; all had to reckon with Marshallian theory, whether to go on to take a distance from it, as Marshall did, or to forge ahead along the most original and promising lines of research it offered. Marshall, who had 'acute awareness of its embeddedness in historically determined totalities' (Becattini 2006: 614) provided a framework which was distinct from the one embraced by other neoclassical economists. In his economics, expectations have an important role to play, so does the notion of the short period as a horizon defined by the nature of choices that the producer can make. His analysis, by assuming the *ceteris paribus* clause to hold, allows one to detect a chain of causes and effects in each individual markets. All these traits provided the fertile ground in which Kahn and Keynes's short period and partial equilibrium analysis developed.

We may also add that his version of the quantity theory, as a demand for money balances, by introducing the possibility of a variable, or even an unstable proportion of money held for transaction purposes, paved the way to the notion of liquidity preference. The notion of liquidity is at the centre of the Cambridge critique of the quantity theory of money; it amounts to denying the separation between monetary and real factors and the determination of the level of price as the outcome of the interplay of a transaction demand for money and an exogenously given money supply.

In Chapter 21 of the *General Theory*, Keynes shows that the quantity theory results apply under very special conditions: far from being a general proposition, it can be applied in very special circumstances which rarely occur in the real world. The level of prices is shown, rather than the outcome of three factors, the level of money wages, technology and the level of demand.

On the demand side, the speculative demand for money, as a function of interest rate is another aspect worth noticing as a feature of the Cambridge approach. We need to be reminded that the liquidity preference is not a relationship, which can be assumed to be stable, as in IS-LM model; it follows that changes in the supply of money bring about changes in the interest rate only if the schedule of the liquidity preference can be thought of as a stable relationship. However—and this was Kahn's main point—it is unsuitable to think of 'a schedule of liquidity preference as though it could be represented by a well- defined curve or by a functional relationship expressed in mathematical terms or subject to econometric processes' and held Keynes responsible for giving way 'to the temptation to picture the state of liquidity preference as a fairly stable relationship' (Kahn [1954] 1972: 90).

These arguments are directed against the 'classical tradition' whereby thrift and capital productivity are the 'real forces' at work in determining the rate of interest, which are conceived as a highly conventional phenomenon, determined by the strength of the desire of individuals to hold money (as protection against an uncertain future) and the quantity of money provided by the banking system. However, the quantity of money necessary to bring about a fall in the rate of interest varies with the circumstances and the state and responsiveness of the market.

Kaldor challenged the alleged exogeneity that is the presupposition of the quantity theory equation. In his *Speculation and Economic Stability* (Kaldor [1939] 1960), he pointed out that the quantity of the money supply in a credit economy comes into existence as a result of bank lending and is extinguished through the repayment of bank loans. This volume of bank lending is limited only by the availability of credit-worthy borrowers. Accordingly, the money supply becomes a passive element varying automatically with the demand for credit. The increase in the supply of money in circulation is the response to increased demand and not an autonomous event. Without credit expansion, the Central Bank's willingness to expand the monetary base will not produce effects on the money supply. It is interesting to note that although we have only scattered passages testifying to Sraffa's monetary views, he certainly shared the idea of the rate of interest as a monetary and a highly conventional phenomenon.

Moreover there is a methodological aspect which make Keynes's and Sraffa's position very close to each other. As it is well known for Keynes in economics 'we cannot hope to make completely accurate generalisations' (Keynes [1936] 1971: 254) because the economic system is not ruled by 'natural forces'. The task of economics is rather to 'select those variables which can be deliberately controlled and managed by central authority in the kind of system in which we actually live' (ibid.).

In the *General Theory*, while the liquidity preference, the propensity to consume, the marginal efficiency of investment, the wage unit and the quantity of money are presented as the 'ultimate independent variables', it is denied that this distinction could ever be general; on the contrary, the division is said to be quite arbitrary from any absolute standpoint (Keynes [1936] 1971: 247). The *General Theory* explains why the level of employment oscillates around 'an intermediate position' below full employment and above the minimum subsistence employment (Keynes [1936] 1971: 254). However, Keynes added:

> we must not conclude that the mean position [of employment] thus determined by 'natural' tendencies, namely, by those tendencies which are likely to persist, failing measures expressly designated to correct them, is, therefore, established by laws of necessity. The unimpeded rule of the above conditions is a fact of observation concerning the world as it is or has been, and not a necessary principle which cannot be changed. (ibid.)

Keynes's stance is very similar to Sraffa's:

> I am convinced that the maintenance of the interest rate by the bank (or) the stock exchange has had its part in the determination of income distribution among social classes [...]. I did not want to commit myself much, and in general I only wanted to signal something in order to avoid the belief that the system is presented as 'foundation' for a theory of the relative supplies of capital and labour! It is *what is denied* that seems important to me: as to what is *affirmatively claimed*, I have no intention to put forward another mechanical theory which, in one form or another, states again that income distribution is determined by natural, or technical or even accidental, circumstances, which in any case are such that they make any action taken by

> either part, in order to modify, futile. [...] I do not see any difficulty in the determination of the rate of profit through a controlled or conventional interest rate, provided that the rate of profit will not be assumed to be determined by external unchangeable circumstances. (SP D3/12/111; quoted in Panico 2001: 301–302)

Finally, Sraffa's critique had implications for the contention that market forces always bring the system to the full employment equilibrium via changes in the wage rate. It was the same battle the Keynesians were fighting.

Heritage There are least three research environments that purportedly draw and build upon the Cambridge tradition, that is, the Marshallian, Post-Keynesian and Sraffian approaches. I draw on Marcuzzo and Rosselli (2016) to present a short review of these developments.

Marshall's concept of 'industrial district, discussed in book IV of the *Principles*, describing 'the concentration of specialised industries in particular localities', pointed to a form of organization governed by trust and co-operation, which characterizes clusters of firms within well-defined regional boundaries in various parts of the world. The district can be seen, then, as a relatively stable community, which has evolved out of a strong local cultural identity and shared industrial expertise. (A recent assessment of the theoretical aspects of this literature can be found in Raffaelli et al. 2010). This attention to the social and historical embeddedness of the economic process within which firms operate is a far cry that has proved to be of great utility in interpreting the peculiarity of several contemporary industrial districts.

Another equally successful endorsement of the Marshallian apparatus draws on his evolutionary vision of the organic development of firms and society at large. Economic progress is seen as the cumulative result of increasing division of labour, of the development of specialized skills, knowledge and machinery and, at the same time, of the ability to coordinate them. Economic change is represented by concepts such as adaptive behaviour, variation and selection through industrial competition. The object of study is a population of firms, each different from the other and continuously evolving, through interaction among themselves and with their social environment. Although this evolutionary approach is not unique to Marshall, having its recognized forefather in Schumpeter, several interesting research trends in cognitive and industrial economics have exploited the richness of this Marshallian tradition.

However, nowadays the best-known and most widespread approach in economics associated with the Cambridge School is Post-Keynesianism, which emerged in the 1960s. In recent years, the insights of Minsky on the causes of the financial meltdown have given more visibility and credibility to an approach which had always stressed the role of uncertainty, as well as the importance of money and income distribution in capitalist economies. The role of effective demand in generating employment, rejection of the idea that public investment crowds out private investment, the monetary nature of the interest rate, mistrust in the flexibility of prices as a way to redress fundamental market imbalances and the importance of cost in generating inflation and of incomes policy in controlling it and fostering growth are the main ingredients of the Post-Keynesian approach.

There is indeed variety within the group of Post-Keynesians, in terms of emphasis and research agenda, while the (smaller) group of Sraffa's followers appears more cohesive and focussed. It is for expository purposes that the division is made here between the two approaches, since many heterodox economists would see no contradiction in endorsing both.

Sraffa's research programme has been carried forward along several different lines. One is the investigation into the properties of the so-called core, that is, the set of equations that determine long-period relative prices and the wage rate or rate of profit, under the assumption that outputs and the alternative techniques that produce them are given. The analytical complexities of the system when joint production is involved and/or the inputs include at least one natural resource have been explored. Another issue that drew the attention of Sraffian scholars is the convergence (or the non-explosive oscillations) of market prices to their long-run positions characterized by the uniformity of the profit rate. Important results have been reached in this field and the related literature is quite large (Kurz and Salvadori 1995).

Another line of research lies in the 'closure of the system' or the determination of the distributive variable which is assumed as given. The classical tradition of assuming constant real wage is rejected and attention is focussed on the rate of profit. Two routes have been pursued here. One, following Pasinetti and his Cambridge growth equation, is to consider the rate of profit determined by the rate of growth of the system, which, in turn, depends on the investment decisions of capitalists. The other route, following Sraffa's suggestion, is to assume the rate of interest to be equal to the rate of profit (allowing for differences in liquidity and risks). In this way, the possibility for monetary policy to impact income distribution—a clear case of non-neutrality of money—is posited.

Note that the two lines of research described previously represent what Pasinetti has labelled as the 'separation theorem', that is, the division between 'those investigations that concern the foundational bases of economic relations—to be detected at a strictly essential level of basic economic analysis—from those investigations that must be carried out at the level of the actual economic institutions' (Pasinetti 2007: 275). The separation concerns not only the objects, but the level of abstraction and generality that the analysis must and can achieve (Garegnani 2002).

Conclusions At the end of this cursory excursus into the history of Cambridge economics, I have left out episodes and figures, such as Austin Robinson, C. Pigou, M. Dobb and D. Robertson, in the earlier period, and R. Goodwin, M. Kalecki and R. Stone, who also made significant contributions to what goes under the name of Cambridge economics. I have focussed on the five economists who epitomize the Cambridge approach to economics, by showing the divergences, differences and commonalities that make them a very composite group. I have also shown that their heritage can be found in contemporary research areas, which make this tradition alive and promising of further developments.

We may conclude by saying that the Cambridge tradition has handed down to us a legacy resting on two pillars. The first is the rejection of the 'classical' conclusion that market forces are always at work to bring the economic system to full employment of resources, implicated by the belief that there is no discontinuity between individual and aggregate behaviour, so that what is good for a single player in the market is good for the whole. The second is the Sraffian theme that the market, taken as synonymous with supply and demand, is a misleading arena for the representation of the rules of production and distribution. Both pillars are needed to travel the road towards an alternative economic theory and economic policy.

References

Becattini, G. 2006. 'The Marshallian School of Economics', in T. Raffaelli, G. Becattini and M. Dardi (eds.), *The Elgar Companion to Alfred Marshall*, Cheltenham, UK and Northampton, USA: Edward Elgar, pp. 664–671.

Bharadwaj, K. 1991. 'History Versus Equilibrium', in I. Rima (ed.). *The Joan Robinson Legacy*, Armonk: Sharpe, pp. 80–103.

Garegnani, P. 1979. 'Notes on Consumption, Investment and Effective Demand: A Reply to Joan Robinson', *Cambridge Journal of Economics*, 3, 181–187.

Garegnani, P. 2002. 'Misunderstanding Classical Economics? A Reply to Blaug', *History of Political Economy*, 34, 241–254.

Kahn, R. [1954] 1972. 'Some Notes on Liquidity Preference', in *Selected Essays on Employment and Growth*, Cambridge: Cambridge University Press, pp. 72–96.

Kaldor, N. [1939] 1960. 'Speculation and Economic Stability', in *Essays on Economic Stability and Growth*, London: Duckworth.

Keynes, J.M. [1936] 1971. 'The General Theory of Employment, Interest, and Money', in E. Johnson and D. E. Moggridge (eds.), *The Collected Writings of John Maynard Keynes*, vol. VII, London: Palgrave Macmillan.

Kurz, H. and Salvadori, N. 1995. *Theory of Production: A Long-Period Analysis*, Cambridge: Cambridge University Press.

Marcuzzo, M.C. 2005. 'Piero Sraffa at the University of Cambridge', *European Journal for the History of Economic Thought*, 12(3), 425–452.

Marcuzzo, M.C. 2012. *Fighting Market Failure: Collected Essays in the Cambridge Tradition of Economics*, London: Routledge.

Marcuzzo, M.C. 2014. 'On Alternative Notions of Change and Choice: Krishna Bharadwaj's Legacy', *Cambridge Journal of Economics*, 38, 49–62.

Marcuzzo, M.C. and Rosselli, A. 2005. *Economists in Cambridge: A Study Through Their Correspondence, 1907–1946*, London: Routledge.

Marcuzzo, M.C. and Rosselli, A. 2016. 'The Cambridge School of Economics', in G. Faccarello and H. Kurz (eds.), *The Handbook of the History of Economic Thought*, Cheltenham: Edward Elgar, pp. 343–357.

Panico, C. 2001. 'Monetary Analysis in Sraffa's Writings', in T. Cozzi and R. Marchionatti (eds.), *P Sraffa: A Centenary Estimate*, London: Routledge.

Pasinetti, L.L. 2007. *Keynes and the Cambridge Keynesians: A "Revolution in Economics" to Be Accomplished*, Cambridge: Cambridge University Press.

Raffaelli T., Nishizawa, T. and Cook, S. eds. 2010. *Marshall, Marshallians and Industrial Economics*, London: Routledge.

Robinson, J.V. 1951. Introduction to *Collected Economic Papers*, Vol. I, Oxford: Blackwell.

Robinson, J.V. [1954] 1964. 'The Production Function and the Theory of Capital', as reprinted in *Collected Economic Papers*, Vol. 2. Oxford: Blackwell.

Robinson, J.V. 1978. Introduction to *Contributions to Modern Economics*, Oxford: Blackwell.
Robinson, J.V. 1979. Introduction to *The Generalization of the General Theory and Other Essays*, London: Palgrave Macmillan.
Robinson, J.V. 1980a. 'Retrospect: 1980', in *Further Contributions to Modern Economics*, Oxford: Blackwell, pp. 131–134.
Robinson, J.V. 1980b. 'Misunderstanding in the Theory of Production', in *Further Contributions to Modern Economics*, Oxford: Blackwell, pp. 135–140.
Sen, M. 2003. *A Traveller and the Road: The Journey of an Indian Communist*, New Delhi: Rupar & Co.
Sraffa, P. 1926. 'The Laws of Returns Under Competitive Conditions', *Economic Journal*, 36, 535–550.
Sraffa, P 1960. *Production of Commodities by Means of Commodities*, Cambridge: Cambridge University Press.

CHAPTER 11

Luigi Pasinetti and the Cambridge Economists

11.1 Introduction

My aim in this paper is to pay tribute to Luigi Pasinetti as an historian of economic thought in general, but in particular with regard to his work on the Cambridge economists.[1] I will refer to some aspects of his interpretations of Sraffa and Keynes, but also of Richard Kahn, Joan Robinson and Nicholas Kaldor, who were Pasinetti's friends, colleagues and companions in arms in various intellectual and academic battles. With them he shared everyday Cambridge life, and he is universally associated with them in terms of a common 'school'—the Cambridge school. My purpose is not to provide a systematic account, but to offer some illustrations of Pasinetti's style of doing history of economic thought and how it developed over time.

This is a revised and extended version of an article I published in Italian in 2007 on the occasion of Luigi Pasinetti's seventy-seventh birthday (see Marcuzzo 2007). I am grateful to two anonymous referees for helpful criticism and suggestions.

Originally publ. in: *History of Economics Review* 60 (Summer), 2014, pp. 15–29; earlier version in *Review of Western Economics* (China Renmin University Press), 4 (1), 2014, pp. 36–47.
Reprint by Springer Nature Switzerland 2024 with kind permission

M. C. Marcuzzo, *Economic Theories, Protagonists and Facts*, Palgrave Studies in the History of Economic Thought,
https://doi.org/10.1007/978-3-031-63949-4_11

Characteristic of Pasinetti's approach to research are respect for sources, accuracy and precise reference to facts and texts, which apply equally to his work as a theoretician and as an historian of economic thought, together with an impeccably rigorous style, sparing in adjectives but rich in details. What I wish to investigate here is the relationship between these two types of research in Pasinetti's work on the Cambridge economists, to see how they evolved over time and to address the more general question of the difference between the approaches of a theoretician and of an historian, offering some concluding thoughts on their nature and scope. To make my point clearer, I follow the chronological order in examining his writings on selected Cambridge authors in Sects. 11.2, 11.3 and 11.4; whilst in Sect. 11.5, I discuss Pasinetti's views on the Cambridge economists as a school.

11.2 Sraffa

In the formulation of the celebrated paper of 1960, 'A mathematical formulation of the Ricardian system', Pasinetti drew extensively on Sraffa's 'Introduction' to Ricardo's *Principles*, together with Kaldor's 1956 article, 'Alternative Theories of Distribution', to reconstruct Ricardo's theory. His interpretation marks a clear distance from previous scholarship, insofar as he makes ample use of Sraffa's critical edition of Ricardo's *Works* (though his analysis was confined to the *Principles*), although he appears to have then been leaning more towards 'rational reconstruction' than 'historical reconstruction' of the history of ideas.[2] Thus, for example, in the 1960 article Pasinetti disregarded the issue and, hence, importance of the 'corn-ratio theory of profits' in the evolution of Ricardo's thought, arguing that it represented, he believed, a 'position [...] very highly vulnerable', and was abandoned by the author 'long before writing the *Principles*' (Pasinetti [1974] 1977: 2n.). Actually, it was Sraffa himself who pointed out that Ricardo 'maintained' this position until 1816—not 'long before', that is, but up to the year immediately preceding the first edition of the *Principles*, when he abandoned it in favour of the labour theory of value. This issue was to loom large in the subsequent literature with historians of economic thought divided between those who accepted Sraffa's reconstruction of 'the rational foundation of the principle of the determining role of the profits of agriculture' (Sraffa 1951: xlix–xxxi) and those who opposed it.[3] It is a typical 'history of economic thought' issue, relating to the quest for the origin of concepts, and their interpretation, textual confirmation and referential context.

At the time, however, Pasinetti was committing himself to a different exegetic exercise which was to last for many years, namely, close scrutiny of *Production of Commodities by Means of Commodities*, which had just appeared in print. The best known product of this endeavour is probably chapter V of the *Lezioni di Teoria della Produzione* of 1975,[4] a text that has stood as a major landmark for many students and scholars approaching Sraffa's book.

Pasinetti's involvement and interest in intellectual history, which is part and parcel of the skills of an historian of economic thought, can be dated to the mid-1980s, when several of his best pieces on the Cambridge economists were written (Pasinetti 1985, 1987a, b, 1991b).

In the 1985 article reconstructing Sraffa's intellectual and human biography,[5] still pervaded by the emotional impact of his death (in September 1983), Pasinetti's flair as an historian emerges, for example, in his accurate account of the context of Sraffa's 1925 original Italian article on the relations between cost and quantity produced. He also presents a telling description of the particular time in Sraffa's life when he faced judgement in a competitive examination for a Chair at the University of Cagliari, as well as the general picture of Sraffa's still essentially Italian world before his final move to Cambridge in 1926. Many years were to pass before Naldi (2001) was able to add some details to this reconstructed picture which, however, has continued to enjoy general consensus over the years.

Sraffa's relations with his contemporaries, Raffaele Mattioli, Antonio Gramsci and Ludwig Wittgenstein, came under the close, searching scrutiny of Pasinetti. As far as I know, the very extensive literature that followed, above all after the Sraffa papers were made available at Trinity in 1994, revealed no significant imprecision nor prompted any major revision, although of course it led to further investigation into certain other aspects of Sraffa's life and work.[6]

The relations between Sraffa and Keynes are a special case, according to Pasinetti, of personal closeness with hardly any intellectual mutual influence. 'It is difficult', he wrote, 'to think of problems on which one might trace a direct influence of Keynes on the development of Sraffa's economic thought. But at the same time I find it equally difficult to find examples to the contrary' (Pasinetti 1985: 327, 1998: 377), The same point is reiterated twenty years later:

> In terms of the concepts associated with Keynes's *General Theory* [Sraffa] was not entirely involved as the others and remained the most critical member of the whole group. The evolution of his thought had started before the *General Theory* and proceeded more on parallel lines, rather than in succession, to the ideas of Keynes. (Pasinetti 2007: 62)[7]

Likewise, he sees relations between Sraffa and the Keynesian economists at Cambridge as lacking in fruitful intellectual communication, summing up with the observation that:

> [...] in the post-second-World-War period [there was a] sort of intellectual independence [...] emerging in Sraffa's relationship with the group of Cambridge Keynesians (notably with Joan Robinson, Richard Kahn and Nicolas Kaldor) [...]. In the post-war period, Sraffa does not use his theoretical scheme to go in the directions along which the whole Keynesian group is moving. [...] At the same time, and similarly, in the 1960's, one could notice many difficulties in the opposite direction, namely on the side of the members of the Keynesian group, to assimilate the ideas contained in Sraffa's book [...] Joan Robinson tried very hard to assimilate the most important propositions of *Production of Commodities*, but I believe she has not been quite successful. Kaldor seems to have remained almost entirely extraneous to it. The same thing may be said of Kahn. (Pasinetti 1985: 329–30, 1998: 380–81)[8]

The question of 'intellectual independence' in Sraffa's relations with Keynes and, later, with the Cambridge Keynesians—whether it reveals a fundamental incompatibility of approach and could therefore have stood in the way of attempts to build a comprehensive framework—is the core issue in Pasinetti's book (2007). I will return to these questions in Sect. 11.4 below.

Apart from the two 1988 texts, one on income distribution, the other on the circular process concept in Sraffa, we have to wait until 2001 to find Pasinetti once again engaged in study of the sources, seeking further elements to add to his historical reconstruction of Sraffa's thought and works. The article in question addresses the issue of 'continuity and change', after an excursus into the Sraffa papers. Pasinetti (2001) is concerned with the context of a discussion on the reasons why Sraffa's 1925 article was not translated into English; in the first place, respecting the author's express wishes, and subsequently in accordance with the decision of the executors of Sraffa's will.[9] Pasinetti himself tells us how he shut himself up in the Wren Library, Trinity, for fifteen days trying 'avidly to read notes and scripts, and files and files of papers' (Pasinetti 2001: 141). The article that emerged is a model of accuracy and conciseness, proposing a periodisation of Sraffa's vast output underlying *Production of Commodities* into three sub-periods (1928–1931; 1941–1945; 1955–1959), taken to correspond to three lines of thought. Subsequent studies by, among others, De Vivo (2004)[10] and Kurz and Salvadori (2005),[11] who spent months at Trinity poring over the Sraffa papers, do not appear to conflict with Pasinetti's approach. Obviously there are other periodisations and interpretations,[12] but Pasinetti's 'brief' archive excursus has come to stand as sound reference for historians of economics thought.[13]

11.3 Keynes

Keynes is the other author whom Pasinetti interpreted on the basis of both rational and historical reconstructions.

The second chapter of Pasinetti's 1974 book (the Italian edition came out in 1977), 'The economics of effective demand', now has the status of a classic in the literature, and as such has received widespread consensus but has also seen a few taking a distance from it in particular in connection with Pasinetti's interpretation of Keynes's marginal efficiency of investment. Here, too, I shall limit my focus to the transformations Pasinetti's interpretations went through in the subsequent works, as a consequence of his approach to the matter from the vantage of the history of economic thought.

In Pasinetti (1974) he presents Keynes's theory of investment with the famous step diagram on the basis of which the various investment projects are ordered in decreasing scale according to the expected rate of profit and the rate of interest. Since, however, the ordering is made by entrepreneurs, who classify the projects according to their expectations, Pasinetti argues that this procedure differs from the marginalist approach where, by contrast, the ordering emerges from the decreasing marginal productivity of the capital. Thus, he writes:

> Keynes's ranking [...] is more akin to Ricardo's ranking of all lands in a decreasing order of fertility than marginal economic elaboration [...] there is absolutely no need to consider Keynes' marginal-efficiency-of-capital schedule as an expression of the marginal productivity theory of capital [which] necessarily entails an inverse monotonic relation between capital

> intensity and the rate of interest [...] In a slump situation the last project to be implemented might well be the least capital intensive of all, and therefore entail a decrease (not an increase) of the average amount of capital per employed labour. (Pasinetti 1974: 43, 1977: 60)

This interpretation has come in for a certain amount of criticism (see Bonifati and Vianello 1998), on the grounds that in Keynes's ordering the returns expected on each investment good are not independent of the quantities of the others, and so relate to intensive rent rather than Ricardo's extensive rent, but this is not the point I mean to settle here.[14] The point is that in this book, in contrast with the practice he would later adopt, Pasinetti makes no use of text or context analysis. Indeed, he cites the *General Theory* only once in relation to Keynes's refusal to adopt 'pseudo-mathematical symbolic methods'.

When he returned to this issue, nearly 20 years later, Pasinetti (1997) took a more wary stance. He pointed out that Keynes could not have benefited from Sraffa's analysis of the neoclassical theory of capital, the only one able to offer a sound critique of the neoclassical investment function, which Keynes was far from endorsing.[15] Pasinetti (1997) makes ample use of textual evidence to the *General Theory* while the characteristics of ordering in the marginal efficiency of investment are fully elaborated. The point on which Pasinetti insists, consistent with the position of some critics, is that it is the determination of the rate of interest independent of the 'quantity' of capital in Keynes's theory which marks the difference with neoclassical theory. He wrote:

> The rate of interest *determines* what the marginal efficiency of the last investment project is going to be. Hence, the rate of interest does influence the total amount of investment to be carried out [...] according to a relation which has the appearance of the orthodox schedule (but a different foundation, because it has no determinate relation with the capital-intensity of the investment projects). Yet, although the rate of interest influences the size of investments, the opposite is not true. (Pasinetti 1997: 208)

As in the case of Sraffa, there is a change in Pasinetti's way of interpreting Keynes, dating from the late 1980s, on gaining access to texts by Keynes and his interlocutors which had been made available with the publication of the thirty volumes of Keynes's *Collected Writings* dated to 1989.

Pasinetti's 1991a article examining the issue of continuity versus discontinuity between the *Treatise on Money* and the *General Theory*, of whether or not a 'Keynesian revolution' occurred in the author's thinking in 1936 is a typical history of thought exercise. In fact, Pasinetti's aim was to contest both the re-evaluation of the *Treatise* as the more important text, at least from the point of view of monetary theory, and the re-wrapping of the *General Theory* as a Walrasian package with the application of simultaneous equations. In doing so, Pasinetti signalled a change in approach when he drew extensively on the textual sources, albeit only those published in volumes XIII, XIV and XXIX of Keynes's *Collected Writings*. The point of contrasting the causality with the simultaneous equation method was also made in his 1974 essay on effective demand, but in Pasinetti (1991a) it is done in the context of a meticulous reconstruction of the steps leading Keynes to his 'revolution'.

11.4 The Cambridge Keynesians

The group of authors examined in this section shared with Pasinetti the common goal of bringing the Keynesian revolution to fulfilment. I will begin with Richard Kahn, to whom Pasinetti was particularly close in the last years of his life.[16]

From the entry in Palgrave (1987a) to the more ambitious article in the *Proceedings of the British Academy* (1991b), Pasinetti's work underlies a great deal of the scholarship upon which the subsequent Kahn literature developed. I wish to stress in particular that it was Pasinetti who first helped reveal who was 'that elusive figure who hides in the Preface to many Cambridge books', to quote Schumpeter's quip, as recorded by Joan Robinson (King's College Archives JVR i/8). There are, of course, points in interpretation of Kahn that may give rise to slightly divergent positions. For example, I am not sure that the study of Kahn's (1989) dissertation 'may well contribute to piecing together the great analytical puzzle of the relations between Sraffa's critique of Marshall's theory of the firm and Keynes's macroeconomic theory, or, to put it in other terms, of the micro-foundations of Keynes's *General Theory*' (Pasinetti 1991b: 427–8). In fact, Keynes seemed to have taken no interest in the topic of Kahn's dissertation and, in turn, Kahn did not pursue the point of assuming imperfect competition when collaborating with Keynes in the writing of *The General Theory*.[17] It has been argued in the literature that Keynes was concerned not to adopt the assumption of imperfect competition, because his main concern of under-employment equilibrium might then be taken to depend on the newly embraced assumption (see discussion in Marcuzzo 1994).

In general, however, and on the particular issue of the importance of Kahn's role in the drafting of the *General Theory*, the evidence shows Pasinetti (and Schumpeter, who first referred to Kahn playing a role approaching that of coauthor) was closer to the mark than Patinkin and Moggridge, who underestimated Kahn's role (see Marcuzzo 2002).

In his 1987 article on Joan Robinson, Pasinetti again shows his flair as an historian of economic thought. His account of characteristic traits of her personality constitutes a lifelike portrait showing a perceptive understanding of that 'mixture of the educational, temperamental and intellectual factors [which] made her one of the leading unorthodox economists of the twentieth century' (Pasinetti 1987b: 213).

The inter-relationship between Robinson and Sraffa has been at the centre of Pasinetti's attention since this article. Pasinetti commented that:

> Piero Sraffa's book appeared too late for Joan Robinson to be able to incorporate it into her analytical framework; and the brave efforts she later made to his effect are not always convincing. At the same time, her *Accumulation of Capital* ventures into fields of economic dynamics which Sraffa does not touch at all. (1987b: 217)

Two questions were raised by Pasinetti both in this article and ten years later.

The first question is why did Robinson always attribute so little importance to the phenomenon of reswitching in her arguments against the theory of the marginal productivity of capital, despite having to some extent 'anticipated' its existence five years before the publication of *Production of Commodities*? The second question is how are we to interpret Robinson's remark that her 'anticipation' of reswitching came as an insight prompted by reading Sraffa's 'Introduction' to Ricardo's *Principles*?

As for the first question, Pasinetti does not give a proper answer, but simply recalls that Sraffa was particularly vexed with Robinson on account of her 'anticipation without analysis' of the curiosum of the neoclassical theory of production, as she had described it in her 1953 article and then later in her 1956 book. Pasinetti's theory is that this vexation accounts for the difficulty Robinson faced in addressing the subject after 1960. Pasinetti (1996a: 215) concluded with the hope that when the Trinity Archive of

Sraffa Papers is opened it would offer further evidence upon which his hypothesis could be verified or not.[18]

Some evidence for Pasinetti's interpretation may in fact be seen in a letter that Sraffa kept in his copy of the *Accumulation of Capital* and which was found amongst his papers, in which Robinson expressed her awareness of her failure to persuade Sraffa of her interpretation:

> Dear Piero: all the work that I have being doing the last 10 years has been much influenced by you – both our conversations in the old days and by your Preface [...] the idea that I had seen in a blinding flash was yours, because it came to me in terms of Ricardo's corn economy; but it was connected with TIME and it now appears is very much alien to your point of view (though to me it seems to fit perfectly well). Since, quite apart from worldly success, I have had a lot of fun. I have a very deep feeling of gratitude to you. The fact that you reject it doesn't affect the case at all. Yours, Joan. (JVR to PS, 18 June 1960, PS papers: D3/12/111/340–1; cit. in Marcuzzo 2005a: 447 n.)

This is confirmation that Robinson dates the insight as to the error in the theory of marginal productivity to 1951. Much more interesting, however, is the clue to what exactly it was that she subsequently saw as being alien to Sraffa's point of view.

In a nutshell, the hypothesis prompted by the letter is that Robinson borrowed from the distinction between 'the two points of view of difference and change', misconstruing it (Sraffa 1951: xlix). This Sraffa reconstructed as the problem addressed by Ricardo, who nevertheless failed to separate the question of the differences in the value of the product due to the conditions of production from that of the change in the value of the product due to variations in distribution.

Robinson identified the distinction between difference and change as contrast and transition between two positions of equilibrium with different quantities of capital: since there can be no knowing whether the quantities of capital are different independently of a knowledge of the rate of profit, we cannot speak of a change, but only of a difference between one equilibrium position and the other (Marcuzzo 2005b: 39–40). For calculation of the marginal productivity, as for transition from one technique to another, a change in the quantity of capital is required, and this necessarily occurs over time. What we can observe—and compare—on the other hand, are two situations with different quantities of capital at the same moment. The reference to 'time' in Robinson's letter to Sraffa can probably be accounted for in this way.

Pasinetti returned to this question only *en passant* in the chapter of his latest book, bearing the fine title, 'The woman who missed the Nobel prize', but added nothing new.[19]

Pasinetti may have dedicated fewer pages to the biographical and interpretative aspects of Kaldor than he did to those of Kahn and Robinson, but they are no less eloquent of the intellectual debt that he recognised as owing to him.[20] Indeed, one of the first essays in intellectual biography by Pasinetti was on Kaldor (1979a),[21] followed in 1985 by a more ambitious paper, which appeared in English (with a few alterations) many years after (Pasinetti 2007). There he paid Kaldor a glowing tribute, arguing that:

> [...] among the major exponents of that school, Kaldor though not originally a pupil of Keynes, was the person who more than anybody else was near to the master, in the global conception of the market economies and in the role which an economist can perform [...] he was a passionate supporter of reforms [and] he was also of the opinion that the defects of the market economies can be corrected by enlightened actions of governments and international cooperation. (Pasinetti 2007: 129–30)

Also, in the case of the smaller group of Cambridge Keynesians the issues of incompatibility of approaches and personal difficulties were a matter of concern for Pasinetti. Between Kaldor on one side and Robinson and Kahn on the other, a taxing atmosphere of tension developed in Cambridge in the 1950s with an uneasy mix of affection, respect, jealousy and rivalry.[22] Kaldor hoped to find in Sraffa 'a sympathetic ear', as we learn from a letter from Geneva addressed to him dated 19 August 1956, immediately after publication of Robinson's *Accumulation of Capital,* in which Kaldor expressed his unwillingness to return to Cambridge the following term because:

> I just couldn't face being bullied by Joan and Kahn about the wonderfulness of Joan's book and how everything must be different from now on! (SP: C/151, cit. in Marcuzzo 2005a: 450n.)

Naturally, Sraffa did not openly take sides with Kaldor and kept well clear of the whole rivalry business. We have no relevant documentation for this, but it seems to me evident and, indeed, noteworthy that Pasinetti was able when at Cambridge at this time to maintain a position of equilibrium and mediation in this environment, which earned him the respect, consideration and friendship of all. The reason for this lies not only in a personal trait but also in Pasinetti's position as an economist and the cultural mission that he had undertaken within the group of Cambridge economists.

11.5 'Cambridge' Economics

The time has come now to consider how Pasinetti interpreted the essential nature of Cambridge economics, impressively combining his flair as an historian with his powers as a theoretician. Let us start with the argument that Pasinetti has propounded since the early 1990s:

> The behaviour of Keynes and the Keynesian group [...] aims at overhauling the foundations of the theoretical structure. The decision has been made to discard and put aside the paradigm of traditional neoclassical theory and lay the foundations for a new construction, a new 'paradigm'. (Pasinetti 1991a: 48)

Here Pasinetti brought in a methodological distinction that, I believe, is indeed the key to understanding the line he has pursued as an historian of economic thought. It is, he wrote, a matter of distinguishing between a 'question of principle' and a 'practical question'. On the evidence of the documents and texts published the former leads to the conclusion that the attitude taken by Keynes and the Cambridge Keynesians was one of 'rejection of the old paradigm and commitment to constructing a new paradigm' (1991a: 49). The latter—which, curiously enough, Pasinetti terms 'practical'—completes the design, filling in the gaps, wiping out the inaccuracies and developing compatible theories. To this task Pasinetti has dedicated all his energies.

Raising these questions at the heart of his 2007 book, Pasinetti held that Joan Robinson, Richard Kahn, Nicky Kaldor and Piero Sraffa formed 'a powerful school on the track of Keynes's economic theory' (2007: 61) and, while recognising that in reality this 'school' consisted of a group in which the strong intellectual and emotional links weighed no less than the differences in culture, attitude and political views, he nevertheless held that there was 'something [...] much deeper, that shaped their intellectual affinities or attractiveness and at the same time gave rise to their strong and stormy personal relationship' (Pasinetti 2007: 63).[23] That 'something much deeper', he held, lay in sharing a common approach to economics. This conclusion, however, is qualified by Pasinetti's assertion that 'Yet one cannot avoid the impression of a fragmentary character of the whole, of a lack of obvious evidence of a unifying overall frame, of an imbalance towards the destructive rather than towards the constructive aspects' (2007: 41).

It seems, then, that if there really is a Cambridge approach to economics, defining it is a task that remains to be accomplished, over and above an examination of the intellectual foundations that characterise what it meant to belong to this group of economists.[24] On this point, Pasinetti seems to concur, having chosen to subtitle his 2007 book 'a revolution in economics to be accomplished'. But I believe it is important to bring it up since it is an issue that has seen and continues to see the economists who identify with the Cambridge tradition divided on the compatibility between the approach taken by Keynes and the Keynesians and that of Sraffa and the neo-Ricardians.[25]

When Pasinetti presents the concept of vertically integrated sectors 'as a quite clear and logical way to accomplish an integration of the two types of economic analysis, associated with the names of Sraffa and Keynes' (1986: 16), he is doing something that is not only legitimate, but also theoretically fecund. But when he goes on to add that these two types of analysis associated with Sraffa and Keynes 'have originally stemmed from the same preoccupations (inadequacy of traditional marginal economics) and have built on the same common ground (classical economics)' (ibid.), he is saddling his proposed reconstruction with a justification that is neither necessary, nor necessarily true. Unlike Sraffa, Keynes was not fiercely opposed to marginal analysis, and he was certainly not enamoured of Ricardo or Marx.

Similarly, when, having written a book to demonstrate that a consistent and common theory can be constructed on the basis of the work done individually by certain Cambridge economists, Pasinetti chooses to entitle it *Keynes and the Cambridge Keynesians*, he is stretching the point since Sraffa, who certainly did not fit the description, is meant to be included. The evidence that there is no common denominator (in terms of theory) enabling us to define a Cambridge school, but rather that Sraffa, Keynes, Robinson, Kahn and Kaldor were a group characterised by cohesion and sharing, is validated by the line of research conducted within the realm of the history of economic thought to which Pasinetti made major contributions, reconstructing the environment that saw concepts and thoughts devised and elaborated by each of the individuals within the group. Interpretation of their individual work and contribution to the pool of ideas identified as the Cambridge school or the Cambridge approach to economics is therefore an exercise in the quest for historical truthfulness. In this Pasinetti also seems to agree, since he writes:

> It is precisely this heterogeneity of feelings and attitudes among the various members of the group that explains their difficulties in acknowledging a comprehensive scheme, which reason and logic would have required from them. Nevertheless I think the *effort must be made, in order to bring these characteristics into sharp relief*, before making any attempt at picking up and trying to sew together the threads of their unaccomplished endeavours. (Pasinetti 2007: 219; my italics)

Historians of the Cambridge group should have no qualms about bringing out the differences, and must continue to cast light on all the evidence that helps us to understand the authors in their historical context. In this theoretical work there is, in a certain sense, more 'freedom' to interpret, integrate and combine concepts and propositions that were quite distinct when formulated.[26] This does not mean making free and easy with the work of the historian, but having a clearer sense of the fact that a different aim is being pursued.

It follows that the search for common elements within the group which could serve as a basis to build a coherent theoretical structure derived from the individual contributions is a legitimate but altogether different exercise, which Pasinetti himself also finds problematic, for he writes:

> The emerging challenge should have been faced long ago by selecting and shaping the theories of Keynes and Sraffa and the developments of Kahn, Robinson and Kaldor (and Goodwin and whoever else have made contributions in the same direction at Cambridge or elsewhere) into a coherent, solid, overall framework. A grand operation of this type has not been accomplished so far. Is this because it is impossible? Or is it because the appropriate time (from any point of view) has been slow to arrive? (Pasinetti 2007: 236)[27]

11.6 Some Final Thoughts

It is part and parcel of the work of the historian to reconstruct theories, personal contributions and circumstances, and the historian must as far as humanly possible respect the context and texts, both published and unpublished. The theoretician, on the other hand, working on the basis of texts and documents but, if necessary, reaching beyond them, takes on the task of constructing a somewhat freer theoretical framework, taking off from the groundwork of the authors studied. In this sense the theoretician is authorised to settle differences and bring together lines underlying different intentions and conceptualisations in the various authors, or in one and the same author.

The theoretical framework to which Pasinetti has dedicated so much of his intellectual efforts is built on his understanding of what Cambridge economics was about and how its scope and aims should be pursued and integrated. As such it is a personal construction which stands, alongside the individual contributions by the Cambridge economists with whom Pasinetti associates himself, as a milestone in the landscape of non-mainstream economics. By its very nature, Pasinetti's construction should not stand in the way of, but rather encourage, further investigations into individual differences and peculiarities within the Cambridge group, including those which may remain to be discovered in the never-ending task of any historical investigation. In this respect, his creative attempt to encompass them in a comprehensive theoretical framework becomes in itself part of their legacy.

Notes

1. He has also dealt with Wicksell and Quesnay, and, more recently, contemporary economists of other schools, like Hicks, Modigliani and Samuelson, recording their features in a varied series of portraits.
2. On the distinction, see Blaug (1999).
3. See Hollander (1979) and Peach (1993, 2001, 2002), for the critique of Sraffa's interpretation, and De Vivo (1985), Kurz and Mongiovi (2002) and Vianello (2002), in its defence.
4. The English edition, *Lectures on the Theory of Production*, was published in 1977.
5. Previously the source on Sraffa had been the book by Roncaglia (1975), the only text combining theoretical analysis with his intellectual biography. Kaldor's 1985 article is clearly subsequent to Pasinetti's and possibly draws on it. In passing, I may add that Kaldor's article contains the improbable conjecture that 'the Editor himself [Keynes] had a hand in the final version' of the 1926 article published in the *Economic Journal* (Kaldor 1985: 624). No such evidence has been found among Sraffa's on Keynes's papers.

6. See, for instance, the *Cambridge Journal Special Issue*: 'New Perspectives on the Work of Piero Sraffa', Volume 36, Issue 6 (November), 2012.
7. This point is not uncontroversial in the literature, especially as far as chapter 17 of the *General Theory*, 'The Essential Properties of Interest and Money', is concerned where some interpreters have seen a clear influence of Sraffa. On Sraffa's annotations in chapter 17, see Kurz (2010).
8. Pasinetti's assertion that Joan Robinson was not entirely successful in assimilating the most important propositions of *Production of Commodities* (1960) does not agree with what is claimed by some Robinson scholars. For a recent evaluation, see Harcourt and Kerr (2009).
9. Pasinetti played a very active part in getting it reprinted in a volume of *Scritti* (that is, 'Writings') by Sraffa for the publishing house il Mulino in 1986 and which was subsequently published in English in the *Italian Economic Papers* of 1992.
10. De Vivo had already outlined the periodisation of the drafting of *Production of Commodities* (1960) in his report to a conference on Sraffa in 1998 (De Vivo 2000: 266–7).
11. The periodisation proposed by Kurz and Salvadori (2005) of 1927–1931, 1941–1946 and 1955–1958, is only slightly different from Pasinetti's.
12. See, for example, an alternative reconstruction by Garegnani (2005) and Rosselli (2005) of the 1927 'watershed'.
13. More recently, Pasinetti (2005, 2006) compares Sraffa respectively with Einaudi and Samuelson and his method on the application of mathematics in comparison with the theoreticians of general economic equilibrium.
14. For a recent defence of Pasinetti's interpretation as being 'a legitimate procedure *in the short period*', see Harcourt (2012: 141).
15. An unpublished letter from Joan Robinson to Richard Kahn dated 18 February 1933 may be used as evidence of Keynes's awareness of the issue: 'Maynard has been trying to find out what the marginal productivity of capital means. He says no reputable writer ever uses it' (King's College Archives, RFK/13/90/1/123–6).
16. I cannot help bringing in a personal note here, for together with Geoff Harcourt, Pasinetti and I ensured that Kahn's papers were kept together, that his 1929 dissertation was published in English, and that, on the other hand, a comment by Kahn on *Production of Commodities*, written during the final years of Kahn's life, should remain unpublished. After his death Pasinetti and I edited together for the Il Mulino publishing house an Italian edition of many of his writings in Kahn (1999).
17. Harcourt (1994: 19) refers to the 'mystery' as to 'why Kahn himself, after having made such remarkable advances in the analysis of actual pricing behaviour in his 1929 dissertation, reverted to short-period Marshallian

theory in his 1931 article and allowed Keynes to do the same in Chapter 21 of the *General Theory*.
18. The Sraffa Papers in the Trinity Archive became available in 1994. Consent to access the archive had yet to be granted as the text was written in 1993, a year before the opening of the Archive, when the book in which Pasinetti's article was going into publication was already in production.
19. Although Pasinetti could draw on neither the Robinson papers nor those of Kahn in his pieces, he nevertheless played a decisive role in preparing the ground for others to do so. Thanks also to his good offices, it has been possible to obtain Bank of Italy funding for the cataloguing of the papers of both (as well as those of Kaldor and Stone) at King's College, the college having declined to bear the financial burden. In return, it was conceded that the microfilms of the papers be given to the Bank of Italy, which then made them available to scholars.
20. The same applies to Richard Goodwin, whom Pasinetti refers to as his 'first teacher' at Cambridge (Pasinetti 1996b: 646).
21. The companion piece in the same year was on Sraffa. See Pasinetti (1979b).
22. For a detailed and scholarly investigation into the relationship between Kaldor and Robinson, see King (1998). King's assessment is that 'it would be quite wrong to think of Kaldor and Robinson as intellectual partners, or even for the most part as close collaborators. Their published work indicates the existence of a certain distance between them, increasing over time to the point of total non-communication and even overt hostility' (1998: 411). His investigation provides further evidence of the difficulty they also had in seeing themselves as part of a common 'school'.
23. Of interest, Pasinetti also commented: 'At the superficial level, it is their determined opposition to the prevailing stream of economic theories and policies that immediately appears as the most striking common feature. But the basic problems remain that of identifying something deeper that can link the many strands of their separate works' (2007: 199).
24. On the definition of 'group' rather than 'school' for the Cambridge economists, see Marcuzzo and Rosselli (2005: 14–5).
25. A sympathetic assessment of the attempts made by Pasinetti is provided by Baranzini and Harcourt (1993: 22) who wrote that '[he] successfully achieved the difficult task of providing a bridge between two different levels of analysis, sharing the same scope but not the method, i.e. that of John Maynard Keynes and Nicholas Kaldor on one side and of Piero Sraffa on the other'. They explained that 'the tentative bringing together of the two complementary schemes' is connected with a) the use of vertically integrated sectors; b) the theory of economic dynamics; and c) the focus on the natural properties of an economic system (1993: 22–24).

26. According to a follower of Pasinetti 'the only way to bridge the gap between Keynes and Sraffa is to set up a coherent set. of principles bringing together the classical view of value and distribution, based upon the labour value principle and the surplus principle of distribution, respectively, and the Keynesian vision of employment and output determination through tire principle of effective demand [...]. This means reasoning, not literally but, in a broad-ranging way, in the spirit of Keynes and Sraffa' (Bortis 2012: 148).
27. He further comments: 'It is indeed surprising to me how insensitive the whole heterogeneous lot of non-orthodox economists have been to the necessity—which appears to me an absolute necessity—of building up an overall, comprehensive, solid, theoretical framework as an alternative to the prevailing orthodox stream' (Pasinetti 2007: 46).

References

Baranzini, M. and Harcourt, G. 1993. 'Introduction' to *The Dynamics of the Wealth of Nations. Growth, Distribution and Structural Change. Essays in Honour of Luigi Pasinetti*. Basingstoke: St Martin's Press: 1–42.

Blaug, M. 1999. 'Misunderstanding Classical Economics: The Sraffian Interpretation of the Surplus Approach', *History of Political Economy* 3: 213–36.

Bonifati, G. and Vianello, F. 1998. 'Il saggio d'interesse come fenomeno monetario e il saggio di rendimento del capitale impiegato nella produzione', in M.C. Marcuzzo and N. De Vecchi (eds), *A cinquant'anni da Keynes: Teorie dell'occupazione, interesse e crescita*. Milano: Unicopli.

Bortis, H. 2012. 'Towards a synthesis in Post-Keynesian economics in Luigi Pasinetti's contribution', in R. Arena and P.L. Porta (eds), *Structural Dynamics and Economic Growth*. Cambridge: Cambridge University Press: 145–80.

De Vivo, G. 1985. 'Robert Torrens and Ricardo's "corn ratio" theory of profits', *Cambridge Journal of Economics* 9: 89–92.

De Vivo, G. 2000. 'Production of Commodities a mezzo di merci: note sul percorso intellettuale di Sraffa', in *Piero Sraffa: Contributi per una biografia intellettuale*, a cura di M. Pivetti, Roma: Carocci: 265–96.

De Vivo, G. 2004. 'Da Ricardo e Marx a Produzione di merci a mezzo di merci', in *Atti dei Convegni Lincei*. Roma: Accademia Nazionale dei Lincei.

Garegnani, P. 2005. 'On a turning point in Sraffa's theoretical and interpretative position in the late 1920s', *The European Journal of the History of Economic Thought* 12: 453–92.

Harcourt, G. 1994. 'Kahn and Keynes and the Making of the *General Theory*', *Cambridge. Journal of Economics* 18: 11–24.

Harcourt, G. 2012. 'Luigi Pasinetti: the senior living heir of the Cambridge School of Economics and the last of the great system-builder', in R. Arena and

P.L. Porta (eds), *Structural Dynamics and Economic Growth*. Cambridge: Cambridge University Press: 137–44.
Harcourt, G. and Kerr, P. 2009. *Joan Robinson*. Basingstoke: Palgrave Macmillan.
Hollander, S. 1979. *The Economics of David Ricardo*. Toronto: Toronto University Press.
Kahn, R.F. 1989. *The Economics of the Short Period*. London: Macmillan.
Kahn, R.F. 1999. *Concorrenza, occupazione e moneta*. Bologna: Il Mulino.
Kaldor, N. 1985. 'Piero Sraffa', *Proceedings of the British Academy* 71: 615–40.
King, J.E. 1998. '"Your position is thoroughly orthodox and entirely wrong": Nicholas Kaldor and Joan Robinson, 1933–1983', *Journal of the History of Economic Thought* 20: 411–32.
Kurz, H. 2010. 'Keynes, Sraffa and the Latter's "Secret Skepticism"', in B. Bateman, T. Hirai and M.C. Marcuzzo (eds), *The Return to Keynes*. Cambridge, Mass: Harvard University Press: 184–204.
Kurz, H. and Mongiovi, G. 2002. 'Interpreting Ricardo: a rejoinder to Peach'. *Cambridge Journal of Economics* 26: 271–80.
Kurz, H. and Salvadori N. 2005. 'Representing the Production and Circulation of Commodities in Material Terms; On Sraffa's Objectivism', *Review of Political Economy* 17: 413–42.
Marcuzzo, M.C. 1994. 'R.F. Kahn and Imperfect Competition', *Cambridge Journal of Economics* 18: 25–39.
Marcuzzo, M.C. 2002. 'The Collaboration between J.M. Keynes and R.F. Kahn from the Treatise to the General Theory', *History of Political Economy* 34: 421–47.
Marcuzzo, M.C. 2005a. 'Piero Sraffa at the University of Cambridge', *European Journal for the History of Economic Thought* 12: 425–52.
Marcuzzo, M.C. 2005b. 'Robinson and Sraffa', in B. Gibson (ed.) *Joan Robinson's Economics*. Cheltenham: Elgar.
Marcuzzo, M.C. 2007. 'Un economista con la passione per la storia. Un ritratto di Luigi Pasinetti per i suoi 77 anni', *Rivista Italiana degli economisti* XII: 107–22.
Marcuzzo, M.C. and Rosselli, A. (eds) 2005. *Economists in Cambridge. A study through their correspondence 1907–1946*. Abingdon: Routledge.
Naldi, N. 2001. 'Piero Sraffa's early approach to political economy: from the gymnasium to the beginning of his academic career', in T. Cozzi and R. Marchionatti (eds), *Piero Sraffa's Political Economy. A centenary estimate*. London: Routledge.
Pasinetti, L. 1974. *Growth and Income Distribution. Essays in Economic Theory*. Cambridge: Cambridge University Press; It. tr. *Sviluppo economico e distribuzione del reddito*. Bologna: Il Mulino, 1977.
Pasinetti, L. 1975. *Lezioni di teoria della produzione*. Bologna: Il Mulino; En. tr. *Lectures on the Theory of Production*. New York: Columbia University Press and London: Macmillan 1977.

Pasinetti, L. 1979a. 'Kaldor, Nicholas, Biographical Supplement', *International Encyclopedia of the Social Sciences*, New York: The Free Press: 366–9.

Pasinetti, L. 1979b. 'Sraffa, Piero, Biographical Supplement', *International Encyclopedia of the Social Sciences*, New York: The Free Press: 736–9.

Pasinetti, L. 1985. 'In memoria di Piero Sraffa: economista italiano a Cambridge', *Economia Politica* 2: 315–31.

Pasinetti, L. 1986. 'Sraffa's Circular Process and the Concept of Vertical Integration', *Political Economy—Studies in the Surplus Approach* 1: 3–16.

Pasinetti, L. 1987a. 'Kahn, Richard Ferdinand', in J. Eatwell, M. Milgate and P. Newman (eds), *The New Palgrave Dictionary' of Economics*, vol. IV, London: Macmillan Press: 1–3.

Pasinetti, L. 1987b. 'Robinson, Joan. Violet', in J. Eatwell, M. Milgate and P. Newman (eds), *The New Palgrave Dictionary of Economics*, vol. IV, London: Macmillan Press: 212–17.

Pasinetti, L. 1991a. 'Dal *Treatise on Money* alla *General Theory*: continuità o rottura?', in J. Kregel (ed.), *Nuove interpretazioni dell'analisi monetaria di Keynes.* Bologna: Il Mulino: 43–51.

Pasinetti, L. 1991b. 'Richard Ferdinand Kahn: 1905–1989', *Proceedings of the British Academy* 16: 423–43.

Pasinetti, L. 1996a. 'Joan Robinson and "Reswitching"' in M.C. Marcuzzo, L. Pasinetti and A. Roncaglia (eds), *The Economics of Joan Robinson*. London: Routledge: 209–17.

Pasinetti, L. 1996b. 'Richard Murphey Goodwin (1913–1996): a pupil's tribute to a great teacher', *The Cambridge Journal of Economics* 20: 645–9.

Pasinetti, L. 1997. 'The Marginal Efficiency of Investment', in Geoffrey Harcour and Peter Riach (eds). *A Second Edition of the General Theory*, vol. 1, London Routledge: 198–218.

Pasinetti, L. 1998. 'Piero Sraffa: an Italian Economist at Cambridge', *Italian Economic Papers*, 1998, vol. 3: 365–83 (English translation of Pasinetti 1985).

Pasinetti, L. 2001. 'Continuity and Change in Sraffa's Thought—An Archival Excursus', in T. Cozzi and R. Marchionatti (eds), *Piero Sraffa's Political Economy—A centenary estimate*. London: Routledge: 139–65.

Pasinetti, L. (with G.P. Mariutti) 2005. *Istituzioni, Mercato e Riforma Sociale*. Atti dei Convegni dei Lincei, n. 274, Roma: Bardi editore: 393–410.

Pasinetti, L. 2006. 'Paul Samuelson and Piero Sraffa—Two prodigious minds at the opposite poles', in M. Szenberg, L. Ramrattan and A.A. Gottesman (eds), *Samuelsonian Economics and the Twenty-First Century*. Oxford: Oxford University Press: 146–64.

Pasinetti, L. 2007. *Keynes and the Cambridge Keynesians: A 'Revolution in Economics' to be accomplished*. Cambridge: Cambridge University Press; It. tr. *Keynes e i Keynesiani di Cambridge. Una 'rivoluzione in economia' da portare a compimento*. Roma-Bari: Laterza, 2010.

Peach, T. 1993. *Interpreting Ricardo*. Cambridge: Cambridge University Press.
Peach, T. 2001. 'Hollander, de Vivo and the "further evidence" for the corn model interpretation of Ricardo: a conspiracy of silence?' *Cambridge Journal of Economics* 25: 685–92.
Peach, T. 2002. 'Interpreting Ricardo: a further reply to Sraffians', *Cambridge Journal of Economics* 26: 281–90.
Roncaglia, A. 1975. *Sraffa e la teoria dei prezzi*. Roma-Bari: Laterza.
Rosselli, A. 2005. 'Sraffa and the Marshallian Tradition', *The European Journal of the History of Economic Thought* 12: 403–24.
Sraffa, P. 1925. 'Sulle relazioni fra costo e quantità prodotta', *Annali di Economia* II.
Sraffa, P. 1951. 'Introduction' to D. Ricardo, *Principles of Political Economy and Taxation*, in P. Sraffa (ed.) with the collaboration of M. Dobb, *Works and Correspondence of David Ricardo*, vol. I, Cambridge: Cambridge University Press.
Vianello, F. 2002. 'The Smithian Origin of Ricardo's Corn-Ratio Theory of Profits: A Suggested Interpretation', *Quaderno di Ricerca*, no. 1, Centro di Ricerche e Documentazione 'Piero Sraffa': Roma.

CHAPTER 12

The "Cambridge" Critique of the Quantity Theory of Money. A Note on How Quantitative Easing Vindicates It

> Economists' understanding of the dynamics of inflation is far from perfect. Reflecting that limited understanding, the predictions of our models often err, sometimes significantly so.
>
> Yellen (2015: 21–22)

Premise In any standard macroeconomics textbooks (i.e., Mankiw and Blanchard to name the most widely adopted), the function of money as a medium of exchange is given prominence and the demand for it is mainly accounted for as a function of the level of income. This quickly establishes that the equation $MV = PT$, or its modified form $M = kPY$, is the key relationship allowing us to determine price levels, at least in the long run. This conclusion is based on the assumptions that:

The author is grateful to an anonymous referee, the editor of the journal, Alessandro Roncaglia, Annalisa Rosselli, and Anna Simonazzi for helpful comments and suggestions.

Originally publ. in: *Journal of Post-Keynesian Economics*, 40 (2), 2017, pp. 260–71. Reprint by Springer Nature Switzerland 2024 with kind permission

M. C. Marcuzzo, *Economic Theories, Protagonists and Facts*, Palgrave Studies in the History of Economic Thought,
https://doi.org/10.1007/978-3-031-63949-4_12

1. The velocity of circulation is constant;
2. The supply of money is exogenous;
3. Variations in the quantity of money have only a short-term effect on output, which in the long run always reaches full employment level;
4. The function of store of value can be neglected.

In Keynes's ([1936] 1973) *General Theory* we find an alternative approach to money and price-level determination, the seeds of which were already planted by Alfred Marshall, cultivated by his followers at Cambridge in the 1930s, and remained the consensus view well into the 1960s. But Milton Friedman and the Monetarists of the 1970s managed to rehabilitate the approach based on the quantity theory and to win over the joint assault later launched by Richard Kahn and Nicholas Kaldor from the House of Lords, in the media and academic journals of the time. In the 1990s, New Classical economists joined forces in favor of restatement of the quantity theory, with Robert Lucas famously summarizing the implications of the theory, writing, "in the long run, money growth should be neutral in its effects on the growth rate of production and should affect the inflation rate on a one-for-one basis" (Lucas 1995: 665).

The restatement of the quantity theory was part of an anti-Keynesian climate that was there to last. For almost forty years the quantity theory regained its hegemony in the academic and economic discourse (traces of it remaining in standard textbooks), whereby the central bank, which is responsible for the supply of money, is said to be able to manage the inflation rate.

Even in macroeconomics textbooks of the so-called neo-Keynesian orientation, we find that an increase in the quantity of money through its effect on spending causes only a short-run increase in output; any increase in output beyond the natural or NAIRU level, brought about by expansionary policies that entail an increase in the nominal stock of money, keeps pushing wages and prices up until the real quantity of money is back to its initial level. So, rather than an alternative approach to price-level determination, the Keynesian approach appears to complement the quantity theory, and is thus valid to explain short-term fluctuations in output and prices.

In the past few years, the quantitative easing (QE) experiment has given us exceptional data to test the validity of this argument. Unlike the influx of silver in sixteenth-century Europe—which is said to have induced belief in the validity of the theory—the unprecedented expansion of the monetary base by the Bank of Japan, Federal Reserve, and European Central Bank have hardly produced any effect on price levels, but only on asset prices. On the contrary the corresponding average annualized inflation rate over that same period, as measured by the personal consumption expenditures price index, not only did not rise, but in the case of Japan and the eurozone showed signs of declining.

Trying to estimate the effects of QE on the economy is said to be difficult because "a host of factors will have been affecting the economy during the crisis period, when most QE programmes are launched [...] most estimation methods require 'heavy' assumptions (e.g., about transmission mechanisms at work) that can dramatically affect the results" (Gros et al. 2015: 20). However, the evidence of no link between monetary expansion and inflation is overwhelming, and most commentators have resorted to "financial frictions" together with "zero-interest rate lower nominal bound" to explain it. As a result, the quantity theory approach is not discarded but said just not to apply in these particular circumstances.

As Brad de Long put it:

> At the zero-interest rate lower nominal bound, [the QT-based] Fisher-Friedman framework breaks down. With no opportunity cost to holding wealth in money rather than in other short-duration safe nominal assets, there is no reason for changes in the money stock to induce any changes in the flow of spending at all. Anybody seeking to model nominal and real income determination must then find another, alternative equilibrium condition to focus on. (De Long 2015)

Furthermore, the vice president of the European Central Bank admitted that "No technical traditional monetarist channels were operating. They did not work either in other cases. This implies that QE is not about the traditional monetarist channels but about new ones, namely signalling and portfolio rebalancing due to financial frictions" (Costancio 2015).

The evidence vindicates old and present critics of the quantity theory and points to the liquidity preference theory as better able to explain the facts: when money is being held as a store of value at the margin, the money banks receive from QE primarily pads out their cash reserves. The financial system has not reacted to the injections of liquidity by augmenting lending and thereby increasing the money supply, while the private sector has been deleveraging and not increasing its borrowing. From both supply and demand considerations, therefore, the link between M (money supply) and *P* (average price) of the quantity theory is severed. The relevant aspect of demand for money neglected by the quantity theory approach is what Keynes called the "speculative" motive, that is, the propensity to hold it in face of uncertainty or negative expectations on future interest rates, leading to possible capital losses. Money is not held for transaction purposes only, but also for its store of value property, as protection against uncertainty. This role of money derives from its liquidity, of which money has more than any alternative asset.

So we must turn to the notion of liquidity to find the appropriate theoretical framework to understand why reasoning based on the quantity theory leads us on a false track.

Kahn and Keynes: Before the General Theory A good starting point is a passage from the Preface to the French edition of the *General Theory,* dated February 1939:

> The following analysis registers my final escape from the confusions of the Quantity Theory, which once entangled me. I regard the price level as a whole as being determined in precisely the same way as individual prices; that is to say under the influence of supply and demand [...]. The quantity of money determines the supply of liquid resources and hence the rate of interest. (Keynes [1936] 1973: xxxiv–xxxv)

Kahn gave the reconstruction of the gradual abandonment of the quantity theory by Keynes in his Mattioli lectures.

> Keynes' long struggle over a period of six years to produce a version of the *Treatise* worthy of publication was directed partly to an escape from the stranglehold of the Quantity Theory of Money in its crude form [...]. Nevertheless, Keynes seems to have been so much under the spell of the Quantity Theory that he could write about his Fundamental Equations as though they were "versions" of the Quantity Theory. (Kahn 1984: 56)

However, in May 1940, the year after publication of the preface to the French edition, we find Keynes writing to Kahn: "I enclose as a specimen the letter I wrote on Christmas Eve, 1917, which is interesting for two reasons—[...] (ii) the fact that even then I was thinking in terms of supply and demand and not of the quantity theory of money!" (RFK 13/57:460).[1]

There were two steps in the process of Keynes's abandonment of the quantity theory approach: the determination of the price level on the basis of aggregate demand and supply and that of the rate of interest on the basis of supply and demand for money. Kahn's multiplier article (Kahn 1931) opened the route toward a price level determination based on aggregate supply and demand curves in providing the terms for analysis of the conditions that see an increase either in the level of prices or in the quantities (or a combination of the two) in aggregate given an increase in demand (in this case, public investments in road building). In fact, these were the appropriate conditions to evaluate the proposal made by Keynes in "Can Lloyd George Do It?" dating to 1929, to implement public works policy as a way out of economic depression. If the level of demand is high, then the productive capacity will already be made good use of, and greater use will entail an increase in costs and thus in prices. But if, on the other hand, the level of demand is low, then plant and equipment will be largely idle and production can therefore be stepped up without any appreciable increase in unit costs and prices (Keynes [1929] 1972).

Although its application was limited there to the consumption goods sector it was clearly a step forward from the *Treatise* framework to the *General Theory*. Kahn himself stated:

> I regard the most important part of my article as being quite different from the view normally taken of it. I dealt with the effect of a higher level of demand on the price-level of consumption-goods by introducing the concepts of the supply curve, and demand curve, of consumption-goods as a whole. This is symptomatic of the *new method*, to be introduced by Keynes eventually in the early drafts of the *General Theory*, of determining price-levels of "output as a whole," or rather consumption-goods and capital-goods as a whole, in terms of demand and supply. (quoted in Patinkin 1993: 659nl7; emphasis added)

Extension of this analysis to output as a whole was accomplished in the discussion of the aggregate supply function as we find it in the lectures given by Kahn in Michaelmas Term 1932, as recorded in the notes taken by Lorie Tarshis.[2] To derive the aggregate supply curve, Kahn starts from determination of the supply cost of each level of output for a single firm. Given marginal and average costs, associated with a given level of output, the supply curve tells us what the price must be in order for the firm that maximizes its profits to be willing to produce precisely that level of output. Unlike the multiplier article, the expected proceeds necessary to induce entrepreneurs to produce a given output are on the vertical axis, while the level of output on the horizontal axis. The aggregate supply curve, drawn in the expected proceeds-aggregate output space, allowed for a straightforward derivation of the level of prices as the ratio of expected proceeds to output. Thus the same forces determine the levels of price and output, with no room left for the quantity of money.

Keynes acknowledged Kahn's contribution:

> It was Mr. Kahn who first attacked the relation of the general level of prices to wages in the same way as that in which that of particular prices has always been handled, namely as a problem of demand and supply in the short period rather than as a result to be derived from monetary factors. (Keynes [1936] 1973, Appendix: 400fn)

In fact, Kahn's opposition to the quantity theory precedes Keynes's and we have evidence of his disdain for it in his letters to Keynes from America (during Kahn's visit from December 1932 to April 1933) where Kahn gives his opinion on the dominant influence of the quantity theory of money in the United States. For instance, he wrote: "I am thinking that the only way to save humanity is to lead a campaign against the Quantity Theory" (JMK L/K: 36[3]). And in a paper he presented to the Political Economy Club when he returned, he added: "the scourge which goes by the name of the Quantity Theory of Money has swept the country" (RFK 3/18/3:15); "my visit to the United States inclines me to ascribe most of the ills of the world to the Quantity Theory of Money" (RFK/3/18/3:16).[4]

By mid-1933 Keynes had grasped the concept of effective demand, although the "precise definition of what is meant by it," was announced to Kahn only one year later,[5] but what was still lacking was the framework in which the different elements of his new theory—the liquidity preference, the output-adjustment mechanism and the wage theory—fit logically together, and provide an alternative determination of the price level and the rate of interest. For this we have to turn to the *General Theory*.

The General Theory In chapter 21 of the *General Theory*, Keynes presents his theory of the determinants of the price level and shows how it stands in relation to the quantity theory and the conditions under which the result of the strict quantity theory—a proportional increase in prices as a consequence of an increase in the quantity of money—actually holds. First, there is the effect of a change in the quantity of money on effective demand and then how the change in effective demand spends itself in increasing output and prices. In other words, the elasticity of changes in prices (P) with respect to a change in the quantity of money (M) is given by the elasticity of changes in effective demand with respect to changes in the quantity of money times the elasticity of changes in prices with respect to changes in effective demand.

Formally

$$e\left(=\frac{M}{P}\frac{dP}{dM}\right)=e_d e_p$$

It is immediately evident that if effective demand increases in the same proportion as the quantity of money, that is, if we assume a constant ratio between effective demand and the quantity of money, namely, if $e_d\left(=\frac{M}{D}\frac{dD}{dM}\right)=1$ prices will increase in the same proportion as the increase in effective demand (D), whenever $e_p\left(=\frac{D}{P}\frac{dP}{dD}\right)=1$ The derivation of e_p gives $e_p = 1 - e_e e_o(1 - e_w)$, where $e_o=\left(\frac{N}{O}\frac{dO}{dN}\right)$ is the elasticity of output in response to changes in employment, $e_w=\left(\frac{D}{W}\frac{dW}{dD}\right)$ is the elasticity of money-wages in response to changes in effective demand, and $e_e=\left(\frac{D}{N}\frac{dN}{dD}\right)$ is the elasticity of employment in response to a change in effective demand.

We then have:

$$e=\frac{M}{P}\frac{dP}{dM}=e_d\left[1-e_e e_o\left(1-e_w\right)\right],$$

$$e=e_d\left(1-e_e e_o+e_e e_o e_w\right).$$

The above expression, according to Keynes, can be regarded as "a generalized statement of the Quantity Theory of Money" (Keynes 1973: 305). Thus the quantitative result is made dependent upon the values of four critical elasticities:

e_d = liquidity factors that determine the demand for money in each situation;
e_w = labor factors that determine the extent to which money-wages are raised as employment increases; and
$e_e e_o$ = physical factors that determine the rate of decreasing returns as more employment is applied to the existing equipment.

Thus, if the public holds a constant proportion of their income in money,

$$e_d = 1$$

if money wages are fixed $e_w = 0$;
if constant returns prevail $e_e e_o = 1$; and
if there is full employment either of labor or equipment, $e_e e_o = 0$.

In fact, there are many conditions under which $\frac{M}{P}\frac{dP}{dM} = 1$. For instance, if $e_d = 1$ and $e_w = 1$, but also:

if $e_d = 1$, $e_w = 0$ and $e_e e_o = 1$

or

if $e_d = 1$ and $e_o = 0$

and of course a variety of other combinations.

However, "on plausible assumptions relating to the real world," according to Keynes, it is very unlikely that the elasticity of the price level with respect to a change in the quantity of money will turn out to be equal to 1, and therefore it is "safe to make the generalization [that] e as a rule [is] less than unity" (Keynes [1936] 1973: 306).[6]

Keynes provided us with a description of a transmission mechanism in which behavioral relationships are ordered according to a clear chain of causes and effects. As Kahn later put it, the novelty of the approach is the view of the monetary and credit mechanism as "a matter of straightforward cause and effect expressed in terms of physical realities" (Kahn [1958] 1972: 145).

The transmission mechanism from monetary to real factors is broken down into a series of steps, which may lead to very different outcomes. For instance, an increase in the quantity of money may not generate a proportional increase in effective demand; the increase in effective demand may not give rise to a predictable rise in wages, and the rise in output and employment and prices may occur in various combinations so that there is more than only one possible outcome.

Keynes's generalization of the quantity theory follows a line of reasoning similar to that employed in the theory of income determination: the quantity theory results apply under very *special conditions:* far from being a general proposition it can be applied in very special circumstances that rarely occur in the real world.

It might well be, however, that the attempted reconciliation with the tradition, as in many other instances of Keynes's tactics against the orthodox view, ended up serving its rehabilitation, as indeed in the aggregate demand (AD) and aggregate supply (AS) models. These models—of which there is more than one variety resulting in a distorted interpretation of Keynes's ideas[7]—became popular in the late 1980s, following the joint effect of monetarism first and the inability of the so-called Keynesian models (IS-LM with Phillips curve) to explain double-digit inflation with unemployment. It was also the effect of the lost battle engaged in by Keynes's close followers against the reinstatement of a quantity theory-based approach.

Kahn and Kaldor: Against the Two Blades of the Monetarist Scissors Already in his "Some Notes on Liquidity Preference," Kahn ([1954] 1972) had outlined the basic elements of his understanding of the working of financial markets. According to his view, in the financial markets there are two kinds of investors: those who hold definite expectations for the future of interest rates and those "who do not have a clue" whether the rate of interest is going to increase or decrease. The same division exists in the mind of the investor himself, who can reveal contradictory preferences and decide to hold money and securities at the same time, while rational behavior (and expected utility theory) would imply a definite choice between the two. Based on this observed behavior, Kahn argues that a finite elasticity of the demand for money relative to the rate of interest is associated not only with the heterogeneity of opinions held by the public divided between bulls and bears but also with the lack of conviction individuals show in their own conjectures. It is as if bullish and bearish sentiments "operated inside each person's mind, one being responsible for his holding securities and one for his holding money" (Kahn [1954] 1972: 88).

So the liquidity preference is not a relationship that can be assumed to be stable. It follows that changes in the supply of money bring about changes in the interest rate only if the schedule of the liquidity preference can be thought of as a stable relationship. However, this is precisely Kahn's main point, that is, "the unsuitability of thinking of a schedule of liquidity preference as though it could be represented by a well-defined curve or by a functional relationship expressed in mathematical terms or subject to econometric processes," and he held Keynes responsible for giving way "to the temptation to picture the state of liquidity preference as a fairly stable relationship" (Kahn [1954] 1972: 90).

In his evidence to the Radcliffe Committee, Kahn restated the argument in relation to the efficacy of monetary policy, since the quantity of money necessary to bring about a fall in the rate of interest varies with the circumstances and the state and responsiveness of the market, where expectations play a crucial role. "If the market likes to help by altering its expectations [...] the authorities will not have to do so much. If the market proves very obstinate and does not believe that they are going to succeed in doing what they are trying to do, then they will have to do much more" (Kahn 1958: 742–743).

In this respect, as observed by Dardi (1994: 104), Keynes and Kahn shared the same conception of monetary policy, not as "the engineering of aggregate variables but a *policy of opinion.*" As for the determination of the level of prices, Kahn insisted that his approach "differs fundamentally from those treatments of the subject which attribute to the quantity or supply of money a direct influence on prices, or an indirect influence on wages and so on prices" (Kahn [1958] 1972: 145); the level of prices, as in Keynes, being the outcome of three factors: "the level of money wages, the state of productive equipment and technical knowledge and efficiency, and the level of demand" (ibid.: 137).

Kaldor also tackled the issue against monetarism from the angle of the supply of money,[8] challenging the alleged exogeneity that is the presupposition of the quantity theory equation. He went so far as to assert that even Keynes, who "retained traces of his old beliefs" in the *General Theory,* is to blame, since "the supply of money is treated as an exogenous constant in the same way as in the quantity theory" (Kaldor 1985: 8).

Kaldor's ideas on the money supply and monetary policy can already be found in his "Speculation and Economic Stability" (Kaldor [1939] 1960).[9] He pointed out that the quantity of money in a credit economy comes into existence as a result of bank lending and is extinguished through the repayment of bank loans; this volume of bank lending is limited only by the availability of creditworthy borrowers. Accordingly, the money supply becomes a passive element varying automatically with the demand for credit.

He developed these points in his evidence to the Radcliffe Committee (Kaldor [1958] 1964) and in several papers in the 1970s and 1980s, where he attacked the monetarist view. The basic error of the quantity theory-based arguments lay—according to Kaldor—in the "assumption that regards the money supply as the *source* of the demand for goods and services" (Kaldor 1985: 4). So, according to Kaldor, the increase in the supply of money in circulation is the response to increased demand and not an autonomous event. Without credit expansion, the Central Bank's willingness to expand the monetary base will not produce effects on the money supply.[10]

In conclusion, the bottom lines of Kahn's and Kaldor's criticisms, are leveled against the two fallacies of the quantity theory-based argument: the assumptions that the money supply is exogenously determined by the monetary authority and that the demand for money, as a proportion of income, is a stable one. Deprived of the two blades of the scissors, the demand and supply of money as independent and stable functions can hardly be considered useful for determining the price level, even assuming a level of income close to full employment.

The notion of liquidity is at the center of the Cambridge critique of the quantity theory; it amounts to denying the separation between monetary and real factors (monetary neutrality) and the determination of the level of price as the outcome of the interplay of a transaction demand for money and an exogenously given money supply.

Conclusion If the quantity theory holds, as long as the velocity of money remains stable, the rate of inflation should equal the difference between the growth rates of money and real gross domestic product. To confront this hypothesis with the data, Graaf (2008) referred to a panel comprising yearly data from 1991 to 2005 across 105 countries and concluded, "these analyses leave no doubt that for our sample period, i.e., the years since 1991, the classical proportionality theorem does not hold." And even more disheartening is the conclusion reached by the author at the end of his review of recent empirical literature on the validity of the quantity theory: "both sceptics and proponents of the quantity theoretical explanation of inflation can refer to sound evidence to support their claims" (Graaf 2008: 26).

Today, the all-time record of money growth expansion by the Bank of Japan, Federal Reserve, and European Central Bank offers an exceptional experiment for testing what has been the pièce de résistance of macroeconomics since the 1970s. We have enough evidence to conclude that quantity theory is a bad predictor of inflation and—at least according to Friedman's own methodological prescription—should be dismissed on this ground.

Even a strong supporter such as Martin Feldstein was forced to admit quite recently: "The low rate of inflation in the United States is a puzzle, especially to economists who focus on the relationship between inflation and changes in the monetary base" (Feldstein 2015: 1; see also Tutino and Zarazaga 2014).

On the other hand, the quantity easing experiment has proved the validity of the Keynes-Kahn-Kaldor arguments: markets have been flooded with liquidity, but rather than inflation we have witnessed a general deflation because of the liquidity trap environment in which the banking system operated, and we observe only inflated asset prices. It is the liquidity preference theory—namely, the idea that the speculative motive is the key determinant of the demand for money in a context of uncertainty—that offers the explanation: if money is being held as a store of value at the margin, the money that banks receive from Central Banks primarily pads out their cash reserves, without ever really entering the economy and therefore having little impact on the price level and real income. The private sector is also struggling to remain liquid in the face of uncertainty and looking for opportunities in asset rather than goods markets.

So two forces are at work: banks' liquidity preference and absence of borrowers in the private sector for investment in the real sector. As Koo remarked:

> Even though a central bank can always inject as much liquidity as it wants into the banking sector via QE, for that money to actually enter the real economy the banks must lend money [...]. But if the private sector as a group is deleveraging, this liquidity cannot enter the real economy because of an absence of borrowers. This means the liquidity remains trapped within the financial system, leaving the central bank with no way to expand the money supply in the real economy. (Koo 2016)

While all major central banks now, at least in practical terms, have shelved the quantity theory since the early 2000s, it has not been dislodged in textbooks and its critics have been too little acknowledged. I hope this note will be seen as a small contribution to rehabilitating the insights of John Maynard Keynes, Richard Kahn, and Nicholas Kaldor.

Notes

1. Kahn Papers, King's College Archives, Cambridge.
2. An outline of Kahn's lecture notes can be found in Kahn's papers (RFK 4/15/4-14).
3. Keynes papers, King's College Archives, Cambridge.
4. Kahn's criticism of the quantity theory before the General Theory is illustrated by what Joan Robinson refers to as his "Quantity Equation for Hairpins." It is worth quoting the relevant passage from her 1933 article: "Let P be the proportion of women with long hair, and T the total number of women. Let $1/V$ be the daily loss of hairpins by earn women with long hair, and M the daily output of hairpins. Then $M = PT/V$ and $MV = PT$. Now suppose that the Pope, regarding bobbed hair as contrary to good morals, wishes to increase the proportion of long-haired women in the population, and asks a student of economics what he had best do. The student sets out Mr. Kahn's equation, and explains it to the Pope. 'All you need do,' he says, 'is to increase M, the daily output of hairpins (for instance, you might give a subsidy to the factories) and the number of long-haired women is bound to increase.' The Pope is not quite convinced. 'Or, of course,' the student adds, 'if you could persuade the long-haired women to be less careless, V would increase, and the effect would be the same as though the output of hairpins had increased'" (Robinson [1933] 1951: 55). See Marcuzzo (2002a).
5. "The fundamental assumption of the classical theory, 'supply creates its own demand,' is that $OW = OP$ [W= marginal prime cost of production when output is 0; P= expected selling price of this output; OP= effective demand] whatever the level of O, so that effective demand is incapable of setting a limit to employment which consequently depends on the relation between marginal product in wage-good industries and marginal disutility of employment. On my theory, $OW \neq OP$ for all values of O, and entrepreneurs have to choose a value of O for which it is equal;—otherwise the equality of price and marginal prime cost is infringed. This is the real starting point of everything" (Keynes [1936] 1973: 422–423). On these and other points addressed here, see Marcuzzo (2002b).

6. Even Keynes, however, appears to be sceptical about the reliability of such a mechanical description: "I do not myself attach much value to manipulations of this kind; and I would repeat the warning, which I have given above, that they involve just as much tacit assumption as to what variables are taken as independent (partial differentials being ignored throughout) as does ordinary discourse, whilst I doubt if they carry us any further than ordinary discourse can" (Keynes [1936] 1973: 305).
7. For a review of the flaws of AS/AD analysis, see Colander (1995).
8. Also Kaldor in his evidence to the Radcliffe Committee (1958) denied that the velocity of circulation could ever be assumed to be constant and determined by factors that are independent of the supply of money or the volume of money payments (see Targetti 1992: 273).
9. Kaldor himself made this claim in an interview to the present author: "I already explained my ideas on the endogeneity of the money supply in 1939" (Kaldor 1986: 73).
10. Drawing on Kaldor, Wray (1990: 73–74) summarized the point: "money is supplied because someone wants it. Money supply and money demand are simply different sides of the balance sheet. From the firm's point of view, money demand is the willingness to go into debt, and money supply is the IOU it issues. Of course, the firm's IOU is not money unless someone is willing to accept it. From the bank's point of view, money demand is indicated by the willingness of the firm to issue an IOU, and money supply is determined by the willingness of the bank to hold that IOU and to issue its own liabilities to finance the purchase of the firm's IOU".

References

Colander, D. (1995), "The Stories We Tell: A Reconsideration of AS/AD Analysis." *Journal of Economic Perspectives*, 9, 169–188.

Costancio, V. (2015), "Panel Discussion on Central Banking with Large Balance Sheets." *2015 US Monetary Policy Forum*, New York. Mimeo, February 27, mimeo.

Dardi, M. (1994), "Kahn's Theory of Liquidity Preference and Monetary Policy." *Cambridge Journal of Economics*, 18, 91–106.

De Long, B. (2015), "On the Fed's Policy of Quantitative Easing Coupled with Promises Not to Let Prices Recover Any of the Ground Relative to Trend They Lost in the Recession: Hoisted from Three Years Ago." Mimeo, January 29 (availableathttp://equitablegrowth.org/feds-policy-quantitative-easing-coupled-promises-not-let-prices-recover-ground-relative-trend-lost-recession-hoisted-three-years-ago/).

Feldstein, M. (2015), "The Inflation Puzzle." (available at www.project-syndicate.org/commentary/low-inflation-quantitative-easing-by-martin-feldstein-2015-05).

Graaf, M. (2008), "The Quantity Theory of Money in Historical Perspective." *KOF Swiss Economic Institute Working Paper*, Zurich.

Gros, D., Alcidi, C. and De Groen, W. (2015), "Lessons from Quantitative Easing: Much Ado About So Little?" *CEPS Policy Brief* no. 330.

Kahn, R.F. ([1931] 1972), "The Relation of Home Investment to Unemployment." In *Selected Essays on Employment and Growth* (pp. 1–27). Cambridge: Cambridge University Press.

Kahn, R.F. ([1954] 1972), "Some Notes on Liquidity Preference." In *Selected Essays on Employment and Growth* (pp. 72–96). Cambridge: Cambridge University Press.

Kahn, R.F. (1958), "Minutes of Evidence Memorandum of Evidence submitted to the Radcliffe Committee." HMSO, London, pp. 739–746.

Kahn, R.F. ([1958] 1972), "Memorandum of Evidence Submitted to the Radcliffe Committee." In *Selected Essays on Employment and Growth* (pp. 124–153). Cambridge: Cambridge University Press.

Kahn, R.F. (1984), *The Making of Keynes's General Theory.* Cambridge: Cambridge University Press.

Kaldor, N. ([1939] 1960), "Speculation and Economic Stability." In *Essays on Economic Stability and Growth* (pp. 17–58). London: Duckworth.

Kaldor, N. ([1958] 1964), "Monetary Policy, Economic Stability and Growth." In *Essays on Economic Policy* (pp. 128–153). London: Duckworth,.

Kaldor, N. (1985), "How Monetarism Failed." *Challenge*, 28, 4–13.

Kaldor, N. (1986), *Ricordi di un economista*, ed. by M.C. Marcuzzo. Milan: Garzanti.

Keynes, J.M. ([1936] 1973), *The General Theory of Employment, Interest and Money.* In E. Johnson and D. Moggridge (eds.), *The Collected Writings of J.M. Keynes*, vol. 7. London: Macmillan.

Keynes, J.M. (1973), *The General Theory and After.* Vol. 13 of E. Johnson and D. Moggridge (eds.), *The Collected Writings of J.M. Keynes.* London: Macmillan.

Keynes, J.M. ([1929] 1972), "Can Lloyd George Do It?" in E. Johnson and D. Moggridge (eds.), *The Collected Writings of J.M. Keynes*, vol. 9 (pp. 86–125). London: Macmillan.

Koo, R. (2016), "Why US Quantitative Easing Worked' Better Than Other QEs." *FT, Alphaville*, July 19.

Lucas, R. (1995), "Nobel Lecture: Monetary Neutrality." *Journal of Political Economy*, 104, 661–682.

Marcuzzo, M.C. (2002a), "The Demise of the Quantity Theory of Money." *History of Economic Ideas*, 10, 49–62.

Marcuzzo, M.C. (2002b), "The Collaboration Between J. M. Keynes and R. F. Kahn from the *Treatise* to the *General Theory.*" *History of Political Economy*, 34, 421–447.

Patinkin, D. (1993), "On the Chronology of the *General Theory.*" *Economic Journal*, 103, 647–663.

Robinson, J. ([1933] 1951), "The Theory of Money and the Analysis of Output." In *Collected Economic Papers*, vol. 1. Oxford: Blackwell.

Targetti, F. (1992), *Nicholas Kaldor: The Economics and Politics of Capitalism as a Dynamic System.* Oxford: Clarendon Press.

Tutino, A. and Zarazaga, C. (2014), "Inflation Is Not Always and Everywhere a Monetary Phenomenon." *Economic Letters* 9, Federal Reserve Bank of Dallas, June.

Wray, R. (1990), *Money and Credit in Capitalist Economies: The Endogenous Money Approach.* Aidershot: Edward Elgar.

Yellen, J. (2015), "Inflation Dynamics and Monetary Policy" The Philip Gamble Memorial Lecture, University of Massachusetts, Amherst (available at www.federalreserve.gov/newsevents/speech/yellen20150924a.htm).

CHAPTER 13

Dear John, Dear Ursula (Cambridge and LSE, 1935). Eighty-eight Letters Unearthed

Introduction Eighty-eight letters were unearthed while sifting through the Hicks papers at the library of the University of Hyogo, Japan, in December 2003.[1] They had been written between September and December 1935, when John Hicks left the London School of Economics (LSE)[2] for Cambridge, having being appointed university lecturer and fellow of Gonville and Caius College, while Ursula (then Webb) was at the

We would like to thank Irini Liakopoulou, Alexandra Saunders, and Emiliano Vendittelli for invaluable research assistance; and Mauro Baranzini, Roger Backhouse, Daniele Besomi, Victoria Chick, Guido Erreygers, Omar Hamouda, Donald Moggridge, Nerio Naldi, Tiziano Raffaelli, Alessandro Roncaglia, and Annalisa Rosselli for comments, suggestions, and help in clarifying various matters. We are also particularly indebted to Sue Howson for her precious help in reconstructing the events and circumstances referred to in the letters. For the relevant information about the people whose names are mentioned in the chapter, we drew extensively on Besomi (2003), Howson (2005), and Moggridge (1992). An earlier version of this chapter, together with the eighty-eight letters between John and Ursula, can be found in Hirai et al. (2005).

Originally publ. in: (With Eleonora Sanfilippo), in R. Scazzieri, A.K. Sen and S. Zamagni (eds.) *Markets, Money and Capital. Hicksian economics for the 21st century*, Cambridge: Cambridge University Press, 2008, pp. 72–91.
Reprint by Springer Nature Switzerland 2024 with kind permission

M. C. Marcuzzo, *Economic Theories, Protagonists and Facts*, Palgrave Studies in the History of Economic Thought,
https://doi.org/10.1007/978-3-031-63949-4_13

LSE, where she had been a student from 1929 and was currently a member of the staff. The letters cover the three months preceding their wedding, which took place in London, on December 17, 1935.

It is a daily exchange, with just the odd interruption marking the days when they would visit each other (mostly at weekends) either in Cambridge or in London. It is a portrait of a marriage in the making, a picture of an academic milieu and a glimpse into British society in the 1930s.

It may be objected that making them public is barely justified by the copyright permission obtained with purchase of the papers, but we sincerely hope that disclosure of them will be accepted as a tribute to—rather than an intrusion into—their relationship.

A few words of justification are also needed on the relevance of the correspondence in reconstructing ideas as well as facts. Most of our understanding of the past is heavily dependent on the sources we have access to. The failure to grasp concepts and debates occurring in more or less remote times is due to our reliance on contemporary language and mindset, and to a lack of knowledge sufficient to place those concepts and debates in their context.[3] Correspondence offers the opportunity to approach opinions, ideas, and feelings in the appropriate setting; it also opens the way for us to retrieve information long wrapped in oblivion. And, of course, it satisfies curiosity—a form of indulgence that is nevertheless the prime mover of any historical investigation.

Cambridge and the LSE What were Cambridge and the LSE like in the mid-1930s? Much has been written about the rivalry between the two economics faculties, divided by style of teaching, intellectual climate, theoretical approaches, and politics. Above all, perhaps, it was a matter of personalities: the domineering influence of John Maynard Keynes and his pupils on the one hand, and Lionel Robbins and Friedrich Hayek with their supporters on the other. The way discussion was organized between students and staff is also worth comparing. First of all there were the two seminars, Robbins's on Monday afternoon (Howson 2005: 22) and Keynes's every other Monday in the evenings during term time.[4] According to one of the accounts by a contemporary, A. K. Dasgupta:

> Lionel Robbins would allocate papers on subjects topical because of some important publication [...] to about eight research students [and] teachers would also be present. The papers would be read, then 'cyclostyled' and discussed in a kind of second-reading debate a week later. Over tea, groups would be formed to discuss a particular paper further in considerable detail.

> Sometimes one paper remained on the seminar agenda for several weeks, with Robbins in the Socratic role [...] In the end, Robbins would turn to the teachers. 'Hicks, do you have anything to say?' Sometimes he did, and sometimes he did not. (Dahrendorf 1995: 298)

Keynes's political economy seminar ('Keynes's club') was run in a different fashion. According to Lorie Tarshis, who was a student there in 1935:

> Kahn [was] invariably present with a sprinkling of other faculty members [...] Sometimes academics from outside Cambridge attended too [and] there was a contingent of students, a very few research students amongst them and perhaps ten or twelve undergraduates. [A paper was read by Keynes or a distinguished visitor, and students whose slips had been drawn were expected to stand up and comment on it; see Plumptre 1947: 370–1; Moggridge 1992: 189; and Skidelsky 1992: 5.] After the students had made their remarks, we all were served tea and fruit cake. Then Keynes asked each of the faculty members and distinguished visitors present whether he wished to speak. And after that Keynes stood up. [...] Sometimes – I guess usually – the paper and the discussion that followed it were merely the springboard from which after gentle criticism and encouragement for the students who had participated, he jumped into any or many related topics – with a wit, a grace and an imagination that were a joy to experience. (Patinkin and Leith 1977: 50–1)

From the many accounts and recollections (see Robbins 1971; Coase 1982; Hicks 1979, 1982a; Kaldor 1986; Thirlwall 1987; Shehadi 1991; Hamouda 1993; Dahrendorf 1995; and Hayek [1963] 1995) we can infer that Robbins's seminar was more cosmopolitan, attracting mostly Continental scholars and visitors passing through London, while Keynes's seminar was much more imbued with the clubby atmosphere that permeated Cambridge societies and colleges. Moreover, the two theoretical approaches favored at the LSE and Cambridge could not be farther apart. Hicks recalls of himself and his LSE colleagues:

> [W]e seemed, at the start, to share a common view point, or even a common faith. The faith in question was a belief in the free market, or 'price mechanism' that a competitive system, free of all 'interferences,' by government or monopolistic combinations, of capital or of labour, would easily find an 'equilibrium.' [...] Hayek, when he joined us, was to introduce into this doctrine an important qualification – that money (somehow) must be kept 'neutral,' in order that the mechanism should work smoothly. (Hicks 1982a: 3)

By contrast, Austin Robinson's account of the making of the Keynesian revolution brings to light the loss of faith in the market mechanism, neutrality of money, and laissez-faire. In particular, he writes: 'We learned to distinguish very clearly [...] between those propositions that are universally true and those propositions that are only true in conditions of full employment [...] [What we learned] was really the integration of value theory and monetary theory into what we now call macroeconomics' (Robinson 1985: 57).

In the mid-1930s the clash between the two faculties of economics was in full spate, with some people totally integrated, others—such as Nicholas Kaldor and Abba Lerner—on the verge of leaving one camp for the other, and yet others—Dennis Robertson, to name but one—already feeling misplaced in their own territory. Meetings between economists from London and Cambridge and academic seminars were more frequent than ever before, providing an arena for confrontation and challenge.

Besides Robbins's and Keynes's seminars there were the much older 'London Political Economy Club,' founded in 1822 (Skidelsky 1992: 22; see also Moggridge 1992: 172), and the 'Economic Club,' attended by people from the LSE and Cambridge and, more generally, economists working in London. The latter was founded in 1891 and was held for a period of time at University College London (*Twenty-eighth Annual Report of The Economic Club* and letter from B. Lander to J. Mair, October 10, 1923, in BEV[5] papers Suppl. 376; see also Moggridge 1992: 175). In 1923—while William Henry Beveridge was president—the Economic Club moved to the LSE[6] (letter from B. Lander to J. Mair, October 12, 1923, in BEV papers Suppl. 376). To these should be added at least three more, extensively referred to in the correspondence between John and Ursula—as we shall see: the so-called 'Joint Seminar,' which started in November 1935, involving mainly research students (but also senior economists) from the LSE and Cambridge; the 'Cambridge Graduate Seminar' (known as 'Sraffa's seminar'), which also saw the occasional participation of people from London; and 'Hayek's seminar,' addressed specifically to Hayek's students.[7]

Let us now look more closely at this environment, where our two characters will be seen living, working, and loving each other, exchanging between themselves accounts of their feelings.

The Meeting Grounds Since the early part of 1933 the younger generations from Cambridge and the LSE had been seeking a meeting ground 'to get together behind the backs of their embattled seniors' (Robinson 1951: viii). In October 1933 a new journal was launched—*The Review of Economic Studies*', the 'children's magazine,' as it was referred to in the correspondence between Keynes, Joan Robinson, and Richard Kahn (see, for example, the letter from J. Robinson to Keynes, September 28, 1937, in JMK[8] papers CO/8/232–5, and the letter from J. Robinson to Kahn, September 13, 1933, in RFK papers 13/90/1/253–5). According to Kaldor, '*The Review* was conceived as an outlet for young writers. Its continuance depended on the extraordinary energy of two people, Abba Lerner and Ursula Webb, who organized printers, produced estimates, read all the proofs and recruited subscribers' (Kaldor 1986: 41).

The most colorful account of one of the meetings of the group behind *The Review* is by Joan Robinson:

> [A] weekend meeting was arranged at an inn half-way between London and Cambridge. Cambridge was represented by Kahn, Austin Robinson and myself, and James Meade who had been back in Oxford for a year [...] Abba Lerner brought three contemporaries (none of whom remained in the profession). It was agreed that there should be no appeal to authority; every point must be argued out on its merits. At the first session, James explained the multiplier; Kahn, who came later, went over it again. Then it was the turn of London. They said that before they could discuss employment they must analyse what would happen if everybody confidently expected that the world was coming to an end in six months' time. [...] The point was to distinguish what capital goods could be consumed in six months, by ceasing replacements from what would have to be left. [...] Next day, Abba asked to go over the multiplier argument. With some help, he repeated it correctly and seemed to be convinced. His companions were quite shocked and were seen afterwards walking him up and down the lawn, trying to restore his faith. (Robinson 1979: xv)

Quite rightly, Ursula commented to Joan Robinson: 'There is something at work emotional or extra-economic, hindering a clearer understanding I really think' (letter from Ursula to J. Robinson, November 13, 1933, in JVR papers vii/201/1).

The confrontation between the two camps was felt as a threat to either group's identity, which had been built up under the spell of Robbins and Keynes. While Cambridge people, notably Keynes, Kahn, Joan Robinson, and Piero Sraffa, each of them with his or her own agenda, were attacking traditional economic beliefs and customs, the LSE people, Hayek, Robbins, Hicks, Allen, and Kaldor were establishing an orthodoxy, based on general equilibrium and intertemporal analysis, highly formalized, and derived from first principles.

There were, in particular, two dividing issues. The first was whether it was legitimate to analyze imperfect competition within a partial equilibrium approach, with no consideration for strategic interaction among agents, as Joan Robinson and, to some extent, Kahn were prepared to do, against which Hicks and Kaldor were raising objections (Rosselli and Besomi 2005).

'I think the problem of imperfect competition is harder, and less important than you do,' wrote John Hicks to Joan Robinson three months after the publication of *The Economics of Imperfect Competition* (Robinson 1933) (letter June 15, 1933, in JVR papers vii/200/1). He maintained the same point later, when writing to her reviewing the matter for his monopoly article (Hicks 1935b): 'I think the real difference between us is that you are more optimistic than I am about the application of the theory of imperfect competition, just because you think that theory is simpler than I do' (letter February 28, 1935, in JVR papers vii/200/25).

The second dividing issue related to the direction of causality between saving and investment and whether it should be reversed when money was explicitly taken into account. Again, it was Ursula who neatly summarized the 'differences' between the two lines of approach:

> I think all the younger people at the school [the LSE] are prepared to admit that saving doesn't directly lead to investment in a monetary economy and that this may have important deflationary effects *at least when uncertainty is rampant* – but this doesn't convince us that investment is not made via monetary saving. (letter from Ursula to J. Robinson, November 13, 1933, in JVR papers vii/201/2: emphasis in original)

By the autumn of 1933 Keynes had abandoned the approach taken in the *Treatise* and was rapidly moving toward that of *The General Theory*, pressed by criticisms and help by Kahn and, to some extent, Joan Robinson and Sraffa (Marcuzzo 2002). Discussion outside the 'inner circle' continued to revolve around the *Treatise*, whose approach had not been greeted favorably by Hicks: writing to Joan Robinson he bluntly remarked, 'I don't like the *method* of analysis [of the *Treatise*]' (letter July 12, 1933, in JVR papers vii/200/12: emphasis in original). Not surprisingly, Hicks's dislike 'for the method of fundamental equations' (letter August 16, 1933, in JVR papers vii/200/19) was shared by Robertson, who was finding in him an ally against the upsurge of the Keynesian revolution.

When his appointment to a lectureship to Cambridge was finalized,[9] however, Hicks was looking forward to the 'improving facilities for thrashing out our differences,' as he wrote to Joan Robinson, adding—with a degree of wishful thinking—that they were 'in any case tending to diminish' (letter February 28, 1935, in JVR papers vii/200/23).

As from November 1935 the Joint LSE and Cambridge Seminar crossed the *Review* board meetings, providing a further outlet for confrontation between the two groups. The Joint Seminar crossed, in particular, with Ursula's activity around *The Review*, organizing the issues and attracting people.[10] In a letter dated November 12, 1935, Ursula wrote to John: 'The following weekend we must have Pearsall[11] on the Sat.[urday] 23, as we are having Douglas [Allen][12] and possibly Maurice Allen[13] on the Sun. [day] (It is the Review weekend).'And on November 13 she wrote to him: 'I had a most friendly note from Hitch,[14] congratulating us. He is evidently very pleased to be asked to join the Review Board [...] and he wants to bring in Oxford to the Joint Seminar, which would be excellent.'[15]

The Move to Cambridge According to Robbins's *Autobiography*, 'Beveridge's insensate hostility to pure theory' forced John in 1935 to leave for Cambridge (Robbins 1971: 129).[16] Hicks, typically, put it rather differently, writing—almost forty years afterwards—that '[b]y 1935, I got so much [from the LSE, where he had been member of staff since 1926] that I needed to go away to put it together. Thus when an opportunity arose for moving [...] I took it' (Hicks 1972).

The opportunity[17] was a post as lecturer at the faculty of economics in Cambridge,[18] for which Pigou warmly invited him to apply.[19] It has been argued (Hamouda 1993) that Hicks had been appointed, under the influence and initiative of Robertson and Pigou, to rein in Joan Robinson, who was all too obsessively propagating the Keynesian creed. This circumstance—according to Omar Hamouda's interpretation—would explain the coldness that Robertson apparently showed toward Hicks when he arrived at Cambridge, as Robertson wanted to avoid any public appearance of being particularly close to Hicks.

On the question of obstructing Joan Robinson's career, the evidence is that, when Keynes stepped in to prevent her proposal to give a course on money for two terms from being turned down (letter from Keynes to C. R. Fay, March 5, 1935, in JMK papers UA/14.2), Pigou supported him and a compromise was reached.[20]

What seems more likely is that Pigou, eager to maintain a certain degree of 'academic pluralism,'[21] favoured Hicks's election in the interest of achieving readjustment between the different orientations within the economics faculty, as well as counteracting Robertson's growing isolation (see Sanfilippo 2005). What is certain is that Robertson felt psychologically supported by Hicks's arrival in Cambridge, and it appears no coincidence that both decided to leave Cambridge at more or less the same time, in the autumn of 1938 (Hicks for Manchester University and Robertson for the LSE).

On the question of the supposed coldness shown toward Hicks by Robertson when they were both at Cambridge, the correspondence between John and Ursula suggests that contact between them was fairly regular: there are several references to Hicks's coming to visit Robertson, discussing with him his papers and work, and being invited by him to a Trinity feast (see, for example, the letters from John to Ursula, October 9 and 28).

Robertson's attitude may be interpreted not as coldness but as the intention to protect Hicks against the growing climate of hostility surrounding him because of his staunch opposition to *The General Theory.* This interpretation finds support in an interview with Hicks in 1983: 'The feud between Keynes and Robertson had already erupted. And they had already sort of cut the relationship, and Robertson kept out of Hicks's way. Hicks told me that was very sweet of Robertson, because Robertson thought that if he was seen associating with Hicks it would be held against him' (N. Shehadi, 'Interview to John Hicks,' 1983, History of LSE Archive, 5).

What is unquestionably true is that, in Cambridge, Hicks felt 'much closer to Robertson than to any other economists' amongst his seniors (Hicks 1982b: 127), not only from a theoretical point of view but also at a personal level, so that he felt himself 'to be temperamentally much closer' to Robertson 'than to the Keynesians' (ibid.).

Hicks supervised about eighteen students of Gonville and Caius College (John to Ursula, October 8), his favorites among them being an American, M. F. Millikan,[22] and a Hungarian, P. T. Bauer.[23] He had a more or less covert agenda, as far as teaching was concerned, with the intention of 'spreading what I think to be sound doctrine among research students here.' He wrote enthusiastically that 'apparently they are already having a prolonged battle about the measurability of utility!' (John to Ursula, November 11).

His interest in 'spreading the sound doctrine' is attested by his willingness to do extra teaching, besides lecturing and supervising: 'I fixed up at the lecture to take a private class of half a dozen of the more promising people coming to my lectures; they want to discuss Indifference Curves, and it will be just as well for me to get to know them' John to Ursula, November 12). Ursula, of course, endorsed the project and provided the necessary encouragement: 'The process of making Cambridge take notice is really progressing very nicely' (Ursula to John, November 12).

While in Cambridge (1935–1938) Hicks lectured on the principles of economics,[24] labor problems,[25] and some leading Continental economists,[26] and was examiner in the tripos for three years.[27] His teaching in the Cambridge faculty left Keynes with a somewhat negative impression. On June 15, 1939, the year after Hicks's departure for Manchester University, Keynes wrote to Pigou:

> I am just at the end of the Tripos examining. The general standard is lower than anything I have previously struck for Part II. The appalling ignorance of even the more intelligent candidates must be partly, I think, due to the breakdown of the curriculum last year through illness and leave of absence. And Hicks's teaching of the Principles has, I think, definitely confused the men and put them further back than as if they had had no such instruction.[28] (In JMK papers EJ/1/6/5–7)

Let us now turn to the issues that were topical in Cambridge and the LSE while the correspondence between John and Ursula was in course.

The Issues Debated During Michaelmas Term 1935 During Michaelmas term 1935 *The General Theory* was going through its final stage. The previous June Keynes had sent the second proofs to Harrod, Hawtrey, Kahn and Joan Robinson. A few of their comments survive, but Hicks is not mentioned in any of the correspondence they exchanged. Moreover, in the letters between John and Ursula there is no reference to the process of the final drafting of Keynes's book.

Hicks must surely have been a total outsider as far as the genesis and evolution of Keynes's ideas from *The Treatise* to *The General Theory* were concerned, which does not, however, mean that their theories (as developing in the spring of 1935) were entirely devoid of points of contact. On the contrary, this letter from Keynes to Hicks, dating to April 2, 1935, clearly testifies a theoretical convergence between their researches, at least on the matter of expectations:

> Your point about the effect of the expectation of the future on current readiness to invest[29] has not yet been published, to the best of my belief, and is on rather similar lines, as I said, to what I shall be publishing in the autumn. I should rather like you to get this on record before my book[30] comes out in the autumn. (Catalogue of the Hicks papers at Oxford, 63)

While writing *The General Theory* Keynes found enthusiastic support in Cambridge from his 'inner circle' (Kahn, J. Robinson, and, much later, Harrod) but strong opposition from his otherwise close friends Sraffa and Robertson. The beginning of 1935 saw Robertson and Keynes engaged in extensive discussion of the first proofs. After reading them Robertson made a swingeingly forthright remark: 'A large part of your theoretical structure is still to me almost complete mumbo-jumbo' (letter February 10, 1935, in Moggridge 1973a: 506).

In particular, three main analytical points underlay the controversy that saw Keynes and Robertson on opposite sides. First of all, there was the question of method. Robertson was accustomed to using a kind of sequential analysis as the only way to address the problems of economic fluctuations, cycle, depression, and, generally speaking, dynamics. He found it hard, for example, to accept Keynes's approach whereby the current level of saving was seen as a function of current income without any reference to the past level of savings—as, indeed, it was hard for him to imagine a theory of investment in which the latter was not linked to the saving decisions made in the previous periods. For the same reason, he had some doubts about the mechanism of the multiplier of investment and, in general, the short-period method, both of which Keynes derived from Kahn. He could not understand how the effect of the multiplier on income could prove instantaneous. Nor was he able to see how Keynes could speak of differences between effective demand and aggregate demand without using any kind of intertemporal method.

The second question concerned the rate of interest. Despite Keynes's arguments to the contrary, Robertson (as in his article in *The Economic Journal*: Robertson 1931) continued to consider the rate of interest as the price bringing the demand and supply of loanable funds into equilibrium, and to consider money like every other good from the point of view of the determination of its price, pointing out that Keynes's theory of liquidity preference put undue emphasis on the speculative motive, at the expense of the transaction motive, for demanding money.

Third came the question of cycle versus long-term stagnation. Keynes was above all concerned with the problem of the tendency of contemporary capitalist economies toward a condition of persistent underemployment of resources, while Robertson, on the other hand, remained ever preoccupied with the 'old' question of business cycle. On at least two of these points (the first and the third), Hicks would surely have been on Robertson's side rather than Keynes's (see, for example, Hicks 1936a, 1956, 1973).

As from March 1935 Robertson's position in Cambridge became rather difficult. There is an interesting exchange between Robertson and Hicks in 1936 showing just how badly the situation had deteriorated. Robertson, commenting on Hicks's review of *The General Theory* (Hicks 1936a), wrote to Hicks:

> It will be a comfort to find somebody who thinks there is a great deal in this book [*The General Theory*] and with whom nevertheless one can discuss – for *entre nous* my trouble is that with the author and his more whole-hearted disciples I can no longer discuss but only be made to feel obsolete and pig-headed for not having seen the light! (Letter May 20, 1936, in DHR papers C4/1.7)

Hicks replied: 'Indeed, I think our differences are less formidable than I feared they might be. I am in whole-hearted agreement with you about the critical view of the book. It is quite nonsense to pretend it is as new as it pretended' (letter May 21, 1936, in DHR papers C18/29.1–2).

Robertson also accused Hicks of having forgotten—together with Keynes—that Pigou and Marshall, in their works, had already dealt with the crucial role of expectations in the economy; Hicks defended himself, writing: 'I am particularly sorry that I should have led you to suppose that

I had joined the ranks of the forgetters' (ibid.; see also Mizen and Presley 1998).

In Michaelmas 1935, however, there might have been at least one possible point of convergence between Hicks and Keynes, the latter having, in the meantime, become very appreciative of Knut Wicksell. He had solicited Kahn's translation of Wicksell's *Interest and Prices,* still in the proof stage at the time. Keynes wrote to Kahn: 'Old Wicksell comes out of it, I think, extraordinarily well. Even at this time of day there are very few dull pages, and he is wonderfully on the right track. It's odd how little influence it has had, and how little progress along these obviously fruitful lines was made in the 30 years after he published it' (letter September 8, 1935, in RFK papers 13/57/137). Hicks would have been pleased but hardly in agreement with this statement, as he had been one of the first to take notice of the Swedish approach (see Hicks 1979; Thirlwall 1987: 25; and Hamouda 1993).

Another admirer of the Swedish economists was Gottfried Haberler, who was on a short visit to the United Kingdom.[31] A controversy had raged between him and Kahn the previous year, and was probably renewed during his visit to Cambridge, as it is hinted at in Hicks's account to Ursula: 'Haberler come to tea, after what I should imagine was a stormy encounter with Kahn at lunch. Our discussion was not at all stormy; we had some pleasant talk about cycle *policy,* where I don't think we had any strong disagreement' (John to Ursula, October 22).

The controversy between Haberler and Kahn (also involving Harrod and, to some extent, Robertson) ran basically on different definitions of saving and the role of inequalities between saving and investment in explaining the cycle. Haberler was closer to Hayek on this, considering saving as a prerequisite for investment; Kahn, on the contrary, had accepted Keynes's reversion of the causality between saving and investment implicit in the multiplier mechanism (Besomi 2000: 359–65). Ursula also showed acceptance of the Hayekian framework of Haberler's analysis:

> We had quite an interesting discussion with Haberler at Hayek's seminar – mostly on the point as to whether a 'horizontal maladjustment'[32] would cause a cumulative deflation – he basing the argument that it would, on the time lag necessary before new investment could take place in other lines, and hence a contraction in the demand for credit and factors would first occur. (Ursula to John, October 23)

Finally, in the autumn of 1935, Joan Robinson was busy writing some 'riders' (Robinson 1979: 185–6) from *The General Theory* and debating with Sraffa whether the rate of interest can actually be negative in a monetary economy (letters December 9 and 11, 1935, in JVR papers vii/43/10–13). The point is related to her 'The Long-period Theory of Employment' and its companion piece, 'The Concept of Zero Saving,' which was included in her *Essays in the Theory of Employment* (Robinson 1937). Once again, it is noteworthy that Hicks—who had just published his 'Suggestion for Simplifying the Theory of Money'—was apparently not consulted by Joan Robinson, and certainly was not cited.[33] It was obvious that Hicks was not going to get a good hearing from Keynes's pupils.

The Letters This correspondence helps fill in the picture of the events and circumstances referred to above. This new evidence comes to us in the form of fragments that can be used to fit in a missing element or fill a gap in the story. For instance, we now have a better understanding of how seminars were organized and their relevance as meeting grounds for young people from Cambridge and the LSE.

There was a proposal, referred to by Ursula, to schedule the 'Cambridge Graduate Seminar' for Sunday 2.30–4.00 to 'give the London people a chance to attend when they liked' (Ursula to John, October 16). It was called 'Sraffa's seminar,' thought it is not clear whether—as was the case with the Cambridge 'circus' (Robinson 1978: xii)—he had been the initiator ('Lerner says Sraffa has promised to be sort of unofficial chairman'; Ursula to John, October 16), or it was related to his being the newly appointed assistant director of research (Marcuzzo 2005), or simply because he was appreciated also by people at the LSE, since—according to Kaldor—his 1926 article had been much discussed at Robbins's seminar (Kaldor 1986: 39).

We also have Ursula's reports of the other seminars, mentioned above. In a letter by Ursula to John, dated November 8, she wrote:

> We had the first Joint Seminar tonight – 26 turned up, of which from Cambridge [David] Champernowne, Bensusan-B[utt],[34] Stone, Singer,[35] Lamberti.[36] We got Fleming[37] to lead off *faut de mieux* at short notice, and a rather technical discussion arose on the imputation of output to various input functions. I think we shall probably do better to stick to monetary theory. But there is no doubt we have got some very good people.

On the London 'economic club' she wrote: 'The Economic Club was quite fun (You are to be made an Honorary Member)—the discussion mostly went on the usefulness of Tintner's[38] assumption that demand depended on price and the rate of change of price. [...] Edelberg[39] once more demonstrated that he had more unknowns than anyone else' (Ursula to John, November 13).

In general, Ursula was anxious that Hicks should attend seminars: 'Will you come to the Joint Seminar Sun.[day]? Hayek will probably be there and probably Sraffa. We shall have to finish up discussing Fleming's article, and then Cambridge must have a look in. We think of "What fixes the rate of interest"' (Ursula to John, November 12). Hicks was reluctant: 'I am a bit shy of turning up at the Sunday seminar without being asked from this end. Do you really think one ought?' (John to Ursula, November 13). Hicks was not too keen on seminar-hopping. On one occasion, he had even failed to realize 'that there was an Economic Club meeting,' wondering 'who was speaking, and what happened' (John to Ursula, November 13). He was more at ease in conversation with selected interlocutors.

As for Hicks's relations with colleagues in Cambridge, we have some interesting accounts. With Pigou he had found it easy to talk economics:

> The thing to do is never to press him, or argue with him; just throw out a remark to see if it tempts him. Then I said to him that I thought the Stationary States [Pigou 1935][40] would be easier to read if he had used more geometry; he said he didn't like geometry, because it was always making you leave out important variables; again he instanced Joan's book as a case in point. It is funny what a general equilibrist he is at bottom! (John to Ursula, October 14)

With Sraffa he seems to have hit it off from the outset: 'Sraffa has been showing me some of his Ricardo treasures' John to Ursula, October 23). He also reported that they 'were in precise agreement' (John to Ursula, October 24) about the paper presented by Joan Robinson at the Political Economy Club meeting on October 21 (see below).

With Kahn and Joan Robinson it was a different story. They had taken upon themselves the task of disseminating Keynesian ideas and launched a campaign of 'tutorage,' whether they were requested to do so (as in the case of Kahn and Harrod; see Besomi 2000: 360–7) or out of proselytizing passion (as in the case of Robinson; see Rosselli and Besomi 2005). This brought strong reactions from people in Cambridge and outside;

some we already know very well (for instance, the reactions of Robertson, Pigou, Robbins, and Hayek), and we can now add John and Ursula to the list. The day after Joan's performance at Keynes's club, John reported to Ursula:

> It was one of the indigestible papers[41] – whole series of rather complex propositions read out rather rapidly – and it left most people pretty bewildered. As far as I could make out – and this is due to subsequent reflection, it was really a fantasia on the Robertsonian theme of satiability of wants, decked out in Keynesian colours, and culminating in a fantastic world where you increased employment 'in the long period' by raising the rate of interest in order to decumulate capital. As a matter of fact, Keynes' own contribution was much more sensible than that of his disciple. He concluded that even if these anticipated perils of too much equipment materialise, and obviously he didn't regard them as very pressing, there were really dozens of things you could do to prevent them becoming serious. (John to Ursula, October 22)

Keynes's opinion of the paper was strikingly different (as was Lerner's[42]). He wrote to Joan Robinson: 'I thought your paper at the [Political Economy] Club was crystal clear and extremely interesting' (letter October 24, 1935, in Moggridge 1973a: 652).

Ursula's reaction was attuned to John's:

> We had a discussion on Joan's paper, at Department tea – on the basis of what Tintner and Lerner had gathered (which didn't agree very well) and what Haberler and I had gathered from you. I loved your description. It doesn't seem to worry either Joan or Kahn that their assumptions are entirely fantastic and in this respect they are on a par with Lerner: one set of assumptions is as worthy of discussion as another. (Ursula to John, October 23)

In the case of Joan Robinson, one cannot help feeling that some misogyny on the part of her colleagues was also at work. It has been noted elsewhere that Robinson

> brought a touch of novelty, her intellectual vitality, temperament and looks attracting attention unknown to the tradition of Cambridge economists. Marshall's wife, who died four years before women were officially accepted in the University of Cambridge in 1948, offered the model of the woman economist who remained a wife in the shade of her husband. Robinson also

> expressed those unconventional attitudes and social criticism that had Cambridge overlapping with Bloomsbury (although this was very much the reserve of King's and Trinity men) [in its] rejection of conformism lapsing into eccentricity. (Marcuzzo and Rosselli 2005: 12)

Pigou's reaction to their getting married is also revealing of the attitude toward women: 'He showed considerable interest in our affairs,' wrote John to Ursula, on October 14; 'we had really maligned him previously. The truth was that the idea of a female economist at once suggests Joan to him. He is really very attached to Austin, and very sorry for him! I assured him that my future wife has a wider range of conversational subjects.' Ursula's reaction shows how she herself thought that a woman economist should behave: 'The poor creature [Pigou] has simply no defences against a woman like Joan. If he can be brought to talk to me I shall try and win his heart by talking about mountains or something like that' (Ursula to John, October 14). At the same time, her approach to women's issues and feelings was awkward: 'The Review sends you its best congratulations on the daughter,' she wrote to Joan Robinson after the birth of her first child. 'It must be a tremendous relief to have all the bother *over*, or terrific fun speculating on the child's capacities and future' (letter July 7, 1934, in JVR papers vii/201/5).[43]

Ursula's style and personality made it particularly difficult for her to penetrate Cambridge diversity. She had not a clue about Sraffa: 'I am sure if one could only get at him he would be most congenial. It is just he wants a quiet life, so doesn't say out loud when he disagrees' (Ursula to John, October 25). At the same time, she was intimidated and annoyed by Joan Robinson.[44] Moreover she was aware that that there was some special bonding among Cambridge people from which she was excluded: 'Dennis Robertson turned up at tea'—she reported—'and I had a very good talk with him, he was much more oncoming than ever before, almost as one Cambridge person to another' (Ursula to John, November 19).

Cambridge was so different that Robertson invented an adjective to describe it: *Cambridge-y*. In a previous work (with A. Rosselli) one of us describes it thus:

> More than in a shared theory, the identity of this group is rooted in motivations, values and habits: perhaps it is common lifestyles and work styles that most aptly and tellingly express these aspects. By work styles we mean the importance attached to correspondence and oral discussion in the process of

> forming ideas and drawing up texts – authoritativeness and authority founded on an internal hierarchy that does not necessarily reflect seniority in terms of age or academic qualification. By lifestyles we mean the importance ascribed to personal relations, affording a framework for scientific intercourse, which explains how so many theoretical divisions left ample safe ground for reciprocal respect and affection. (Marcuzzo and Rosselli 2005: 15)

For the Hickses, 'belonging to Cambridge' was never a goal, but perhaps—we may conclude—it was never an option either.[45]

A Marriage in the Making 'Their marriage was a marriage of opposites. He was shy, she was outgoing; she was direct, he was subtle. She protected him and organized their lives. Their loyalty to each other was unswerving.' So Robin Matthews (1994: 13) depicts the enduring and 'ever-green' union between John and Ursula.

Many personal recollections by generations of scholars from all over the world who had the opportunity to become acquainted with the Hickses directly and visit their house (see, for example, Hamouda 1993; Samuelson 2001; and Simkin 2001) reflect the image of a couple still much involved in each other and very well suited. We cannot read into the letters, which were exchanged during the three months before their marriage, the secret recipe of so fortunate a relationship, which belongs entirely to the protagonists and their capacity for renewing their mutual interest over the years, but we can glean some of the ingredients of their successful encounter.

First and foremost, it was a matter of intellectual companionship: she was evidently fascinated by John's brilliance of mind, and he was attracted by her energy and determination, as well as her capacities. They were both stimulated by the opportunity to share in depth their interest in economics.[46] This was not all, though. They had much in common:[47] their passions for poetry (see, for example, the references to Dante Alighieri and John Donne, in the letters they exchanged on October 9 and 10), literature in general, and theater, as well as their interest in political affairs. They also shared the same curiosity about visiting other countries and finding out about different cultures, which saw them traveling far and wide around the world.

In addition to all this, they held genuine physical attraction for each other. They shared their existences profoundly and in all respects, participating in each other's family events and professional successes or failures.

Ursula never missed a chance to let him know how very proud she was of him and his scientific and academic achievements.[48] He, too, took a close interest in the development of her career, as for example when Ursula wrote to him (letter December 3) that her teaching job at the LSE would not be renewed,[49] and he replied: 'I am so sorry to hear… about your lectures. […] I hope you are not too disappointed. But let us comfort ourselves by the thought that it would anyhow have been only a temporary arrangement, and the main job of seeing that you do in the future get some teaching, will certainly have to go in other directions' (John to Ursula, December 4).

She was also protective and supportive toward him in a manner and to a degree that could not simply be put down to the fact that she was eight years his senior.[50] She genuinely liked taking care of him, well aware of his real needs, intelligently reinterpreting without actually questioning the traditional role of a wife of the times.

From the letters we also know that she was in charge of all their financial affairs; she also took care of all the details in fitting out their house, called Campden,[51] which they had just bought in September 1935, and of organizing their wedding party. She guided him in all practical questions, and he seemed perfectly happy to follow her directions scrupulously. For all these reasons we can well imagine the aching loneliness John must have experienced when she died in 1985, four years before him.

Concluding Remark The sheer richness of this correspondence, greatly enhancing our knowledge of the Cambridge and LSE environment of the period, has helped us—as indeed we hope it will help our readers—to overcome the feeling of a breach of privacy, of intimacy violated. It confirms the importance of primary sources in dealing with historical matters and therefore of the invaluable worth of personal archives. They should be preserved and made public, to record the past and to foster knowledge, as best we possibly can.

Notes

1. The research was undertaken by M.C. Marcuzzo and A. Rosselli as part of a joint project with the Japanese group on Cambridge economists, in collaboration with T. Hirai, Y. Hakamata and T. Nishizawa (see www2u.biglobe.ne.jp/~olympa/cambridge/hyoushi/), who made possible access to

and digital reproduction of the letters. The letters were later catalogued, indexed and transcribed by E. Sanfilippo. Copyright of the correspondence between John and Ursula Hicks is with the University of Hyogo.

2. Hicks taught at the LSE from 1926 to 1935 (Hicks 1982b: 5).
3. Personal papers are among the most important archival sources for historians. It is a shame to disperse them in separate batches. The Hicks papers—like the Harrod papers, which were sold in seven batches (see Besomi 2003: xxxi)—are, sadly, a case in point. They are at present divided into two batches, one held at the University of Hyogo, the other at the Hicks Foundation in Oxford.
4. Robbins's seminar started in 1929 (Robbins 1971: 131; Howson 2005: 3) and Keynes's seminar yet earlier, around 1909 (Skidelsky 1992: 5).
5. References to the Beveridge Papers are given as BEV, according to the classification of the catalogue of the London School of Economics Archives, London.
6. According to the 'rules' of the club, '[I]ts object [... is] the study of Economics' and the 'Club meetings are held on the Second Tuesday in each month at 8 p.m.' The list of the members in 1922 included, for example, Beveridge (president from 1922 to 1924), Harold Laski, and Marjori Tappan Hollond from the LSE, Keynes, Herbert Foxwell, and Alfred Marshall from Cambridge, and members of the Treasury such as Ralph Hawtrey and Henry Higgs (*Twenty-eighth Annual Report of The Economic Club*, in BEV papers Suppl. 376). In November 1935—when John and Ursula corresponded—Hayek was elected as president of the 'Economic Club,' and Hicks had just resigned as one of the honorary secretaries. In 1936–1937 some of the members, besides Hicks and Beveridge, were Lionel Robbins, G. L. S. Shackle, and Nicholas Kaldor, and also R. G. D. Allen, Hugh Dalton, and Evan Durbin (*Forty-first* and *Forty-second Annual Report of The Economic Club*, in BEV papers Suppl. 376).
7. For a reconstruction of the seminars that took place in that period at the LSE, see also McCormick (1992: 29).
8. References to the Keynes, Kahn, Kaldor, J. Robinson, and Dennis Robertson papers are given as JMK, RFK, NK, JVR, DHR respectively, according to the classification in their respective catalogues at King's College and Trinity College, Cambridge.
9. From the Faculty Board Minutes: 'The Appointments Committee meeting of Monday 18th February 1935 unanimously agreed to offer the vacant lectureship to Mr J. R. Hicks as from October 1st 1935, and to recommend to the General Board that the probationary period of 3 years be waived in Mr Hicks's case, in view of his academic standing and teaching experience in the University of London' (FB Mins. V. 118, 27).

10. Kaldor confirms that these seminars were reserved to research students and sometimes coincided with a meeting of *The Review* board (Kaldor 1986: 41).
11. Charles William Pearsall (1880–1939), economist from South Africa.
12. Sir Roy George Douglas Allen (1906–1983), economist and mathematician.
13. William Maurice Allen (1908–1988), economist.
14. Charles Johnston Hitch (1910–1995), economist.
15. According to a contemporary witness, 'subsequently "Oxford" was added to the seminar's title [London and Cambridge Economic Seminar] and it sometimes met there' (Brown 1988: 36). An indirect confirmation of it can also be found in the oral recollection of Elizabeth Durbin, reported in Ebenstein (2001).
16. This dislike of theoretical economics is confirmed by Beveridge's comments on the activities of the economics department at the LSE, quoted by Robbins in his 'Note on the Director's Reflections' (probably of November 1935), in which Beveridge is reported as saying: 'The academic developments [theoretical and mathematical] of the school within the range of my special interests [economics] have not been those which I myself should have favoured' (NK papers 2/31/102).
17. From the Faculty Board Minutes: 'The Appointments Committee meeting of Friday 23 November 1934 unanimously agreed to advertise in the Reporter that the Committee expect shortly to appoint to a University Lectureship, covering economics, economic history, or political science. Applications to be submitted by 1st February 1935' (FB Mins. V. 118, 13).
18. As from October 1, 1935, the list of members of the Cambridge faculty of economics was as follows: A. C. Pigou (professor of political economy), D. H. Robertson (reader), P. Sraffa (assistant director of research), Joan Robinson (faculty assistant lecturer); lecturers: L. Alston, C. G. Clark, M. Dobb, C. W. Guillebaud, J. R. Hicks, M. Hollond, R. F. Kahn, E. A. G. Robinson, J. Rowe, G. F. Shove, W. Thatcher (*Cambridge University Reporter*, October 1, 1935: 5).
19. Forty-four years later Hicks gave this explanation of his move to Cambridge: 'I went there in consequence of an invitation from Pigou, and it was because of the friendship I had already formed with Robertson that I was attracted' (1984: 285).
20. In March 1935 Joan Robinson proposed to the faculty board (which Robertson chaired at the time) to lecture a two-term course on money for second-year students, while Robertson gave the lectures to the third-year students on the same subject. Robertson firmly opposed Robinson's lecturing: he feared, not without grounds, being ridiculed by her before his

own students. Fay intervened in order to defend Robertson's point of view (letter from C. R. Fay to Keynes, March 2, 1935, in JMK papers UA/14.2). Keynes sided most decidedly in favor of Robinson, however, and in the end she taught a two-term course: applications of monetary theory (two hours per week in Michaelmas and Lent terms) followed in Easter term by a course on some problems of economic theory. The courses taught by Robinson were, however, included in the list of lectures for part II of the Economic Tripos, so that neither of them appeared as preliminary to Robertson's course on money (Moggridge 1992; Naldi 2005).

21. A similar preoccupation would be expressed by Pigou a few years later, in 1938, about the editorial policy of *The Economic Journal*, which led him to a clash with Keynes (Bridel and Ingrao 2005).
22. On November 7 he wrote to Ursula: 'My Mr Millikan brought me an essay this evening on the theory of interest, which was really excellent. I was tremendously cheered by it.' And again, on November 11: 'He does continually go up in my estimation.' He was a research student—not registered for a degree—whom Hicks supervised for one year (May 20, 1935, FB Mins. V. 118, 64).
23. P. T. Bauer took a first in part I of the economic tripos in 1935.
24. Michaelmas and Lent terms 1935, 1936, 1937 (on leave in Lent term 1938).
25. Easter terms 1936, 1937.
26. Easter term 1937.
27. In 1934 Hicks had been appointed as external examiner in part II of the economic tripos, when R. Bryce and L. Tarshis took firsts. He was examiner in part II for 1935, when D. Bensusan-Butt, S. Dennison, R. Stone, and R. Simon took firsts. He was also examiner for the preliminary exam in economics in 1936. He was also appointed as examiner for part II in the tripos 1937 (October 19, 1936, FB Mins. V. 118) but he resigned at the beginning of 1937 'owing to pressure of work' (January 25, 1937, FB Mins. V. 118). He was examiner in part I for 1938.
28. Keynes's negative opinion did not concern only Hicks's teaching. On *Value and Capital* a few months earlier Keynes wrote to Kahn: 'I don't think I have ever read a book by an obviously clever man, so free from points open to specific criticisms, which was so utterly empty' (letter from Keynes to Kahn, 11 April 1939, in RFK papers 13/57/411).
29. Keynes was probably referring to 'A Suggestion for Simplifying the Theory of Money' (Hicks 1935a).
30. *The General Theory*, which in fact appeared only in January 1936.
31. Haberler, then working at the League of Nations in Geneva on his *Prosperity and Depression* (Haberler 1937), asked for leave permission from October 14–18 to go to London to give a series of four lectures on busi-

ness cycle research, present situation and future outlook. He also asked for two more days of leave to go to Cambridge and Oxford to visit 'competent economists' (League of Nations, Haberler personal file; we are indebted to Daniele Besomi for this information). From the correspondence between John and Ursula we learn that Haberler gave the first of his lectures at the LSE on October 14 (letter from Ursula to John) and that, during his stay, he went for one day to Cambridge (letter from Ursula to John, October 16).

32. In a letter from Robertson to Hicks dated November 13, 1934, when Hicks was still at the LSE, discussing the different conceptions of equilibrium that Keynes, Gunnar Myrdal, Erik Lindahl, Hicks, Hayek, Haberler had, together with their different conceptions of the adjustment mechanisms (horizontal or vertical), Robertson wrote: 'I'm depressed by the hardness of it all, and the lack of fundamental agreement between the people' (in DHR papers C4/1.3).
33. Later, Joan Robinson did cite Hicks in her *Essays* (1937); in one case, however, Keynes suggested 'a slight modification of what you say about Hicks' (Moggridge 1973b: 147).
34. David Miles Bensusan-Butt (1914–1994), economist.
35. Hans Wolfang Singer (b.1910), economist.
36. Mario Lamberti Zanardi (1900–1945), economist.
37. Albert Grant Fleming (1887–1943), economist.
38. Ursula is probably referring to the paper 'The Theory of Monopoly, with Reference to Time,' which Gerhard Tintner (1907–1983) presented at the session of November 13, 1935, of the Economic Club *(Forty-second. Annual Report of The Economic Club,* in BEV papers Suppl. 376).
39. Victor Gregory Edelberg, economist.
40. Hicks reviewed the book for *The Economic Journal* (Hicks 1936b).
41. The paper was on the 'The Long-period Theory of Employment.'
42. 'Lerner reports very well of Joan's paper,' Ursula wrote to John on October 22.
43. Another interesting glimpse into British society is provided by the correspondence between Ursula and John (letters of November 26–27), which give us an idea of how an educated couple faced sexual issues in the 1930s: by reading a book on sex written and recommended to Ursula by a gynecologist after a medical check-up just before their marriage. Through these exchanges we also learn that they planned to have children, although none ever materialized.
44. To John she wrote: 'It was very satisfactory not only to have a good talk with Joan but to convince her that someone else may be right' (Ursula to John, November 12).
45. 'He [Hicks] didn't enjoy Cambridge at all,' according to Shehadi ('Interview to John Hicks,' 1983, History of LSE Archive, 5).

46. Their professional partnership was particularly intense in the 1940s and 1950s (Hicks 1984: 287–8), leading to some joint articles and other work.
47. They each expressed this concept differently. Ursula wrote: 'What a new meaning all the poems and the songs one has loved take on when there's somebody really to attach them to, at least when the somebody is you. It's just wonderful to feel that we can be together, not just through lots of ordinary interests but right through all of us' (Ursula to John, October 11). John, in his own way, wrote: 'It is nice that we can be partners in economics..., but thanks heaven it is not only that!' (John to Ursula, October 24).
48. For instance, in the letter of November 13 she wrote to John: 'Laski drew me aside this afternoon and said "I want to tell you I have been hearing such golden opinions of John at Cambridge" [...] specifically the opinion [of graduates and undergraduates] was that you were making things that had never been clear before, suddenly stand straight by showing their connections and real significance. Isn't it nice? (But no more than I suspected).'
49. Ursula spent seven years at the LSE, as a student from 1929 to 1932, then as a PhD student in economics, and finally as a lecturer (though only for a brief period) in 1935 (obituary of Lady Hicks, *The Times*, 18 July 1985; David 1973).
50. When they married she was thirty-nine and he thirty-one.
51. It was the last house on the west side of Trumpington Road, just within the southern boundary of Cambridge.

References

Besomi, D. (2000) 'On the Spread of an Idea: the Strange Case of Mr Harrod and the Multiplier,' *History of Political Economy*, 32 (2, Summer), 347–79.

Besomi, D. (2003) 'Editorial Introduction,' in D. Besomi (ed.), *The Collected Interwar Papers and Correspondence of Sir Roy Harrod*, vol. I, Cheltenham, Edward Elgar, xxxi–xliv.

Bridel, P., and B. Ingrao (2005) 'Managing Cambridge Economies: the Correspondence between Keynes and Pigou,' in M.C. Marcuzzo and A. Rosselli (eds.), *Economists in Cambridge: A Study through Their Correspondence, 1907–1946*, London, Routledge, 149–66.

Brown, A. J. (1988) 'A Worm's Eye View of the Keynesian Revolution,' in J. Hillard (ed.) *J. M. Keynes in Retrospect: The Legacy of the Keynesian Revolution*, Aldershot, Edward Elgar, 18–44.

Coase, R. H. (1982) 'Economics at LSE in the 1930s: a Personal View,' *Atlantic Economic Journal*, 10 (1, March), 31–4.

Dahrendorf, R. (1995) *A History of the London School of Economics and Political Science, 1895–1995*, Oxford, Oxford University Press.

David, W. L. (ed.) (1973) *Public Finance, Planning and Economic Development: Essays in Honour of Ursula Hicks*, London, Macmillan.

Ebenstein, A. (2001) *Friedrich Hayek: A Biography*, New York, Palgrave.

Haberler, G. (1937) *Prosperity and Depression*, Geneva, League of Nations.

Hamouda, O.F. (1993) *John R. Hicks: The Economist's Economist*, Oxford, Basil Blackwell.

Hayek, F. A. [1963] (1995) 'The Economics of the 1930s as Seen from London,' in B. Caldwell (ed.) *The Collected Works of F. A. Hayek*, vol. IX, *Contra Keynes and Cambridge: Essays, Correspondence*, London, Routledge, 49–63.

Hicks, J. R. (1935a) 'A Suggestion for Simplifying the Theory of Money,' *Economica*, new series, 2 (5, February), 1–19 [reprinted in J. R. Hicks (1967a) *Critical Essays in Monetary Theory*, Oxford, Clarendon Press, 61–82].

Hicks, J. R. (1935b) 'Annual Survey of Economic Theory: the Theory of Monopoly,' *Econometrica*, January, 1–20 [reprinted in J. R. Hicks (1983a) *Collected Essays on Economic Theory*, vol. III, Classics and Moderns, Oxford, Basil Blackwell, 131–52].

Hicks, J. R. (1936a) 'Mr Keynes's Theory of Employment,' *Economic Journal*, 46 (June), 238–53.

Hicks, J. R. (1936b) 'Review of A. C. Pigou, The Economics of Stationary States,' *Economic Journal*, 46 (March), 98–102.

Hicks, J. R. (1956) 'Methods of Dynamic Analysis,' in *25 Economic Essays in Honour of Erik Lindahl*, Stockholm, Ekonomisk Tidskrift, 139–51 [reprinted with addendum in J. R. Hicks (1982a) *Collected Essays on Economic Theory*, vol. II, *Money, Interest and Wages*, Oxford, Basil Blackwell, 219–35].

Hicks, J. R. (1972) Prize lecture, Nobel banquet, Stockholm, December 10.

Hicks, J. R. (1973) *Capital and Time: A Neo-Austrian Theory*, Oxford, Clarendon Press.

Hicks, J. R. (1979) 'The Formation of an Economist,' *Banca Nazionale del Lavoro Quarterly Review*, September, 195–204 [reprinted in J. R. Hicks (1983a) *Collected Essays on Economic Theory*, vol. III, *Classics and Moderns*, Oxford, Basil Blackwell, 355–64, and in J. R. Hicks (1984a) The Economics of John Hicks: Selected Papers (introd. D. R. Helm), Oxford, Basil Blackwell, 282–90].

Hicks, J. R. (1982a) 'Introductory: LSE and the Robbins Circle,' in J. R. Hicks (1982a) *Collected Essays on Economic Theory*, vol. II, Money, Interest and Wages, Oxford, Basil Blackwell, 3–10.

Hicks, J. R. (1982b) 'A Note on Robertson,' in J. R. Hicks (1982a) *Collected Essays on Economic Theory*, vol. II, *Money, Interest and Wages*, Oxford, Basil Blackwell, 127–31.

Hicks, J. R. (1984) *The Economics of John Hicks: Selected Papers* (introd. D.R. Helm), Oxford, Basil Blackwell.

Hirai, T., M. C. Marcuzzo, T. Nishizawa, and E. Sanfilippo (eds.) (2005) *The Letters between John Hicks and Ursula Webb September-December*, 1935, Working Paper no. 207, Institute for Economic and Business Administration Research, University of Hyogo, Tokyo.

Howson, S. (2005) 'The Robbins Circle,' draft paper presented at the American Society for the History of Economics annual conference, Tacoma, WA, June 24.

Kaldor, N. (1986) Ricordi di un economista (ed. M. C. Marcuzzo), Milan, Garzanti.

McCormick, B. J. (1992) *Hayek and the Keynesian Avalanche*, London, Harvester Wheatsheaf.

Marcuzzo, M. C. (2002) 'The Collaboration between J. M. Keynes and R. F. Kahn from the Treatise to the General Theory,' *History of Political Economy*, 34 (2, Summer), 421–47.

Marcuzzo, M. C. (2005) 'Piero Sraffa at the University of Cambridge,' *European Journal of the History of Economic Thought*, 12 (3, September), 425–52.

Marcuzzo, M. C., and A. Rosselli (eds.) (2005) *Economists in Cambridge: A Study through Their Correspondence, 1907–1946*, London, Routledge.

Matthews, R. C. O. (1994) 'In Memoriam,' in H. Hagemann and O. F. Hamouda (eds.) *The Legacy of Hicks: His Contributions to Economic Analysis*, London, Routledge, 12–15.

Mizen, P., and J. R. Presley (1998) 'Keynes, Hicks and the Cambridge School,' *History of Political Economy*, 30 (1, Spring), 1–16.

Moggridge, D. E. (ed.) (1973a) *The Collected Writings of John Maynard Keynes*, vol. XIII, *The General Theory and After: Preparation*, London, Macmillan.

Moggridge, D. E. (ed.) (1973b) *The Collected Writings of John Maynard Keynes*, vol. XIV, *The General Theory and After: Defence and Development*, London, Macmillan.

Moggridge, D.E. (1992) *Maynard Keynes: An Economist's Biography*, London, Routledge.

Naldi, N. (2005) 'Robertson and the Great Divide: the Correspondence between Kahn, Kaldor, J. Robinson and Sraffa,' in M. C. Marcuzzo and A. Rosselli (eds.) *Economists in Cambridge: A study through Their Correspondence, 1907–1946*, London, Routledge, 371–87.

Patinkin, D., and J. C. Leith (eds.) (1977) *Keynes, Cambridge and The General Theory*, London, Macmillan.

Pigou, A. C. (1935) *The Economics of Stationary States*, London, Macmillan.

Plumptre, A. F. W. (1947) 'Keynes in Cambridge,' *Canadian Journal of Economics and Political Science*, 13 (3, August), 366–71.

Robbins, L. (1971) *Autobiography of an Economist*, London, Macmillan.

Robertson, D. H. (1931) 'Mr Keynes' Theory of Money,' *Economic Journal*, 41 (September), 395–411.

Robinson, E. A. G. (1985) 'The Cambridge "Circus" (2),' in G. C. Harcourt (ed.) *Keynes and His Contemporaries*, London, Macmillan, 52–7.

Robinson, J. (1933) *The Economics of Imperfect Competition*, London, Macmillan.
Robinson, J. (1937) *Essays in the Theory of Employment*, London, Macmillan.
Robinson, J. (1951) *Collected Economic Papers*, vol. I, Oxford, Basil Blackwell.
Robinson, J. (1978) *Contributions to Modern Economics*, Oxford, Basil Blackwell.
Robinson, J. (1979) *Collected Economic Papers*, vol. V, Oxford, Basil Blackwell.
Rosselli, A., and D. Besomi (2005) 'The Unlooked for Proselytiser: J. Robinson and the Correspondence with Sraffa, Harrod and Kaldor,' in M.C. Marcuzzo and A. Rosselli (eds.) *Economists in Cambridge: A Study through Their Correspondence, 1907–1946*, London, Routledge, 309–23.
Samuelson, P. A. (2001) 'My John Hicks,' in K. Puttaswamaiah (ed.) *John Hicks: His Contributions to Economic Theory and Application*, New Brunswick, NJ, Transaction, 1–4.
Sanfilippo, E. (2005) 'Keynes's Valuable Opponent and Collaborator: the Correspondence between Keynes and Robertson,' in M. C. Marcuzzo and A. Rosselli (eds.) *Economists in Cambridge: A Study through Their Correspondence, 1907–1946*, London, Routledge, 58–76.
Shehadi, N. (1991) 'The LSE and the Stockholm School in the 1930s,' in L. Jonung (ed.) *The Stockholm School of Economics Revisited*, Cambridge, Cambridge University Press, 377–89.
Simkin, C. (2001) 'John and Ursula Hicks: a Personal Recollection,' in K. Puttaswamaiah (ed.) *John Hicks: His Contributions to Economic Theory and Application*, New Brunswick, NJ, Transaction, 5–15.
Skidelsky, R. (1992) *John Maynard Keynes: The Economist as Saviour 1920–1937*, London, Macmillan.
Thirlwall, A. P. (1987) *Nicholas Kaldor*, Brighton, Wheatsheaf Books.

PART IV

Cambridge Protagonists: Keynes, Joan Robinson and Sraffa

CHAPTER 14

On Alternative Notions of Change and Choice. Krishna Bharadwaj's Legacy

14.1 Premise

The consumption and production of goods is the kind of human activity to which the term 'economic' is applied; in most societies these activities are mediated through exchange and in capitalist societies exchange is performed in organised markets. In the history of economic thought, a range of different conceptions have been put forward to explain how individuals interact in markets and various accounts have been advanced of ways to understand which are the incentives and the constraints affecting their behaviour and decision making.

In neoclassical theories, choices in consumption and production are conceptualised through reasoning at the margin. Under the *ceteris paribus* assumption, i.e. that everything else remains unchanged, this method provides the means to measure the effects of a small (technically, infinitesimal)

This is a revised version of the Twentieth Krishna Bharadwaj Memorial Lecture delivered at the Jawaharlal Nehru University, Delhi, on 12 March 2012. I am grateful to two anonymous referees of the *Cambridge Journal of Economics* for helpful criticism and suggestions.

Originally publ. in: *Cambridge Journal of Economics*, 38 (1), 2014, pp. 49–62. Reprint by Springer Nature Switzerland 2024 with kind permission

M. C. Marcuzzo, *Economic Theories, Protagonists and Facts*, Palgrave Studies in the History of Economic Thought, https://doi.org/10.1007/978-3-031-63949-4_14

variation in quantities of selected variables, such as utility and cost, which are compared with the relevant prices to determine the optimum choice by individuals. The optimal choice framework is in fact the basis upon which price and quantities are simultaneously determined in the neoclassical world.

The marginal method requires that a particular type of change be enacted, i.e. that an *experiment* be carried out varying the quantity of the selected variable, keeping all the others constant. Individuals are said to equate marginal quantities, found through a *hypothetical* change brought about by the agent or the observer, to the given prices of goods and factors.

On the other hand, the *observed* changes in economic variables are said to be the outcome of the behavioural response to changes in prices and are brought about through individuals' quantity adjustments in response to these price changes. It is precisely the conception of absence of price incentives for a change in quantities that characterises the neoclassical notion of equilibrium.

Krishna Bharadwaj, following upon the work and insights of Sraffa, made substantial contributions to our understanding of what is implied in the neoclassical notion of change and its related notion of choice; in this respect she appears closer to the spirit of Sraffa's critique of neoclassical theory than many others. Unlike Keynes, Kahn, Kaldor and Joan Robinson—the protagonists of the so-called Cambridge school with whom Sraffa was personally close, while remaining secretive on his own work—Bharadwaj fully rejected the marginal approach and the theory hinging upon it. She also supplemented important elements in building an alternative approach, based on classical political economy, which is free from the need to employ marginal magnitudes and does not require hypothetical or potential changes to determine the resting positions of economic variable; by this means she endeavoured to rescue the notion of choice from the parable of 'preferences' by giving it more meaningful contents, allowing for consideration of habits, customs and power relationships.

In order to substantiate these claims in Sects. 14.2 and 14.3, I summarise Sraffa's main arguments against the marginalist theory, turning to the contribution of Bharadwaj in Sect. 14.4. In Sect. 14.5 I review the controversy on some methodological points regarding the critique of neoclassical economics that saw Joan Robinson on one side and Garegnani with Bharadwaj on the opposite side. In the final section I draw some conclusions on Bharadwaj's legacy, on the occasion of the 20th anniversary of her death.

14.2 'Change' and 'Difference' in Sraffa's Published Work

In his published writings Sraffa made few references to the reasons behind his objections to the marginal method, but he did make several references to the notion of change in neoclassical economics (Marcuzzo and Rosselli 2011). In the Preface to *Production of Commodities by Means of Commodities*, the reader is warned that the book 'is concerned exclusively with such properties of an economic system as do not depend on changes in the scale of production or in the proportions of "factors"'. In this respect the work is presented as an alternative to the 'marginal approach' which 'requires *attention to be focused on change*, for without change either in the scale of an industry or in the "proportions of the factors of productions" there can be neither marginal product nor marginal cost' (Sraffa 1960: v, emphasis added).

The second warning given in the Preface is 'to avoid mistaking spurious "margins for the genuine article"', adding that the 'sure sign of their spuriousness' is 'the absence of *the requisite kind of change*' (Sraffa 1960: v, emphasis added).

Finally, the interpretative key to the book is to be sought in the critique of the theory which has its foundation in the marginal method:

> It is [...] a peculiar feature of the set of propositions now published that, although they do not enter into any discussion of the marginal theory of value and distribution, they have nevertheless been designed to serve as the basis for a critique of that theory. (Sraffa 1960: vi)

The nature of marginal analysis in classical political economy and neoclassical theory and the distinction between spurious and pure margins had been discussed by Sraffa in his 1925 article, although the article did not include the argument that a particular kind of change was required in one type of margin, i.e. the case of intensive cultivation of land when successive doses of capital and labour are applied to the fixed factor, but not in the other case, i.e. that of extensive cultivation when lands of different degrees of fertility are cultivated side by side. Sraffa simply mentioned the 'truth and generality' (1925: 19; 1998: 15) of the extensive margin case upon which the Ricardian theory of rent is based, unlike the case of the intensive margin upon which the neoclassical theory of distribution rests.[1]

The 1925 article was unavailable in English until after Sraffa's death, although an unofficial translation, prepared by J. Eatwell and A. Roncaglia in the mid-1970s, circulated privately and was made available only in 1998 (Sraffa 1998).[2] The issue of the two types of margins was not discussed in the 1926 article. Thus with the exception of a passing reference to the 'two points of view of change and difference' in the Introduction to Ricardo's *Principles* (Sraffa 1951), to which I will return below, the discussion of the type of change required in neoclassical theory remained undisclosed and appeared in print only in 1960. On the other hand, Sraffa's unpublished papers contain a wealth of material relating to the claims made in the Preface and it is to these we have to turn to have a better understanding of the claims. Before we do so, however, we need to consider how and when these papers became available to us.

Soon after Sraffa's death in September 1983, Bharadwaj and Garegnani undertook 'the initial work of scouring and inventorying the manuscript material [...] more detailed scrutiny followed with systematic listing of the manuscripts [...] which served as a basis to microfilm them at the University Library in 1987. This work took practically all the time that Prof Bharadwaj and [Garegnani] were able to dedicate to the manuscripts up to the summer of 1987' (Garegnani 1998: 151–2).

The plan for publishing the papers, as conceived in 1987, contemplated that the first volume comprising the manuscripts of 1927–1931 (which saw a turning point in Sraffa's thinking; see Garegnani 2005) was to be edited by Bharadwaj, 'whose work on the writings of Piero Sraffa, together with her personal friendship and informal theoretical discussion with him is well known, and who had for some time collaborated extensively with [Garegnani]' (ibid.: 152).

Bharadwaj's health conditions subsequent to 1987, which led to her premature death in 1992, prevented her from playing a regular part in the publication project.[3] The Sraffa papers were made available for scholarly access in late 1993,[4] but their publication is still awaited.[5] From 1983 to 1993, access to the manuscripts was restricted and few were able to appreciate their importance.

14.3 'Change' and 'Difference' in Sraffa's Unpublished Writings

What the unpublished writings revealed at the outset and was immediately clear to Bharadwaj and Garegnani (Garegnani 1998) on inventorying them was that in autumn/winter 1927–1928, while preparing for the lectures he was to give at Cambridge, Sraffa made the path-breaking discovery that classical political economy and neoclassical economics rested on alternative theories of value and distribution; only the latter explains distribution and relative prices by means of the equilibrium of the two opposing sets of forces, demand and supply for factors of production; the former determines shares of product other than wages (which are exogenously given) as a residuum or surplus simultaneously with the determination of the relative prices of commodities.[6] On the basis of this discovery he started working on his 'equations', which form the backbone of was to become his *Production of Commodities* many years later.

The question of how change and choice are conceptualised in neoclassical economics appeared quite early in the context of this discovery. In one of the manuscripts of the period 1927–1928, possibly where there is the first mention of the 'Difference (simultaneous) versus Change (succession in time)', Sraffa wrote:

> The general confusion in all theories of value [...] must be explained by the failure to distinguish between two entirely distinct types of questions and the universal attempt of solving them both by one single [...] theory.
>
> The two questions are:
>
> 1) what determines the (difference in the?) values at which various commodities are exchanged in a given market *on a given instant*?
>
> 2) what determines the changes in the values of commodities *at different times*? (e.g. of one commodity). (Sraffa Papers, D3/12/7, quoted in Garegnani 2005: 471–2, emphasis added)

And he continues:

> The first problem gives rise to a geometrical theory, the second to a mechanical one [...] Marshall's theory of value, with its increasing and diminishing costs and marg[inal] utility, scissors, pillars and forces, can only be understood as an attempt to solve the first question in terms of the second. (Sraffa Papers, D3/12/7, quoted in Garegnani 2005: 472)

The same point, but related to the theory of distribution, is reiterated more than 30 years later in one of the many extant drafts of the Preface to *Production of Commodities*:

> The fundamental difference is that the *extensive* (different qualities of land) is truly a purely *timeless*, or geometrical representation: all the different lands exist simultaneously, at one instant, they and their products can be ascertained, distinguished and measured at one instant, without changing anything in the present arrangements.
>
> On the contrary, the *intensive* (successive doses of capital and labour on a piece of land) diminishing returns do not exist at any one instant. We can only find these diminishing returns by *change*, or movement: that is to say, we require *time*. (Sraffa Papers, D3/12/13/23(2), quoted in Marcuzzo and Rosselli 2011: 227–8)

In a contemporaneous manuscript dated 1–3 January 1958 and inscribed as 'Margins and margins', which he might have considered including in his book, Sraffa made the same point, returning to his earlier distinction between the point of view of difference and change:

> The names usually given to the two types [of rent], 'extensive' and 'intensive', conceal rather than describe the essence of the distinction. This is that the first is based on the *difference* between situations which are mutually compatible and can coexist at the same time, since they involve the payment of different rents on different qualities of land; while the second is based on *changes* in the situation on a single quality of land which represent a transition from one to another state, the two states being incompatible and mutually exclusive, since they determine two different rents on the same quality of land. The former compares two or more 'returns' existing side by side within a given set of circumstances: the latter compares successive returns obtained in different circumstances – it implies a comparison between the actual return and a potential *alternative* return. (Sraffa Papers, D3/12/46/50, quoted in Marcuzzo and Rosselli 2011: 228)

Finally, Sraffa reiterated the same point as late as 17 August 1965, when he was still trying to carry out his project for a comprehensive critique of marginal theory:

> Another aspect [...] is that in the first case [intensive rent] there is only a decrease of product in time with the increase of the doses: at any instant of time no difference can be seen. Whereas in the second case [extensive rent]

> the difference in productivity is noticeable at any instant. The first is a case of change, which takes time to happen: the second is a difference between simultaneous product. (Sraffa Papers, D3/12/42/5, quoted in Marcuzzo and Rosselli 2011: 228)

As argued more in detail elsewhere (Marcuzzo and Rosselli 2011), objections to the reasoning at the margin in the neoclassical theory of value and distribution were raised by Sraffa over his entire working life. They fall into three categories:

(i) In order to observe the marginal product one has to perform an experiment, i.e. to bring about *a change in the existing situation* and to give rise to a *new* situation. The assumption is then made that the two situations do not differ but for the change in the variable considered. This is unwarranted since comparing the effects of an *induced* change in a given situation does not have the same degree of certainty as the case of comparing *observable* differences in two existing situations.

(ii) Since differences in two products can be compared only when the same circumstances occur, we cannot infer that the effect of an increase/decrease in the variable factor is the measure of a marginal product; more certainly it is the measure of the effect of a new combination of *all* the factors involved, namely an increase or decrease in the *average* product.

(iii) Only observable differences in situations existing at the same time, which do not require any change to be brought about, can constitute a legitimate basis for deriving functions relating prices and quantity. It is the *hypothetical* nature of such relations that is questioned, incorporating as it does the assumption that such relations remain constant under any circumstances, as the law of demand and supply implies.

In conclusion, Sraffa's objections were raised against the claim of generality and universality of the relationship between prices and quantities, or of the functional forms of demand and supply equations required for the existence and stability of equilibrium in neoclassical theory. These objections do not apply to reasoning based on observed magnitudes and measurable entities involved in exchange and production processes, where the resting positions of the variables involved can be ascertained without invoking alternative (non-observable and non-measurable) configurations.

Bharadwaj readily grasped the implication of these arguments for alternative notions of change and choice in her theoretical and applied work. To her contribution I now turn.

14.4 Bharadwaj's Intellectual Closeness to Sraffa

Bharadwaj's intellectual and personal closeness to Sraffa and the Cambridge group is well known among scholars and is best recalled with her own words:

> a fellowship to work at Cambridge in 1967 [...] gave me the unique opportunity to communicate with Piero Sraffa and with other scholars including Joan Robinson, Maurice Dobb, Richard Kahn, Nicky Kaldor, Luigi Pasinetti, Pierangelo Garegnani and with a group of young economists from England and Europe interested in the revival of classical and Marxian theory. My association with Piero Sraffa until his death in 1983 radically altered my theoretical perspective in economics. (Bharadwaj 2000: 59)

In fact her intellectual encounter with Sraffa took place four years earlier,[7] in 1963, when she was asked to review *Production of Commodities*, a review that was so very positively received by the author that it marked the beginning of a close association and developed into friendship.

It is indeed surprising that a young economist, miles away from Cambridge and Sraffa's own milieu, could have 'correctly grasped the main lines of the argument, and also guessed some of the directions in which [...] the criticism of marginalism should be developed' as Sraffa wrote back on receiving the review (Piero Sraffa to Krishna Bharadwaj, 8 September 1963 in Sraffa Papers vi, 3, (i) 391, D3/12/111/42 quoted in Omkarnath 2005: 463). The 'guess' of the directions in which the criticism of marginalism should be developed became Bharadwaj's lifetime research endeavour and guided her applied work; the privilege of having discussions with Sraffa and access to his unpublished writings made it all the more unique and valuable.

Bharadwaj expanded upon Sraffa's 1960 brief reference to *the requisite kind of change* implied in the marginal method already in her R. C. Dutt lectures (Bharadwaj 1978, 1986). There are two editions[8] of this little book which were published at an interval of several years; they are almost identical, although the second version contains some additions and alterations, which I consider somewhat interesting.[9] It is mainly in the second of the three lectures, entitled 'The Shift to Supply and Demand Theories: Some Methodological Implications', that the thrust of her arguments emerges.

The role of change in supply-and-demand theories is to allow convergence towards equilibrium and to provide the optimum solution for the individual choice; it must therefore be conceived as following a predetermined path. Thus the direction of change required (i.e. the assumption that demand and supply are well-behaved functions) imposes 'constraints which operate against an effective handling of problems of change' (Bharadwaj 1986: 3). Historical changes, i.e. those observed in the real world, are descriptions of 'events ex post facto' that may occur outside the strictures of the predictive relation between price and quantity described by supply-and-demand functions, which are necessary for the stability of equilibrium. She writes:

> Thus, a statement about one position (at equilibrium) is tied up with a theory *specifying in exact terms* the behaviour of the system under 'change' away from that position, even though these variations may be considered 'hypothetical' or theoretically confined to the infinitesimally small (or to points 'in the neighbourhood') [...] The prices of production in the classical theory, in contrast, do not posit and therefore do not depend for their stipulation upon the postulate of actual or 'potential' change. (Bharadwaj 1986: 39)

And again:

> The classical system [is] more general in scope and versatile in dealing with historic-specific factors [because] 'it does not commit itself through its theoretical structure to any rigid form and direction of change [...] [on the contrary, neoclassical theory] sought to explain a single observed situation in terms of potential changes – and as brought about by the balancing of marginal quantities operating through the principle of substitution. In order to be consistent with these explanations, the changes had to be in a direction and of the type postulated by theory'. (ibid.: 63–4)

On the contrary, neoclassical theory 'sought to explain a single observed situation in terms of potential changes—and as brought about by the balancing of marginal quantities operating through the principle of substitution. In order to be consistent with these explanations, the changes had to be in a direction and of the type postulated by theory' (ibid.: 63–4).

To illustrate the distinction between economic propositions depending upon change and those which do not Bharadwaj referred to the analogy with propositions in geometry and mechanics, considering the two cases of the 'extensive' and 'intensive' margins.[10] Here is where I believe the discussions with Sraffa and access to his unpublished papers helped her towards a firmer grasp on the matter. The distinction between geometry and mechanics was drawn by Sraffa in his early manuscripts, as we have seen, and it is an analogy that he must often have made reference to in his subsequent work and conversations.

She interpreted Sraffa's message as a rejection of the neoclassical theory of choice based on reasoning at the margin, as requiring a particular type of change, which is hypothetical rather than observed. So the direction of change is assumed under the *ceteris paribus* clause rather than discovered through factual evidence or historical reconstruction. The framework of supply and demand constrains the analysis within a given relationship between prices and quantities required for the well-behaved functions, while the price mechanism is endowed with all the explanatory power of choices, leaving little or no room for customs, habits and social conventions.

On the contrary, freedom from the marginal approach and supply-and-demand apparatus allows consideration of other factors besides price incentive, exogenous preferences and given endowments.

Four points marked Bharadwaj's endorsement of alternative notions of 'change' and 'choice':

(i) changes in wages, methods of production and social demand are not explained as 'arising solely due to relative price fluctuations' (Bharadwaj 1991: 86);
(ii) there are multiple constraints operating on the individuals, as demanders and suppliers: 'these include the physical and material resources at the individual's command as well as those systemic constraints that circumscribe his or her feasible options' (ibid.: 87);
(iii) 'not all individuals are equally or uniformly placed in terms of the power to make decision or in terms of the influence their decision can exert' (ibid.: 87); and
(iv) inequalities cannot be reduced to a matter of resource endowment, but must be understood in terms of the 'systematic discrimi-

nation which occurs in the exchange systems originating from social distinctions such as class, caste or sex' (Bharadwaj 1990: 22).

This methodology guided her analysis of the Indian economy, as several scholars in the field have recognised. In her study on the condition of production in Indian agriculture (Bharadwaj 1974), she made substantial advance over the mainstream interpretations, because:

> She classified the peasantry according to their access to land, as well as to the nature of exchange involvement in the agrarian situation where competitive capitalist markets have not yet emerged. She also attempted to stratify peasants according to their status in production and their corresponding involvement in exchange under conditions of uneven commercialization. (Knell and Ramaswamy 1995: 110)

Of similar recognised importance is her notion of 'interlinked markets', so called 'because the terms of contracts in two or more agrarian markets are interlocked such that the feasible choices of the weaker party to the transaction are *ex ante* severely constrained' (Omkarnath 2007: 396).

In conclusion, her methodology was firmly based on observation and the discovery of regularities in the particular social formation she aimed to identify. Not all changes in quantities are the outcome of the principle of substitution nor do they involve mainly allocative variations in response to changes in relative prices by optimising agents. The notions of change and choice can be rescued from the neoclassical strictures and, thanks to the classical approach reconstructed by Sraffa, given new meaning and applications.

14.5 Alternative Interpretations

The nature of the criticism of the marginal approach, and its implications for supply-and-demand analysis and the notions of change and choice, was not easy to detect in Sraffa's sparse remarks in his published writings well after the publication of *Production of Commodities,* whose meaning and significance baffled many interpreters.

In fact, Sraffa's distinction between 'difference' and 'change' surfaced in 1951 in his Introduction to Ricardo's *Principles*. There, Sraffa referred to 'the two points of view of difference and of change' (Sraffa 1951: xlix) to clarify two different effects on the relative value of two commodities of different proportions or durabilities of capital employed in their production. He wrote:

> First, that of occasioning a *difference* in the relative values of two commodities which are produced by equal quantities of labour. Second, that of the effect which a rise of wages has in producing a *change* in their relative value. (Sraffa 1951: xlvii)

This change, which is said to be 'apparent' as 'due solely to change in measurement' (ibid.: xlviii), in relative values can be ascertained at different moments in time, while the difference in the values of commodities due to the different proportions of capital and labour employed in their production can be ascertained at the same moment in time. Time is thus implied in the notion of change, but not in the notion of difference and the same tool of investigation—as Ricardo tried to do with his invariable measure of value—cannot be employed to trace the implications of these two types of comparisons. The same applies to neoclassical theory, where variations at the margin are used as a means to ascertain changes as well as differences in goods and factors price. *Changes* as opposed to *differences* in values or prices require different procedures for comparisons.

The full implication of the arguments contained in the Introduction remained clouded until their full exposure with the publication of *Production of Commodities*, with only exception of Joan Robinson who on two occasions made reference to it.

In the second essay *On Re-Reading Marx*, written shortly after reading Sraffa's Introduction to Ricardo's *Principles*, there is a cryptic remark in which Joan Robinson described the nature of supply-and-demand curves in determining equilibrium, as 'a metaphor based on space' of 'a process which takes place in time' (Robinson 1973: 138).[11] Her reading of Sraffa's distinction between the point of view of change and difference was made more explicit in her celebrated 1953 article on the production function, which opened the capital controversy.

In the 1953 article Joan Robinson pointed up the neoclassical failure to distinguish between changes in the conditions of producing a given output, when the quantity of capital is altered, from changes in the value of that capital due to variations in wages and profits. The implication she drew is that 'different factor ratios cannot be used to analyse changes in the factor ratio taking place through time', because in time the *value* of the quantity of capital may change as a consequence of a change in distribution and the same quantities were not being comparing. She concluded that 'it is impossible to discuss changes (as opposed to differences) in neo-classical terms' (Robinson 1978: 89).

Robinson interpreted the 'points of view of difference and of change' as a distinction between legitimate as opposed to illegitimate comparisons between two equilibria, with different amounts of capital; since changes in the value of capital may occur simply because of a change in the rate of profit, it is impossible to know whether the quantity of capital has changed in the transition from one position to another. Thus she drew the conclusion that equilibrium positions could only be compared as differences and never described as changes from one position to another.[12]

However, in the Introduction Sraffa takes the question of measurement of the quantity of capital to pertain only to the question of measuring 'the magnitude of aggregate of commodities', i.e. to the *apparent* change in the quantity of output to be distributed whenever there is a change in its value due to a change either in wages or in profits. Sraffa does not take it to pertain to the question of the impossibility of comparing two different aggregates of commodities at two different points in time because of the impossibility of singling out the effects of a change in distribution, as Joan Robinson seemed to take it. It is not the time element that makes the analysis of change impossible in neoclassical terms, but the circularity in the measurement of capital unless the rate of profit is determined simultaneously.

After the publication of *Production of Commodities*, Joan Robinson became aware of the misunderstanding[13] of her reading of the Introduction, but still defended her distinction between the 'two point of views of difference and of change' as resting on the distinction between logical and historical time, claiming that reasoning in logical time is common to both general equilibrium theory and Sraffa's system, while the language of Keynes is in historical time.

Joan Robinson's main line of attack on the neoclassical theory was levelled against the notion of equilibrium and the impossibility of dealing with historical time, rather than against the inconsistencies in the theory of supply and demand (Robinson 1979: xiv). She remained unconvinced by the theory of prices of production and objected to the method of *Production of Commodities*, because 'there is no causation and no change' and 'the argument is conducted strictly in terms of comparisons of logically possible positions' (Robinson 1980a: 132). She felt it to be more promising to rely on Keynes, who, 'at the opposite extreme to Sraffa, discusses only events' (Robinson 1980b: 139) and discusses them 'in terms of processes taking place in actual history' (Robinson 1979: xiv).

This issue gave rise to the controversy with Garegnani on the question as to where the dividing line of the alternative to neoclassical economics lay. Garegnani rebutted Robinson's critique of Sraffa's approach; he argued that the assumption of irreversibility in time that Robinson points out is implicit only in the method of supply-and-demand analysis, in which the tendency towards equilibrium is described as movements along those curves. But Garegnani explains that the same assumption is not made when comparing two long-term equilibrium positions determined by a 'classical' theory of prices and distribution (Garegnani 1979).[14]

Bharadwaj sided with Garegnani in the controversy with Joan Robinson and, while sharing some of his arguments, her distancing from Robinson had characteristics of its own. She agreed with Robinson that history, namely the process involving actual and irreversible as opposed to potential and reversible changes, has to be rescued from neoclassical theory and brought back into economic analysis, but how is this best done?

She commented that 'The success of the notion of "instantaneous or hypothetical change" in mechanics does not validate its use in economic theory as a *general* representation of change' (Bharadwaj 1980: 50) and defended the method of comparison between long-term positions as legitimate method of analysis of change.

On the contrary, Robinson objected to the method of comparisons of classical political economy and to Sraffa's method as showing no substantial difference from the neoclassical equilibrium method in their neglect of disregard of uncertainty and disregard of expectations, which are the guiding forces of economic behaviour. With her typical terse prose (which is a good match for Robinson's), Bharadwaj summarises Robinson's 'theorem of non-existence' in the following passage:

> with uncertainty present, no system not already in equilibrium can achieve equilibrium; while a system already in equilibrium could not but have 'perfect foresight' by virtue of its being in such a state. Thus, since uncertainty of expectations is ever present, a state of equilibrium cannot exist. (Bharadwaj 1991: 94–5)

Bharadwaj made two objections to Robinson's criticism of the equilibrium (in the sense of the long-term position) method. First, a meaning conceptualisation of the equilibrium concept does not entail that the corresponding prices and the uniform rate of profit actually rule at any particular moment in time. It is rather the tendency towards it, driven by the forces believed to be 'persistent', that is argued for. Second, it is not denied that uncertainty of expectations has a role to play, but rather that:

> We need to discover [the] objective basis of different states of expectations and we need to know what systematic objective outcomes arise from these different states of expectations. (ibid.: 95–6)[15]

The point being made is that since expectations work in patterns, because imitation and mutuality play an important role, 'broadly uniform behaviour' (ibid.) can be detected and should be made part of the analysis. Thus her emphasis on the 'objective basis' is to be interpreted as refusal to appeal to non-observable entities, such as individual utility functions, and instead to look to custom, social norms and the like. Investigation into decision making under uncertainty, opinion formation and subjective evaluation of future events is not banned from the theory; rather, it is claimed that the theoretical framework of neoclassical theory is not endowed to address the issue.

14.6 The Legacy of Krishna Bharadwaj

Bharadwaj was intellectually closer to Sraffa than the group of economists considered part of the so-called Cambridge school.

The critique that Keynes, Kahn, Kaldor and Joan Robinson raised against the neoclassical paradigm went together with their apparently unquestioning acceptance—at least at a disaggregate level—of marginal analysis. True, Kaldor and Robinson in later years rejected the notion of equilibrium, but without severing the connection with supply-and-demand theories. Kahn championed the 'marginal principle' for the determination of price and output for the single firm and was instrumental in persuading Keynes to adopt the marginal approach in the *General Theory* (Marcuzzo 2002).[16] Keynes never rejected increasing marginal costs in the *General Theory* and this led him to adopt assumptions, such as the inverse relationship between employment and real wages, which brought conclusions that he later admitted were at variance with facts.[17] I have argued elsewhere that Sraffa's estrangement from Cambridge economics and his refusal to engage in discussion of his own work with those who were among his closest friends can be accounted for by a political, social and cultural gulf (Marcuzzo 2005b).

On the other hand, both Keynes and Kahn dropped the 'maximising rule' when analysing entrepreneurs' behaviour in financial markets and regarding investment decisions. Given the element of uncertainty and the various degrees of conviction with which opinions are formed and held by individuals, they viewed the decision process as leading not so much to an optimum solution as, rather, to a condition reached when sufficiently strong motives to do otherwise are lacking. No appeal to the marginal principle was deemed necessary here. Moreover, Keynes's principle of effective demand explicitly rejects the idea that flexibility in prices and wages may restore full employment equilibrium. The related concept of the multiplier is based precisely on the presumption that quantity adjustments follow an exogenous increase in aggregate demand in the presence of underutilised resources.

This is the basis upon which the two strands of Cambridge economics, one stemming from Sraffa and the other from Keynes, find common ground in the post-Keynesian world.[18] To this enlarged family, Bharadwaj—who pointed up many important insights by Keynes,[19] Kalecki[20] and Robinson[21]—never refused to belong, while remaining firmly on the Sraffian side.

In looking back to her own work, with typical understatement and economy of words,[22] she wrote:

> I have [...] attempted to combine my critique of economic theory and the reconstruction of the classical (including Marxian) approach with the analysis of historical change in the course of development. (Bharadwaj 2000: 62–3)

She claimed for herself only to have 'tried to lend accuracy and sharpness to earlier critiques directed against the utilitarian and subjective basis' of supply-and-demand theories (ibid.: 61). In fact she did much more than that; she offered concrete examples of the fruitfulness of the alternative approach in her applied work. As Schefold remarked in the 1995 Memorial Lecture, she 'was one of the few followers of Sraffa who took the implication of the openness of the theory seriously in that she actually tried to relate her applied work to the historical perspective of the theory which she helped to elaborate' (Schefold 1998: 20).

This methodology also fuelled her 'unswerving radicalism', as it was aptly described by a close friend:

> She was deeply conscious of the reality of social exploitation in this [India] country, and extremely sensitive to and disturbed by what she saw as the rise of authoritarian tendencies and of communal and caste sentiments in recent years. Activists of the women's movement, the trade-union movement and the broader political movement on the left found in her a staunch and consistent ally. They never had to explain anything to her when they went with letters and petitions on issues as diverse as the Muslim women's bill, the amendment to the dowry act, or the Mandal question. She had already anticipated their arguments and reached further than they had on the basis of a more subtle and complex understanding of social issues. (Patnaik 1992: 67)

Amit Bhaduri's closing words in the obituary understandably express a feeling of irremediable loss:

> Her intellectual excellence [...] combined with rare human qualities [...] shone quietly to illuminate many dark patches of our lives – for her circle of friends, for her professional colleagues and for her students. That light has gone out. (Bhaduri 1992: 14)

Twenty years after her death, that light is still shining and will continue to shine for many generations to come.

Notes

1. 'Thus the truth and generality of the law of diminishing returns is much greater if it is based on the variety of the prices of land than if it is based on the variety of the doses of capital and labour, or on the variety of purposes for which equal doses can be used.'
2. The story of Sraffa's refusal to have an English translation published during his lifetime (Sraffa 1925: 19, 1998: 15) is told by Pasinetti (2001); an account of Sraffa's reasons is given by Garegnani (2005).
3. It has been suggested that Bharadwaj was in fact denied the editorship at an early stage of their collaboration (Omkarnath et al. 2011: 29). Harcourt described the ordering of Sraffa's papers a 'mammoth' task that put an enormous strain on her, to the extent that it was 'a significant factor leading to her final illness' (1993–1994: 308).
4. 'In all they number 115 archival entities consisting of notebooks, folders of notes, typescripts and proofs' (Smith 2012: 1292).
5. After Garegnani's death in October 2011, John Eatwell has been nominated Sraffa's literary executor.

6. The basis of Sraffa's distinction radically differs from other characterisations of the difference between classical and neoclassical economics proposed by earlier marginalist authors, such as Jevons, Wicksteed and Marshall.
7. Bharadwaj stated that she had been made ready for it by Joan Robinson: 'During my stay at Cambridge [USA, 1961–1962], Professor Joan Robinson arrived on her famous trip to launch her attack on the aggregate production function and the neoclassical theory of distribution, and to debate with Professors Samuelson, Solow and other neoclassical theorists. At that time my approach to neoclassical theory was primarily formed in the context of the theory of development—siding against its static resource-allocative, individual-centred analysis. My interest in the distribution theory was rekindled by this controversy between the two Cambridges. As a critic of the marginal productivity theory of distribution, I became more pointedly aware of the capital-theoretic debate. I did not then know of the more fundamental critique of economic theory heralded by Piero Sraffa's work' (2000: 57).
8. There is also a working paper version (1976) which is extant among the Krishna Bharadwaj papers now held in the Nehru Memorial Museum & Library in New Delhi, India.
9. Comparing the 1976, 1978 versions with that of 1986, we notice, for example, that in the earlier versions the supply-and-demand theories are more often referred to as the 'method of equilibrium analysis'.
10. She quotes from the 1925 article (Sraffa 1998), but not in connection with this argument.
11. 'If you read Mr. Sraffa's Introduction to the Principles you will see how right I am' (Robinson 1973: 145).
12. It should be noted that at the time of the 1953 article, Joan Robinson still considered comparisons between two equilibrium positions as opposed to movement from one position to another a legitimate exercise, which she later repudiated in her attack on the equilibrium method *tout court*.
13. See the letter from Joan Robinson to Piero Sraffa, 18 June 1960: 'Dear Piero: I thought that the idea that I had seen in a blinding flash was yours, because it came to me in terms of Ricardo's corn economy; but it was connected with TIME and it now appears is very much alien to your point of view (though to me it seems to fit perfectly well)' (Sraffa Papers, D3/12/111/340-41, quoted in Marcuzzo 2005a: 40).
14. Another appropriate response to the idea that Sraffa's system is timeless can be found in Roncaglia (1978: 119): 'Sraffa's analysis is not static, but rather [...] it represents a "photograph" of a particular moment of a system's development. This is something rather different [from neoclassical static theories] for it does not abstract from time. Instead, time is

taken into account by the fact that any particular moment of time is determined by its past history, and serves as the determining factor of the next moment in time'. However, in her last paper, published posthumously, Joan Robinson adopted a different perspective on Sraffa's system, arguing that it does not 'represent a stationary state of an equilibrium position. It is simply the position that has been reached, "today", as a result of accumulation of stocks and of technical knowledge over the past history' (Robinson 1985: 164). On this point see Martins (2013).

15. Bharadwaj's argument is reminiscent of a point made by Sraffa in an unpublished note dating from summer 1929, where he recognised the importance of expectations when based on objective elements, such as 'an average which eliminates individual differences'. I am indebted to a referee to drawing my attention to the existence of such a note and to Jonathan Smith for locating it.
16. His endorsement of the principle was mainly the outcome of his investigation into the *Economics of the Short Period* (Kahn 1989) and the result of his collaboration with Joan Robinson between 1930 and 1933, during the writing of her *Economics of Imperfect Competition.*
17. The increasing marginal cost assumption led Keynes to conclude that real and money wages varied in the opposite direction in the cycle, implying the existence of an inverse relation between employment and real wage.
18. There have been several attempts to bridge the two Cambridge strands. The most recent and authoritative example is Pasinetti (2007).
19. See her article 'On Effective Demand: Certain Recent Critiques' (Bharadwaj 1989: 275–97).
20. 'Kalecki sought to develop an integrated view of the processes of pricing, investment, production and income-employment generation, as operating under monopoly capitalism' (Bharadwaj 1977: 983).
21. '[Joan Robinson's] trenchant criticisms exposed the logical hurdles that the neoclassical theory faced in its notion of the aggregate production function, the marginal productivity explanations of distribution, the conceptualization of the choice of the techniques, etc.' (Bharadwaj 1991: 81).
22. Roncaglia notes in an obituary that 'Krishna very much enjoyed talking with her friends: about economics, politics, India, about her daughter and friendships in common—but very rarely did she speak about herself' (1993: 187).

References

Bhaduri, A. 1992. Krishna Bharadwaj, *Economic and Political Weekly*, vol. 27, nos 10–11, 490.

Bharadwaj, K. 1974. *Production Conditions in Indian Agriculture as Reflected in the Farm Management Studies*, Cambridge, UK, Cambridge University Press.

Bharadwaj, K. 1977. Michael Kalecki, *Economic and Political Weekly*, vol. 12, no. 25, 983–4.

Bharadwaj, K. 1980. *On some Issues of Method in the Analysis of Social Change*, Mysore, University of Mysore.

Bharadwaj, K. 1986. (2nd ed). *Classical Political Economy and the Rise to Dominance of Supply and Demand Theories*, Calcutta, Orient Longmans.

Bharadwaj, K. 1989. *Themes in Value and Distribution: Classical Theory Reappraised*, London, Unwin Hyman.

Bharadwaj, K. 1990. Paradigms in development theory: plea for 'labour-ist' approach, *Economic and Political Weekly*, vol. 25, no. 4, 20–8.

Bharadwaj, K. 1991. History versus equilibrium, in Rima, I. (ed.), *The Joan Robinson Legacy* (pp. 80–103), Armonk, Sharpe.

Bharadwaj, K. 2000. Krishna Bharadwaj, in Arestis, P. and Sawyer, M. (eds), *A Biographical Dictionary of Dissenting Economists* (pp. 55–64), 2nd edn, Aldershot, Elgar.

Garegnani, P. 1979. Notes on consumption, investment and effective demand: a reply to Joan Robinson, *Cambridge Journal of Economics*, vol. 3, 181–7.

Garegnani, P. 1998. Sui manoscritti inediti di Piero Sraffa, *Rivista Italiana degli Economisti*, vol. 3, 151–6.

Garegnani, P. 2005. On a turning point in Sraffa's theoretical and interpretative position in the late 1920s, *European Journal for the History of Economic Thought*, vol. 12, 453–92.

Harcourt, G. 1993–1994. Krishna Bharadwaj—a memoir, *Journal of Post Keynesian Economics*, vol. 16, 299–311.

Kahn, R. F. 1989. *The Economics of the Short Period*, London, Macmillan.

Knell, M. and Ramaswamy, S. 1995. Krishna Bharadwaj and the revival of classical theory, in Rima, I. (ed.), *The Classical Tradition in Economic Thought* (pp. 107–12), Aldershot, Elgar.

Marcuzzo, M. C. 2002. The collaboration between J.M. Keynes and R.F. Kahn from the *Treatise* to the *General Theory*, *History of Political Economy*, vol. 34, 421–47.

Marcuzzo, M. C. 2005a. Robinson and Sraffa, in Gibson, B. (ed.), *The Economic Legacy of Joan Robinson* (pp. 29–42), Cheltenham, Elgar.

Marcuzzo, M. C. 2005b. Piero Sraffa at the University of Cambridge, *European Journal of the History of Economic Thought*, vol. 12, 425–52.

Marcuzzo, M. C. and Rosselli, A. 2011. Sraffa and his arguments against marginism, *Cambridge Journal of Economics*, vol. 35, 219–31.
Martins, N. O. 2013. Sraffa, Marshall and the principle of continuity, *Cambridge Journal of Economics*, vol. 37, 443–62.
Omkarnath, G. 2005. 'Value through exogenous distribution': a review article in 1963, *Economic and Political Weekly*, vol. 40, 459–64.
Omkarnath, G. 2007. The formation of capabilities, *Indian Journal of Human Development*, vol. 1, no. 2, 389–99.
Omkarnath, G., Limakumba, W. and Thomas, A. 2011. Pierangelo Garegnani: a tribute, *Economic and Political Weekly*, vol. 46, no. 52, 28–9.
Pasinetti, L. 2001. Continuity and change in Sraffa's thought: an archival excursus, in Cozzi, T. and Marchionatti, R. (eds), *Piero Sraffa's Political Economy: A Centenary Estimate* (pp. 139–56), London, Routledge.
Pasinetti, L. 2007. *Keynes and the Cambridge Keynesians*, Cambridge, UK, Cambridge University Press.
Patnaik, U. 1992. Krishna Bharadwaj, *Social Scientist*, vol. 19, no. 223, 63–7.
Robinson, J. 1973. A lecture delivered at Oxford by a Cambridge economist, in *Collected Economic Papers*, vol. IV, Oxford: Blackwell, pp. 254–63.
Robinson, J. 1978. The production function and the theory of capital, in *Contribution to Modern Economics*, Oxford, Blackwell, pp. 76–90.
Robinson, J. 1979. *The Generalization of the General Theory and Other Essays*, London, Macmillan.
Robinson, J. 1980a. Restrospect: 1980, in *Further Contributions to Modern Economics* (pp. 131–4), Oxford, Blackwell.
Robinson, J. 1980b. Misunderstanding in the theory of production, in *Further Contributions to Modern Economics* (pp. 135–40), Oxford, Blackwell.
Robinson, J. 1985. The theory of normal prices and the reconstruction of economic theory, in Feiwel, G. (ed.), *Issues in Contemporary Macroeconomics and Distribution* (pp. 157–65), Albany, New York Press.
Roncaglia, A. 1978. *Sraffa and the Theory of Prices*, New York, Wiley.
Roncaglia, A. 1993. Krishna Bharadwaj, 1935–1992: in memoriam, *Metroeconomica*, vol. 44, 187–94.
Schefold, B. 1998. The creation of economic theories and the history of economic thought: reflections on the work of Krishna Bharadwaj, *History of Economic Ideas*, vol. 6, 7–25.
Smith, J. 2012. Circuitous processes, jigsaw puzzles and indisputable results: making best use of the manuscripts of Sraffa's *Production of Commodities by Means of Commodities*, *Cambridge Journal of Economics*, vol. 36, no. 6, 1291–301.
Sraffa, P. 1925. Sulle relazioni fra costo e quantità prodotta, *Annali di Economia*, vol. 2, 277–328.
Sraffa, P. 1926. The laws of return under competitive conditions, *Economic Journal*, vol. 36, 535–50.

Sraffa, P. 1951. Introduction, in Sraffa, P. and Dobb, M. H. (eds), *The Works and Correspondence of David Ricardo*, vol. I (pp. xiii–lxii), Cambridge, UK, Cambridge University Press.
Sraffa, P. 1960. *Production of Commodities by Means of Commodities: Prelude to a Critique of Economic Theory*, Cambridge, UK, Cambridge University Press.
Sraffa, P. 1998. On the relations between cost and quantity produced, English translation by J. Eatwell and A. Roncaglia, in Pasinetti, L. (ed.), *Italian Economic Papers*, vol. III (pp. 323–63), London, Oxford University Press.

CHAPTER 15

Sraffa and His Arguments Against 'Marginism'

Why do economists lay so much emphasis on the Margin? (Paper 6, Qual. Examinations 1925, p. 119 in Sraffa Papers D1/4/12)[1]

Our metaphysics is in fact embodied in our technique; the danger lies in this, that when we have succeeded in thoroughly mastering a technique, we are very liable to be mastered by her. (Sraffa Papers D3/12/4.15)

An earlier and very incomplete version of this paper appeared in Marcuzzo (2006). We wish to thank, for their comments, the participants in seminars and conference sessions where it was presented: STOREP Conference (Lecce, 2006); European Society for the History of Economic Thought Conference (Oporto, 2006); History of Economic Society conference (Toronto 2008) and the seminar at the Sraffa Center of the University of Rome III (2007) and University of Salento (2008). We are in debt to Marco Dardi, Franco Donzelli, Heinz Kurz and two anonymous referees for detailed criticism. We are grateful to Pierangelo Garegnani for permission to quote from the unpublished papers of Piero Sraffa. The usual disclaimers apply.

Originally publ. in: (With Annalisa Rosselli), *Cambridge Journal of Economics*, 35 (1), 2011, pp. 219–231.
Reprint by Springer Nature Switzerland 2024 with kind permission

M. C. Marcuzzo, *Economic Theories, Protagonists and Facts*, Palgrave Studies in the History of Economic Thought, https://doi.org/10.1007/978-3-031-63949-4_15

15.1 Introduction

In this article we explore the nature of Sraffa's criticism of the use made of the marginal method in economics (or 'marginism' as he often called it).[2] The method—as we hardly need remind readers—consists in allowing for small variations in one variable, while keeping the others constant, to determine the optimal choice of the economic agent. It is on this method that Marshall's demand and supply functions of goods and factors are constructed. These are the objects of Sraffa's criticism.

Our aim here is to show that marginism, as the specific target of Sraffa's criticism, is a constant element in his thought, and that his arguments against it remained fairly unchanged from the 1920s to the 1960s, although they show varying degrees of elaboration during the different phases of his research activity.[3]

Sraffa's habit of drawing upon argumentations and observations made in previous years, retrieving scraps of paper and notes written even decades before, makes reconstructing the genesis and evolution of his reasons for rejecting marginism no easy task. In the first place, it was only in the 1940s that Sraffa got into the habit of dating his notes in a systematic way; second, the notes were for ever being sorted and re-sorted, and the chronological order of writing thus, inevitably, lost; third, the literature (De Vivo 2000; Gilibert 2003; Garegnani 2005; Rosselli 2005; Kurz 2006) offers contrasting interpretations of the phases of change in Sraffa's thought on specific points, such as the influence that came with his perusal of Marx and the classical economists, or how far his initial concurrence with Marshall actually went. In particular, it is very hard to trace out a path in his progress over the years before 1925, distinguishing an initial phase and point of arrival, so what we offer here is a tentative reconstruction pending further investigation when the relevant papers are fully edited in a hopefully not too distant publication.

We have organised the paper thus: in Sect. 15.2 we examine Sraffa's unending quest for measurable and observable entities in economics in his unpublished papers, investigating the reasons why he believed that marginal method did not satisfy his criteria of scientific method; in Sect. 15.3 we review the relevant published writings to seek further clues to Sraffa's position and, in the final considerations of Sect. 15.4, we sum up our findings, listing Sraffa's arguments and criticism.

15.2 The Quest for 'Measurable' and 'Observable' Economic Magnitudes

Preoccupation with measurement of economic magnitudes is a hallmark of Sraffa's thinking and we see it recurring throughout his writings. A time span stretching from the writing of his notes in the early 1920s (see his endorsement of Sidgwick's statement on 'the necessity of unit of measurement, not for measurement, but for conception' in D1/20/5) to his contribution to a conference in Corfu in 1958 saw Sraffa in quest of a measurement criterion valid in theoretical analysis that should prove univocal, in contrast with the approach in statistical investigation, which requires some arbitrary choices as in the case of selecting weights in constructing index numbers.[4]

Sraffa's position on measurement of economic variables is clearly stated in 1929, while he was working on the equations that would become *Production of Commodities by Means of Commodities.* Here Sraffa claims that in economic theory there are three types of magnitudes. First are those that are observable and measurable in production and consumption processes (acres of land, tons of grain, etc.). This type is illustrated by the contrast Sraffa drew between the notions of cost in Petty and Marshall, in the notes for the course on Advanced Theory of Value, which he gave in 1928–1931:

> For Petty and the Physiocrats cost [...] is a stock of material that is required for the production of a commodity [...]. This cost is therefore something concrete, tangible, and visible, that can be measured in tons or gallons. It stands therefore at the opposite extreme of Marshall's cost, which is absolutely private to each individual, and can only be measured (if at all) by means of the monetary inducement required to call forth the exertion. (D2/4/3/21)

Second, there are the purely subjective magnitudes (such as sacrifice or utility), which are not observable and cannot be measured. This is not to say that for Sraffa there are no subjective or purely mental forces at work in the real world of economics (such as expectations, beliefs, or motivations), but only that these 'magnitudes' are neither observable nor measurable. Among the notes taken in May-July 1928, we read:

> [...] superstitions have an influence on facts, and have to be taken into account as such by the economist. But the recognition of the fact that the opinions of the actors have an influence must not lead the economist to believe that they are all the real facts themselves, or much less their objective explanation, as Marshall does. (D3/12/9/32)

According to his notes of Winter 1927–1928, in this distinction between the two types of magnitudes lies the difference between classical political economy and modern economics; the former dealt with

> 'material things' that have existed in the past. Modern economics deals with the second class, i.e. hopes for the future, such as utility, abstinence, disutility, etc.; these things, it must be noticed, refer only to the foresight of future acts. (D3/12/10/61.1)

Finally, there are the third type of magnitudes which are features of controlled experiments only, although Sraffa—as we shall see—questions the very possibility of carrying the experiment out. All marginal magnitudes, together with the demand and supply curves which are built upon them, belong to this class. They share the nature of being a sequence of mutually exclusive alternatives which do not exist *at the same time*. For example, we cannot observe the same piece of land simultaneously cultivated by n and $n + 1$ units of factor, as we cannot observe two alternative quantities supplied (or demanded) in the same instant. As Sraffa noted in October 1929:

> [...] [demand and supply curves, marginal productivities, which form the basis of Marshall's theory, (or, rather, Pareto's)] do not exist at any one moment, nor during any period of the recurrent steady process of production and consumption. They are alternatives, only <u>one</u> of which can exist in any one position of equilibrium, all the others being thereby excluded [...] Therefore they cannot be found by merely observing the process or state of things, and measuring the quantities seen. They can only be found by experiments [...]. But the experiments have an entirely different significance: they actually <u>produce</u> facts which would otherwise not happen at all; if the experimenter did not step in first to produce them, and then to ascertain them, they would remain in the state of 'unknown possibilities', which amount to the deepest inexistence. (D3/12/13/3)

The idea that marginal magnitudes have no place in the real and that their very existence depends on the performance of an experiment, was also a constant in Sraffa's reflections, recurrent in his notes in the years subsequent to 1928–1929, to which the long passage quoted above dates back.

For instance on November 3, 1955, when he resumed working on his book after completing the edition of Ricardo's *Works and Correspondence*, he wrote:

> The most striking feature of the marginal theory of distribution is that it asserts that the method of production and the quantities of the factors of production determine the distribution. And yet, if we suppose that a man from another planet came down to see the system postulated by the marginal theory, he would never, by observation, no matter how searching, succeed in discovering the determinants of distribution. He would himself have to bring them into the open by changing the proportions of the factors, and then observe them. He could discover them by experiment, but never by pure observation. (D3/12/42/86)[5]

These doubts about the existence of marginal magnitudes appear particularly evident in the final period of drafting *Production of Commodities*, subsequent to 1955. In a text of which we have a great many versions we find the following observation:

> But while the former [the average product] can be discovered by observation, the marginal product can only be found by comparing two successive average products, which are incompatible and can exist only in different circumstances and at different times.
>
> The question is, are the potential, hypothetical returns which would be obtained by additional doses part of the existing situation? [...]. (D3/12/46)

Thus Sraffa questions the legitimacy of using magnitudes in economic theory, such as marginal magnitudes, whose existence has to be brought about by experiment. They cannot be used to explain phenomena, since—Sraffa held in 1929—'only really happening things [i.e. "excluding inexistent possibilities"] can be real causes and determine effects' (D3/12/13/1.2). It would be like setting out to explain a natural phenomenon attributing its cause to substances that do not exist in nature but can only be created artificially. Note that marginal magnitudes do not come within the category of the counterfactual, or propositions regarding happenings that cannot be subjected to experiment (what would have happened to European history if Napoleon had won at Waterloo?).[6] Unlike in the counterfactual case, measuring production upon adding the *n* + 1*th* factor *can* be done. However, even granting—which Sraffa does not—that marginal magnitudes could be brought to life by experiment, the question still remains whether they can be used successfully for the purposes for which they are created.

Having established that marginal magnitudes are not of natural occurrence but, if anything, the result of an experiment, Sraffa questions the feasibility of the experiment required. He wrote in October 1929:

> These experiments cannot be carried out (and never have been, as a matter of fact) for various reasons: 1) the practical difficulties, 2) the lack of definition of the conditions to be required, which are always summed up in the absurd 'other things being equal'. (D3/12/13/3)

The fact that the experiment necessary to bring about marginal magnitudes could not be carried out was a constant concern for Sraffa, well after publication of *Production of Commodities* in 1960. As he wrote on 1 January 1963, setting out the reasons for this impossibility more clearly:

> [...] in mechanics if the experiment is repeated in similar circumstances (say, on the elasticity of a metal) the same results will be obtained. But with supply and demand, even if the external circumstances were the same, the result would be different because man learns from experience, or at any rate is changed by it, forms and transforms habits, etc. (D3/12/42/10)

These observations have a general application to social sciences,[7] but Sraffa's contribution consists in questioning the validity of reasoning at the margin, specifically in economics. In the case of marginal productivity theory by means of the 'experiment' measurement is made of the product obtained with *n* + 1 units as compared with that obtained in the preceding instance with *n* units, but what we measure is only the difference between two products. Can it really be claimed that the variation in production brought about by the 'experiment' measures the marginal productivity or, in other words, the contribution to production attributable solely to the *n* + 1*th* unit of the factor? It might be, perhaps, if the *ceteris paribus* condition held, but it is precisely this condition that Sraffa considered highly questionable. The assumption that 'all the rest remains equal' can indeed be interpreted in two ways. Literally, it means that all the other factors and the other units of the same factor continue to be in exactly the same employment (symmetrically, in the case of consumption, the equivalent assumption is that there is no difference in the use to which the other goods are put before and after the addition of one unit) In this case the change in production (or utility) is the result both of the additional quantity and of the different proportion in which the factors of production (or the consumption goods) are combined. How can we 'disentangle' the contribution of the additional unit? This is the problem identified by Robertson (1931: 45–6) as the 'impossibility of disentangling the specific product of the various factors of production', namely how to impute the variation in production to the variation of the factor employed.[8] What we observe is only the difference between two products and not the marginal product (or the marginal utility) of the marginal unit. Alternatively, we may assume that the combination of factors (or goods) is always optimal and that factors or goods are put to a different use when one unit is added, although their quantity is always the same. Even neglecting what is meant by 'same quantity' in the case of capital, *a fortiori* we have no grounds to conclude with certainty that the marginal variation is the contribution of the marginal unit. (This is known in the literature as 'Hobson's objection', see below.)

Does Sraffa think that infinitesimal calculus, introduced into mechanics by Leibnitz and Newton—should be rejected in economic analysis? To answer this question, we can draw on his own judgement of the use of infinitesimal calculus. Sraffa originally viewed the adoption of sophisticated techniques from mechanics positively as facilitating progress in economic science. He believed they could be used to establish a hierarchy between the direct and indirect effects of a cause, identifying the latter as infinitesimals of a higher order, and thus negligible.[9] However, this positive orientation waned somewhat when he realized that the tool had ended up by prevailing over the content. From being a strength, the analogy built by Marshall between economics and mechanics with the aim of improving the scientific status of economics became a weakness.[10] It so happened that Sraffa was almost persuaded to publish the paper 'Margins and margins',[11] where he engaged in full-blown criticism of marginism and which appeared to him as 'disjoined and perhaps inconclusive expressions of dissent from the "marginalist" theory of value and distribution', by the argument that 'I feel however fortified by the echo of criticisms which are being made of the theory of mechanics on which the marginal approach is entirely based' (4 January 1958, D3/12/49/7).

At the same time, however, Sraffa asserted that the end of Newtonian physics could not be used as an argument against marginism, just as

Newton's authority could not be invoked in support of Marshall. He was aware that the *continuum*, a basic assumption of classical mechanics, had lost its central position in contemporary physics.[12]

Sraffa held that change in economic realities hardly ever manifested itself in the form of infinitesimal variations in magnitudes that leave the overall structure unchanged. In a celebrated example in the *Principles*, Marshall represented the process in the railway manager's choice of productive technique thus:

> [...] an alert manager is constantly weighing the net product in saving of time and of annoyance to passengers, that will accrue from the aid of a second guard on an important train and considering whether it will be worth its costs. (Marshall 1920: 5)

Sraffa never found this representation convincing, and made reference to it on various occasions over the years. He eventually wrote on 29 March 1963:

> This suggests that his [the alert manager's] main task is to sack a porter here, add a coach to a train there, or shorten a platform elsewhere. The idea is that the process of change can be reduced to a continuous process, like shortening platforms, 'a penny is the basis of a million', and so a process of shortening, adding, sacking in detail is the route from one position to another. In Marshall's view the 'alert Dr. B' never needs to take bird's eye view of his enterprise. (D3/12/42/12)

However, Sraffa does not seem to have been satisfied with criticising the continuity hypothesis for its lack of realism, but went on to demonstrate the logical impossibility of continuity in the production function with infinitesimal variations in one factor alone if there were more than two factors. For example, on 29 March 1963 he wrote:

> Marshall is constantly on the defensive against objections to continuity based on facts [...]. This is not the basis on which this [my argument] is based. That can be granted in detail, wherever it is possible; it is against the logical possibility of the type of continuity assumed. That type is only possible with two factors.[13] (D3/12/42/12)

His criticism of the continuity hypothesis does not, therefore, concern the hypothesis of infinite divisibility of the factors, but the 'logical' possibility of continuity or, in other words, the possibility that by continually varying the quantity of a factor, both the product and the proportions between the factors go through continual variation. This is a matter that Sraffa had dwelt upon ever since his earliest reflections on the possibility of defining the marginal product, which he expressed in a lengthy comment on Marshall's example of the 'marginal shepherd', namely a herd in the care of shepherds without the support of any capital, investigated by Marshall to define the marginal productivity of labour.[14] Sraffa's objections to the continuity hypothesis appear to have something to do with the perplexity he had always experienced over a comment made by Marshall in a celebrated note to the *Principles* on Hobson's criticism of marginalism. The page where the footnote appears (Marshall 1920: 409n.) is one of the most heavily annotated in Sraffa's copy of the *Principles*. Hobson had observed that when the quantity of a factor increases we cannot attribute the variation in the total product solely to the increased quantity of the factor, thus speaking of the 'marginal productivity of the factor'. In fact, the productivity of the factors whose quantity is maintained constant changes nevertheless, since these factors now combine in different proportions with the variable factor. Marshall had claimed that this effect was 'negligible', given that the variation in productivity (a second derivative) is an infinitesimal of higher order than the product variation (a first derivative). Sraffa never found Marshall's reply truly convincing[15] and continued to dwell on the point even after publication of *Production of Commodities*, which makes no explicit criticism of continuity. Nevertheless, the foundations were laid with demonstration that there may correspond to infinitesimal variations in the rate of profit variations in productive methods that are not 'close', but characterised by very different quantities of the means of production employed.

However, study of variations does find a place in Sraffa, since he does not rule out scientific analysis of observable 'margins'—the elements, that is, that Ricardo takes into account in determining extensive rent. This is an issue that Sraffa returned to on various occasions with slight differences in argumentation, and we shall return to it now, in our examination of which of his arguments against marginism are to be found in his published writings.

15.3 Against Marginism in the Published Writings

Just how do the unpublished writings cited in the preceding sections, dating to various periods in Sraffa's intellectual progress, help us towards a better understanding of his arguments against marginism? To answer this question we focus in this section on examining what his published writings have to tell us about the issue. Our reference here is to the 1925 and 1926 articles and to *Production of Commodities by Means of Commodities*.

The 1925 article can be taken as the starting point of Sraffa's analysis of marginism, since the preparatory notes contain nothing of any importance that did not appear in the published version, and the preceding writings—which, however, show that Sraffa began to take an interest in the issue of marginal productivity very early—offer no significant references to the matters under discussion here.

In the 1925 article Sraffa's focus is manifestly on the objective elements of economic reality, in order to distinguish them from other elements thrown up by the particular type of theory employed to analyse them. We might take, for example, the passage where Sraffa questions whether the classification of industries on the basis of increasing, decreasing or constant returns depends 'on objective circumstances inherent in the various industries, or instead, on the other hand, is dependent on the point of view of the person acting as the observer' (Sraffa 1925: 278, 1998: 324); he goes on to point out that 'the idea of interdependence between quantity produced and the cost of production of a commodity produced under a competitive conditions is not suggested by experience at all' (Sraffa 1925: 279, 1998: 325).[16]

More specifically entering into his criticism of marginism are two particular arguments, one taken up in *Production of Commodities*, the other dealt with in a footnote. The first has to do with the distinction Wicksteed made between margins that he calls 'spurious', which depend on the varying productivity of heterogeneous doses of a factor, and 'pure' margins, in which the marginal productivity depends not on the nature of each single dose of the factor, all being homogeneous, but on the overall number used (Wicksteed 1914: 18–20). The classical example is the Ricardian definition of extensive and intensive rent. The former arises from the different fertility of lands, all of which can be simultaneously cultivated, while the latter is the outcome of application of successive identical doses of capital and labour to the same plot of land. The final point Sraffa comes to in his considerations on the issue is found in the Preface to *Production of*

Commodities, where he acknowledges that Wicksteed's distinction is not groundless, although Sraffa reverses Wicksteed position. It is only 'spurious' margins—which Wicksteed preferred to exclude from economic analysis—that can find a place in Sraffa's theory, legitimised with the consideration that they are indeed observable given the objective fact of their existence. As he observes:

> Caution is necessary, however, to avoid mistaking spurious 'margins' for the genuine article. Instances will be met in these pages which at first sight may be indistinguishable from examples of marginal production; but the sure sign of their spuriousness is the absence of the *requisite kind of change*. (Sraffa 1960: v, italics added)

The revealing words in this passage are 'the requisite kind of change', which draw attention to the nature of variations implied by the marginalist theory.[17] However, in the 1925 article Sraffa denied the foundation that Wicksteed had given to his distinction between spurious and pure margins. He aimed at demonstrating that decreasing marginal productivity does not constitute a physical law deriving from the technical conditions of production, but results from the rational behaviour of the economic agent. It is he/she who decides to use techniques or factors of production in decreasing order of productivity.[18] Thus Wicksteed's distinction between the 'functional' productivity curve (with homogeneous factor) and the 'descriptive' curve (based on the heterogeneity of the factor) is groundless since 'the "functional curve" merely transfers the "difference in nature", and therefore the "arbitrary" ordering from the doses themselves to their modes of utilization' (Sraffa 1998: 337). As Sraffa wrote in the notes written in preparation of the 1925 article, it is like ordering a row of soldiers according to their different height or arranging soldiers of the same height on the steps of a stair. In both cases the decreasing order is the result of a choice (D1/40). Thus Wicksteed's rejection of descriptive curves fails to convince Sraffa, although he does not raise any explicit criticism of the functional curves.

Between the initial formulation in the 1925 article and the final version in *Production of Commodities*, Sraffa made a more thorough exploration of the characteristics of marginal analysis, and the turning point came at the end of the 1920s.

A crucial element in this rethinking was the distinction between *change* and *difference*, which played a key role in Sraffa's formulations at a very early stage of his work on *Production of Commodities*[19] and presented in his Introduction to Ricardo's *Principles.* It seemed quite clear to Sraffa that the change in the quantity of the factor used giving rise to the marginal product for the determination of intensive rent called for the introduction of time.[20] As he wrote in the summer of 1929:

> The fundamental difference is that the extensive (different qualities of land) is truly a purely timeless, or geometrical representation: all the different lands exist simultaneously, at one instant, they and their products can be ascertained, distinguished and measured at one instant, without changing anything in the present arrangements.
>
> On the contrary, the intensive (successive doses of capital and labour on a piece of land) diminishing returns do not exist at any one instant. We can only find these diminishing returns by change, or movement: that is to say, we require time. (D3/12/13/23.2)

In the final stage of drafting *Production of Commodities*, Sraffa returned to the topic of intensive and extensive rent in 'Margins and margins', which he might have considered including in the book. The distinction between the two kinds of margins still appears important to him to clarify the difference between his approach and that of marginism, and again the difference is grounded, as it was in 1929, on the observability and measurability (or lack thereof) of the two types of productivity. There he wrote:

> The names usually given to the two types, 'extensive' and 'intensive', conceal rather than describe the essence of the distinction. This is that the first is based on the difference between situations which are mutually compatible and can coexist at the same time, since they involve the payment of different rents on different qualities of land; while the second is based on changes in the situation on a single quality of land which represent a transition from one to another state, the two states being incompatible and mutually exclusive, since they determine two different rents on the same quality of land. The former compares two or more 'returns' existing side by side within a given set of circumstances: the latter compares successive returns obtained in different circumstances—it implies a comparison between the actual return and a potential alternative return. (D3/12/46/50)

Consistently, even intensive rent in *Production of Commodities* is dealt with by assuming two methods of production which coexist on the same land at the same time. As Sraffa reiterated as late as 17 August 1965, when he was still trying to carry out his project of a complete critique of marginal theory:

> Another aspect, not mentioned by Wicksteed, is that in the first case [intensive rent] there is only a decrease of product in time with the increase of the doses: at any instant of time no difference can be seen. Whereas in the second case [extensive rent] the difference in productivity is noticeable at any instant. The first is a case of change, which takes time to happen: the second is a difference between simultaneous product. (D3/12/42/5)

The second argument against marginism to be found in the 1925 article, albeit confined to a footnote (Sraffa 1998: 358–9fn), relates to the nature of the demand and supply curves. They must indicate the value of the dependent variable for each supposed value of the independent variable, at least in the neighbourhood of equilibrium. Here Sraffa does not go into criticism of the Marshallian determination of equilibrium, obtained by means of the marginal method, although he does make it quite clear that

> If the supply curve is to be considered one of the elements that determine price, it is not sufficient that *only the point of equilibrium* is significant. At least those points in the immediate vicinity must *also* be significant; since these represent precisely the forces that will be set in motion when an accidental shift of the equilibrium position occurs, and that would tend to re-establish that position. (Sraffa 1998: 358)

However, the determination of a curve is remote from every element of observation, entering, rather, into the realm of those experiments that he was to dwell on later. Much later, in one of the versions of the above-mentioned note on 'Margins and margins', Sraffa commented thus on the nature of the curves of the marginal analysis:

> This is nothing less than a declaration of faith in universal determinism, for nothing less can support the belief in the <u>actual existence</u> of a prescribed path which must inevitably be followed, whether by the consumer or by the producer, such as is described by the demand- and supply-curves: for no observation, however minute, of the <u>existing</u> situation (in our case, of the existing methods of production) can bring out the path along which they must move in any given circumstances. (D3/12/46/52)

It should be noted that neither of the two arguments (distinction between pure and spurious margins, determinism) finds its way into the 1926 article, although—as we have seen—they remain the object of intensive and continuous reflection in the unpublished writings. In *Production of Commodities* it is only the result that emerges, clear enough as far as intentions are concerned but rather less so in respect of reasons against marginism. In the preface Sraffa stated quite explicitly that he did not want to bring the changes typical of marginal analysis into his work: 'The investigation is concerned exclusively with such properties of an economic system as do not depend on changes in the scale of production or in the proportions of "factors" '(Sraffa 1960: v). He does state explicitly that:

> It is however a peculiar feature of the set of propositions now published that, although they do not enter into any discussion of the marginal theory of value and distribution, they have nevertheless been designed to serve as the basis for a critique of that theory. (Sraffa 1960: vi)

However, his reasons for rejecting the marginal method find no explicit expression apart from the following passing observation, where he refers to the impossibility of observing the magnitudes deriving its application:

> In a system in which day after day production continued unchanged in those respects, the marginal product of a factor (or alternatively the marginal cost of a product) would not merely be hard to find—it just would not be there to be found. (Sraffa 1960: vi)

Thus we have, it seems, ample confirmation that the arguments against marginism were formulated above all in the unpublished writings, and that the part of his critique that Sraffa chose to publish in explicit form was very small.[21]

15.4 Final Considerations

The requirement that in economics entities be observable and measurable, as we have shown in Sect. 15.2, is a hallmark of Sraffa's critical work. These convictions may have come to him from his studies in the natural sciences (physics and chemistry in particular), which Sraffa pursued from the 1920s (see Kurz and Salvadori 2005), or from his early endorsement of Marxism in his university years (Naldi 2008). To understand the epistemological position held by Sraffa would require investigation of a thoroughness that has not been attempted here. Rather, we have sought to document Sraffa's unending quest for measurable and observable economic magnitudes throughout his unpublished writings and offer some evidence of his constant concern with it.

Starting from the early notes of the 1920s to the crucial period 1927–1928,[22] while preparing for his lectures and dwelling upon the nature of classical political economy, to the Autumn of 1929 when working at his 'equations', he struggled with his argumentations against marginism. When he resumed working on *Production of Commodities*, these concerns were still there and resurfaced in papers dated 1963.

All these writings have remained unpublished, raising the question of why exactly Sraffa was not satisfied with them, but casting no doubts on the strength of his convictions. It seems to us that Sraffa's objections against reasoning at the margin are rooted in his firm conviction that since marginal magnitudes are not observable in nature, their existence could and should be doubted.

Marginal magnitudes have no spontaneous existence and therefore must be created by experiment. However, Sraffa was convinced neither of the possibility of the experiment nor of the *ceteris paribus* condition this experiment requires. To begin with, the comparison between the two alternative situations that cannot coexist at the same time entails the possibility that circumstances may change between the first and second observation. Moreover, even in the simplest possible case of production—as in Marshall's example of the 'marginal shepherd'—the employment of the $n + 1th$ shepherd does not imply that the n shepherds continue in exactly the same occupation, and their different occupation contributes to the product variation as much as the marginal shepherd.

Sraffa's argument is even more evident in the case of consumption of n identical objects; even if we could calculate the difference between the utility of 101 and 100 handkerchiefs which are in the drawer of a consumer (see Ferrante 2006), we cannot conclude that this difference is attributable to the 101st handkerchief since the remaining handkerchiefs also contribute towards it. When we set about measuring the effect of an additional unit, we do not obtain the contribution of the marginal unit but the difference between two total values.

Over the years Sraffa refined and honed his critique as the focus of his analysis shifted towards construction of his own theory, which did not require marginal magnitudes to determine prices. *Production of*

Commodities demonstrates the non-necessity of marginal analysis by constructing a counter-example. To Sraffa's mind, however, this was only the 'prelude' to the critique proper, as the subtitle to his work clearly indicates. The fully formulated critique, based on the arguments reconstructed here, was to follow. One of the many drafts of the preface, bearing the date of 14 December 1957, makes so much quite clear:

> The sketch now submitted to the public has grown out of a projected critique of the marginal theory of production and distribution, to which it was to serve as foundation. It has however seemed better to publish this material by itself so that it may be judged on its own merits. The critique may, or may not, follow later. (D3/12/46/29)

Production of Commodities was never meant to compete with neoclassical analysis in terms of scope and generality. It was meant to show, as in other approaches (from input-output analysis to game theory), that we can do without it.

Notes

1. References are to the catalogue of Sraffa's papers conserved at Trinity College, Cambridge. Abbreviations and symbols, which are frequent in Sraffa's papers, have been substituted with the full forms for easier reading.
2. See, for example, the notes of December 1942 (D3/12/29); 31 January 1955 (D3/12/49); 16 February 1957 (D3/12/42); 11 August 1963 (D3/12/42).
3. Sraffa's research activity on his own theory progressed in steps, with long intervals in-between when he focussed his attention on Ricardo's edition, before the publication of *Production of Commodities by Means of Commodities* and a short period afterwards. Three periods have been identified: 1927–1931; 1941/1942–1945; 1955–1958 (see Kurz 1998; Pasinetti 2001: 142–3; De Vivo 2000: 267). His work on marginism was particularly intense in the late 1920s and late 1950s.
4. In his contribution to a conference in Corfu in 1958, Sraffa is reported as having observed that: 'One should emphasize the distinction between two types of measurement. First there was the one in which the statisticians were mainly interested. Second, there was measurement in theory. The statisticians' measures were only approximate and provided a suitable field for work in solving index number problems. The theoretical measures required absolute precision. Any imperfections in these theoretical

measures were not merely upsetting, but knocked down the whole theoretical basis' (Lutz and Hague 1961: 305).

5. Similarly, he wrote on 7 December 1955: 'The experiments that are suggested by theory to "ascertain" it [i.e. the marginal product] must be directed in the first place to "make" [create] it (whether they can succeed in doing so is another matter)' (D3/12/42; second square brackets in the original).
6. Sen (2003) considers marginal and counterfactual analysis to be the same thing, and argues that it is Sraffa's objection to counterfactuals that explains his aversion to marginal analysis. Ferrante (2006) holds the contrary and argues that marginal notions are not necessarily counterfactual, but can be conceived as factual changes which refer to different instants of time. 'By paraphrasing Sraffa's own terms: in a system which does change, the marginal product is there to be found; but no counterfactuals are needed to make such a statement' (Ferrante 2006: 5).
7. In a similar vein, it has been stated that only in closed systems, 'meaning those in which event regularities or correlations occur, […] an experimenter succeeds in isolating/insulating an intrinsically stable mechanism from the effects of countervailing factors. Under such conditions a regularity can be produced correlating the triggering of the mechanism with its unimpeded effects. Two conditions for guaranteeing a closure are apparent in this experimental case. The first is that we are dealing with a mechanism that is intrinsically constant. The second is that a situation can be engineered ensuring that this mechanism, if triggered, acts in relative isolation. We can refer to these as conditions as respectively the intrinsic and extrinsic closure conditions' (Lawson 2009: 126–7).
8. Given the good personal relationship between Sraffa and Robertson (Naldi 2005), there might have been some exchange on these issues between them. For a good discussion of Robertson's article, see Trabucchi (2008).
9. See the following comment of November 1927: 'His [Marshall's] one contribution is the intelligent application of Leibnitz and Newton analysis to economics' (D3/12/11/11).
10. See comment of 10 January 1963, on Marshall's motto in the *Principles* ('*Natura non facit saltum*'): 'It is Marshall's usual false analogy with Newtonian mechanics' (D3/12/42/8).
11. Actually, we have a great many versions of this typescript among the notes used in the drafting of the preface to *Production of Commodities*. Whether or not it was meant to form part of the preface, we cannot tell.
12. On the inside cover of his own copy of Schrödinger (1952), Sraffa, as usual, noted the pages he found most interesting. Among the passages indicated thus we find: 'We must not admit the possibility of continuous observation. Observations are to be regarded as discrete, discontinuous

events' (p. 27), and: 'If you envisage the development of physics in the last half century, you get the impression that the discontinuous aspect of nature has been forced upon us against our will' (p. 54).

13. The same idea of the applicability of marginal analysis only in particular cases finds expression in a note written in the same period, where we read: 'Where marginism goes astray is in (falsely) assuming [...] that it has general applicability, whereas in fact it only applies exceptionally (in cases where partial change is feasible, there is independence, the whole is not affected)'(D3/12/42/9).
14. "[...] where it is question of adjustments or proportions, the marginal product of any one agent is meaningless: we have to consider the marginal effect of the changing proportion of all" (D1/4/76). References to the 'marginal shepherd' appear frequently in Sraffa's papers (see also D3/12/10).
15. It would be beyond the scope of this paper to reconstruct Sraffa's thoughts on this point, and would certainly prove no simple task. There can, however, be no doubting the fact that his thoughts frequently returned to the topic (see, for example D1/4; Sraffa 1925: fn 64; D3/12/3). At an early stage Sraffa found Marshall particularly ambiguous on this point, having failed to specify where he referred to gross or net product of the marginal factor.
16. For the relevant citations from the early published works, showing Sraffa's objectivist convictions, see Salvadori and Signorino (2006) on the recurrent use of the words reality ('realtà') and concrete reality ('realtà concreta') in the 1925 article (Sraffa 1925: 286, 298, 303, 307, 310, 325, 326, 327 and 328) and similar expressions in the 1926 article. However, the authors also note a greater caution in Sraffa's use of such expression in *Production of Commodities.*
17. Bharadwaj (1990: 53) has pointed at the importance of the 'subtle shift' in the method of economic analysis implied by the shift from the observable changes in production of the extensive rent to the hypothetical changes of intensive rent.
18. The relevance of Sraffa's criticism of Wicksteed is highlighted in Roncaglia (1978: 104–107).
19. See Garegnani (2005: 470ff.) for a thorough discussion of the two manuscripts 'part of a group on a folder marked in Sraffa's handwriting with a generic dating "after 1927"—the second of which is entitled "Difference (simultaneous) vs. Change (succession in time)"'. According to Garegnani Sraffa would have reached a better understanding of the implications of his 'equations' by distinguishing between (simultaneous) differences in prices for the same commodity and changes in the price of that commodity as a result of an exogeneous event.

20. As Sraffa pointed out in a note written on New Year's day 1963, taking up once again his discussion of the nature of Marshallian curves, only referred to in passing in the 1925 article: '[Marshall acknowledges] that if with an increase of output the costs would follow one, declining, path, when output relapsed, costs would follow a different path, not rising as high as the original level: but he does not draw the inevitable conclusion that what he draws are historical, not equilibrium, diagrams' (D3/12/42/11).
21. Pasinetti identifies three streams of thought among Sraffa's papers: (i) the historical reconstruction; (ii) the critique of 'aberration brought into existence by marginal economic theory'; (iii) the construction of a theory that goes back to classical political economy. Only the third was accomplished (see Pasinetti 2001: 143–5).
22. See Garegnani (2005) on Sraffa's turning point in his theoretical and interpretative position which led to his approach to classical and neo-classical political economy.

References

Bharadwaj, K. 1990. Return to Classical Theory, in Bharadwaj, K. and Schefold, B. (eds), *Essays on Piero Sraffa. Critical Perspectives on the Revival of Classical Theory*. London, Routledge.

De Vivo, G. 2000. Note sul percorso intellettuale di Sraffa, in Pivetti, M. (ed.), *Piero Sraffa. Contributi per una biografia intellettuale*, Roma, Carocci.

Ferrante, V. 2006. 'Common Sense' on Margins: From Value to Distribution, *Rivista Italiana degli Economisti*, 11: 119–44.

Garegnani, P. 2005. On a turning point in Sraffa's theoretical and interpretative position in the late 1920s, *European Journal for the History of Economic Thought*, 12: 453–92.

Gilibert, G. 2003. The equation unveiled: Sraffa's price equations in the making, *Contributions to Political Economy*, 22: 27–40.

Kurz, H. 1998. Against the current: Sraffa's unpublished manuscripts and the history of economic thought, *European Journal for the History of Economic Thought*, 5: 437–51.

Kurz, H. 2006. 'Sraffa's Equations "Unveiled"? A comment on Gilibert', mimeo.

Kurz, H. and Salvadori, N. 2005. Representing the production and circulation of commodities in material terms: on Sraffa's objectivism, *Review of Political Economy*, 17: 413–41.

Lawson, T. 2009. Contemporary economics and the crisis, *Real-world Economics Review*, no. 50: 122–31.

Lutz, F.A. and Hague, D.C. 1961. *The Theory of Capital*, London, Macmillan.

Marcuzzo M.C. (ed.) 2006. 'The Cambridge Approach to Economics: a re-invented tradition?' Discussion Paper, no. 52, Dipartimento di Scienze Economiche, Università di Roma, La Sapienza.

Marshall, A. 1920. *Principles of Economics*, 8th edn., London, Macmillan.

Naldi, N. 2005. Robertson and the great divide. The correspondence with Kahn, Kaldor, J. Robinson and Sraffa, in Marcuzzo, M.C. and Rosselli, A. (eds), *Economists in Cambridge. A Study through Their Correspondence, 1907–1946*, London, Routledge.

Naldi, N. 2008. Archival research and the reconstruction of Piero Sraffa's intellectual biography: an interim report, in Leeson, R. (ed.), *Archival Insights into the Evolution of Economics*, Vol. I, London, Palgrave Macmillan.

Pasinetti, L. 2001. Continuity and Change in Sraffa's Thought: An Archival Excursus, in Cozzi, T. and Marchionatti, R. (eds), *Piero Sraffa's Political Economy. A Centinary Estimate*, London. Routledge.

Robertson, D.H. 1931. Wage-grumbles, in Robertson, D.H., *Economic Fragments*, London, P.S. King & Son.

Roncaglia, A. 1978. *Sraffa and the Theory of Prices*, London and New York, Wiley.

Rosselli, A. 2005. Sraffa and the Marshallian Tradition, *European Journal for the History of Economic Thought*, 12: 403–23.

Salvadori, N. and Signorino, R. 2006. Piero Sraffa: the economic reality, the economists and the economic theory. A suggested interpretation, in Marcuzzo, M.C. (ed.) 'The Cambridge Approach to Economics: a re-invented tradition?' Discussion Paper, no. 52, Dipartimento di Scienze Economiche, Università di Roma, La Sapienza.

Schrödinger, E. 1952. *Science and Humanism, Physics in Our Time*, Cambridge, Cambridge University Press.

Sen, A. 2003. Sraffa, Wittgenstein and Gramsci, *Journal of Economic Literature*, 41: 1240–55.

Sraffa, P. 1925. Sulle relazioni fra costo e quantità prodotta, *Annali di Economia*, 2: 277–328.

Sraffa, P. 1926. The laws of returns under competitive conditions, *Economic Journal*, 36: 535–50.

Sraffa, P. 1960. *Production of Commodities by Means of Commodities*, Cambridge, Cambridge University Press.

Sraffa, P. 1998. On the relations between cost and quantity produced, in L. Pasinetti (ed.), *Italian Economic Papers*, Bologna, Il Mulino and Oxford, Oxford University Press.

Trabucchi, P. 2008. 'Capital as a single magnitude in some writings of the early 1930s', Paper presented at the ESHET Conference, Prague, mimeo.

Wicksteed, P.H. 1914. The Scope and Method of Political Economy in the light of the 'marginal theory' of Value and Distribution, *Economic Journal*, 24: 1–23.

CHAPTER 16

Joan Robinson's Challenges on How to Construct a Post-Keynesian Economic Theory

> To me, the expression *post-Keynesian* has a definite meaning; it applies to an economic theory or method of analysis which takes account of the difference between the future and the past.
>
> J.V. Robinson (1978a: 78)

16.1 Premise

There is a generation of economists for whom Joan Robinson is no more than a name buried in a footnote in old-fashioned microeconomic textbooks, linking her to the notion of imperfect competition. For my generation, it is a name reminding us of the "revolutionary" spirit of the 1960s and early 1970s, when she became an icon of various strands of heterodoxy. Challenged by Marxists and Neoclassicals alike, she gained universal respect, as amply evidenced by the standing ovation at the American Economic Association meeting in 1971, when she gave the Richard T. Ely lecture entitled "The Second Crisis in Economic Theory".

Originally publ. in: *Annals of the Fondazione Luigi Einaudi*, LIII (Winter), 2018, pp. 121–35.
Reprint by Springer Nature Switzerland 2024 with kind permission

M. C. Marcuzzo, *Economic Theories, Protagonists and Facts*, Palgrave Studies in the History of Economic Thought,
https://doi.org/10.1007/978-3-031-63949-4_16

Now, 35 years after her death, on August 3rd 1983, and on the occasion of the Japanese translation of Pasinetti's book, which includes one of the best short portraits[1] of Joan Robinson by someone who knew her personally and indeed very well, it is right to remember her as that "mixture of the educational, temperamental and intellectual factors [which] made her one of the leading unorthodox economists of the twentieth century" (Pasinetti 1987: 213, now in Pasinetti 2007: 101).

In this paper I have chosen to re-examine some of the challenges raised by Joan Robinson in constructing a Post-Keynesian economic theory, and I intend to provide some assessment of their relevance today. Rather than dwell on her criticisms of neoclassical economics and of the Neoclassical synthesis, on which much has already been written (even though, unfortunately, not taken on board by mainstream economics), I will focus here on her arguments concerning how to construct a Post-Keynesian economic theory, possibly now forgotten or at any rate neglected. My reasons are that I believe there is still much to be learnt, and by reviving them to offer once again a tribute to an intellectually bold and courageous mind.

In a letter written in a bleak mood following a nervous breakdown, Robinson wrote to Richard Kahn:

> I have realised more than ever after this do how much one's whole personality is involved in one's 'purely intellectual' work. I think the reason I have done so much more with a much weaker brain than any of us is because of my extremely simple minded attitude. (letter of 3 November 1952 in RFK Papers, 13/90/5/352–5)

At the time she was 49 years old, and although she had already produced four books (Robinson 1933, 1937a, 1937b, [1942] 1966), one of which had brought her international recognition, and published more than 100 articles (Marcuzzo 2002), she had made herself known mainly for her fierce defence of Keynesian economics within and outside the Faculty of Economics and Politics, where she was still a Reader at the time. She had been struggling to gain acceptance in the all-male club of economists, and to have a voice among such towering Cambridge intellectuals as Keynes, Kahn, Sraffa and Robertson, to name but a few.

In the following 30 years she would engage in numerous battles, mainly against mainstream economics, but also against what she labelled as "bastard Keynesians", and becoming involved in a series of controversies with Marxists and neo-Ricardians alike, producing, especially from the 1970s, a great number of papers defending her own understanding of what should be discarded and rebuilt in economics. Although towards the end of her life she was overcome by a pessimistic mood[2] and her posthumously published work had the telling title "Spring Cleaning", she left as her legacy the project of "throwing out all self-contradictory propositions, unmeasurable quantities and indefinable concepts and reconstruct a logical basis for analysis" (Robinson 1985: 160).

Pasinetti is one of the few economists who fully accepted the challenge. At the heart of his 2007 book, he called for

> selecting and shaping the theories of Keynes and Sraffa and the developments of Kahn, Robinson and Kaldor (and Goodwin and whoever else have made contributions in the same direction at Cambridge or elsewhere) into a coherent, solid, overall framework. (Pasinetti 2007: 236)

Like Joan Robinson, Pasinetti felt that conceptual differences and heterogeneity of attitudes among the economists of different inspiration and background should not stand in the way of constructing an alternative to neoclassical economics.

In this paper I review some of Robinson's criticisms of heterodox economics in the tradition of Marx and Sraffa and I conclude with an assessment of her "constructive" side, namely proposals regarding the basis on which a Post-Keynesian economics should be constructed.

16.2 Marx and the Marxists

Just a few months before she wrote the above-mentioned letter, Sraffa's *Introduction* to Ricardo's *Principles* had been published. Robinson, unlike many of her Cambridge colleagues, was ready for it. Since 1940 she had been studying Marx[3] (Robinson 1973b: x). She claimed that she "began to read *Capital*, just as one reads any book, to see what was in it" (Robinson [1942] 1966: vi). Maurice Dobb was one of her "tutors",[4] but Kalecki was the main influence. She wrote that Piero Sraffa used to tease her by saying that she "treated Marx as a little-known forerunner of Kalecki" (ibid). In Dec. 1941 she published the article "Marx on Unemployment", in which she explicitly recognised that "Mr. Kalecki's epigram 'The tragedy of investment is that it causes crisis because it is useful' has a close affinity with Marx: 'The real barrier of capitalist production is capital itself'"

([1948] 1951: 134].[5] In fact, when her booklet *Essay on Marxian Economics* came out in 1942, Kalecki's comment was highly appreciative:

> I think that your analysis of Marx is very valuable: it has shown that one conception in his writing is a quite consistent theory; while Marxists who wanted to show that everything is right and consistent failed to show even that. (MK to JVR, 30.7.1942, JVR Papers: vii)

But the book provoked strong reactions from orthodox and Marxist scholars alike.[6] The main conclusion of the book, while revaluing many points of Marxian analysis, was rejection of Marx's value theory; for this reason she has "been treated as an enemy by the professed Marxists ever since" (Robinson [1978b] 1979a: 276).[7]

The problem of the theory of value became the central issue in Robinson's review of the book edited by P. Sweezy, *On the Close of the Marxian System*, which included the essays by Böhm-Bawerk, Hilferding and Bortkiewicz on the "contradiction" between the first and the third volume of *Capital*. In her review, Robinson took a negative view of any attempt "to solve the problem of transformation". She wrote:

> The theory of value, in the narrow sense of a theory of relative prices, is not the heart of Marx's system [...] and nothing that is important in it would be lost if value were expunged from it altogether. (Robinson [1950] 1951: 148)

However, she recognized the importance of the value theory for characterization of the key features of the capitalist system, arguing that:

> it was a mistake for Marxists to allow themselves to be lured onto the terrain of price theory, where the orthodox economists could score some hits (though their own analysis of prices is far from satisfactory). The Marxists should have said: Do not worry about prices. We will get around to that later. Meanwhile we are interested in the mode of production, the rate of accumulation, and the distribution of income. We have a theory of the share of profit – the rate of exploitation. The *share* of profit is far more important than the *rate* of profit. The *share* of profit is something that actually happens and affects people's lives – the *rate* of profit is a mental calculation. [...] The theories that Marx put forward in terms of *value* are the indispensable basis for a treatment of the economics of capitalism, which the orthodox school fails to provide. (Robinson [1977] 1980a: 185–186)

The other point in which she was interested was whether or not a theory of effective demand existed in Marx. She maintained that:

> though Marx explicitly repudiated Say's law as childish nonsense, yet he no more than Mill or Marshall admits the divorce between decisions to save and decisions to invest, which, in Keynes's system, appears as the root cause of crises and unemployment. (Robinson [1948] 1951: 141)

Her conclusion is therefore that, although Marx addresses the problem of unemployment through "the reserve army of labour", in his system the "problem of effective demand does not arise" (ibid.).

These two questions, the repudiation of the theory of value for the determination of relative prices and the assertion that in Marx there is no room for a deficiency of effective demand, are hotly debated even today. In fact, Robinson's criticisms did not, and still do not, meet with approval in Marxist literature, although, after the publication of Sraffa's book, her point about the relevance of the labour theory of value for the determination of relative prices gained acceptance among several commentators. An example is provided by Lippi, who stated that:

> in line with Joan Robinson's view [...] Marx theories can be better appreciated by getting rid of labour value [...] and nothing important is lost if labour values are dropped. (Lippi 1996: 106–7)

Similarly, although many commentators have claimed that in Marx there is a clear understanding that it is in the nature of a monetary economy to have a separation of sales and purchase which may generate a level of insufficient demand (for a recent exposition, see Bellofiore 2018[8]), another recent assessment of Marx's theory of crises argues along lines closer to Robinson's position. It is claimed that in Marx the inevitability of general gluts ensues from

> not the use of money and the separation of sale and purchase, but massive interconnectedness [...]. A severe profit squeeze in a leading sector (whether originating in intermediate good prices, market demand, rising wages or rising use of fixed capital) necessarily turns into a general glut. (Persky 2018)

These, however, remain exceptions within the Marxist camp, where the theory of value is seen as essential to an understanding of the issues which Marx addresses. See for instance, a recent presentation:

> The key to the continuing relevance and analytical strengths of Marxist political economy lies in its capacity to provide a framework of analysis for unifying disparate insights into and critiques of the contradictions of capitalism across the social sciences. The instrument for forging that unity is Marx's theory of value. (Fine and Saad-Filho 2018)

16.3 Sraffa and the Neo-Ricardians

The evidence that study of Marx provided Joan Robinson with the key to understanding Sraffa's Introduction to Ricardo's *Principles* is to be found in a collection of three short essays, *On Re-reading Marx*, in which she said:

> [The Introduction] caused me to see that the concept of the rate of profit on capital is essentially the same in Ricardo, Marx, Marshall and Keynes. (Robinson [1953] 1973a: 247)

In these essays she argued that, unlike in the short period, in the long period capital changes and the question "what is the quantity of capital" cannot be avoided; the point was taken up in her famous 1954 article, which is widely regarded as the starting point of the capital theory controversies. Since the question of Joan Robinson's priority in the criticism of neoclassical capital theory was raised, it may be helpful to quote what she wrote to Kahn in 1975:

> It is true that I anticipated Piero's publication but only because I had more or less worked it out for myself from his Introduction to Ricardo's *Principles* – the corn economy. (Letter of 25 February 1975 in RFK papers: 13/90/10/191–2)

Thus she pointed up the neoclassical failure to distinguish between changes in the conditions of producing a given output when the quantity of capital is altered from changes in the value of that capital due to variations in wages and profits.

The implication she drew is that "different factor ratios cannot be used to analyse changes in the factor ratio taking place through time", because in time the value of the quantity of capital may change as a consequence of a change in distribution and the same quantities were not being comparing. She concluded that "it is impossible to discuss changes (as opposed to differences) in neo-classical terms" (Robinson [1954] 1978c: 89).

These arguments persuaded her of the inadequacy of supply and demand analysis in dealing with the passing of time—which is irreversible—as if it were a movement in space. She claimed that the lesson that she had learned concerned questions of time. She would argue the point with Sraffa, who evidently disagreed, as an unpublished letter makes clear:

> Dear Piero: all the work that I have being doing the last 10 years has been much influenced by you – both our conversations in the old days and by your Preface. When I went off my head I thought that the idea that I had seen in a blinding flash was yours, because it came to me in terms of Ricardo's corn economy; but it was connected with TIME and it now appears is very much alien to your point of view (though to me it seems to fit perfectly well). Since, quite apart from worldly success, I have a lot of fun. I have a very deep feeling of gratitude to you. The fact that you reject it doesn't affect the case at all. Yours, Joan. (JVR to PS, 18 June 1960, PS papers: D3/12/111/340–1; see Marcuzzo 2005)

The distinction between historical and logical time for Joan Robinson brought with it repudiation of the notion of equilibrium—in particular the concept of long-run equilibrium—which is the hallmark of the classical approach for some of Sraffa's followers and therefore, according to them, also the key to Sraffa's production prices. Her criticisms run as follows:

> *When* is the long-run position with prices corresponding to a uniform rate of profit? Is it in the future or in the past? Or only in a journal article?
>
> I certainly agree that, in any actual situation, there is a share of wages (though it is not unambiguously measurable) and there is a stock of means of production (though it is a job lot of past vintage). I concede that we might imagine that we could detect the ghost of a long-run rate of profit that would correspond to the momentary actual situation if it were permanent (though it is necessarily in the course of changing). Perhaps the succession of values of this ghost could be traced through historical time, to see whether it has had a falling tendency. But there are so many indeterminacies in such a calculation that probably anyone who attempted it would only get

> an answer corresponding to his preconceptions, whatever they might be. (Robinson [1980b] 1980a: 128)

It is the *expectation* of profits as opposed to the equalization of the rate of profit which, according to Robinson, "is the operative force". And she added: "The very description of equilibrium implies that correct decisions were made in the past" (ibid.).

It is the critique of the concept of equilibrium itself, and not only of neoclassical equilibrium, which she sees as the legacy of Keynes (and Marx).[9] She wrote:

> The concept of equilibrium is incompatible with history. It is a metaphor based on movements in space applied to processes taking place in time. In space, it is possible to go to and from and remedy misdirection, but in time, every day, the past is irrevocable and the future unknown. (Robinson 1979c: xiv)

It follows that this is where Joan Robinson saw the main line of attack on the neoclassical theory as lying, and not between two alternative explanations of prices and distribution, as the neo-Ricardians had it. Moreover, she objected that in Sraffa:

> there is no room here for short-period "Keynesian" movements in the level of utilisation of stocks of inputs or employment of labour. The language of change may be used, for it is difficult to describe a map without using the language of moving about on it, but essentially the argument is conducted strictly in terms of comparisons of logically possible positions. (Robinson [1980c] 1980a: 132)

This is why she felt it more promising to rely on Keynes who, "at the opposite extreme to Sraffa, discusses only events" (Robinson [1979b] 1980a: 139) and discusses them "in terms of processes taking place in actual history" (Robinson 1979c: xiv).

In conclusion, Robinson objected to the method of comparisons in classical political economy and Sraffa because they showed no substantial difference from the neoclassical equilibrium method in their neglect of uncertainty and disregard of expectations, which she claimed are the guiding forces of economic behaviour.

How were these criticisms met?

Garegnani insisted that the assumption of irreversibility in time is implicit only in the method of supply and demand analysis, whereby the tendency towards equilibrium is described as movements along those curves, while the same assumption is not made when comparing two long-run equilibrium positions determined by a "classical" theory of prices and distribution. (Garegnani 1979).

Krishna Bharadwaj also responded with two objections to Robinson's criticisms. First, the equilibrium concept does not entail that the corresponding prices and the uniform rate of profit actually rule at any particular moment in time. It is, rather, the tendency towards it, driven by the forces believed to be persistent, that is argued. Second, while not denying that uncertainty or expectations had a role to play, Robinson followed Sraffa in defending an objective method of analysis, which does not invoke non-observable entities, such as individual utility functions, but rather considers customs, social norms and the like (see Marcuzzo 2014a).

16.4 Post-Keynesian Economic Theory

Notwithstanding her criticisms, Robinson argued for an integration of Sraffa's results into a Marshallian and Keynesian framework, so as to give birth to a true alternative to neoclassical economics, which she labelled Post-Keynesian:

> The classical tradition, revived by Sraffa, which flows from Ricardo through Marx, diluted by Marshall and enriched by the analysis of effective demand of Keynes and Kalecki. (Robinson 1973b: xii)

Over the years, she unsuccessfully tried to convince the Keynesians that the gulf between Keynes and Sraffa could be bridged. Similarly, she unsuccessfully tried to convince the "Sraffians" that there was no incompatibility with Keynes' theory.[10] She must, however, have been aware of the difficulty of achieving such an integration when she wrote:

> The post-Keynesian theory reaches back to clasp the hands of Ricardo and Marx, skipping over the sixty years of dominance of neoclassical doctrines from 1870 to the great slump. This accounts for the paradox that post-Keynesian analysis derives equally from two such apparently incompatible sources as Piero Sraffa's interpretation of Ricardo and Michal Kalecki's interpretation of the theory of employment. (Robinson [1974] 1978c: 126)

She pointed out that she saw it only as an apparent paradox:

Because Keynes was trying to understand how the economy works, he was unwittingly following the line of Ricardo and Marx, who were engaged in the same quest, each trying to understand the operation of capitalism in his own day. Keynes was clearing up a particular element in it (effective demand) that Ricardo had ignored and Marx imperfectly understood. This explains the apparent paradox that the post-Keynesians in Cambridge find an affinity with the classics (Robinson [1979d] 1979a: 115).

But what are the ingredients of this integration?

The first is "negative" or critical awareness of the weakness of the neo-classical notion of equilibrium resulting from the balancing of demand and supply schedules. Although she was concerned more with challenging the notion of equilibrium as such, since "it cannot be used to discuss the *effects* of *change*. It can only deal with *comparisons* of imagined *differences*" (Robinson [1978d] 1978c: xix) than with rejecting the construction of demand and supply as based on marginal calculation (as Sraffa did), she nevertheless admitted that:

> The post Keynesians must make use of Sraffa to build up a type of long-period analysis which will prevent neoclassical equilibrium from oozing back into the *General Theory*. (Robinson [1978a] 1980a: 82)

Although Sraffa "was completely successful in his aim of providing a basis for the critique of neoclassical theory", Robinson was convinced that *Production of Commodities by Means of Commodities* provided "a very narrow basis for constructive analysis" (Bhaduri and Robinson 1980: 64).

So where is the suitable basis?

Surprisingly, the foundation stone is drawn from Marx:

> The schema for expanding reproduction provide a very simple and quite indispensable approach to the problem of saving and investment and the balance between production of capital goods and demand for consumer goods. It was rediscovered and made the basis for the treatment of Keynes' problem by Kalecki and reinvented by Harrod and Domar as the basis for the theory of long-run development. (Robinson [1955] 1978c: 66)

Then there is also a bit of Ricardo, and she approvingly refers to Pasinetti (1974: ix) to support the inclusion of Ricardo in the reconstruction project, as saying "Keynes' theory of effective demand, which has remained so impervious to reconciliation with marginal economic theory, raises almost no problem when directly inserted into the earlier discussions of the Classical economists".

Hence Ricardo (with the help of Sraffa) "provides the basis for a theory of the rate of profit on capital" (Robinson [1974] 1978c: 133), because

> the concept of the rate of profit on capital is essentially the same in Ricardo, Marx, Marshall and Keynes; while the essential difference between these, on the one side, and Walras, Pigou and the latter-day textbooks on the other, is that the Ricardians are describing an historical process of accumulation in a changing world, while the Walrasians dwell in timeless equilibrium where there is no distinction between the future and the past? (Robinson [1978d] 1978c: xi)

However, for Joan Robinson the function of Sraffa's prelude to a critique is "mainly negative—to knock out the marginal productivity theory and clear a space where a Marxian analysis of modern problems can grow up" (Robinson [1975] 1980a: 122).

More difficult to understand is the inclusion of Marshall as a forefather of Post-Keynesian economics. But let us see her reasons:

> Marshall retained something of the classical tradition. His world is inhabited by businessmen, housewives, workers, trade union leaders, bankers and traders [...] he was studying a recognizable economy in a particular phase of its historical development, in which recognizable classes of the community interact with each other in a particular framework of law and accepted conventions. (Robinson [1974] 1978c: 131]

The constructive element of Post-Keynesian economics, for Joan Robinson, comes from "Kalecki's version of the *General Theory*, rather than Keynes'" (Robinson [1975] 1980a: 122). Of course, at the early stage of the Keynesian revolution she championed Keynes and later defended him against what she called the "bastard Keynesians", or the Neo-classical synthesis as it also known. However, in later years she saw Kalecki's approach as better suited to the project of constructing a Post-Keynesian theory.

For this she gave two reasons: (a) Kalecki's background as a Marxist allows for a better integration of Marx's important intuitions (such as the reproduction schemes, the reserve army of labour; (b) Kalecki's dual approach to price determination—supply and demand and competition for primary commodities, and mark-up and monopolistic competition for industrial goods—are more respondent to the reality of the contemporary world (Robinson [1978d] 1978c: xx).

Thus Kalecki's version was "in some ways more truly a *general* theory than Keynes's", because he brought "imperfect competition into the analysis and emphasized the influence of investment on the share of profits" (Robinson [1972] 1978c: 5). Nevertheless, she felt that what was missing (the role of money, uncertainty and the multiplier) in Kalecki could and should be supplemented by Keynes.

16.5 Conclusions

Joan Robinson felt that Post-Keynesian theory was a project to be accomplished, rather than a construction which had been completed. She also foresaw that it might take time to do it. She wrote:

> Post-Keynesian theory has plenty of problems to work on. We now have a general framework of long- and short-period analysis which will enable us to bring the insights of Marx, Keynes and Kalecki into a coherent form and apply them to the contemporary scene, but there is still a long way to go. (Robinson [1978a] 1980a: 85)

In this respect Joan Robinson's position is close to that of Pasinetti, who chose to subtitle his 2007 book "a revolution in economics to be accomplished" and had previously maintained that the two types of analysis associated with Sraffa and Keynes "have originally stemmed from the same preoccupations (inadequacy of traditional marginal economics) and have built on the same common ground (classical economics)" (Pasinetti 1986: 16).[11]

Pasinetti, in particular, sees the concept of vertically integrated sectors "as a quite clear and logical way to accomplish an integration of the two types of economic analysis, associated with the names of Sraffa and Keynes" (ibid.).

In Joan Robinson's position, there is, however, a less clear indication of how exactly this bridge between the two theories could be forged. She wrote:

> We now have a more or less satisfactory theory of prices in a short period situation, with given plant embodying technology, given money wage rates

> and given expectations. And we have an analysis of long-period normal prices corresponding to a uniform rate of profit on capital. But all important and interesting questions lie in the gap between the two. (Robinson [1978d] 1978c: xx)

She did not seem to find any difficulties in making Kalecki's price determination or Keynes's consistent with Sraffa's production prices, as she once wrote bluntly to Kahn:

> Cannot we agree on Piero's prices for the long run and on Keynes' prices for the short run and leave it at that? (letter of 19 May 1961 in RFK Papers 13/90/6/199–200 (see Marcuzzo 2003)

Several of Joan Robinson's challenges have been addressed by the enlarged family of what we now term Post-Keynesian economics, which is a very composite group of people often at odds with each other, but I think united in the belief that Joan Robinson is the leading and iconic figure with whom most of them could identify. She may not have laid down the reconstructive part of the project of an alternative to neoclassical economics in full detail, but she was very compelling in denouncing its inconsistencies and inadequacy for an understanding of the real world. Moreover, her analysis was particularly forceful in pointing out the ideological elements embodied in any economic theory (also in those whose views she endorsed),[12] urging us to disentangle the ideology and extract the logic rather than the axe-grinding of the arguments.

She was not herself immune from one-sidedness, as a delightful account of having her as Supervisor in Cambridge has revealed (Waterman 2003). She could come across as opinionated, but she conveyed that commitment to the search for truth which wins awe and respect, also by critics and opponents.

Notes

1. An enthusiastic but balanced, approving but not uncritical book-length assessment of Joan Robinson's intellectual achievements can be found in Harcourt and Kerr (2009).
2. In one of her last interviews she is quoted as saying: "I have spent my life in economic theory and it has come to pieces in my hands" (*National Times*, Feb. 1983).

3. In an unpublished paper Robinson recalls the story of her involvement with Marxism: "In 1936 I published a review of a book by John Strachey (brother of the more famous Lytton) who had set up as a populariser of Marx—*The Nature of Capitalist Crisis*—I accused him of presenting the labour theory of value in terms of Say's Law, ignoring Keynes and treating Hayek as the representative of academic economics. He replied that it was absurd for someone who had never read Marx to talk about him. We each felt that the other had made a fair point. He began to read Keynes and I read Marx" (JVR papers: i/10.1).
4. See the exchange of letters between January and May 1941 in JVR papers: vii.
5. The first two paragraphs of the 1941 article, "Marx on Unemployment", were integrated in the 1948 article, "Marx and Keynes", from which the quotations are taken.
6. The attitude towards Marx in the academic circles of the time was described by Joan Robinson in the following terms: "In those days most of my academic colleagues in England thought that to study Marx was a quaint pastime (though Keynes, who was allergic to Marx's writings, received my *Essay* kindly) and in the United States it was disreputable" (Robinson [1966] 1942: vi).
7. However, see the following episode narrated by Asimakopulos (1984: 407): "Brus and Kowalik recall that the first time they met Robinson was at an official function for a group of visiting economists in Poland the day after the events of June 1956, when workers in Gdansk and Poznan had risen up against the authorities and provoked bloody reprisals. The atmosphere was heavy with unexpressed thoughts about the events, but only vacuous comments about the value of exchanges of views were being made—Robinson could not let things stand without stating the need to find out what had happened and why. 'Until that time we had thought of Joan Robinson as a left Keynesian bent on confronting Marxism with difficult questions. But at that moment she acquired a moral authority which she retained all her life. Joan Robinson was a person who awakened conscience and asked questions which disturbed complacency whether it be the complacency of academic or of Marxist orthodoxy' (Brus and Kowalik 1983: 244)".
8. "The possibility of crisis arises when money is hoarded, because of the pessimistic prospects of capitalist-entrepreneurs or money-capitalists, and brings with it unsold commodities and involuntary unemployment. Crisis is a 'break' in the circuit—a point that encompasses both Keynes's view of crisis as the result of a rise in liquidity preference (failure to 'close' the circuit), and circuitists' view of crisis as an outcome of capitalist-entrepreneurs' reluctance to invest (failure to 'open' the circuit)" (Bellofiore 2018: 39).

9. "For me, the main message of Marx was the need to think in terms of history, not of equilibrium" (Robinson 1973b: x).
10. This saw it as reparation for an original sin: "The book [PCMC] was not published until 1960. Sraffa had shown a draft to Keynes in 1928. Keynes evidently did not make much of it and Sraffa, in turn, never made much of the *General Theory*. It is the task of post Keynesians to reconcile the two" (Robinson [1978a] 1980a: 81).
11. I have elsewhere expressed my doubts as to whether this is a historically accurate reconstruction of the origin and nature of Keynes's and Sraffa's "preoccupations" (see Marcuzzo 2014b).
12. See Robinson ([1955] 1978c: 71) for a skilful excursus on the ideological elements in Marx, Marshall and Keynes, which can be reversed leading to paradoxical conclusions, namely: "Marx's analysis of capitalism shows its strong points, although his purpose was to attack it. Marshall's argument inadvertently shows the wastefulness of capitalism, although he meant to recommend it. Keynes in showing the need for remedies to the defects of capitalism also shows how dangerous the remedies may be".

References

Asimakopulos A. 1984, "Joan Robinson and Economic Theory", *BNL Quarterly Review*, 37 (151): 65–95.

Bellofiore R. 2018, "The Multiple Meanings of Marx's Value Theory", *Monthly Review*, 69: 31–48.

Bhaduri A. and Robinson J.V 1980, "Accumulation and Exploitation: An Analysis in the Tradition of Marx, Sraffa and Kalecki", in J.V. Robinson, *Further Contributions to Modern Economics*, Oxford: Blackwell: 64–77.

Brus W. and Kowalik T. 1983, "Socialism and Development", *Cambridge Journal of Economics*, 7: 243–255.

Fine B. and Saad-Filho A. 2018, "Marx 200: The Abiding Relevance of the Labour Theory of Value", *Review of Political Economy*, 30 (3): 339–354.

Garegnani P.A. 1979, "Notes on consumption, investment and effective demand: a reply to Joan Robinson", *Cambridge Journal of Economics*, 3: 181–187.

Harcourt G.C. and Kerr P. 2009, *Joan Robinson*, Basingstoke: Palgrave Macmillan.

Lippi M. 1996, "Joan Robinson on Marx's Theory of Value", in M.C. Marcuzzo, L. Pasinetti and A. Roncaglia (eds.), *The Economics of Joan Robinson*, Routledge: London: 101–111.

Marcuzzo M.C. 2002, "The Writings of Joan Robinson", in the Palgrave Archive edition of *Joan Robinson, Writings on Economics*, vol. 1, London: Macmillan: xxxii–lxxiii.

Marcuzzo M.C. 2003, "Joan Robinson and the Three Cambridge Revolutions", *Review of Political Economy*, 15: 545–560.

Marcuzzo M.C. 2005, "Robinson and Sraffa", in B. Gibson (ed.), *The Economic Legacy of Joan Robinson*, Cheltenham: Elgar: 29–42.

Marcuzzo M.C. 2014a, "On Alternative Notions of Change and Choice. Krishna Bharadwaj's Legacy", *Cambridge Journal of Economics*, 38: 49–62.

Marcuzzo M.C. 2014b, "Pasinetti and the Cambridge Economists", *History of Economics Review*, 60: 15–29.

Pasinetti L. 1974, *Growth and Income Distribution*, Cambridge: Cambridge University Press.

Pasinetti L. 1986. "Sraffa's Circular Process and the Concept of Vertical Integration", *Political Economy—Studies in the Surplus Approach*, 1: 3–16.

Pasinetti L. 1987, "Joan Violet Robinson", in J.L. Eatwell, M. Milgate and P. Newman (eds.), *The New Palgrave. A Dictionary of Economics*, vol. 4, London: Macmillan: 212–17.

Pasinetti L. 2007, *Keynes and the Cambridge Keynesians*, Cambridge, UK: Cambridge University Press.

Persky J. 2018, "Say's Law, Marxian Crisis Theory and the Interconnectedness of the Capitalist Economy", *Review of Political Economy*, 30 (3): 269–283.

Robinson J.V. 1933, *The Economics of Imperfect Competition*, London: Macmillan.

Robinson J.V. 1937a, *Essays in the Theory of Employment*, London: Macmillan.

Robinson J.V. 1937b, *Introduction to the Theory of Employment*, London: Macmillan.

Robinson J.V. [1942] 1966, *An Essay on Marxian Economics*, London: Macmillan.

Robinson J.V. 1948, "Marx and Keynes", in Robinson 1951: 133–145.

Robinson J.V. 1950, "The Labour Theory of Value", in Robinson 1951: 146–151.

Robinson J.V. 1951, *Collected Economic Papers*, vol. I, Oxford: Blackwell.

Robinson J.V. 1953, "Essays 1953: Introduction", in Robinson 1973a: 247–248.

Robinson J.V. 1954, "The Production Function and the Theory of Capital", in Robinson 1978c: 76–90.

Robinson J.V. 1955, "Marx, Marshall and Keynes", in Robinson 1978c: 61–75.

Robinson J.V. 1972, "The Second Crisis of Economic Theory", in Robinson 1978c: 1–14.

Robinson J.V. 1973a, *Collected Economic Papers*, vol. IV, Oxford: Blackwell.

Robinson J.V. 1973b, "Preface" to J.A. Kregel, *The Reconstruction of Political Economy: an Introduction to Post-Keynesian Economics*, London: Macmillan, pp. ix–xiii.

Robinson J.V. 1974, "History versus Equilibrium", in Robinson 1978c: 126–136.

Robinson J.V. 1975, "Survey: 1960s", in Robinson 1980a: 112–122.

Robinson J.V. 1977, "The Labour Theory of Value", in Robinson 1980a: 183–191.

Robinson J.V. 1978a, "Keynes and Ricardo", in Robinson 1980a: 78–85.

Robinson J.V. 1978b, "Formalism vs Dogma", in Robinson 1979a: 275–279.

Robinson J.V. 1978c, *Contributions to Modern Economics*, Oxford: Blackwell.

Robinson J.V. 1978d, "Reminiscences", in Robinson 1978c: ix–xx.

Robinson J.V. 1979a, *Collected Economic Papers*, vol. V, Oxford: Blackwell.
Robinson J.V. 1979b, "Misunderstanding in the theory of production", in Robinson 1980a: 135–140.
Robinson J.V. 1979c, "Introduction" to *The Generalization of the General Theory and Other Essays,* London: Macmillan.
Robinson J.V. 1979d, "Thinking about Thinking", in Robinson 1979a: 110–119.
Robinson J.V. 1980a, *Further Contributions to Modern Economics*, Oxford: Blackwell.
Robinson J.V. 1980b, "Debate: 1970s", in Robinson 1980a: 123–130.
Robinson J.V. 1980c, "Retrospect: 1980", in Robinson 1980a: 131–134.
Robinson J.V. 1985, "The Theory of Normal Prices and Reconstruction of Economic Theory", in G.R. Feiwel (ed.), *The Theory of Normal Prices and Reconstruction of Economic Theory*, London: Macmillan: 157–165.
Waterman A.M.C. 2003, "Joan Robinson as a Teacher", *Review of Political Economy*, 15: 589–596.

CHAPTER 17

Fighting Austerity. Why After 80 Years the *General Theory* is Still Relevant Today

In the aftermath of the 2007–2008 crisis, the name of Keynes has again entered the list of economists to be read, whose ideas are to be taken seriously. After over twenty-five years of ostracism, spent praising the efficiency of free markets and running econometric tests to prove that economic policies are either ineffectual or even irrelevant, there has been an upsurge in the wave of references to Keynes in the media. Unfortunately, this has not been reflected in the academic scene, still dominated by the macroeconomics of anti- or pre-Keynesian inspiration that took hold between the 1970s and 1980s.

To reclaim the topical importance of *The General Theory of Employment, Interest and Money*, I would like to begin by pointing out how the space assigned to government intervention has shrunk in contemporary public opinion; it was the "policy space" opened up by Keynes's denunciation that market laws are neither natural nor unchangeable. The guiding spirit

---

Lecture delivered as *Jean Monet Conference*, in the Faculdade de Ciencias Económicas—UFMG in Belo Horizonte on June 1, 2017. An earlier and shorter version has been published in Italian in *Moneta e Credito*, vol. 70 n. 277 (March 2017), pp. 7–19.

Originally publ. in: *Brazilian Keynesian Review*, 3 (1), 2017, pp. 14–24. Reprint by Springer Nature Switzerland 2024 with kind permission

M. C. Marcuzzo, *Economic Theories, Protagonists and Facts*, Palgrave Studies in the History of Economic Thought, https://doi.org/10.1007/978-3-031-63949-4_17

of the Keynesian Revolution is that full employment is a goal which can be pursued not by following the free market rules, but by reshaping them by means of public intervention. This message was widely accepted for thirty years as from the end of the Second World War by all the advanced countries which actively engaged in full employment and welfare policies, and subsequently abandoned with the neo-liberal Restoration which saw the dogmas of individualism and de-regulation prevailing.

In reclaiming the topical importance of the *General Theory*, we should of course take into consideration the changed circumstances of today's world when compared to those of twenty—let alone eighty—years ago, although there are notable similarities between the Great Depression of the 1930s—Keynes's world—and our contemporary crisis.[1] A corresponding similarity is to be seen between the economic theory prevailing before Keynes's times and that of our own times (see Wray 2013).

The return to Keynes I would like to see, arguing for its topical relevance, is firstly in the realm of method. In a famous letter to George B. Shaw, written a few weeks before the publication of the *General Theory* in February 2016, Keynes announced it as a book "which will largely revolutionise [...] the way the world thinks about economic problems" (Keynes 1971–89, CWK XIII: 492). And in the same letter he added:

> When my new theory has been duly assimilated and mixed with politics and feelings and passions, I can't predict what the final upshot will be in its effect on action and affairs. But there will be a great change. (Keynes 1971–89, CWK XIII: 493)

Rather than invoking the "scientific" aspect of his theory, Keynes turned to "politics and feelings and passions", to anticipate how his message would be received. A couple of years later, in a letter to Roy Harrod, recalling the story of Newton's discovery of the law of gravity on observing an apple fall to the ground while sitting in the garden of Trinity College, Cambridge, Keynes listed the questions that an economist should be asking: for instance, whether

> the fall of the apple to the ground depended on the apple's motives, on whether it is worth while falling to the ground, and whether the ground wanted the apple to fall, and on mistaken calculations on the part of the apple as to how far it was from the centre of the earth. (Keynes 1971–89, CWK XIV: 300)

Economics—Keynes wrote—"deals with introspection and with values [...] it deals with motives, expectations, psychological uncertainties" (Keynes 1971–89, CWK XIV: 300), whose scope is neither "constant nor homogeneous". There cannot be an analogy with physical sciences, because they aim at discovering regularities from which to derive general laws, while economics is expected to capture the effects of decisions taken in an uncertain environment and with different degrees of information. So the object of economic theory is that of developing a logical way of thinking about factors, which are "transitory and fluctuating" (Keynes 1971–89, CWK XIV: 297).

When Keynes states in the *General Theory* that the level of employment oscillates around "an intermediate position" below full employment and above the minimum subsistence employment (Keynes 1971–89, CWK VII: 254), he explains that this position "is a fact of observation concerning the world as it is or has been, and not a necessary principle which cannot be changed" (ibid). The point made here is that in economics "we cannot hope to make completely accurate generalisations" (ibid.) because the economic system is not ruled by "natural forces" that economists can discover and order in a neat pattern of causes and effects. The task of economics, according to Keynes, is rather to "select those variables which can be deliberately controlled and managed by central authority in the kind of system in which we actually live" (ibid.).

Keynes's critique is directed against a conception of economics as scientific study of society modelled on the method of the physical sciences, and it is a plea to start investigating the problems involved in seeking to bring about desired end states. Only by exposing the fallacy of the analogy of economic laws with physical laws does it become possible to promote values and attitudes to change society. Keynes wrote:

> it is many generations since men as individuals began to substitute moral and rational motive as their spring of action in place of blind instinct. They must now do the same thing collectively. (Keynes 1971–89, CWK XVII: 453)

Letting individuals be guided by self-interest alone—as in Adam Smith's parable of "the butcher, the brewer and the baker", whose pursuit of individual profit produces a social good—is not a principle of general validity, because there are not always forces to harmonize individual interests and, moreover, aggregate economic behaviour does not have the same outcome as individual economic behaviour. If the goal is to change the environment within which individuals operate, we ought to change the way we see the economic problem. This could be achieved, according to Keynes, through the power of persuasion. In a letter to T.S. Eliot of 5 April 1945, he wrote:

> [...] the main task is producing first the intellectual conviction and then intellectually to devise the means. Insufficiency of cleverness, not of goodness, is the main trouble [...] the full employment policy by means of investment is only one particular application of an intellectual theorem. (Keynes 1971–89, CWK XXVII: 384)

And earlier on, in a famous speech to the House of Lords on May 23, 1944, he wrote:

> [for the last twenty years] I have spent my strength to persuade my countrymen and the world at large to change their traditional doctrines and, by taking better thought, to remove the curse of unemployment. (Keynes 1971–89, CWK XXVI: 16)

Clearly, by "better thought", Keynes meant a theory which, among other things, made the elimination of unemployment possible, rejecting the doctrine that whatever unemployment there is—as long as it is market generated—is a level which the same market forces—if unimpeded by "rigidities" (any of these: prices, wages, interest rate) would re-establish in the long run. This is the reason why in modern macroeconomics this level has been labelled as "natural".

In the aftermath of the Second World War we witnessed a transformation of economic theory into a set of models which, although at the cost of extreme simplification, were thought able to capture the fundamentals of the economic system they were describing; it was believed that models enabled empirical verifications of the variables and offered the means to provide the tools for policy intervention.

The stress on forecasting, measurement, empirical testing was meant to enhance the scientific aspect of economics, where "scientific" again implied resemblance to the physical science, to their rigour and predictive power.

After Lionel Robbins (1932) had declared that ethics and political philosophy considerations should be banned from economic theory, Karl Popper in the 1930s (Popper [1935] 1959) vindicated the idea that economics could be a science only if value-free and with predictive power.

In the following two decades Friedman's insistence on prediction as the only test for economic theories and Samuelson's mathematization of economics gave a new boost to the faith in imitation of the physical sciences as far as the chosen method of scientific inquiry is concerned.

It is now apparent that this conception of what constitutes a good economic theory has not proved reliable, having had—especially in the recent crises—many examples of the inadequacy of mainstream theory in understanding let alone predicting forthcoming events. If facts are identified with empirical estimates of models that are believed to incorporate the progress made in the economic literature, it is clear that these "facts" are heavily dependent on the choice of the models and the methodology employed to find them. The relationship between facts and theory becomes opaque and we may reasonably challenge the motives behind the discovery of "facts", for they tend to be recognized or ignored according to the ebbs and flows of academic fashions. Let me take an example that is recent history.

My example is the multiplier—the heart of the Keynesian theory of effective demand—which has a story of alternate acceptance and rejection in its over 70 years of existence. It is a formula telling us that every increase in autonomous expenditure (for instance private or public investment or exports) generates—through induced expenditure (net consumption, i.e. allowing for taxation and imports)—an increase in income greater than the initial expenditure, provided there are capacity underutilisation and unemployment. This is why the formula is called the "multiplier", because typically it gives a number greater than 1.

Deficit spending, i.e. a level of public spending greater than tax revenue—is justifiable on two counts: a) because it creates income; b) because it generates the savings and tax revenues (both functions of the level of income) necessary to finance the initial investment. The consensus on this proposition lasted for almost 30 years until it was seriously challenged by the Monetarist assault of the late sixties. Building on his (and Franco Modigliani's) earlier work on the consumption function, Milton Friedman, on the basis of empirical estimate, showed that the independent variable in the consumption function was not current income, but income that can be assumed to be perceived as permanent over an individual life-time.

When consumption is made a function of permanent rather than current income, the value of the multiplier becomes much smaller, with the result that the whole idea that an increase in autonomous expenditure is expansionary was lost, sowing the seeds for mistrust of fiscal policy as a means to reach full employment. This, which came to be named The Monetarist Counterrevolution, was taken further by Robert Lucas and the New Classical economists well into the 1990s, meeting with feeble defence by the New Keynesians, who relegated the efficacy of the multiplier to the very short period, when prices and wage rigidities prevented the system from getting into full employment equilibrium.

Until the outbreak of the 2007–2008 crisis the majority of the economic profession in prestigious universities and institutions such as the World Bank and the IMF, and in influential media such as the *Financial Times* and the *Economist*, agreed that the scant value of the multiplier was conclusive proof of the limited or even null impact of public expenditure on the level of income and employment. The classical arguments against short-term policy interventions—the lags in making economic policy and further lags in the implementation and effects after the policy is enacted—coupled with the assumptions on the countering effects of expectations and actions of rational agents who observe the government's policy process, had made it appear practically impossible for policymakers to time fiscal policy actions to jumpstart the economy.

In the 1950s and 1960s, when Keynesianism was at its height, the multiplier was generally assumed to be about 2. Then, in the 1990s and 2000s, these estimates gradually dropped, leaving the consensus range about 0.5–0.7. However, the value of the multiplier was again closer to 1 after the crisis. In fact, in 2009 the estimates by both the IMF and the European Union showed the value of the multiplier in the range of 0.9 and 1.7 (Marcuzzo 2014). At last the multiplier is multiplying again, since it cannot be denied against the evidence of the effects of drastic cuts in public expenditure brought about by austerity programmes in Europe.

This is just one example of how empirical evidence to a great extent depends on the nature of the models that are constructed to find it, and also on the behavioural assumptions embedded in these models. In orthodox economics, consumers are said to pursue their individual maximizing utility over an infinite time horizon and with full knowledge of possible outcomes and perfect foresight. This is precisely the opposite of consumer behaviour as viewed in Keynes's macroeconomics, where perfect foresight and full rationality are not deemed acceptable assumptions, because probability calculus is not applicable: when there is uncertainty, as is the case in human affairs in general and in economic matters in particular, such calculation is not feasible.

The assumption of perfect foresight was discredited after the events of 2007–2008. This meant bringing some modifications into the standard macro-models to incorporate limited rationality and knowledge, imperfections and rigidities in the goods, labour and financial markets. However, these modifications were made within a theoretical apparatus which remains unchanged in its main features and, in any case, still quite the opposite of the way Keynes understood and described economic behaviour, which was never imputed to abstract economic agents, but always to individuals who have specific functions and characteristics.

Consumers, entrepreneurs or speculators always make their decisions in the face of uncertainty; therefore, according to Keynes, their behaviour cannot be described as guided by an optimizing rationality, as the utilitarian tradition would have it. Economic choices require evaluation of the available information, which is often contradictory or ambiguous and most of the time insufficient to offer enough elements to predict the future course of events. In each specific case the evidence we collect bears different "weight" in the argument we use to make our choices, on the basis of our knowledge and experience.

However, decision-making in a context of uncertainty should not imply the impossibility of making decisions according to reason, although the reason involved here is not the rationality employed in orthodox economic theory. Keynes was not only a great economist, but an investor on a large scale, for himself, his college and insurance companies; at King's College Archives, several unpublished papers document his investment strategy and philosophy, showing how painstakingly he collected and carefully reviewed all the evidence before making his choices (Cristiano and Marcuzzo 2018).

Keynes's rationality—which is not to be confused with optimizing choice—should be interpreted as "reasonableness", a concept describing the attitude to adopt in situations where following the rationality implied by economic theory might lead to very unsatisfactory outcomes. Keynes refers to it when dealing with the questions of the War Reparations imposed on Germany, insisted upon by the victorious powers after the First World War, and again in the negotiations on the repayment of loans to Great Britain made by the United States during the Second World War. And the question continues to arise: was it "reasonable" not to rescue Lehman Brothers but to let it go bankrupt?

So far I have been arguing on the relevance of the *General Theory* as a revolution in economic thinking; now I would like to move on to a more specific issue, namely when and whether government intervention is called for to correct market forces, since this is what is usually, and in an unqualified way, understood as the Keynesian message.

Adam Smith had already shown how rules and limitations are needed to prevent market failures: on defence, education and other "public goods" the market simply does not deliver the best. This is not the crux of the matter in the case of Keynes's subversion of the mainstream approach, but rather the role of effective demand in generating, income, increasing production and guaranteeing employment. It is the low level of effective demand, not the rigidity of money wages, which accounts for underemployment equilibrium.

Contrary to the opinion of the mainstream economists, Keynes does not assign to prices (wages and interest rate included) the task of adjusting supply and demand to bring the system to full employment equilibrium. Only by supporting a high level of demand, through policies designed to do so, can this goal be attained.

However, Keynes was not in favour of indiscriminate deficit-financed public investments: in the *General Theory* we do find an apology for government intervention, but this is to be interpreted in terms of the need to control the total level of investment, through direct or indirect action by a public or semi-public body, always taking into account market incentives, and favouring a climate of business confidence. This is clearly spelt out by Keynes:

> If the State is able to determine the aggregate amount of resources devoted to augmenting the instruments and the basic rate of reward to those who own them, it will have accomplished all that is necessary. (Keynes 1971–89, CWK VII: 378)

Similarly, on the origin and structure of the welfare state, Keynes's ideas were not represented faithfully (see Backhouse and Bateman 2012). He was not in favour of high taxes to pay for social benefits and pensions, the costs of which ought to be borne by the employers, whose interest was to have a fit and healthy labour force (Keynes 1971–89, CWK XXVII: 224). He was in favour of making the State accountable to the taxpayer for the goods and services provided, associating "as closely as possible the cost of particular services with the sources out of which they are provided", for he believed that "this is the only way by which to preserve sound accounting, to measure efficiency, to maintain economy and to keep the public properly aware of what things cost" (Keynes 1971–89, CWK XXVII: 225).

He helped Beveridge to draft the Social Insurance and Allied Services, the 1942 Beveridge Plan, as it was called, and gave his support it to having it approved. Keynes was appreciative of the "new features" of Beveridge's Plan, namely "the extension of the social security benefits and contributions to the whole of the population, and not merely to the present contributory classes" (Keynes 1971–89, CWK XXVII: 252), but he was concerned about the budgetary aspects of it. However, while both Keynes and Beveridge were preoccupied with the moral and social problems deriving from unemployment, they looked for solutions along different paths. For Beveridge, it was the human fight against scarcity, the plague of cycles in production and business confidence—as unpredictable as weather and natural calamities, as he saw them (Harris [1977] 1997). Social insurance was meant to disjoint individual coverage from general economic performance. Keynes, on the other hand, thought that by making the future dependent on the economic success of an active social investment policy it would be possible to free individuals from the deprivations deriving from unemployment.

Keynes did not believe in the idea embraced by Malthus and Mandeville that opulent consumption by the rich provided the source of income and employment and, therefore, the key to economic growth. In the *General Theory* consumption is seen as the necessary means for the well-being of society; the propellant, so to speak, in the machinery to boost employment and income. However, Keynes sees two major problems related to consumption. The first is satiation, which he believed derived from a "fundamental psychological law", according to which "men are disposed, as a rule and on the average, to increase their consumption as their income increases, but not by as much as the increase in their income" (Keynes 1971–89, CWK VII: 96). It follows that, since "the larger our incomes, the greater, unfortunately, is the margin between our incomes and our consumption", the government must find ways to fill the gap, unless it accepts a level of unemployment sufficient "to keep us so poor that our consumption falls short of our income by no more than the equivalent of the physical provision for future consumption which it pays to produce to-day" (Keynes 1971–89, CWK XXVII: 105).

The second problem with consumption is how best to bring about the desired increase in the propensity to consume in order to sustain aggregate demand. The means could be found in a fiscal policy aiming at more equitable distribution of incomes (Keynes 1971–89, CWK XIV: 16), thereby increasing aggregate consumption. However, this is a policy that is bound to come up against opposition, and by no means easy to implement. Alternatively, fiscal policy can be directed to boosting aggregate consumption through public expenditure, entrusting the government with "the task of adjusting to one another the propensity to consume and the inducement to invest" (Keynes 1971–89, CWK VII: 380) or "making public investment a counterweight to fluctuations of private investment" (Keynes 1971–89, CWK XXVII: 381).

Keynes's love of paradoxes lies behind the famous example that, as Joan Robinson tells us, was meant "to penetrate the thick walls of obscurantism of the old laissez-faire orthodoxy" (Robinson 1964: 91). The suggestion was for the Treasury to bury bottles filled with banknotes and let private individuals lease the ground, dig out the bottles and pocket the money (Keynes 1971–89, CWK VII: 129). This is clearly a paradox, against the view that every operation should make a full profit or not be done at all. Keynes's makes his point—it does not matter how public money is spent, as long as it is spent, since it will generate income and, through the multiplier, the savings necessary to finance the initial expenditure—to illustrate a principle, not to provide a blueprint of "useful" public work schemes. Keynes spelt it out clearly:

> it would, indeed, be more sensible to build houses and the like; but if there are political and practical difficulties in the way of this, the above would be better than nothing. (Keynes 1971–89, CWK VII: 129)

The political difficulties mentioned by Keynes arise mainly from "the education of our statesman on the principles of the classical economics". Moreover, expenditure on useful goods and services may not always be equally practical: "Two pyramids, two masses for the dead, are twice as good as one; but not two railways from London to York" (Keynes 1971–89, CWK VII: 129). Moreover "unless the rate of interest is falling *pari passu*" with the marginal efficiency of investment there is a limit to the possibility of increasing the stock of wealth by means of "useful" forms of loan expenditure. Waste results not when expenditure is channelled to objects which are not "useful", but when they are not "economically" viable.

In Keynes's work we find many sarcastic comments on common prejudices against public spending, which can equally well be applied to today's defences of austerity programs. I would like to mention at least two:

> the man who regards all this [loan-financed public works, particularly public expenditure on housing] as a senseless extravagance which will impoverish

the nation, as compared with doing nothing and leaving millions unemployed, should be recognized for a lunatic. (Keynes 1971–89, CWK XXI: 338)

And again:

When we have unemployed men and unemployed plant and more savings than we are using at home, it is utterly imbecile to say that we cannot afford these things. For it is with the unemployed plant, and with nothing else, that these things are done. To have labour and cement and steel and machinery and transport lying by, and to say that you cannot afford to embark on harbour works or whatever it may be is the delirium of mental confusion. (Keynes 1971–89, CWK XIX: 765–766)

The two pillars of the Welfare State—distrust of market forces and, with it, reliance on government intervention to bring about full employment on the one hand, and lack of confidence in the power of liberalism to achieve economic security and social stability on the other, came from different traditions: Beveridge, the heir to the Fabians, relied on neoclassical economic theory, while Keynes, the revolutionary economist, relied on reformed liberalism for his social policy (Marcuzzo 2010).

Keynes's approach to the way to fight unemployment should not identified with the welfare state, nor with indiscriminate public spending, with no concern for the government budget, nor with attributing the causes of unemployment to the rigidity of wages and prices, nor indeed with all the other distortions of the *General Theory* we find in the literature, showing how little it was read or understood.

Keynes's message needs to be adapted to the present domestic and international circumstances, but it is still topical in its appeal to those common good values which markets are sometimes unable to deliver. Keynes was confident that addressing market failures was possible by placing in charge of institutions created for the purpose people—often chosen among his group of friends—who were of high moral standards and fortitude.

While Keynes rejected consequentialism in ethics, he endorsed consequentialism in his political philosophy, to the effect that rules have to be set for given goals. The relevant question becomes how these goals are chosen and how rigid or fixed these rules should be. Keynes rejected the abstract and formal character of rules, claiming that we should try to reduce the social damage caused by conventions and engage in substituting them with other, less socially harmful conventions.

It follows that, for Keynes:

> The reformer is not he who would impose his own values on society, but he who understands better than others the potential for change in the moral conventions of society itself, and acts in order to affect such change. (Carabelli and De Vecchi 1999: 291)

Two questions then arise: a) where does the "better understanding" of the reformer come from; b) which are the appropriate actions to change the moral conventions of society.

The answers to these questions are scattered among Keynes's early writings on ethics and politics and his mature work in economics, but they can also be gathered by reviewing his activities as policy adviser and even his practical experience in various institutions. It is in particular on the importance Keynes attributed to expert advice, to "superior knowledge", and his elitism that I mean to focus attention.

A good starting point is a passage from a famous letter to Hayek:

> Dangerous acts can be done safely in a community which think and feels rightly, which would be the way to hell if they were executed by those who think and feel wrongly. (Keynes 1971–89, CWK XXVII: 987–8)

To think and to feel "rightly" or "wrongly" is contingent on two elements: knowledge and values. Skidelsky labelled Keynes "a meritocratic elitist" (Skidelsky 2009: 223), and he was not the only one to take this view. O'Donnell makes the interesting point that:

> Keynes's elitism [is] of an essentially intellectual variety, as distinct from those elitisms stemming from political, financial or military power. With individual varying in abilities, and with rationality linked to logical insight and knowledge, the presumption is strong that those with greatest mental power and education will have the greatest capacity in their given fields. (O'Donnell 1989: 66)

And he concludes that "Elitism is always a possible companion of intuitionist philosophy" (ibid.). It was the belief in the rationality of ends as well as means that led Keynes to value "superior knowledge" as the guide to political actions. Superior knowledge can be acquired through experience and education, and only those who have acquired it can be entrusted with the management of affairs or enactment of reforms.

The *rational* pursuit of individual interest in economics, according to the utilitarian creed, does not guarantee the collective good, which Keynes identified with full employment. It is an assumption that leads to a logical fallacy, which Keynes identifies as the fallacy of composition. For instance, attempts to reduce real wages or increase the saving of individuals on the basis of an individual rationale will not achieve the aim if undertaken by all, since aggregate prevails over individual effect. Another example is when the level of aggregate demand is kept drastically low within a country to satisfy the *reasons* of the victor or creditor, leading to a deflationary potential for *all* the economies. Thus, lack of reasonableness leads to consequences not only morally reprehensible but also economically disastrous for anyone who has sought guidance solely from the individual point of view.

In Keynes's economics the impasse of failure to achieve the aggregate effect of full utilisation of resources can be remedied with a set of direct and indirect instruments designed to overcome individual inertia and generate the level of demand necessary to raise the level of employment. Much has been written on the extent to which Keynes endorsed state intervention (Marcuzzo 2010; Backhouse and Bateman 2012). It is worth recalling the main points here.

Keynes's argument is summarized in the need for fiscal stimulus to boost the economy from the depths of recession; the burden of the deficit is not seen as the main drawback for government intervention, but as a condition necessary to address a failure in aggregate demand. This argument does not, however, imply unqualified government intervention. Government expenditure is to be finalised to provide enough investment to counterweight a decline in private investment and a level of consumption insufficient to generate the level of aggregate demand necessary to maintain full employment.

Although Keynes's mistrust of the smooth working of market forces came long before the *General Theory*, the case for intervention is made there forcefully in the case of aggregate demand failure. However, the policy message in the *General Theory* is to sustain the level of investment—more "stabilizing business confidence" (Bateman 1996: 148) than debt-financed public works. His reliance on "socializing investment" rather than fiscal policy aiming at smoothing out consumption levels over the cycle shows his concern for the size of the deficit and the importance attributed to market incentives to bring about the desired level of employment. "If the State is able to determine the aggregate amount of resources devoted to augmenting the instruments [of production] and the basic rate of reward to those who own them," he wrote in the *General Theory*, "it will have accomplished all that is necessary" (Keynes 1971–89, CWK VII: 378).

His "vision" of the future of capitalist society rested on the belief that freedom from economic constraints would allow the vast majority of the population to pursue happiness and enjoyment in their lives. "It is not any fear of a failure of physical productivity to provide an adequate material standard of life that fills me with foreboding," he remarked, addressing the House of Lords in February 1943:

> The real problems of the future are first of all the maintenance of peace, of international cooperation and amity, and beyond that the profound moral and social problems of how to organize material abundance to yield up the fruits of a good life. (Keynes 1971–89, CWK XXVII: 261)

Keynes rejected utilitarianism, both in ethics and politics, and he did not endorse consequentialism in his ethical philosophy, but he accepted it in his political philosophy, the purpose of which, he believed, was to provide reasons for action.

According to Keynes, the goal of an ethically rational society could be achieved by overcoming the economic and moral obstacles that encumbered contemporary society. For Keynes persuasion—the primary tool of political action—provided the means to given ends. These means were to be grounded in sound knowledge and experience, which are the basis of trust and confidence in expert advice and council. He wrote:

> The first condition of successful control and useful interference of whatever kind from above is that it must be done with knowledge. (Keynes 1971–89, CWK XIX: 643)

Keynes's view of economics, whereby full employment was the instrument or "social primary" means to a good life, was intertwined with his consequentialism in politics.

In conclusion, his prescription for a better society lies in setting rules and limitations in the market arena, not letting individual self-interest prevail, and putting some governing bodies in charge of filling the gap when deficient aggregate demand occurs, so that the acquisition of material goods and the fruition of the enjoyments of life be not a privilege of the few but the conquest of civilization. There are at least two reasons why the ideas put forward by Keynes in the 1930s are still relevant for the world of today. The first, and perhaps the most important, is the global recession which has been persisting since 2008–2009 and even now is showing only a few timid signs of recovery, forcefully reminding us of the events which prompted Keynes to look for solutions to mass unemployment and economic disruption. The second is the still pervasive free-market ideology that inspired the policies and behaviour that played no small part in fuelling the crisis. The traditional remedies to cure the 1930s recession—reliance on market mechanisms and balancing the budget—have been resurrected in the present times, and while criticism of the austerity policies is gaining momentum Keynes's arguments still fail to be widely and fully accepted. It is time we woke up to them.

Note

1. See Sylos Labini (2009), Temin (2010), Shapiro (2012) and Eichengreen (2012).

References

Backhouse, R. and Bateman, B. (2012), "Keynes and the Welfare State", *History of Economic Thought and Policy*, 1(1), pp. 7–19.

Bateman, B. (1996), *Keynes's Uncertain Revolution*. Ann Arbor: University of Michigan Press.

Carabelli, A. and N. De Vecchi (1999), "'Where to draw the line'? Keynes versus Hayek on Knowledge, ethics and economics", *Journal of the History of Economic Thought*, 6(2), pp. 271–296.

Cristiano, C. and Marcuzzo, M.C. (2018), "John Maynard Keynes: The Economist as Investor", *Review of Keynesian Economics*, 6(2), pp. 266–281.

Eichengreen, B. (2012), "Economic History and Economic Policy", *The Journal of Economic History*, 72(2), pp. 289–307.

Harris, J. ([1977] 1997), *William Beveridge. A Biography*, 2nd ed. Oxford: Clarendon Press.

Keynes, J.M. (1971–1989), E. Johnson and D. E. Moggridge (eds.), *The Collected Writings of John Maynard Keynes* (CWK), London: Macmillan.

CWK VII, *The General Theory of Employment, Interest, and Money*

CWK XIII, *The General Theory and After: Part I, Preparation*

CWK XIV, *The General Theory and After: Part II, Defence and Development*

CWK XVII, *Activities 1920–22: Treaty Revision and Reconstruction*

CWK XIX, *Activities 1920–29: The Return to Gold and Industrial Policy*

CWK XXI, *Activities 1931–39: World Crisis and Policies in Britain and America*

CWK XXVI, *Activities 1941–46: Shaping the Post-War World: Bretton Woods and Reparations*

CWK XXVII, *Activities 1940–46: Shaping the Post-War World: Employment and Commodities*

Marcuzzo, M.C. (2014), "Whatever happened to the Keynesian multiplier?" in R. Baranzini and F. Allisson (eds.), *Economics and Other Branches: In the Shade of the Oak Tree. Essays in Honour of Pascal Bridel*, London: Pickering & Chatto, pp. 157–68.

Marcuzzo, M.C. (2010), "Whose Welfare State? Beveridge vs Keynes" in R. Backhouse and T. Nishizawa (eds.), *No Wealth but Life: Welfare Economics and the Welfare State in Britain 1880–1945*, Cambridge: Cambridge University Press, pp. 189–206.

O'Donnell, R.M. (1989), *Keynes: Philosophy, Economics and Politics. The Philosophical Foundations of Keynes's Thought and Their Influence on his Economics and Politics.* London: Macmillan.

Popper, K. ([1935] 1959), *The Logic of Scientific Discovery*, London: Hutchinson.

Robinson, J. (1964), *Economic Philosophy,* Harmondsworth: Penguin Books.

Robbins L. (1932), *An Essay on the Nature and Significance of Economic Science*, London: Macmillan.

Shapiro, N. (2012), "Keynes, Steindl, and the Critique of Austerity Economics", *Monthly Review*, 64(3), pp. 103–13.

Skidelsky, R. (2009), *Keynes. The Return of the Master.* Public Affairs: New York.

Sylos Labini, P. (2009), "Le prospettive dell'economia mondiale", *Moneta e Credito*, 62(245–248), pp. 61–89.

Temin, P. (2010), "The Great Recession and the Great Depression", *NBER Working Paper*, 15645, January.

Wray, R. (2013), "The Dismal State of Macroeconomics and the Opportunity for a New Beginning" in J. Davis and W. Hands (eds.), *The Elgar Companion to Recent Economic Methodology*, Cheltenham: Eward Elgar, pp. 452–72.

Index[1]

[1] Note: Page numbers followed by 'n' refer to notes.

M. C. Marcuzzo, *Economic Theories, Protagonists and Facts*, Palgrave Studies in the History of Economic Thought,
https://doi.org/10.1007/978-3-031-63949-4

GPSR Compliance
The European Union's (EU) General Product Safety Regulation (GPSR) is a set of rules that requires consumer products to be safe and our obligations to ensure this.

If you have any concerns about our products, you can contact us on

ProductSafety@springernature.com

In case Publisher is established outside the EU, the EU authorized representative is:

Springer Nature Customer Service Center GmbH
Europaplatz 3
69115 Heidelberg, Germany

www.ingramcontent.com/pod-product-compliance
Lightning Source LLC
Chambersburg PA
CBHW071538201025
34223CB00051B/66
* 9 7 8 3 0 3 1 6 3 9 4 8 7 *